THOMAS ALFRED WALKER

A HISTORY
OF THE
LAW OF NATIONS

VOLUME I

Elibron Classics
www.elibron.com

Elibron Classics series.

ISBN 0-543-97802-8 (paperback)
ISBN 0-543-97801-X (hardcover)

This Elibron Classics Replica Edition is an unabridged facsimile of the edition published in 1899 by the University Press, Cambridge.

A HISTORY

OF THE

LAW OF NATIONS

London: C. J. CLAY AND SONS,
CAMBRIDGE UNIVERSITY PRESS WAREHOUSE,
AVE MARIA LANE:
AND
STEVENS AND SONS, LIMITED,
119 AND 120, CHANCERY LANE,
LAW PUBLISHERS AND BOOKSELLERS.

Leipzig: F. A. BROCKHAUS.
New York: THE MACMILLAN COMPANY.
Bombay: E. SEYMOUR HALE.

A HISTORY

OF THE

LAW OF NATIONS

BY

THOMAS ALFRED WALKER, M.A., LL.D.

FELLOW AND TUTOR OF AND LECTURER IN HISTORY IN PETERHOUSE, CAMBRIDGE.

VOL. I.

FROM THE EARLIEST TIMES TO THE PEACE OF WESTPHALIA, 1648.

Cambridge:
AT THE UNIVERSITY PRESS.
1899

Cambridge:
PRINTED BY J. AND C. F. CLAY,
AT THE UNIVERSITY PRESS.

PREFACE.

I AM acquainted with but three noteworthy attempts at the writing in the English language of a History of International Law. The earliest, the tentative effort of Robert Ward, is represented by two highly useful and interesting but incomplete volumes published in 1795. The later work of Hosack is slight and formless. Wheaton's *History of the Law of Nations in Europe and America from the Earliest Times to the Treaty of Washington*, 1842, excellent as it is in its handling of two centuries, touches but lightly upon the pre-Grotian history, and has moreover been long unprocurable by the majority of readers. Under these circumstances the ordinary English inquirer in this branch of study must seek his information either in foreign texts or, under, it may be, the guidance of the late Mr W. E. Hall's monumental general treatise, in the embarrassingly rich literature of State Papers, Memoirs and Collections of Treaties. Convinced that in the prosecution of the historical method will be found the only really satisfactory way to the right understanding of the character and claims of International Law, I have embarked upon the attempt to write a brief History of the foundation and development of International Law as a science. I have in the present volume endeavoured to trace the gradual evolution of the State System of the modern civilised World and to mark the sources of that composite Law of Nations of which Grotius in the seventeenth century is commonly deemed to have been the Father. In a second volume I hope to follow System and Law in their later expansion. Having incorporated in the text considerable portions of a volume published in 1893 I have retained, in a secondary place, its title of "The Science of International Law."

In the preparation of the work I have been frequently indebted to Professor Laurent's ample *Histoire de l'Humanité* and to the keen research of Professor Nys. Local references will, I trust, make clear my obligations in these and other quarters.

In this last connection I would say that, in spite of much criticism, I have pursued my former practice of constant citation. I have recourse to citation, not only as pointing to the sources of my personal authority for particular statements, but as directing to stores of further information which might possibly otherwise escape the student who would prosecute research into wider fields. I have, moreover, no desire to affect originality where the merit has been that of another.

I would remark with regard to the method I have followed in confining attention in the volume now issued to the international relations of Europe, that I am far from disregarding thereby the claims which might be preferred in a History of Civilisation on behalf of certain States of the East. Indeed I would express my belief that an examination initiated into the history of China and Japan, of Persia and of India—an examination which I have some hope may be ere long initiated by one better qualified for the work than myself—would reveal the fact that the recent appearance of one at least of the peoples of the Orient amongst the States of the International Circle represents but the renewal of a connection severed by long centuries of Barbarian cleavage.

Lastly, I must ask indulgence for some inconsistencies in the spelling of proper names which have, I find, escaped correction.

T. A. WALKER.

PETERHOUSE, CAMBRIDGE,
October, 1899.

LIST OF SOME BOOKS AND EDITIONS REFERRED TO OR CONSULTED IN VOL. I.

Aquinas, *Summa Totius Theologiae.* Antwerp, 1626.
Augustine, *Opera.* 10 vols. Paris, 1614.
Austin, John, *The Province of Jurisprudence Determined.* 2nd Ed. London, 1861.
„ *Lectures on Jurisprudence.* 2 vols. 4th Ed. London, 1879.
Bargès, J. J. L., *Histoire des Beni Zeiyan, Rois de Tlemcen.* Paris, 1852.
Bassompierre, Ambassades du Mareschal de. Cologne, 1668.
Bayard, The Good Chevalier sans Peur et sans Reproche, History of. London, 1883.
Bentham, J., *Fragment on Government.* 2nd Ed. London, 1823.
„ *Principles of Morals and Legislation.* Oxford, 1879.
Bentivoglio, Cardinal, *Historical Relation of the United Provinces of Flanders. Rendered into English by Henry, Earl of Monmouth.* London, 1652.
„ *Compleat History of the Wars of Flanders.* London, 1654.
Berwick, Memoirs of the Marshal Duke of. Written by Himself. 2 vols. London, 1779.
Birch, T., *Historical View of the Negotiations between the Courts of England, France and Brussels from the Year* 1592 *to* 1617. London, 1749.
Bodin, J., *De Republica Libri Sex.* Paris, 1586.
„ *Les Six Livres de la République.* Lyons, 1593.
Boroughs, Sir John, *The Soveraignty of the British Seas.* London, 1651.
Bougeant, P., *Histoire des Guerres et des Négociations qui précédèrent le Traité de Westphalie.* 2 vols. Paris, 1727.
Bradford, W., *Correspondence of the Emperor Charles V. and His Ambassadors at the Courts of England and France.* London, 1850.
Brienne, Mémoires du Comte de. 3 vols. Amsterdam, 1719.
Brunus, Conradus, *De Legationibus.* Mayence, 1548.
Bryce, J., *The Holy Roman Empire.* 5th Ed. London, 1875.
Burgus, *De Dominio Ser. Genuensis Reip. in Mari Ligustico Libri II.* Rome, 1641.
Busbequii, A. Gislenii, Omnia quae exstant. Elzevir, 1633.
Busbequius, A. G., The Four Epistles of. London, 1694.
Cabala sive Scrinia Sacra. London, 1654.

Callières, *De la Manière de négocier avec les Souverains.* 2 vols. London, 1750.
Camden, *The Historie of the Most Renowned and Victorious Princesse Elizabeth, late Queene of England.* London, 1630.
Canonici, Corpus Juris. Ed. A. L. Richter. 2 vols. Leipzig, 1839.
Carleton, Letters from and to Sir Dudley. 2nd Ed. London, 1775.
Castelnau, Michael de, *Memoirs of the Reigns of Francis II. and Charles IX.* London, 1724.
Church and Brodribb, *Annals of Tacitus.* London, 1876.
Clark, E. C., *Practical Jurisprudence.* Cambridge, 1883.
Commines, The History of Philip de, Knight, Lord of Argenton. 4th Ed. London, 1674.
Condé, J. A., *History of the Dominion of the Arabs in Spain.* 3 vols. London, 1854.
Conringii, Hermanni, Opus de Finibus Imperii Germanici. Frankfort and Leipzig, 1693.
Consolato del Mare, Il. Venice, 1584.
Creighton, M., *History of the Papacy.* 5 vols. London, 1882—1894.
Crusades, Chronicles of the. London, 1848.
Dalton, C., *Life and Times of Sir E. Cecil, Viscount Wimbledon.* 2 vols. London, 1885.
Davila, H. C., *History of the Civil Warr of France.* London, 1678.
Dumont, J., *Corps Universel Diplomatique du Droit des Gens.* Amsterdam, 1726—31.
Eginhard, *Vita et Gesta Karoli Magni.* Cologne, 1521.
,, *Annales Regum Francorum Pipini, Karoli, Ludovici.*
Fanshaw, Sir Richard, Original Letters of. London, 1702.
Finett, Sir John, *Finetti Philoxenis.* London, 1656.
Finlay, *History of the Byzantine and Greek Empires.* 2 vols. Edin. and London, 1853, 4.
Flassan, *Histoire Générale et Raisonnée de la Diplomatie Francaise.* 7 vols. Paris, 1811.
Fowler, Warde, *The City State of the Greeks and Romans.* London, 1893.
Freeman, E. A., *Historical Geography.* 2nd Ed. London, 1882.
,, *History of Federal Government.* London, 1863.
Froissart, *Chronicles of England, France, Spain and the adjoining Countries.* Translated by Thomas Johnes. 2 vols. London, 1839.
Gentilis, Albericus, *De Legationibus Libri Tres.* London, 1585.
Gibbon, E., *Decline and Fall of the Roman Empire.* 6 vols. London, 1776—88.
Grotius, Hugo, *De Jure Belli ac Pacis Libri Tres.* Paris, 1625.
,, ,, ,, ,, Amsterdam, 1689 and 1712.
,, *Of the Rights of War and Peace.* 3 vols. London, 1715.
,, *De Rebus Belgicis, or The Annals and History of the Low-Country Warres.* London, 1665.
Grotius, Hugo, *Mare Liberum.* Leyden, 1633.

Grotius, Hugo, *Mare Liberum.* Amsterdam, 1689 and 1712.
Guicciardini, Francesco, *The History of Italy.* Translated by Austin Parke Godard. 3rd Ed. 10 vols. London, 1763.
Guizot, F., *History of Civilisation.* 3 vols. London, 1882.
Hall, W. E., *International Law.* 3rd Ed. Oxford, 1890.
Hallam, H., *View of the State of Europe during the Middle Ages.* 8th Ed. 2 vols. London, 1841.
Hammond, *Political Institutions of the Ancient Greeks.* London, 1895.
Henry IV., surnamed the Great, King of France and Navarre, The History of. By the Bishop of Rodez. Made English by F. D. London, 1663.
Hodgkin, T., *Italy and Her Invaders,* 476—535 A.D. 4 vols. Oxford, 1885.
Holland, T. E., *Jurisprudence.* 2nd Ed. Oxford, 1882.
" *Studies in International Law.* Oxford, 1898.
Hooker, Richard, The Works of. London, 1705.
Hosack, John, *Rise and Growth of the Law of Nations.* London, 1882.
Hostiensis, Henrici a Segusio Cardinalis, Aurea Summa. Cologne, 1612.
Intelligencer, The Swedish. London, 1632.
Isidori Hispalensis Episcopi, Originum sive Etymologiarum Libri Viginti. 1585.
" *Historia sive Chronicon Gothorum.* Paris, 1579.
James, The Court and Character of King. Collected and perfected by Sir A. W. London, 1651.
Jenkinson, Charles, Earl of Liverpool, *A Discourse on the Conduct of the Government of Great Britain in respect to Neutral Nations.* London, 1801.
Jordanes, *De Origine Actuque Getarum Liber.* Basle, 1531.
Josephus, Flavius, The Works of. Translated into English by Sir Roger L'Estrange, Knight. London, 1733.
Kaltenborn, Von, *Die Vorläufer des Hugo Grotius.* Leipzig, 1848.
Koran, The. Translated from the Original by George Sale. 2 vols. London, 1812.
Laurent, F., *Études sur l'Histoire de l'Humanité.* 18 vols. Paris, 1865—80.
Lawrence, T. J., *The Principles of International Law.* London, 1895.
[Macchiavelli], *The Works of the famous Nicholas Machiavel, Citizen and Secretary of Florence.* London, 1675.
Maine, Sir H. S., *Ancient Law.* London, 1876.
" *Early History of Institutions.* London, 1875.
" *International Law.* London, 1888.
" *Village Communities.* London, 1876.
Mallet, M., *Northern Antiquities.* Translated by Bishop Percy. By J. A. Blackwell. London, 1847.
Manning, William Oke, *Commentaries on the Law of Nations.* London, 1839.
" " " " Ed. Sheldon Amos. London, 1875.

Martens, Charles de, *Causes Célèbres du Droit des Gens.* 5 vols. Leipzig, 1859.

Melvil, Sir James, of Halhill, The Memoirs of. By George Scott, Gent. London, 1683.

Mer, Les Us et Coûtumes de la. Rouen, 1671.

Monstrelet, The Chronicles of. Translated by T. Johnes. 13 vols. London, 1810.

Montaigne, Michael, Lord of, *Essays.* Translated by John Florio. London, 1613.

Montluc, The Commentaries of Messire Blaize de, Mareschal of France. London, 1674.

Muirhead, James, *Historical Introduction to the Private Law of Rome.* Edinburgh, 1886.

Murphy, J. C., *The History of the Mahometan Empire in Spain.* London, 1816.

Nani, B., *Histoire de la République de Venise.* 4 vols. Cologne, 1682.

Niebuhr, B. G., *The History of Rome.* Translated by J. C. Hare and C. Thirlwall. 3rd Ed. 2 vols. London, 1837.

Nys, E., *Les Origines de Droit International.* Brussels and Paris, 1894.

Ockley, Simon, *History of the Saracens.* 2 vols. Cambridge, 1757.

Oldendorp, Johann, *Juris Naturalis Gentium et Civilis εἰσαγωγή.* Antwerp, 1539.

Oman, C., *The Dark Ages.* London, 1895.

Ompteda, D. H. L. von, *Litteratur des Volkerrechts.* Ratisbon, 1785.

Orosius, Paulus, *Historiarum adversus Paganos Libri VII.* Paris, 1517.

Pardessus, J. M., *Us et Coûtumes de la Mer.* 2 vols. Paris, 1847.

Procopius, *De Bello Gothorum Libri III.* Basle, 1531.

„ *De Bello Persico et Vandilico Libri IV.* Basle, 1531.

REPORTS—

Coke, Sir E., Reports.

Croke, Sir G., *Reports of Select Cases adjudged in the reigns of Elizabeth James and Charles.*

Dyer, Sir James, *Reports of Cases in the Reigns of Hen. VIII., Edw. VI., Q. Mary and Q. Elizabeth.*

Kelyng, Sir John, *Report of Divers Cases in Pleas of the Crown adjudged and determined in the reign of the late King Charles II.*

Rolle, *Cases en le Court del' Banke le Roy.*

Salkeld, William, *Reports of Cases adjudged in the Court of King's Bench* (1689—1712).

Saunders, Sir Edmund, *Reports of Pleadings and Cases in the Court of King's Bench* (1666—72).

Revue de Droit International et de Législation Comparée. 1869—

Robertson, William, *The History of the Reign of the Emperor Charles V.* 3 vols. London, 1769.

Rose, H. J., *A New General Biographical Dictionary.* 12 vols. London, 1857.

Rushworth, John, *Historical Collections. Part I.* London, 1659.
Rymer, T., *Foedera, Conventiones, Litterae.* 3 vols. London, 1816—30.
Schardius, S., *Sylloge Historico-Politico-Ecclesiastica.* Strasburg, 1618.
Schmauss, *Corpus Juris Gentium Academicum.* 2 vols. Leipzig, 1730.
Sédillot, *Histoire Générale des Arabes.* 2 vols. Paris, 1877.
Selden, John, *Mare Clausum seu de Dominio Maris.* London, 1635.
" *Mare Clausum; the Right and Dominion of the Sea.* Translated by J. H., Gent. London, 1663.
Sismondi, J. C. L. Simonde de, *Histoire des Francais.* 31 vols. Paris, 1821—44.
Solorzano, Joannes de, *De Indiarum Jure.* Madrid, 1629.
Soto, Dominic, *Libri Decem de Justitia et Jure.* Lyons, 1582.
Suarez, *Tractatus de Legibus ac Deo Legislatore.* Antwerp, 1614.
Sully, Mémoires du Duc de. 6 vols. Paris, 1827.
State-Papers from 1501 *to* 1726, *Miscellaneous* (Hardwicke Papers). 2 vols. London, 1788.
Strype, John, *Life of Sir John Cheke.* London, 1705.
Thirlwall, C., *History of Greece.* 8 vols. London, 1845.
Vattel, E., *Le Droit des Gens ou Principes de la Loi Naturelle.* 2 vols. Leyden, 1758.
Victoria, Franciscus a, *Relectiones Theologicae Tredecim.* Lyons, 1586.
Villehardouin, The Chronicles of Geoffrey de. Translated by T. Smith. London, 1829.
Walker, T. A., *Manual of Public International Law.* Cambridge, 1895.
Ward, Robert, *An Enquiry into the Foundation and History of the Law of Nations in Europe.* 2 vols. London, 1795.
Warnefridus, Paulus, *De Longobardorum Origine et Gestis Libri VI.* Basle, 1532.
Welwood, J., *Memoirs of the most material Transactions in England for the last Hundred Years preceding the Revolution in* 1688. London, 1700.
Westlake, John, *Chapters on the Principles of International Law.* Cambridge, 1894.
Wheaton, H., *Elements of International Law.* Ed. A. C. Boyd. London, 1880.
Wicquefort, *The Rights, Privileges and Office of Embassadors and Public Ministers.* Translated into English by Mr Digby. 2nd Ed. London, 1740.
Wynne, William, *The Life of Sir Leoline Jenkins.* 2 vols. London, 1724.
Zosimus, *Historiae Novae Libri VI.* Translated into Latin by J. Leunclavius. Basle, 1531.

ERRATA.

p. 9, line 33. For *commands* read *command.*
p. 30, chapter heading. Read *The Evolution of International Law—Antiquity and the Middle Ages.*
p. 57, in margin. Before *International Law* insert II.
p. 110, last line. For (1010) read (1110).
p. 112, line 37. For *began* read *begun.*
p. 114, line 15. For *Henry VII.* read *Henry VI.*
p. 115, in margin. For *Oakley* read *Ockley.*
p. 161, line 37. For *Granville* read *Grenville.*
p. 163, in margin. Read Boroughs, *Soveraignty of the British Seas.*
p. 173, line 8. Read *whosoever.*
,, last line. For *explains* read *explain.*
p. 194, line 13. Read *Mansfeld.*
p. 196, in margin. For *militate* read *militates.*
p. 199, line 10. For *her* read *their.*
,, in margin. For 1510 read 1501.
p. 206, line 30. For *definition* read *definitions.*
p. 244, line 27. For *interests* read *interest.*
p. 305, in margin. For (II) read (III).

CONTENTS.

INTRODUCTION.

CHAPTER I.

The Name "International Law."

CHAPTER II.

The Evidence of International Law.

PART I.

CHAPTER I.

The Evolution of International Law—Antiquity and the Middle Ages.

CHAPTER II.

The Evolution of International Law—Birth of Territoriality.

CHAPTER III.

The Evolution of International Law.—The Forerunners and the Prophet of International Law.

THE SCIENCE OF INTERNATIONAL LAW.

INTRODUCTION.

CHAPTER I.

THE NAME "INTERNATIONAL LAW."

If rules of conduct are observed between State and State are they fitly styled *International Law?*

Bentham, *Morals and Legislation*, Chap. 17, § 2.

§ 1. THE term *International Law* was proposed by Jeremy Bentham as the most appropriate English designation for the body of rules denominated by Germans and Frenchmen *Völkerrecht* or *Droit des Gens.* The suggestion met with singular favour, insomuch that *International Law* has amongst English-speaking peoples well-nigh altogether superseded the once familiar *Law of Nations.*

The felicity of the victorious phrase has, however, not passed unchallenged. The term is by its employers used to denominate certain rules which are asserted to be observed *between states.* Its propriety is questioned commonly upon the ground that, states being independent, a rule which is observed between states is, in so far as it is international, not properly a law, while, in so far as it is properly a law, it is not international. The term International Law, in a word, involves, it is said, a contradiction.

Austin denies to International Law the name of Proper Law.

§ 2. "Laws Proper, or Properly so-called, are commands: laws which are not commands, are laws improper or improperly so-called."

So says John Austin in the outset of that remarkable work which made of its author the accepted prophet in terminology of well-nigh every English Law School.

"Those essentials," he subsequently declares, "of a "law proper, together with certain consequences which "those essentials import, may be stated briefly in the "following manner:—

"1. *Laws properly so-called* are a species of *com-* "*mands.* But being a Command, every law properly so- "called flows from a determinate *source* or emanates from "a *determinate author.* In other words, the author from "whom it proceeds is *a determinate* rational being, or a "*determinate* body or aggregate of rational beings. For "whenever a Command is expressed or intimated, one "party signifies a wish that another shall do or forbear: "and the latter is obnoxious to an evil which the former "intends to inflict in case the wish be disregarded. But "every *signification* of a wish made by a single individual, "or made by a body of individuals *as a body or collective* "*whole*, supposes that the individual or body is *certain* or "*determinate.* And every intention or purpose held by a "single individual, or held by a body of individuals as a "body or collective whole, involves the same supposition.

"2. Every *sanction properly so-called* is an eventual "evil *annexed to a command.* Any eventual evil may "operate as a motive to conduct: but, unless the conduct "be commanded and the evil be annexed to the command "purposely to enforce obedience, the evil is not a sanction "in the proper acceptation of the term.

"3. Every *Duty properly so-called* supposes a com- "mand by which it is created. For every sanction properly "so-called is an eventual evil *annexed to a command.* "And duty properly so-called is obnoxiousness to evils of "the kind."

Province of Jurisprudence determined, Lect. v. p. 182.

In a word, Laws Proper are a species of command. And command implies (1) a determinate author, (2) a direct expression of desire on the part of that author, and (3) a determinate eventual evil or sanction to be incurred by non-compliance with that expression of desire.

It follows that, if states are *independent*, rules of conduct between States are excluded from the category of Law Proper, for such rules of conduct are necessarily devoid alike of determinate author and of determinate sanction.

Austin leaves us in no doubt as to his full recognition of this conclusion.

"International Law supposes," wrote he in a marginal note, "a Law of Nature: i.e. a law obligatory upon all "mankind, but wanting the political sanction. If there "be no law without that sanction, the admitted maxims "for the conduct of international transactions are not Law, "but Ethics. Each State may, however, adopt an International Law of its own; enforcing that law by its "tribunals, or by its military force (at least) as against "other nations. This, however, is not International, but "National or Civil Law; i.e. in regard to the sanction. "For in regard to the subject, and (where there is good "faith) to the object, it may be styled international. If "the same system of International Law were adopted and "fairly enforced by every nation, the system would answer "the *end* of law, but, for want of a common superior, could "not be *called so* with propriety. If courts common to "all nations administered a common system of International Law, this system, though eminently effective, "would still, for the same reason, be a *moral* system. "The concurrence of any nation in the support of such "tribunals, and its submission to their decrees, might at "any moment be withdrawn without *legal* danger. The "moral system so administered would of course be "eminently precise." *Jurisprudence*, II. p. 594.

Are we to be content quietly to accept Austin's positions, and deny the name of Law to those rules of conduct by which the mutual dealings of civilised states have been for centuries and still are regulated?

The question thus raised is not one of mere logomachy, but of vital practical interest in the field of foreign politics.

Lawrence, *Principles of International Law*, p. 25.

§ 3. It may be said that to engage in a controversy upon this point is to engage in mere logomachy. If this were the case, if the question were merely one of terminology debateable amongst and interesting the members of English-speaking Law Schools alone, the international jurist might indeed spare himself much singularly tedious labour.

But unfortunately the discussion, or at least the conclusion of the discussion in the view of Austin and his followers, has not been confined to the Law Schools and to the treatises of legal philosophers. It will suffice to cite but one of many examples of the appearance of John Austin's theorem in the field of practical politics.

Illustration.

"I confess," said the Marquis of Salisbury, replying to a resolution in the English Upper House advocating the establishment of a Court of International Arbitration, "I "confess—and I think it is the general feeling—that "deeply as everybody sympathises with the object my "noble friend has in view, and earnestly as we must desire "to see the day when the horrors of war may be prevented "by the establishment of some species of international "arbitration, it is very far from us now, and further ap- "parently than it was some years ago. No one, I think, "can watch the progress of affairs on the Continent of "Europe, and the tendency of various states, without "seeing that the pacific spirit has not increased, and that "the chances of avoiding war are not more favourable "than they were.......I think, my lords, we are misled in "this matter by the facility with which we use the phrase "*International Law*. International Law has not any "existence in the sense in which the term *law* is *usually* "understood. It depends generally upon the prejudices "of writers of text-books. It can be enforced by no "tribunal, and therefore to apply to it the phrase *law* is "to some extent misleading, and I think has given rise "to the somewhat exaggerated hope with which those "persons who hold the views of my noble friend approach "this matter." *The Times*, July 26, 1887.

The criticisms on International Law advanced by John Austin may be in themselves, as the late lamented Sir Henry Maine remarked in one of the last lectures which he was fated to deliver, "very interesting and quite innocuous," but when they pass outside the schools into the Cabinet, and into the public speeches of responsible Foreign Ministers, by the employment of the weapon of "mere logomachy" the peace of the world is put in jeopardy. "Popular fame does not enter into nice distinctions." Maine, *International Law*, p. 49. Bentham, *Fragment on Government*, Preface, xxv.

It is this consideration which makes it important for English-speaking races that the true facts of Austin's position should be clearly understood.

§ 4. Now either words are meaningless or they bear a meaning. But if, as is obvious, they be at root mere names, mere conductors for the conveyance of ideas, any usage of any kind is, from the purely *logical* standpoint, equally good with any other, provided only that that usage be consistent: any naming is grammatically valid, provided only that it fulfil the end of naming, that it at once distinguish and describe. Are Austin's positions maintainable? Maine, *Early History of Institutions*, p. 374.

Austin accordingly is free to lay it down that the appropriate field of his science of Jurisprudence is one division alone of those rules which commonly go by the name "Laws"; that that Jurisprudence is a science of conduct, and of *human* conduct, and that its field is limited to Laws being rules of human conduct set by determinate man in virtue of *political superiority*, political superiority implying Sovereignty and so a State. Answer. Possibly, in point of logic,

And he may, with a view to precision and exact definition, describe this division of the wide field of "Laws" commonly so-called by one distinct and special name, whether "Positive Law," the term which he actually adopts, or any other. Nay, he may, if he will, apply the term "Proper Law" exclusively and solely to such rules as, being set by a determinate superior, and so imposing a duty upon a determinate inferior, operate by means of a determinate sanction. He is free herein to advise, but he is not free to dictate, to deny the validity of the application of the name "Law" to such other varieties of rule as have hitherto enjoyed the appellation, to characterise a wider employment of the term as "mere jargon."

Even should a novel term be taken, a term to which frequent usage has not as yet sanctified any special and commonly received interpretation, there must be equal liberty for all. The one man may create the name for a special end, but popular usage will decide the fate of the creation. And when the word is no new one, but well-known and well-worn, considerations other than logical come into play, and to the condition of consistency is added the element of intelligibility: then we have to do not alone with empty words, but with speaking language.

but not in the field of Practice.

The term "Proper" is in this latter case. It is a word which common speech has already appropriated. And, if the term "Proper" have indeed any meaning determinate and intelligible, that meaning involves the notion of exclusion. "Laws Proper," if we speak the language of intelligence, are *true* laws, and "Laws Properly so-called" are laws *truly and fitly designated*, rules of conduct, that is, to which, and to which *alone and exclusively*, the epithet, or name, "laws" does in correct and exact parlance, and *as of right*, belong.

"Laws Proper, or Laws Properly so-called, are commands." So to assert is to assert the present existence of some certain test, some canon of precise speech, by which the propriety of the application of the substantive term may be measured or known.

And it is clear that that test or canon can be but one or other of two. Either the application is appropriate because it is in harmony with the usage of the past, or it is appropriate because it is surpassingly convenient for the future.

To assert that any term is appropriate having regard to the usage of the past is to assert that, as a fact, a certain idea has been wont to be in that past conveyed by that term.

To assert that any term is appropriate by reference to the future is to assert that a certain idea should, on grounds of surpassing convenience, be conveyed by that term in the time to come.

But, if Austin assert that, as a fact, the idea which in the past was wont to be conveyed by the term "law" was the idea of command, he asserts that which is not.

And if he assert that the notion of command should, on grounds of surpassing convenience, be conveyed in future by the term "law," he advances an assertion which some of us at least may well deem incapable of support.

If a term have meaning in past usage, that meaning must be sought in History and in Philology, in the common speech of the people and in the page of the Classic or standard author.

If a term be proposed to be employed by reference to the surpassing convenience of the future, the employment must be rested upon considerations of utility, must be considered with respect to the furtherance of the greatest happiness of mankind.

History, Philology and Usage unite with Practical Convenience against Austin.

Grammatically and historically, in its origin and in its application, "Law" and its concomitants and equivalents have been in no wise restricted to the meaning "command." Philology unites with History, common language with common experience, and the united testimony stands clear against Austin.

And if Austin rest the justification of his terminology upon utility, upon manifest practical convenience[1], what shall we say of an usage which, logical although it be, alike weakens the bonds of State control by the depreciation of

[1] Holland, *Jurisprudence*, p. 43. "It is *convenient* to recognise as laws only such rules as are enforced by a sovereign political authority, although there are states of society in which it is difficult to ascertain as a fact what rules answer to this description."

Constitutional, and facilitates the excuse of international wrong-doing by the degradation of International, Law? How shall the convenience of scientific definition weigh in the world's scale with the inconvenience of lawlessness and turmoil?

It is incumbent upon us in our turn to support our assertions of fact.

I. The Historical Objection to Austin's Analysis of Law as Command. *All* Law is not Command.

§ 5. The first main objection to Austin's analysis of "Law Proper" rests for its justification upon the hard facts of History. Austin's definition, however apt it be to the circumstances of modern state life, has no universal application. For albeit in the present day laws may be, and laws commonly are, the declaration of the will of determinate authors, determinate lawgivers, such lawgivers commonly passing under the style of sovereigns, it has been, and is, by no means possible at all times to point out any such determinate lawgiver.

In the Patriarchal Household we have Command,

If we turn to Ancient Society, to that society wherein was quickened the germ of the Aryan State, we discover communities independent and under the undisputed governance of determinate rulers; but those communities approach not to the proportions of a State nor those rulers to the style of Sovereigns. Probably the Family is nomadic: probably its numbers are but few. Here then there is no field for "Positive Law." But in such an association have we "Proper Law?" Theoretically indeed we might in the government of the Household discover rules of conduct answering to Austin's definition. We have command, and that command imposed by a determinate human superior upon an inferior formerly obliged to obey, and we have determinate eventual evil attached to noncompliance on the part of the determinate individual who is obliged to, or under the duty of, obedience. But, in actual fact, the government of the Paterfamilias partakes not of the character of regular law, but of special command.

but it is "Particular Command."

Maine, *Ancient Law*, pp. 14 et seqq.

When we pass beyond the Family it would seem essential that the conduct of the members of the community should be regulated by something more than mere arbitrary command: when we pass beyond the Family we, in fact, enter naturally upon the sphere of political organisation and of Law. Yet when we examine primitive associations larger than the Family, and popular society as advanced in political life as were the Germans of Tacitus, we find nothing of the character of Austinian "Law": we find rulers, but these rulers are not legislators, but judges: we find Councils of Elders, but these again are not lawmakers, but assessors, advisers of the Headman or the Monarch: we find popular assemblies, but these are not legislative Parliaments, but the meetings of the Host, the meetings of the whole free people in arms for deliberation as to some external movement, or for the supervision of the customary land distribution. *Plusque ibi boni mores valent quam alibi bonae leges.*

Early Law is Custom.

Germania, VII. and XI.

The rules of conduct operating amongst primitive peoples are not commands issued, or set, by a Sovereign one or body, and sanctioned by a definite penalty to proceed from the one or body, and to be incurred by the offender. Primitive Law is Custom, Custom observed on account of its antiquity or on account of its supposed Divine origin. Custom is a Law in itself: its own legislator and its own sanction.

And, turning to certain of the empires of the hide-bound East, the late Sir Henry Sumner Maine has shown that there, too, while there exists a certain well-recognised head, which head sends his delegates into various portions of his vast territories, the subjects of those territories are in no way indebted to that head, nor yet to his delegates, for anything in the nature of fixed rules or ordinances. Arbitrary command there is, indeed, on occasion, commands of Akbar or of Runjeet, but, so long as the imperial and vice-regal demands for tribute are met with reasonable acquiescence, the regular life of the people is limited, not by any general command of the Emperor, or his delegates, but by mere Custom.

So too the Law of certain modern Oriental States.

Early History of Institutions, Lectures XII. and XIII.

"Without the most violent forcing of language," says

Maine, "it is impossible to apply these terms, *command*, "*sovereign*, *obligation*, *sanction*, *right*, to the customary "law under which the Indian village-communities have "lived for centuries, practically knowing no other 'law' "civilly obligatory. It would be altogether inappropriate "to speak of a political superior commanding a particular "course of action to the villagers. The council of village "elders does not command anything, it merely declares "what has always been, nor does it generally declare that "which it believes some higher power to have commanded; "those most entitled to speak on the subject deny that "the natives of India necessarily require divine or political "authority as the basis of their usages; their antiquity "is by itself assumed to be a sufficient reason for obeying "them. Nor, in the sense of the analytical jurists, is "there *right* or *duty* in an Indian village-community; a "person aggrieved complains not of an individual wrong, "but of the disturbance of the order of the entire little "society. More than all, customary law is not enforced "by a sanction. In the almost inconceivable case of dis-"obedience to the award of the village council, the sole "punishment, or the sole certain punishment, would "appear to be universal disapprobation."

Village Communities, pp. 67, 68.

On this it has been observed:—

Professor Holland's criticism upon Sir Henry S. Maine's view of Indian Society.

"With reference to the relation of a great Oriental "taxgathering empire to the village customs of its sub-"jects, or to the more distinctly formulated laws of a "conquered province, it is necessary to draw a distinction. "Disobedience to the village custom or the provincial law "may either be forcibly repressed, or it may be acquiesced "in, by the local authority. If it be habitually repressed "by such local force as may be necessary, it follows that "the local force must, if only for the preservation of "the peace, be supported, in the last resort, by the whole "strength of the empire. In this case the humblest "village custom is a law which complies with the require-"ment of being enforced by the sovereign. If, on the "other hand, disobedience be habitually acquiesced in, the "rules which may thus be broken with impunity are no "laws; and, so far as such rules are concerned, the tax-"gathering empire is lawless, its organisation consisting "merely of an arbitrary force, acting upon a subject mass "which is but imperfectly bound together by a network of "religious and moral scruples." T. E. Holland, *Jurisprudence*, p. 42.

An answer. But the very gist of Maine's argument is that disobedience to village custom is repressed by "local force," and by local force only. Little it profits to know that such and such "must be," if such and such in actual fact *is* not. Respect for village custom *is* maintained by local force, but it is the force not of arms but of opinion, a force practically sufficient for the purpose, and a force which binds together village society more perfectly than would the fear of interference on the part of "the whole strength of the empire." To one to whom the notion of absolute recalcitrance would be inconceivable, the idea of applying for the support of "the whole strength of the empire" to punish the refractory would be foreign indeed. To appeal from village social opinion to "the whole strength of the empire" represented by the Central Head would be in effect to appeal from a stronger to a weaker power. It may be that "local force must...be supported, in the last resort" by such whole strength, but for the villagers themselves "the whole strength of the empire" speaks in the custom itself, and not by the bared sword of the absent and distant ruler.

The opinion of an indeterminate body is often more effective as a sanction than are the penalties imposed by determinate legislation. A law observed must be in *some* way enforced, and, if observance cease in any community, that community is doubtless *so far* "lawless." But the truth is that the opinion of an indeterminate body is often a sanction far more effective than are the penalties annexed by the determinate legislator. In the most strongly centralised community the success or failure of a legislative measure will depend upon the fact that it is, or is not, a reflection of current popular opinion. The free use of criticism will secure the speedy repeal of a hateful edict, unless indeed that edict be supported by the free use of the axe or the scimitar, the knout or the bayonet, and even so, in the fulness of time, it may behove the tyrant to reckon with the agents of his tyranny, Praetorians or Mamelukes, Janissaries or Strelitzes.

Modern Sovereignty is determinate or fairly determinable: not so all Sovereignty.

Sovereignty, doubtless, being the union of independence with supremacy, is an essential characteristic of every true state. But the wielding of sovereign powers may be committed to one or to many, and not everywhere and at all times is it possible to point out the sovereign delegate, or representative, with instantaneous precision: not everywhere and at all times is it possible to predicate of any person or body of persons forming part of a political whole, or community, that he or they are habitually obeyed by the bulk of the members of that whole, and at the same time habitually obey no external human power. Not everywhere and at all times is it possible to designate any one person, or any certain aggregate of persons less than the whole, as possessed of exclusive legislative authority. The modern sovereign is, in truth, fairly determinate, and the modern sovereign combines distinctly functions executive and legislative. But in such a state of society as that described by Maine, there is rule, and rule effectively enforced, but it is not command set by a determinate author to a human being formerly obliged to obey; there, while we may identify no determinate legislator, so neither may we point out any one person, or body of persons *less than the whole*, as at once representing the unity of the race, and admittedly and habitually supreme within. Sovereignty may, like gravity, have existed from all time, but of its existence, as that of gravity, men were for a long season ignorant, and ascribed its operations to other causes. If the apple fell it was but obeying the everlasting laws of God; if rules of conduct were observed, they were observed spontaneously, unquestioned, as the law primaeval, the Æ, the eternal, the unbroken custom, the θέμις, the foreordained of Heaven.

Observance precedes Command, and the Administrator the Law-Giver. And even when the people dissatisfied with the judge call for a king, and a Saul stands head and shoulders above the congregation, it by no means appears that he is regarded as absorbing in himself exclusive legislative and executive functions: Sovereign he may be, judge in peace and leader in war, but he is not Law-Maker.

Austin's position is not saved by the proposition that "Whatever the Sovereign permits he commands."

Nor is the definition of Austin rendered applicable to the facts of universal politics by the admission of the thesis that "whatever the Sovereign permits he commands." For permission predicates power to refuse assent, and willing abstention from its exercise. Permission may be held equivalent to command, where one, having the power to ordain the contrary, or another course, knowingly assents to the line of conduct actually pursued; and assent may be tacit or express. But there is no permission where there is no power, or where there is no adverting mind. Permission is grounded in forbearance, not in mere omission. Silence may be admitted as consent when the possession of the power of effective speech has first been plainly shown.

Early History of Institutions, p. 363.

The proposition is inadmissible.

Its admission imports confusion of ideas.

A reasonably profitable classification can hardly well be rested upon a confusion of ideas in common usage distinct. Command and permission, observance and enforcement are notions commonly understood, and commonly clearly distinguished. Austin himself saw that it was only remotely and indirectly that even such Permissive Laws as Laws repealing laws "are often or always imperative." And in common speech "permission" clearly falls short alike of "command" and of "enforcement."

The Indian Sovereign, be he Rajah or Emperor, may be allowed to *permit* when he has proved his power to extend to the subversion of village custom: to paint him *commanding* the observance of that custom is to assert that which is not.

And historically Sovereign Enforcement is in the same case as Sovereign Command.

And the society, be it modern Indian or be it ancient Irish, which knows no specially consecrate and recognisable sovereign ordainer, is equally ignorant of specially consecrate and recognisable sovereign enforcer. The Village

Council administers and declares, and Village Society enforces; the Rajah neither permits nor commands, nor yet enforces. The Brehon declares the law: it may be shrewdly suspected that he sometimes *makes* the law which he proclaims: superstition may even lend some slight enforcement to his declarations: but the Brehon is not a sovereign but a judge.

II. The Philological Objection to Austin's analysis of Law as Command.

Clark, *Practical Jurisprudence*, Chapters II.—VII.

§ 6. The second main objection to the Austinian analysis is founded upon the evidence of Philology. Words are to-day mere titles, but words have root-meanings. And, if words may speak for themselves by these root-meanings, Obligation precedes Command with the Indo-European.

"Obligation" precedes "Command" in root-meanings: Greek,

Maine, *Ancient Law*, Chap. I. Holland, *Jurisprudence*, pp. 13, 14 n.

The Greek has his "Law": he acknowledges the reign of Θέμις, of Δίκη and of Νόμος. Θέμις, the earliest of these in point of time, is "ordinance," "the appointed," but it is the ordinance of Heaven made known to men through the inspired mouth of some Hellenic Dubhthach, some priestly or royal judge, touched by the sanctifying hand. Δίκη is "judgment," the "indicated," the "revealed": while Νόμος is pure "Custom."

Roman,

The Roman, again, has his three jural conceptions, *Jus*, *Lex* and *Rectum*. But *Jus* (the abstract) is not "the *jussum*," but "that which joins," so "the binding," and "the proper."

Lex (the concrete) is "that which binds," or, may be, "the read-out," whether in rogation or otherwise. *Rectum* is not "the commanded" (*rego*), but "the straight" (Sanskrit *Riju*), while to do wrong is "to twist," to wrench, to adopt crooked courses. And so the derivatives *Diritto*, *Derecho*, *Droit*, which descend through the late *Directum*, bring down, like *Right*, *Recht* and *Richter*, the root notion of "physical straightness."

English.

The primitive English law was Æ, "the eternal," "the everlasting," the descended from old time. The Saxon recognised law also in the Dóm, "the judgment"; he recognised it, too, in the Asetnis, "the ordinance"; but that which he finally accepted at the hand of his Danish conqueror was none of these, but Lagu, "Law," "that which lies."

"In the unconscious definitions of law," says Dr Clark, "furnished by those early names of it, which I have been "examining, different conceptions of *law* present them-"selves not only in different nations but in the same. "The nearest approximation to a uniform or pervading "idea is certainly not so much that of *enactment, position,* "and *command,* as of *antiquity, general approval* and *usage*: "where an original notion of *ordinance* does appear, it is "not human but divine.

"That which is *fitting, orderly* or *regular* (*jus*); that "which is *observed* (*witoth*); that which is *from ever-"lasting* (*æw*)—these are the earliest ideas of law which "we can find in the language of the Romans, the Goths, "and the Anglo-Saxons or early English. Some notion of "external institution in *witoth,* some notion of divine "authority in *æw,* may not unreasonably be imagined "or inferred, but are certainly not expressed in these "names. The word of moral approbation in that 'pri-"'maeval antithesis,' *Right* and *Wrong,* does not originally "designate *law,* although the sentiment expressed by "that word may be, in some languages, assumed to be "part of the basis of law, on sufficient etymological "grounds.

"The difficult Greek νόμος, a comparatively late name "in the sense under consideration, expresses, if I am right "in my explanation of it, simple *usage*: but the oldest "Greek conception of law is θέμις, the *ordinance* of heaven "—a view exactly coinciding with the well-known tradi-"tion of the Hindus.... The body of primaeval law or cus-"tom, though independent of human *institution,* is, in the "earliest times, conceived as the subject of human *admi-"nistration.* The *Judex* declares what is *jus,* the δίκη or "declaration of the θεμίζων furnishes a name for justice, "and the widespread word of moral approval, *right,* "becomes, through the agency of the *richter* a name for "*law*. The mere act of setting or appointing is all that "appears to be expressed in the Gothic and early English "names for judge—*staua* or *dema*—the latter of which "may indeed be confined to the special setting by way of "*judgment*. It is in the stage of judicial declaration that "what was by *general opinion* ancient, fitting, customary "or right, becomes so much of the same as will be recog-"nised, and as a natural sequence enforced, by a common "officer.... Neither the θέμιστες nor the *domas* are gene-"ralisations got by some logical process out of individual "decisions; nor are they the decisions themselves, as "original sources. They are *previously existing principles* "*or rules*, declared by the judge, who *assigns or selects* the "right one."

Clark, *Practical Jurisprudence*, pp. 90—92.

"*Observance* with our Gothic ancestors, in *witoth*: "*immemorial customs* with our Saxon ancestors, in *æ*, "appear to be their first ideas of law. In the case of "the former our knowledge begins and ends with one "literary work: in the case of the latter we can trace a "development of institutions and ideas not very dissimilar "from that appearing in Greek phraseology. The pro-"spective rules to guide judicial decision (*domas*) resemble "the Greek θέμιστες, while the more general *asetnissa* "may be compared with the θεσμοί. The name which "has, with us moderns, supplanted the rest, the northern "*lagu*, if treated, in England, as equivalent to the native "*dom*, may have somewhat lost its original signification. "But that signification must have been rather one of "custom, than, as in the *domas* and θέμιστες of ordi-"nance."

Clark, *Practical Jurisprudence*, pp. 75, 76.

The term law then translates into English a long succession of other terms, which have been employed by various peoples from time to time to express their conception of a particular notion. The analogies set forth have been various, but the consistent notion to be extracted from all is not command but obligation, not imposition but observance, conduct and orderly conduct. The fundamental basis of Law as evidenced by Philology is observance:

the determinate imposer and the determinate sanction are but mere modern accidents.

To limit to a modern narrow idea an old wider denomination is actually to import confusion.

It might be well, indeed, to distinguish by specially appropriate names between rules accompanied by, and rules devoid of, those modern accidents; but to attempt a distinction after the manner of Austin by confining the ancient appellation to the rules of the new model, and denying it to the old, is but to add to that confusion in terminology which Austin would fain see disappear.

III. The Objection to Austin's Analysis of Law as Command derived from Common Usage: the term Law has not been by writers in general restricted to Command.

§ 7. By speakers and writers of every tongue throughout all time to the present day, the term "law," its equivalents and concomitants, have been familiarly employed, and employed not with any rigid restriction to command imposed by determinate superiority to determinate inferiority, and enforced by determinate sanction, but with every shade of meaning, from the wide high-sounding generalisations of Montesquieu and Hooker to the trite and narrow delimitations of Hobbes and his admirer Austin.

Hooker, *Ecclesiastical Polity*, I. 3.

Austin admits the facts of common usage, but he denies its propriety, its precise and philosophic character; he challenges in fact the presumption, which stands clear in support of the older and more usual terminology. Upon him lies the onus of proof of the position he would establish.

IV. Austin seeks to justify his terminology on the score of Utility.

And this Austin does not fail to recognise, and strives to justify himself, in some degree, upon that utilitarian ground which alone is open to him, the surpassing advantages ensuing to mankind from the acceptance of his postulates; upon the ground that his delimitation is that which is demanded by considerations of highest philosophical and logical convenience; that by the acceptance of that delimitation alone can be laid the foundations of a complete science of law, can the field of jurisprudence and morals be rescued from the prevailing deluge of "muddy speculation," shall we be preserved from "the most foolish conceits" of lawyers like Ulpian, from the

Austin, *Jurisprudence*, I. p. 90
I. p. 215.

Austin, *Jurisprudence*, I. p. 216.

I. p. 217.

"misleading and pernicious jargon" of those moderns who still affect Natural Law, and the "fustian" of authors like Hooker.

But here he confuses the "is" with the "ought to be."

It were, perhaps, enough to urge in reply, that Austin is herein guilty of that very confusion of the *is* with the *ought to be*, which he so often and rightly denounces. To contend that men *should* employ exact language is matter of opinion: to assert that they *do* is matter of fact.

"Laws proper, or properly so-called, are commands; laws which are not commands are laws improper or improperly so-called."

So to assert as matter of fact is to give the lie to all History. So to assert as matter of advice is to prefer the logic of the school to the peace of the human race.

And, although his usage has the merit of neat terminology,

§ 8. It is upon this narrow ground that must be fought out the final issue.

For other than English-speaking peoples, for peoples who have to do with *Droit des Gens* or *Völkerrecht*, the difficulty is non-existent. Is it well at this stage of our English legal History to refuse the name Law to the rules which regulate the mutual dealings of States?

its deleterious practical consequences must secure its rejection.

To confine the term Law to the commands of determinate human authority, to commands enforced by determinate sanctions, would doubtless facilitate the framing of a formally faultless Science of Jurisprudence. But, on the other hand, to deny to any rule the name of Law, on whatever ground, would be in the popular mind to deprive it of all that peculiar halo of respectful reverence which has undoubtedly attached to the term in the passing of the ages. Either a rule governing human conduct is law or it is not; if it is not law, it is not binding. So argues the average man, "the man in the street," and it is useless to talk to him of the obligation of morality, more particularly if he be taught that the test of morality is utility. The popular mind, as Austin's master, Jeremy Bentham, saw, does not draw fine distinctions. Were it not for its deleterious practical consequences we might be content to leave the great legal precisian in the undisturbed enjoyment of his logic and his verbal purism, but, if the choice must indeed be made, rather let us seek out some other unoccupied route to legal scientific perfection[1] than, by claiming as private a hitherto public highroad, block the way of a progressive International Law. Rather let us have peace and peacefulness without the blessings of neat terminology than precise language and therewith the spirit of lawlessness. It is well to have a formally faultless Science of Jurisprudence: it is better to have English-speaking peoples displaying ready obedience to the dictates of Honour, Justice and proved Utility enshrined in the rules known as the Law of Nations or International Law.

[1] Why cannot students of Jurisprudence expunge from their science the term *Proper* as applied to a special field of Law?

CHAPTER II.

THE EVIDENCE OF INTERNATIONAL LAW.

Civilised States have in their mutual dealings observed rules of conduct: evidence available to prove the allegation.

§ 9. THE preceding pages have, it is hoped, sufficiently established the allegation that rules of conduct observed by States in their dealings with each other were, assuming such rules to exist, fitly styled International Law.

It remains to establish that such rules have been in fact observed. Before proceeding with the attempt, however, it were advisable to consider the nature of the evidence available for it.

The evidence purely historical.

§ 10. The proof of the allegation can, it is clear, be only furnished by History and direct observation. So the available authorities are every written document, every record of act or spoken word which presents an authentic picture of the practice of states in their international dealings. But these, having very various relative values, must be carefully classified.

Wheaton's classification of the authorities of International Law.

§ 11. Wheaton classifies the "sources" of International Law under six heads:—

(1) Text writers of authority, showing what is the approved usage of nations, or the general opinion respecting their mutual conduct, with the definitions and modifications introduced by general consent;

(2) Treaties of peace, alliance and commerce declaring, modifying or defining the preexisting international law;

(3) Ordinances of particular States prescribing rules for the conduct of their commissioned cruisers and prize tribunals;

(4) The adjudications of international tribunals, such as boards of arbitration and courts of prize;

(5) The written opinions of official jurists, given confidentially to their own governments;

(6) The history of wars, negotiations, treaties of peace, and other transactions relating to the public intercourse of nations.

Wheaton, *Elements*, I. i. § 15.

These are all sources of law in the same way, namely, in so far as we may extract from them authoritative evidence of what has been and is the accepted practice of states. The sole source of law in the language of Austin is actual observance.

(1) Text writers as authorities.

§ 12. Text writers, when they do their duty, are simply the impartial historians of International Law. To them it belongs to note actual facts and events, and to extract from them broad principles for the future guidance of mankind. The authority they possess, they possess not as judges, but as skilled observers and relaters, and that authority will increase or decrease, accordingly, according as their representations present, or do not present, an accurate picture of actual practice. When the text writer becomes a theorist, it is time for men to look askance at his opinion; and when he becomes, as he too often does become, the advocate of the special view of a particular people, his arguments must be treated as the arguments of counsel in a court of law. Greater authority is wont to be assigned on the Continent to the opinions of jurists than in England and America, but even in English and American courts the views of certain writers, more particularly the authorities of the classic period from Grotius to Vattel, are at times freely cited in support of special arguments. In the end, nevertheless, the text writer is a good witness, and speaks with convincing authority, when he speaks of past facts, not when he ventures upon moral advice. Gentilis, Grotius, Puffendorf, Zouch, Bynkershoek, Leibnitz, Wolf, Vattel and the rest, were great men in their generation, but they were not advisedly makers of law. Their opinions may have passed, and undoubtedly in many cases did insensibly pass, into the opinion of their age, and became reflected in practice, but that honour they owed to the strength of their intellect and the soundness of their appreciation of the moral needs of their time. And their successors are in like case.

Their evidence commonly second hand.

The information of the text writer is commonly second hand.

(2) First hand authorities:—

§ 13. Amongst first hand authorities must be classed the actual statements of officers, ministers and judges personally and directly engaged in international affairs and in the administration of the appropriate law.

(i) Official declarations of Law Officers and Ministers, and official instructions.

§ 14. The declarations of official jurists cannot be taken as absolutely unassailable statements of correct principles of International Law, even as set out in the usage of the state of the declarant, the interests of state-craft being only too apt to vitiate the arguments of the state lawyer, as the *Exposition des Motifs* of the Prussian Commission of 1751 may well be admitted to testify; but such declarations do naturally constitute a fair reflection of current legal opinion in the particular state. And to such declarations may at least be applied with reasonable certainty the rule of law which attaches a special value to "declarations against interest." Where, that is, the law officer of a Government, being consulted by his superiors on the legal character of their claims against a foreign state, has in confidence reported adversely to those claims, it is no unreasonable assumption that his report covers an indisputable proposition of International Law as hitherto generally received.

Amongst such declarations may be specially cited the published Opinions of American Attorneys-General, and similar opinions of British Law Officers scattered through numerous Blue Books.

The same view concerning declarations against interest may be applied to the despatches of Foreign Ministers and Diplomatists found in collections of State Papers, although these in the nature of things hold a brief for a national case.

Official instructions to the commanding officers of public armed forces or to responsible civil servants must be taken as setting forth the understanding of current International Law held by their framers. Thus we have in England Instructions by the Lords of the Admiralty and Orders in Council, and in the United States the invaluable *Instructions for the Government of United States' Armies in the Field.*

(ii) Adjudications of municipal courts.

§ 15. The adjudications of the municipal courts of any one country must naturally speak with a less weight of international authority than would the decisions of a specially appointed international court; but, fortunately for the world's peace, national judges like Lord Stowell in England and Marshall, Story and Kent in the United States have been found capable of rising superior to the admonitions of purely national interest, and of responding to the call of a world patriotism. When the judgments of Scott[1] are freely quoted in the Courts of America, and American reports are cited before British judges, we have to do with authorities more than municipal. And when to the high value attached in Great Britain and America to legally decided precedent is coupled the principle that the judgment of the highest court of the land is absolutely binding until the law be changed by express legislative enactment, the invaluable character of the reported decisions upon international questions of the American Supreme Court, and of our own Admiralty Court and House of Lords, becomes abundantly evident. They show in the most authoritative fashion not only what has been, but what upon the very strongest grounds of presumption will be, the practice of the particular states, that practice enshrining understanding of general International Law.

(iii) Adjudications of international tribunals.

§ 16. In recent years an increasing desire has been displayed in some quarters to secure the reference of

[1] See the Admiralty Reports of C. Robinson, Edwardes, and Dodson.

international disputes to the arbitration of mixed courts, whether of specially selected arbitrators appointed *ad hoc* for the settlement of a particular quarrel, or of a permanent board established for the resolution of any questions of international law which may chance to arise between particular peoples.

So early as July 8, 1873, a resolution in favour of international arbitration was, on the motion of Mr Richard, carried by a majority of 10 in the British House of Commons against the full strength of the Liberal Government of the time. On Nov. 24 in the same year, the Italian Government having accepted a resolution to the same purpose moved by Signor Mancini, it was unanimously adopted. And the example thus set was followed by the Second Swedish Chamber on March 21, 1874, by the U. S. Congress on June 17, 1874, by the Second Chamber of the Dutch States General on Nov. 27, 1874, and by the two Belgian Houses on Jan. 20 and Feb. 17, 1875.

Manning, *Law of Nations*, Ed. S. Amos, Ch. XIV.

Revue de Droit Int. 1875, p. 79.

Recent efforts in the direction of permanent Courts of International Arbitration.

Certain practical steps have lately been taken in the direction of the establishment of a permanent system of arbitration amongst a limited number of Powers.

On May 24, 1883, Congress approved an Act which authorized the President of the United States to invite the several other Governments of America to join the United States in a Conference "for the purpose of discussing and recommending for adoption some plan of arbitration for the settlement of disagreements and disputes that may hereafter arise between them."

The Washington Congress, 1890.

Parl. Papers, United States, No. 9 (1893), p. 3.

Invitations having been issued in pursuance of this Act, a Pan-American Conference composed of representatives of eighteen Governments met in Washington in 1890. The Conference adopted three Reports. The first recommended the conclusion by the Governments represented at the Congress of a uniform Treaty adopting arbitration as a principle of international law for the settlement of differences between American nations, and laying down rules for the establishment of a Court of Arbitration for the decision of any question so arising.

The signatories of this treaty would bind themselves to regard arbitration as obligatory in all cases, the sole questions reserved being those which, in the judgment of any one of the nations involved in the controversy, might imperil its independence, in which event arbitration should for such nation be optional only.

The second Report recommended the bringing of the subject of arbitration to the notice of the nations of Europe with a view to their adoption of a similar method for the settlement of disputes between them and any American Power; while the third advised that the principle of conquest should not be recognised during the continuance of the Treaty of Arbitration as admissible under American public law, all cessions of territory or renunciations of the right of arbitration made under threat of war or in the presence of an armed force during this period being declared null and void.

The recommendations of the delegates did not remain unfruitful. The form of Arbitration Treaty recommended by them was promptly signed by ten of the Powers represented at the Conference, including Bolivia, Ecuador, Guatemala, Haïti, Honduras, Nicaragua, Salvador, the United States of America and the United States of Brazil. The treaty is to remain in force for twenty years from the date of the exchange of ratifications, and subsequently will remain in force on each of the contracting nations until formally denounced by it, a year's notice being required before such denunciation can operate to release the denouncing Power. *Parl. Papers, United States,* No. 9 (1893), pp. 8, 9.

In transmitting the Reports of the Conference to Congress on Sept. 3, 1890, President Harrison expressed the opinion that the ratification of the treaties contemplated by them would constitute "one of the happiest and most "hopeful incidents in the history of the Western Hemi-"sphere." **Message of President Harrison, Sep. 3, 1890.**

Meanwhile on Feb. 14, 1890, the Senate of the United States (the House of Representatives concurring) resolved that the President be requested to invite "from time to **Resolutions of Congress,** "time as fit occasions may arise, negotiations with any "Government with which the United States has, or may "have, diplomatic relations, to the end that any differences "or disputes arising between the two Governments which "cannot be adjusted by diplomatic agency may be referred "to arbitration, and be peaceably adjusted by such means."

Parl. Papers, United States, No. 9 (1893), p. 1.

And on July 23, 1892, Mr Sherman introduced a Bill into the Senate authorising the President to appoint a Commission to visit other Governments "for the purpose "of instituting negotiations with them for the creation of "a Tribunal for International Arbitration, or other appro-"priate means whereby all difficulties and disputes between "nations may be peaceably and amicably settled and wars "prevented."

Parl. Papers, United States, No. 9 (1893), p. 15.

The pacific sentiments thus expressed have not been confined to the other side of the Atlantic.

and of the House of Commons.

On July 28, 1893, Lord Rosebery was able to transmit to Sir J. Pauncefote, to be communicated to the Government of the United States, a copy of a resolution of the House of Commons of June 16.

"Resolved,—That this House has learned with satis-"faction that both Houses of the United States' Congress "have, by Resolution, requested the President to invite, "from time to time, as fit occasions may arise, negotiations "with any Government with which the United States "have or may have diplomatic relations, to the end that "any differences or disputes arising between the two "Governments which cannot be adjusted by diplomatic "agency may be referred to arbitration and peaceably "adjusted by such means; that this House, cordially "sympathising with the purpose in view, expresses the "hope that Her Majesty's Government will lend their ready "cooperation to the Government of the United States "upon the basis of the foregoing Resolution."

Parl. Papers, United States, No. 9 (1893), p. 16.

The Anglo-American Arbitration Treaty, 1896–7.

And within the last four weeks (Dec. 1896) as the result of the Venezuelan Boundary difficulty, a general treaty for the settlement by arbitration of disputes arising between the two Powers has been signed by England and the United States.

The omens are propitious: nevertheless we yet await a Permanent International Court.

Such determinations as we have had by Special Courts of International Arbitration have in several notable cases staved off the horrors of war. They have been on occasion deprived of much of their value as expositions of International Law by the introduction into the treaties under which the tribunals were set up of particular clauses. Great Britain, for example, when going before the Geneva Tribunal on the "Alabama Claims," whilst agreeing to be bound by the Three Rules of the Treaty of Washington, expressly denied their obligatory character at the time when the referred occurrences took place. But, where such special stipulations are non-existent, the value of a judgment by the selected representatives of a number of neutral Powers can hardly be over-estimated, and, even where they exist, the decision is all-important within the limits laid down, not only as the expression of *opinion* by a tribunal as impartial as the world can produce, but as the laying down of the *law* by specially qualified selected judges. The judgment of a magistrate is not deprived of its character as a correct exposition of law by a skilled and faithful interpreter, because the bailiff of the court would be unequal to the task of compelling obedience to the decision, should one or other of the parties be disposed to dispute its terms.

Value of judgments of Special International Tribunals of Arbitration.

§ 17. Treaties are the most authoritative of international acts. But treaties are of various kinds, and the value of a treaty as evidence of International Law depends upon its particular quality, upon the parties, their objects, and, in some degree, upon their circumstances.

(iv) Treaties and the General Acts of International Conferences.

In general, treaties may be classed as of two kinds.

Treaties are

(*a*) There are treaties declaratory of International Law as understood by the parties. Such treaties are unfortunately rare, but their value, where they exist, is

(*a*) declaratory or

all the greater, and that value increases with the number and importance of the contractors. Amongst such may be classed the Declaration of Paris, 1856. "Privateering is "and remains abolished." "Blockades to be binding must "be effective." "The neutral flag covers enemies' goods, "with the exception of contraband of war." These are clear authoritative statements of general International Law, although not every civilised State may have yet expressed its formal adhesion to them, whether by word or practice. With such declarations must be classed the formally ratified General Acts of International Congresses.

(β) stipulatory.

(β) There are stipulatory treaties. These may be of mere passing interest, acts dictated by the temporary position of the parties, but of no value as expositions of International Law; or they may contract for the observance by the parties of a particular international practice. In this last case the necessity for express contract demonstrates at least the non-existence of an universal international practice in the sense stipulated for: it may prove that practice exists to a contrary effect, or merely that general practice does not fully secure the observance of the conduct desired. In point of obligation such agreements operate only as between the contracting parties. The mere fact that a vast number of such treaties have been entered into in the same sense does not make the practice stipulated for general International Law. At most it marks the growth of a general international desire.

Their value as evidence of practice.

Treaties, then, like other recorded public acts, afford evidence as to the existence of certain rules observed as International Law, but, according to their character, the evidence afforded is positive or negative in tendency: they may declare the existence, or they may demonstrate the non-existence of sufficient recognition to justify the regarding of a particular rule as a binding principle of International Law.

Interpretation of Treaties.

The interpretation of a treaty is but a special instance of the interpretation of a contract, and calls for the application of well-known canons.

§ 18. The importance of non-official testimony is not to be overlooked. Biographies, private letters, and the reports of newspaper correspondents have often a special value as conveying the accounts of eye-witnesses of actual international events. (v) Private Correspondence, Biographies, &c.

PART I.

CHAPTER I.

THE EVOLUTION OF INTERNATIONAL LAW.

The proof that rules of conduct have been observed between state and state involves the determination of: (1) The states observing the rules, (2) The rules themselves.

§ 19. THE student approaching for the first time the pages of History to seek unguided for the proof of the existence of an International Law, and thereby necessarily for some detailed knowledge of its dictates, will be apt to be repelled. In the first place the field of his labour is colossal, it being no less than the legal history of all civilised peoples, the history indeed of humanity from a particular standpoint; in the second place, the first view of international practice will probably present to him but a faint notion of fixed rule: it will convey merely the idea of a seething mass of inconsistent precedents and contradictory dicta; and it will be only slowly that there will rise before his eyes in the international field the large outlines of a legal system as connected and consistent as that which occupies any other position of the field of legal science.

The seizing of two simple facts will go far to clear his vision. He must recognise the fact that (1) a *corpus* of International Law at any period must be the creation of the then prevalent International System, that is, of the prevailing conception of a state and of the bonds binding state to state; and (2) that civilisation is progressive. An attempt to demonstrate the existence of rules of conduct between state and state at any one time will necessarily involve (*a*) an attempt to define the field within which the rules in question have operated, that is, to determine the communities between which they have been observed, (*b*) an attempt to point out some, at least, of the actual rules so observed.

I. International Law of Antiquity before the rise of the Roman World Empire.

§ 20. International Law, being the embodiment of state practice, might, it is clear, date from the birth time of states, or from the time when one state, become aware of its own corporate existence, found itself by the necessities of international intercourse obliged to accord recognition to the same quality in other communities. And Antiquity in point of fact offered for centuries a fair field for International Law until the rise of the World Empire of Rome reduced into subjection, with many Eastern peoples, all the nations of the West.

(*a*) *The Israelites.*

§ 21. The most ancient state whose records have been preserved to us in a condition of fair completeness is that of the Israelites. The Jewish international history is typical of that of many Oriental peoples fated to be absorbed into the Empire of Hadrian and Antoninus. The Israelites come before us as a people thirteen centuries or more before the birth of Christ with a polity fresh from the hands of its framer, the Law-giver Moses, the leader of a migration from Egypt. Applied in the first instance to wandering tent-dwellers, that polity retained on the settlement in Canaan the clear signs of its origin. Israel established in the Promised Land wears under the influence of Religion the form of a pure Theocracy, but, constructed upon the expansion of a Patriarchal Household, its political lines are those of a Confederation of independent kindred tribes. The International System of the ancient Israelite, therefore, is that of an independent tribal people surrounded by similar populations obeying various forms of government. The Israelites are, in the view of their historians and teachers, a Chosen Race of brother tribes

(i) The International System of the Jews a system of tribal communities.

clearly marked off from the surrounding Heathen. This fact colours all their international dealings. There was one law for Jew and Jew, another for Jew and Gentile. The eleven tribes in the day of the Judges refused to destroy utterly the recalcitrant Benjamites. After the division of Israel into two kingdoms commonly mutually hostile a clear distinction was drawn between the relation of the kindred tribes and general international practice. Shemaiah the prophet forbade Rehoboam of Judah to fight against the "brethren" of Israel. When Pekah of Israel had carried off in a successful invasion a vast number of the subjects of Ahaz of Judah, the captives were, upon the demand of the prophet Oded and of leading nobles of Ephraim, courteously returned to their own homes.

1. An inner international circle of kindred tribes recognised.

Judges xxi.

2 Chron. xi. 4.

2 Chron. xxviii.

A tie of common descent was recognised as existing between Israel and Edom, the offspring of Esau, and that tie deterred the migrating Israelites from forcing a way through the territory of that unfriendly people, although it failed to prevent subsequent wars of subjection.

Numb. xx.

Dwelling in the Debateable Land of Canaan, the meeting ground of the Egyptian and successive great Syrian Empires, the Tribes were compelled again and again to submit to a foreign yoke. The Ten of the North and the Two of the South were successively carried off into distant captivity (μετοικεσία) from which only a remnant returned. But, whilst the tribes of the Dispersion never lost their marked peculiarities, the returning Exiles restored their State in strict adherence to their ancient principles, and under the shadow of the successive Empires of Persia, of Alexander, of the Seleucidae and the Roman, the Jew retained his primitive pride of race. In later times he showed some willingness to make converts to his Faith, but the foreigner admitted to the full privilege of the Jewish Citizenship was to the last a proselyte adopted into the Jewish people after submission to the rite of circumcision. Common descent, in fact, constituted for the Jew the test of nationality, and suggested the first faint outline of an inner International Circle. Amongst peoples

Joseph., *Antiq. of the Jews*, xiii. 9.

outside this circle a distinction was drawn between the Seven Nations, the original occupiers of the Promised Land, and other foreign communities.

2. Amongst foreign peoples a distinction drawn between the Seven Nations and other States.

Treatment of the Seven Nations.

Towards the Seven Nations the policy enjoined by the Jewish Law Giver was very definite. "When the Lord "thy God," said Moses, "shall bring thee into the land "whither thou goest to possess it, and hath cast out many "nations before thee, the Hittites, and the Girgashites, "and the Amorites, and the Canaanites, and the Perizzites, "and the Hivites, and the Jebusites, seven nations greater "and mightier than thou; and when the Lord thy God "shall deliver them before thee; thou shalt smite them, "and utterly destroy them; thou shalt make no covenant "with them, nor shew mercy unto them: neither shalt "thou make marriages with them; thy daughter thou "shalt not give unto his son, nor his daughter shalt thou "take unto thy son." Deut. vii. 1–3.

But this command was confined in its operation to the tribes expressly designated. "When thou comest nigh "unto a city to fight against it, then proclaim peace unto "it. And it shall be, if it make thee answer of peace, and "open unto thee, then it shall be, that all the people that "is found therein shall be tributaries unto thee, and they "shall serve thee. And if it will make no peace with thee, "but will make war against thee, then thou shalt besiege "it: and when the Lord thy God hath delivered it into "thine hands, thou shalt smite every male thereof with "the edge of the sword: but the women, and the little "ones, and the cattle, and all that is in the city, even all "the spoil thereof, shalt thou take unto thyself; and thou "shalt eat the spoil of thine enemies, which the Lord thy "God hath given thee. Thus shalt thou do unto all the "cities which are very far off from thee, *which are not of "the cities of these nations*. But of the cities of these people, "which the Lord thy God doth give thee for an inheritance, "thou shalt save alive nothing that breatheth; but thou "shalt utterly destroy them; namely, the Hittites, and the "Amorites, the Canaanites, and the Perizzites, the Hivites, "and the Jebusites, as the Lord thy God hath commanded "thee."

Deut. xx. 10—17.

(ii) General International Practice of the Israelites. (a) The Law of Peace. Fair treatment of the resident alien.

§ 22. With peoples other than the Seven Nations the Israelites freely entered into friendly relations, admitting and protecting the foreign sojourner and carrying on an extensive commerce. Hiram of Tyre was an ally of David; under Solomon Jewish trading vessels became known in distant ports; later kings of Israel secured the right to establish trading quarters in foreign cities, and granted similar privileges to alien merchants[1].

Cf. Tac. *Hist.* v. 5.

Care for the faith of treaties.

Care for the faith of treaties was a marked characteristic of the Jews, insomuch that, having been inveigled into a convention with the Gibeonites, they admitted them as tributaries in direct contravention of the command of Moses as to dealings with the Canaanitish tribes. The Jewish national history is fairly free from that treachery[2] in international dealings which was a common feature in the public proceedings of other Asiatic peoples. More than one of the noble Asmonean house in later days lost his life by his confidence in Syrian fidelity.

Josh. ix.

Recognition of the sanctity of Ambassadors.

The Israelites recognised the sanctity of the legatine character. David resented by a peculiarly severe war the insults proffered to his ambassadors by Hanun, king of Ammon.

2 Sam. x.

The reception of the foreign refugee.

The reception of David by Achish of Gath may perhaps be cited as proving the early acknowledgment amongst the peoples of Palestine of the claims of the foreign refugee.

1 Sam. xxi., xxvii.

(b) The Law of War. Jewish war practice severe.

The war practice of the Israelites was terribly severe. Warring against Midian on their way to the Promised Land they slew all the males, took captive the women

[1] Ahab obtains from Benhadad I. the right to "make streets" in Damascus, a right exercised by Rezon of Syria, Benhadad's father, in Samaria. 1 Kings xx. 34.

[2] More than one Jewish hero or heroine stooped, however, to the crime of assassination, e.g. the assassination by Ehud of Eglon, king of Moab (Judg. iii.), the murder of Holofernes by Judith, and the praise by Deborah of the base act of Jael (Judg. iv.).

and children, carried off all cattle and goods and burnt the cities. This barbarity did not, however, satisfy the relentless Moses, who ordered a further massacre. The command of utter destruction directed against the Seven Nations was, although not absolutely, yet with fair completeness, executed. Not only was no quarter given but captive kings were put to death in cold blood. "Now "go and smite Amalek," ran the order of Samuel to Saul, "and utterly destroy all that they have, and spare them "not; but slay both man and woman, infant and suckling, "ox and sheep, camel and ass." Saul disobeying by the preservation of the cattle and of the Amalekitish king, Samuel pronounced sentence against him and "hewed "Agag in pieces before the Lord in Gilgal."

Refusal of quarter; Numbers xxxi. killing of women and children; Numb. xxi.; Josh. vi., vii., x., xi. slaughter of prisoners; 1 Sam. xv. 3. 1 Sam. xv. 33.

David smote Moab "and measured them with a line, "casting them down to the ground; even with two lines "measured he to put to death, and with one full line to "keep alive."

2 Sam. viii. 2.

The Israelites on occasion descended to the mutilation of their defeated foes. The men of Judah cut off the thumbs and great toes of Adonibezek. Even David took barbarous trophies of slain Philistines.

and mutilation. Judg. i. 1 Sam. xviii. 27.

The declamations of Psalmist and Prophets ring with references to ferocious barbarities.

Ps. 137; Is. xiii. 16, 18.

But savage as was the Jewish war practice it was no worse than that of the neighbouring states. The slaughter of all able-bodied warriors and the carrying off of women and children into captivity was in accordance with the universal practice of Antiquity.

The Jewish practice not worse, but rather better than that of contemporary peoples. Amos i. 3, 13; ii. 1.

Adonibezek, the mutilated king of Bezek, had himself dealt with conquered chieftains as the men of Judah dealt with him.

Judges i. 7.

The Philistines sent the head of Saul as a ghastly trophy through their cities, nailing his body to the wall of Bethshan.

1 Sam. xxxi. 9, 10.

"I know," says Elisha to Hazael of Damascus, "the "evil that thou wilt do unto the children of Israel: their "strong holds wilt thou set on fire, and their young men "wilt thou slay with the sword, and wilt dash their "children, and rip up their women with child." "But "what is the dog thy servant," replies the unabashed Hazael, "that he should do *this great thing?*" Eastern monuments tell a sad tale of ancient belligerent barbarity, and the Fathers of History complete the picture.

2 Kings viii. 12, 13.

Herod. I. 86; IV. 62; VI. 32.

Signs of an improving practice.

Moreover there are not wanting signs of the recognition by the Israelites of the claims of a milder practice.

The proposition of the king of Israel to smite the forces of the entrapped Syrians in Samaria was doubtless in accordance with general views of international right, but Elisha's question, "Wouldest thou smite those whom thou hast taken captive with thy sword and with thy bow?" and the consequent release of the prisoners seem to suggest the appearance of improved counsels.

2 Kings vi. 22.

The Mosaic command concerning fruit-bearing trees the germ of a Law of War.

In one particular the Mosaic Code anticipated in curious fashion modern limitations upon the exercise of belligerent force.

"When thou shalt besiege a city a long time, in making "war against it to take it, thou shalt not destroy the trees "thereof by forcing an axe against them: for thou mayest "eat of them, and thou shalt not cut them down (for the "tree of the field is man's life) to employ them in the "siege: only the trees which thou knowest that they be "not trees for meat, thou shalt destroy and cut them down; "and thou shalt build bulwarks against the city that "maketh war with thee, until it be subdued." It would not be too much to say that herein we see the beginning of a definite Law of War.

Deut. xx. 19, 20.

When the allied kings of Israel, Judah and Edom warred against the revolted tributary king of Moab (circ. 895 B.C.), the Israelites by direct command of Elisha "beat down the cities, and on every good piece of land "cast every man his stone, and filled it; and they stopped "all the wells of water and felled all the good trees," until the despairing Moabitish monarch offered his eldest son a burnt sacrifice upon his city wall, "and there was great "indignation against Israel."

2 Kings iii. 25–27.

§ 23. Ancient Greece in the days of her glory and down to the Macedonian Conquest (338 B.C.) consisted of a number of petty commonwealths jealously guarding each its independence (αὐτονομία) against its neighbours and against the non-Hellenic foreigner. Many or all of these commonwealths were historically traceable to earlier tribal arrangements common to all members of the great Aryan family, Athens in particular referring her greatness to the συνοικισμός of what were doubtless village communities. But to the Greek mind the State was ἡ πόλις, the city. The name reveals the conception which colours all Greek history. The state, Athens or Argos, possessed lands, made territorial conquests and planted distant colonies, but the city was all, her territories were adjuncts necessary indeed but subordinate. The state too was necessarily an aggregation of human beings, but although these human beings were conceived to be bound together by ties of common descent, it was as free citizens that they enjoyed the full benefits of state life. With the single exception of Sparta, state life in civilised Hellas centred in a walled town: and at the walls of the city Greek patriotism stayed till the days of Philip and of the Achaean League.

(β) *The Greeks.* (i) The International System of Ancient Greece: a system of City States.

Warde Fowler, *The City State of the Greeks and Romans*, Chap. I. Hammond, *Political Institutions of the Ancient Greeks*, Chap. II.

The Greek conceived of an autonomous city commonwealth with her Perioikoi and her dependent colonies, and he went no further. After the victory of Salamis (480 B.C.) Athens assumed of right that leadership (Ἡγεμονία) of the Hellenic communities which the incompetence of proud and selfish Sparta was content tamely to resign; but the states in her confederacy speedily found that the Athenian hegemony was in fact supremacy, and that for them the contribution of the free ally was tribute paid to a mistress. And when Sparta, putting herself forth as the champion of autonomy, succeeded by the help of the Great King's gold in the subjugation of her rival, she too failed —and failed ignominiously and more deservedly—in the very hour of her triumph. The Spartan lauded autonomy, but he practised tyranny, and, chafing under the brutal

Greek independence was the independence of the city,

rule of Spartan harmosts, Greece regretted the days of the milder Athenian sovereignty. The Greek knew in fact no other form of commonwealth than a free or a subject city and the sway of a tyrant, whether king of Macedon or Great King in Susa. A Leonidas might die battling not for Lacedaemon alone but for Hellas against the Mede, or a Kallikratidas curse the policy which brought Spartan commanders to beg their hoplites' pay at the doors of Persian satraps, but the Greek patriot of the ordinary mould was unable to extend his patriotism beyond his city commonwealth and the community of citizens. The history of the mutual relations of the Greek states is the history of the alternation of independence and subjection amongst cities whose citizens were in fact or in theory members of families of approved descent. The genius which enabled Thebes to overthrow the tyranny of Sparta was the genius of two only of her citizens: the glory of Thebes was born, and died, in Pelopidas and Epaminondas; and Hellenic unity came behind the spears of the conquering Macedonian phalanx.

and Greek patriotism was bounded by the city wall.

Xen. *Hellen.* I. c. 6, 7. Plutarch, *Lysander*.

Dion. Hal. II. 17.

The International Law of such a people could, it is clear, be hardly more than an intermunicipal law.

Greek International Law an intermunicipal law.

What traces do we in fact find amongst the Greeks of the recognition of an International Law?

(ii) International Law of the Greeks:—

§ 24. The Greek, drawing a clearly marked distinction between Hellene and Barbarian, recognised the sway of a Law of the Hellenes (τὰ νόμιμα τῶν Ἑλλήνων), which was stricter and more humane than that acknowledged by or as applicable to mankind at large (τὰ πάντων ἀνθρώπων νόμιμα).

Thuc. I. 3; I. 118. Plutarch, *Pericles*, c. 17.

The Greek International Circle.

The Athenians, fortifying the temple at Delium, were held by the Boeotians to have thereby outraged τὰ νόμιμα τῶν Ἑλλήνων, and the restoration of their slain was refused until its evacuation. The law forbade Greeks, so pleaded the Plataeans before their merciless judges, to slay prisoners freely surrendering; ὁ δὲ νόμος τοῖς Ἕλλησι μὴ κτείνειν τούτους.

Thuc. IV. 97. Diod. XIX. 63.

Thuc. III. 58.

This distinction of Hellene and Barbarian, like that of Jew and Gentile, may be taken as tracing the lines of a primitive International Circle. Dion. Hal. I. 31; IV. 25.

§ 25. Within the Hellenic circle the common Oracles and the common Games, over and above common language, common Gods and local propinquity, encouraged friendly communication and tended to extend the feeling of unity. (1) The "Law of the Greeks."

The Amphiktionic Council, which has been by some erected into a board of international arbitration after the model of the Kantian scheme, was in truth a religious, not a political, assembly, but nevertheless did operate as a symbol of international good fellowship, and to a certain degree as an active international agent. An Amphiktiony was in essentials a confederation of neighbouring States for the protection of some common temple and its worship, and to the providing of that protection were mainly directed the terms of the Delphic Amphiktionic oath. That oath even went the length of prohibiting the utter destruction of an Amphiktionic town, and the cutting off of the water supply of a besieged city; but this early attempt at a restraint of mutual violence was more necessary than effectual, and when the Delphic Amphiktionic league was active in lay matters, it worked rather as the engine of encroaching Macedon than as a court of international equity. The Amphiktiony as an international institution. Freeman, *Federal Government.* Thuc. I. 112. Laurent. II. 86. Aeschines, *De Falsa Leg.* 115.

"A review," says Thirlwall, "of the history of the "council shows that it was almost powerless for good, "except perhaps as a passive instrument, and that it was "only active for purposes which were either unimportant "or pernicious. In the great national struggles it lent no "strength to the common cause; but it now and then "threw a shade of sanctity over plans of ambition and "revenge. It sometimes assumed a jurisdiction, uncertain "in its limits, over its members; but it seldom had the "power of executing its sentences, and commonly com-"mitted them to the party most interested in exacting "the penalty. Thus it punished the Dolopes of Scyrus "for piracy, by the hands of the Athenians who coveted "their island. But its most legitimate sphere of action "lay in cases where the honour and safety of the Delphic "sanctuary were concerned; and in these it might safely "reckon on general cooperation from all the Greeks."

Thirlwall, I. pp. 435, 436.

(a) International Law within the Greek Circle in time of peace.

The mutual relations of the Hellenic cities in time of peace were characterised by rigid exclusiveness. Everywhere throughout Hellas citizenship was a privilege religiously protected against the foreign intruder, although not everywhere as at Megara admission to the suffrage was equivalent to entry upon the roll of the city Gods.

Dion. Hal. II. 17. Arist. *Polit.* III. c. 5. Plutarch, *Pericles*, c. 37. Laurent. II. 192, 304.

The foreigner at Athens,

The Athenians were justly reputed the most hospitable of the Greeks; but even at Athens the Metoikos, the domiciled alien, while he enjoyed the protection of Athenian laws through the agency of his patron (προστάτης), was subjected to special taxation, and was liable to compulsory service in the ranks of the hoplites, or even on the benches of the fleet.

Thuc. III. 16; Laurent. II. 114.

and at Sparta.

Sparta, in the days of her early severity, refused to admit strangers to reside within her precincts, and forbade her citizens to take up their abode abroad. But Xenophon, lamenting as an admirer of the Constitution of Lycurgus the decay of Spartan manners, remarks that, whereas in old time Sparta guarded herself by the Xenelasia against the corruption of her citizens by association with foreigners, the Lacedaemonians of his degenerate day were the most forward of men to make themselves governors (ἁρμοσταί) of foreign cities. Greek care for the stranger appeared at its best in treaties for the mutual administration of justice to the sojourning foreigner, and in international conventions for the establishment of mixed tribunals or even for the grant of Isopolity.

Laurent. II. 112; Plut. *Ages.* 10; Plut. *Lycurg.* 27; Thuc. I. 144.

Xen. *De Rep. Laced.* XIV. 4.

The Symbolon.

Arist. *Polit.* III. 1. 3; III. 5. 10; Xen. *Hellen.* I. 26; Laurent. II. 121; Polyb. XVI. 26.

The Xenia.

The Hellenes, like their neighbours, and like most half-civilised peoples, attached high sanctity to the guest tie, and the noble institution of the Xenia, extended from the mutual relations of private individuals to the public reception of representatives of States, was a prototype of the consulates of modern times. But in contrast to such examples of progress may be cited drastic customs like the

Thuc. I. 136, 137. Polyb. V. 37. Herod. II. 182.

Polyb. V. 95. Thuc. I. 13; II. 29; V. 43. Laurent. II. 119.

Athenian Androlepsia, whereby the relatives of a citizen murdered by a foreigner were empowered to seize three fellow-countrymen of the murderer, and hold them for judicial condemnation to compensation, or even the death penalty.

Androlepsia.

Demosth. c. *Aristocr.* § 96. Vattel, II. 18 § 351.

Amongst the less civilised Greek peoples the conception of international duty was primitive indeed. The Greek coastmen and islanders, like our own Saxon ancestors and the Scandinavian Vikings, at first regularly practised piracy and held it no disgrace. Hellenic maritime history begins with Mare Clausum. Minos, the first lord of the sea, obtained his title to supremacy by ridding the seas of pirates. The Greek built his city back from the sea as some preventive against piratical surprise. In the days of Thucydides the Ozolian Locrians, the Aetolians and the Acarnanians habitually plundered and raided the neighbouring lands, imitating the Carians and Phoenicians across the ocean, who were practised pirates. The Illyrians and Aetolians retained the character of freebooters until Hellas yielded to the Roman conqueror.

Prevalence of Piracy amongst less civilised Greeks.

Thuc. I. 5.

Thuc. I. 4, 8. Cf. Herod. I. 171.

Thuc. I. 7.

Thuc. I. 5, 8; II. 32.

It is by its war practice that the state of international legal advancement of a people may be most easily gauged, and Greek war practice was, even in purely Hellenic contests, terribly severe.

(*b*) International Law within the Greek Circle in time of War.

The herald and the trophy were inviolate, and truces were fairly observed. The Sacred Truce of Olympia was an early Truce of God. But the Greek temper too often got the better of rule. For the citizen soldier life had no value, and he wreaked his vengeance in frightful fashion. Pitiless ravage and destruction marked his path. Private individuals belonging to the enemy state caught in the field, or upon the seas, were ruthlessly slaughtered, and there were not wanting instances wherein not only allies, but unarmed neutrals, shared the fate of the merchants of the belligerent city in whose company they were found. No mercy could be looked for by the defenders of a stormed city, and even a capitulation might purchase for the women and children, and the stranger but the poor privilege of

Severity of Greek War practice.

Thirlwall, I. p. 441; Polyb. IV. 73, 74.

Thuc. II. 12; III. 24.

Thuc. I. 29, 54, 105; II. 22, 79, 84.

Thuc. I. 114; II. 19, 23, 25, 31, 47, 66; III. 7. Plutarch, *Pericles*, c. 34.

Thuc. I. 67; III. 32.

Thuc. II. 68; IV. 57.

Thuc. I. 29. Arist. *Polit.* I. c. 6. Thuc. I. 30; II. 5; III. 32; V. 116. Plut. *Lys.* c. 13; *Alcib.* c. 37. Thuc. III. 68. Thuc. V. 116. Thuc. III. 36—50.

slavery. Prisoners of Hellenic race were slaughtered by thousands in cold blood, and the fate of the survivors of the hapless Platæa, sons of the men whose appearance on the field at Marathon had roused to wildest enthusiasm the heart of Hellenic patriotism, offers but one of many examples of the influence of the spirit which guided the conquerors of Melos, and narrowly failed of moving the conquerors of Mytilene, which signed the death warrant of Nikias and the poor remnant of the great Sicilian expedition. Alexander sacked and razed Thebes and sold thirty thousand of her citizens into slavery. The most polished of the Hellenes were capable of decreeing the maiming of captives, and the Samians in the days of Pericles, in reprisals for similar wanton conduct on the part of their opponents, branded Athenian prisoners with insulting emblems. Even Solon, like Belisarius in later days, could poison the water-supply of a besieged city, and an Athenian captain could lead a troop of barbarous Thracians to the massacre of every soul in a defenceless and peaceful country town[1].

Plut. *Alex.* c. 11. Plut. *Lys.* c. 9. Plut. *Pericles,* c. 26. Thirlwall, I. 437. Thuc. VII. 29.

(2) The "Law of all Mankind."

§ 26. In his relations with peoples outside the Hellenic pale the Greek recognised the obligation of certain rules, though these were ill-defined. The slaughter by the Athenians and Spartans of the envoys of Persia was clearly an admitted breach of custom, intended, as it would appear, rather to proclaim in the most forcible fashion the character of the struggle upon which the culprits were prepared to enter than to express the Greek view of international right. And Xerxes recognised and bowed to the sway of a general law, whatever its character, when, refusing the proffered retribution of the Greeks, he declined to transgress "the laws of all mankind" (τὰ πάντων ἀνθρώπων νόμιμα). So it is the law with all men (νόμος ἐν πᾶσιν ἀνθρώποις) that, when a town is taken in war, goods captured belong to the captors. It may be that on

Herod. VII. 136. Cf. Thuc. I. 67.

[1] True such conduct was "worthy only of barbarians." It may be likened, perhaps, to the employment of Red Indians in Anglo-American warfare in the days of Chatham.

closer examination these laws reveal themselves rather as laws *universal*, rules of conduct observed by all men as men, than as laws *international*, rules of conduct observed by men as state members towards the members of another political aggregate, but, whatever their origin, *τὰ πάντων ἀνθρώπων νόμιμα* did fulfil for Greeks and Eastern despots the functions of an International Law. International Law so apprehended was rude and primitive enough. It might in its earliest stages justify the wildest tortures of Druid and Moloch priest, cruelties worthy of Iroquois or Aztec or negro of Dahomey, the crucifixion of the invading hostile sovereign or the insulting of the corpse of a fallen Hector, but it was something to have it recognised that the intercourse of men, members of diverse communities, was not absolutely lawless. And when, beside the vague and fleeting World Law, the law of all humanity, came to be recognised a law special to certain peoples, when the distinction was drawn between the progressive and the stationary, between civilisation and barbarity, and the Greek bowed to the sway of *τὰ νόμιμα τῶν Ἑλλήνων*, the lines of an International Circle appeared, and Hope dawned upon the darkness.

Xen. *Cyrop.* 7. 5. 73.

Law Universal rather than Law truly International, but still *a* law.

Thuc. I. 110. Herod. I. 86; IV. 62, 64. *Iliad*, XXII. 254, 337, 395.

And the International Law of the Greeks, we may unhesitatingly conclude, was an improving law. The Athenians did not hesitate to immolate Persian prisoners before the battle of Salamis (480 B.C.) as an offering to Bacchus the Devourer: the Thebans before Leuctra (371 B.C.) could not bring themselves to offer a human sacrifice, deeming it barbarous and impious. The average Greek general ravaged and burned without mercy, confounding in a common fate the soldier and the peasant; but Xenophon depicts his ideal king as making an agreement with his foe that the labourers on the land should be let alone on either side, and the operations of war confined to those bearing arms.

The Greek International Law a progressive law.

Plutarch, *Pelop.* cc. 21, 22.

Xen. *Cyrop.* 5. 4.

§ 27. In Ancient Rome, as in Greece, the root of the prevailing conception of the State was that of citizenship.

(γ) *The Romans.*

The Roman conception of the State.

Rome under her kings and in her early republican days was a City-State (*civitas*), one of many Italian independent societies. One by one her neighbours passed under her conquering yoke; tract after tract of Latin, Etruscan, Umbrian and Campanian land was added to the Roman

Vell. Pater. I. 14.

ager publicus; and Roman *coloniae*, like military outposts, securely established the ever-tightening bonds of Roman control; but down to the outbreak of the struggle with Carthage (264 B.C.) Rome continued a city commonwealth queening it over daughter communities and dependent or subject Italian townsmen and rustics, who enjoyed various degrees of civil and political right under capitulation with, or grant from, their iron-handed mistress. The First Punic War gave to Rome the first of a long list of foreign *provinces*, but distant conquests left her still the Eternal City, and even the Social War, in which she was fain to overcome by yielding to the Italians the Roman franchise they claimed (89 B.C.), only added to the number of the citizens in eight of her thirty-five voting tribes.

(*a*) Rome as a petty Italian State.

§ 28. In the first period of her history, when Rome was one of several Italian petty states, there was room for the adoption by the Roman of some such conceptions of international obligation as those which prevailed amongst

Her attitude towards the Foreigner.

the Hellenes. And in point of fact the practice of Rome in her external relations during this period reveals features similar to those distinguishable in the international practice of the Hellenic commonwealths. It was only in prehistoric times that every stranger was the Roman's enemy (*hostis*). Early Rome was a march city, and, in all likelihood, a trading emporium, and long before her growing wealth and military greatness had attracted to her thronging streets crowds of admiring or profit-seeking *peregrini*, the Roman was brought into constant friendly

1. Hospitality and Patronage.

Laurent. III. 1, 3.

contact with the foreigner. The guest-tie, public and private, was an institution known at Rome as in other communities of the Ancient World[1]. Roman citizens

[1] The tie existed between Scipio Africanus and Syphax as between Syphax and Hasdrubal, the son of Gisgo. King Eumenes was bound by

entered into the private relationship with inhabitants of distant towns; Roman patricians were proud of the title of patron of a foreign people; whilst upon specially favoured individuals or communities, who had deserved well of the state, were conferred the benefits of the Roman public hospitality (*hospitium*). And not only did the Roman Senate enter into treaties upon terms of equality with Tarentines and Samnites, not only were foreigners from time to time freely admitted to Latin or even to Roman civic rights, but the Roman magistrates directly provided for the enforcement at Rome of the legal rights of the alien visitor. The alien had, indeed, no part in the Roman *Jus Civile*; he was refused the *connubium* and *commercium* as well as the *jus suffragii* and *jus honorum* of the citizen, but the praetor administered for all foreign sojourners resident at Rome a regular system of equity. This system was *Jus Gentium*.

Dion. Hal. VIII. 3, 30.

Sallust, *Catil.* 41.

T. Liv. v. 28, 30; VII. 20.

Dion. Hal. II. 16.

2. *Jus Gentium* as a system of (1) Private International Law,

The history of *Jus Gentium* will, perhaps, continue to furnish matter for controversy amongst modern jurists, but whatever may have been the origin of *Jus Gentium*, whether as a conscious abstract of the laws common to the nations of the Roman world made by Roman magistrates for, and applied to the disputes of, the foreign visitor, or whether it was at the outset a purely Roman Equity, a place in international legal history belongs to a conception which marks the recognition by the Romans of the necessity for the application in certain cases by Roman Courts of legal maxims other than those of *Jus Civile*. The Roman possessed, in fact, in his *Jus Gentium* a system of Private International Law.

Maine, *Ancient Law*, Chap. III. Clark, *Practical Jurisprudence*, Chap. XIII. Austin, *Jurisprudence*, Lect. XXXI.

Maine, *Ancient Law*, p. 49.

Inst. I. 3. 2, 3.

Jus Gentium, however, included for the Roman rules of a different order.

(2) Public International Law.

An assault upon an ambassador or herald was a violation of *Jus Gentium*. Some relations of King Tatius, the colleague of Romulus, having ill-used the envoys of the Laurentes, the Laurentes, according to Livy, commenced

T. Liv. IV. 17, 19, 32; VI. 19; IX. 10; XXI. 25; XXXIX. 25.

the tie of hospitality at once to the Rhodian State and to each individual Rhodian. T. Liv. XXIX. 23, 29; XXX. 13; XXXVII. 54. Herod. II. 182.

T. Liv. I. 14. proceedings "according to the law of nations" (*jure gentium*). Envoys of the expelled Tarquin having been detected at Rome in a plot for the restoration of the kingship, their fellow-conspirators were thrown into chains, but, with regard to the legates themselves, after some discussion, the "law of nations (*jus gentium*) prevailed," and they were allowed to go free. T. Liv. II. 4.

On the other hand, the action of the Roman ambassadors sent to call upon the Gauls to refrain from attacking Clusium, in taking part in battle against the invaders, was a breach of the "law of nations" (*jus gentium*), and Quintus Fabius, the chief offender, although his surrender to the Gauls was improperly refused, was subsequently put upon his trial at Rome, and only escaped condemnation by voluntary death. T. Liv. v. 36, 51; VI. 1.

T. Liv. XXI. 10. Sallust, *Jug.* 22.

In these and numerous similar instances the terms employed are doubtless those of the historian of the Augustan age, but the facts related clearly demonstrate the recognition by the Romans from the earliest times of certain rules of practice, which, at any rate subsequently, known as *Jus Gentium*, trenched upon the field now occupied by Public International Law.

Jus Gentium was not law *international* but law *universal*.

§ 29. In *Jus Gentium* in its more public sense the Roman approached most nearly to our modern International Law. But *Jus Gentium*, even in so far as it protected the ambassador, was not in conception law *international*. *Jus Gentium* was at root law *universal*: the foundation of the system was community of observance by men of whatsoever nationality, by men as law-abiding human beings, not by men as members of different bodies politic. The Greek tutor explained this common observance, if the Roman pupil had not himself already conceived of some such ascription, by reference to a certain *Jus Naturale* or φυσικὸν δικαίον, a law which Nature herself had implanted in man, immutable and unchangeable, exact justice, self-evident to the individual exercising the right reason or the moral faculty with which he was

Aristotle, *Rhet.* I. 13.

Dig. I. 1. 9.

Cic. *De Offic.* III. 5, § 23; 17, § 69.

endowed; but it was the *general recognition* of this law, its character as rule acknowledged by all peoples who observed any law, which first caught the Roman eye. Church and Brodribb, *Annals of Tacitus*, I. 42, note. Tac. *Ann.* I. 142.

§ 30. The Romans observed a regular ceremonial with regard to the declaration of war, the making of peace and the framing of treaties. These rules constituted a special system, the *Jus Fetiale*, the guardianship of which was committed to a special body of officials, the College of Fetials. 3. *Jus Fetiale.* Dion. Hal. II. 52.

No war was in Royal and early Republican Rome deemed rightly (*pie, jure*) waged unless after the rejection of a formal demand of redress preferred with ornate ceremony by a Roman herald (*fetialis*) to the offending people. In default of satisfaction within thirty-three days after this demand, the herald was despatched to declare war by the hurling of a javelin dipped in blood into the territory of the foe. This form was referred by tradition to Ancus Martius or Numa, and the ancient people of the Aequicolae, a tradition which at any rate covers the fact that the ceremonial was at once antique and not exclusively Roman. Similar formality attended the conclusion of conventions, treaties made by *fetiales* by order of and in the name of the Roman people being held to require the ratification of the *paterpatratus*. The repudiation of the capitulation of the Caudine Forks was attempted to be justified by some Roman authorities on the ground that it was a mere unratified convention and not a peace[1]. The Roman declaration of war. T. Liv. I. 22; IV. 30; VII. 32; X. 45; XLII. 47. Dion. Hal. IX. 60. Cic. *De Offic.* I. 11. T. Liv. I. 32. Dion. Hal. II. 52. and the Roman treaty. T. Liv. XXX. 43. T. Liv. I. 24; IX. 5.

The infraction of formally contracted treaties was deemed by all right thinking Romans a breach of the most sacred of religious obligations and a particular cause of divine resentment. T. Liv. IX. 1; XXXIV. 31. Flor. III. 11. Dion. Hal. VIII. 2. Tac. *Hist.* IV. 57.

§ 31. The war practice of the petty Italian state was terribly severe. 4. *Jus Belli.*

[1] *Itaque non, ut vulgo credunt, Claudiusque etiam scribit, foedere pax Caudina, sed per sponsionem, facta est.* T. Liv. IX. 5.

The Roman war practice permits devastation, T. Liv. VIII. 1; XXIII. 41; XXIV. 20. T. Liv. V. 24; VI. 31.

Hostile territory was ravaged without scruple with fire and sword. Warring against the Faliscians and Capenatians the Roman forces wasted the country, "leaving "not a fruit-tree nor a vegetable": so likewise in war against the Volscians.

refusal of quarter, T. Liv. II. 16. slaughter and enslaving of captives, T. Liv. IX. 14.

Victory did not always stay the hand of slaughter in the open field. The Romans, fighting against the Auruncians, refrained from slaughter after battle no more than in the heat of action, and put the prisoners indiscriminately to death. When they defeated the Samnites after the capitulation of the Caudine Forks, they "slew without "distinction those who resisted and those who fled, the "armed and unarmed, freemen and slaves, young and old, "men and cattle."

special severity in the case of storm, T. Liv. II. 17; VI. 10; VII. 19; IX. 31. T. Liv. IV. 29, 34; V. 22; XXVII. 19; XLII. 63. of revolters and of deserters. T. Liv. XXVIII. 19, 20; XXX. 43. Flor. III. 19. Polyb. I. 7. Sallust, *Jug.* 56. Dion. Hal. V. 43; VI. 30.

Towns carried by storm suffered cruelly. The leaders in the defence, and even all the males who survived the tumult of the assault, were not unfrequently put to death in cold blood; the common herd of the inhabitants, men, women and children were regularly sold *sub corona* to merchants who followed in the train of the Roman legions. The armed defenders of a town which freely surrendered were habitually similarly enslaved. Rebels and deserters were treated with yet greater rigour, they being not merely put to death, but previously cruelly scourged and mangled. Hostages were in imminent danger of the like savage handling should their fellow-citizens violate their faith.

But the Roman "Law of War" did imposebounds on absolute savagery. Cic. *De Offic.* I. 11. T. Liv. V. 27, 28. Flor. I. 12.

The Romans of the Augustan age nevertheless ascribed to their ancestors a certain *Jus Belli*, which at any rate set a bound to absolutely unlimited savagery. When the treacherous tutor of the sons of the leading men of Falerii led his charges into the camp of the Roman besiegers, Camillus declared, according to Livy, that, whilst between the Faliscians and Romans there did not exist the form of society established by human compact, there did and ever would exist that implanted by nature. "There are," he said, "laws of war as well as of peace; "and we have learned to enforce them not less justly "than bravely[1]." And the traitor, stripped and with hands bound behind his back, was handed over to the boys to be driven back into Falerii by rods supplied by the Roman hero. It was this conduct which, according to the historian, induced the Faliscians to make peace, they being "conquered by justice and good faith."

Harsh as was the Roman practice it displayed the reign, and a particular respect for the letter, of law. The circumstances attending the repudiation of the Caudine capitulation show this Roman characteristic, however inadequate in point of fact was the measure of restitution offered to the magnanimous foe.

It displays respect for the letter of the law.

T. Liv. IX. 9.

The Roman soldier, who refrained from mocking a defeated foe by the erection of a trophy, looked with particular disfavour on treachery or breach of pledged faith. Mucius Scaevola in early days was but one of three hundred young Roman nobles who bound themselves by oath to attempt the assassination of Porsena; but the Roman Fabricius rejected with scorn the offer of the physician of Pyrrhus to poison his master.

Roman contempt of treachery

Flor. III. 2. T. Liv. XXII. 6; XXXIV. 31.

T. Liv. II. 12.

T. Liv. XLII. 47. Amm. Marcell. XXX. 1.

Truces were freely granted, not only for the burial of the dead, and for negotiation, but for prolonged periods of time; and their violation was strictly condemned.

and breach of faith.

T. Liv. XXX. 25, 37; XXXIII. 11, 12; XXXIV. 35. Dion. Hal. IX. 36, 58.

It is only by comparing the Roman with contemporary non-Roman war-practice that the soldier of the great Republic can fairly be judged. And when we find the Samnites not merely slaying, but previously torturing, the men of a town reduced by famine; the Lucanians mutilating in horrible fashion the body of the slain Epirote king Alexander; the Gauls of Northern Italy carrying off as trophies the heads of the slain, and fashioning the skull of a Roman consul into a libation cup for their temple service; we recognise the Roman as a civiliser even in his severity. In the eyes of the polished Hellene the war-practice of the Romans was particularly mild.

Compared with contemporary war-practice the Roman was not unduly severe.

T. Liv. IX. 31.

T. Liv. VIII. 24.

T. Liv. X. 26; XXIII. 24.

[1] *Sunt et belli, sicut pacis, jura; justeque ea, non minus quam fortiter, didicimus gerere.*

(*b*) Rome as a Mediterranean Power.

§ 32. In the second period of her history Rome became a Mediterranean power.

The rivals, Rome and Carthage, were members of a group of states representative of ancient civilisation, which, marching in common upon the Mediterranean seaboard, were hemmed around by marauding barbarian tribes with whom they waged a practically perpetual war.

A true International Law becomes possible.

Polyb. XVIII. 46.

1 Macc. viii.

When Rome, become the mistress of Italy, wrestled to the death with Hannibal, proclaimed the liberation of Hellenic cities from the yoke of Philip, or conferred the title of friend and ally upon Attalus of Pergamus, Judas Maccabaeus, or the Numidian Masinissa, a fair field existed for a true International Law.

Polybius as an authority upon international practice.

§ 33. For a view of the international practice of the beginning of the period we are peculiarly fortunate in the possession of the "Histories of Polybius." Polybius of Megalopolis, the son of Lycortas, the friend and successor of Philopoemen, the heroic Strategos of the Achaean League, was born about 200 B.C. Himself early admitted amongst the foremost statesmen of the League, employed on various embassies, and in 169 B.C. commander of the Achaean cavalry, he was an eyewitness of the relentless advance of the Roman power amongst the States of Greece which followed upon the defeat of Philip (197 B.C.) and of Antiochus (191 B.C.). Carried off with a thousand other Achaeans to Italy after the final overthrow of Perseus at Pydna (168 B.C.) on a trumped-up charge of illicit assistance of the Macedonian king, and detained for sixteen years (167–151 B.C.) at Rome, where he acted as tutor to the sons of the noble Aemilius Paulus and contracted a close intimacy with his younger pupil, the famous Publius Scipio Aemilianus, he had peculiar opportunities for the study of the institutions of Rome and of the policy of the Roman Senate. Himself a soldier, accompanying Scipio to Carthage and present at the pillage of Corinth by Mummius (146 B.C.), he witnessed in active operation the Roman "Law of War." Subsequently a chief actor in the settlement of the affairs of his harassed native land, an acute observer, and an energetic traveller and collector, he became the second Father of International History in the West, and as such an invaluable witness as to the state of International Law. Shuckburgh, *Histories of Polybius*, Introduction.

He draws the clear outline of a true International Circle.

In his pages we seem to see clearly defined for the first time the outlines of a true International Circle, a distinct society of civilised states of very considerable extent. We recognise Great Powers in Rome, Carthage, Macedon, Syria and Egypt, with the Oriental monarchy of Parthia and the short-lived semi-Greek kingdom of Bactria; second-rate states in the free and confederate commonwealths of Continental and Sporadic Hellas, including the powerful naval republic of Rhodes, and in the independent kingdoms of Asia Minor, Pergamos, Bithynia, Cappadocia, Pontus and Paphlagonia; semi-barbarous principalities in Illyria and Numidia.

Amongst the Greeks there still linger traces of the ancient distinction between Hellene and non-Hellene. In the mouths of patriotic Hellenic orators and even of excited Macedonian soldiers the Roman himself is a barbarian[1]; but the cosmopolitan Polybius has no difficulty in extending the boundaries of civilisation, and distinguishing Roman, Carthaginian, Egyptian, Syrian, Macedonian and Bactrian from the barbarians round about. Polyb. IV. 45; V. 104. Polyb. XI. 5. Dion. Hal. VII. 3, 4, 70. Polyb. XVIII. 22.

He distinguishes between civilised and barbarous peoples.

Amongst the various Great Powers, and even amongst the Greeks themselves, there exist varying degrees of social advance. The Illyrians have been pirates from time immemorial. The Aetolians live by raiding in time of peace, and on the outbreak of war between any neighbouring states spoil indiscriminately both belligerents, without care for friend or ally. The Epirotes are not above acting Polyb. I. 65; X. 27—31; XI. 34; XXXIV. 10; XXXV. 2. Polyb. II. 8; V. 95. Polyb. IV. 3, 16; XVIII. 5; XXX. 11.

[1] The attempt of Dionysius of Halicarnassus to prove the Romans to have been descended from Greeks is a curious proof of the permanence amongst the Hellenes of the old prejudice. Dionysius classes the Egyptians without hesitation as Barbarians. Dion. Hal. VII. 70. The Egyptians in their turn placed all foreigners in the same category. Herod. II. 158.

Polyb. II. 6. in cooperation with these predatory pests. The Cretans are
Polyb. XIII. 8. not only pirates but treacherous in the last degree, and cruelly slaughter neighbours of kindred race in spite of
XXVIII. 15. ties of friendship, common institutions and sworn treaty.

But the most lawless of these front rank peoples are
Polyb. I. 65, 67; II. 7; X. 1; XVIII. 37; XXIII. 10; XXV. 6; XXXIII. 7. distinguishable from Mauretanians, Iberians, Thracians, Ligurians, Bruttians, Scythians, Bastarnae and Gauls, who are all absolute barbarians.

Amongst the civilised peoples he recognises the existence of

Amongst the civilised peoples Polybius notes the sway of two legal conceptions of international interest: "the laws of war" (οἱ τοῦ πολέμου νόμοι) and "the common laws of mankind" (οἱ κοινοὶ τῶν ἀνθρώπων νόμοι).

(1) "the Laws of War;"

Polybius remarks with regret on the general disuse in his day of the custom dictating formal declaration of war. Some slight traces of old-fashioned morality remain,
Shuckburgh's *Polybius*, XIII. 3. he observes, among the Romans; for they do formally
Polyb. IV. 26, 36; IV. 53; XXII. 4. declare war and make sparing use of ambuscades. The Greeks frequently authorise the exercise of reprisals in lieu
Polyb. II. 58. of, or as preliminary to, actual war[1].

The "laws of war" are stern enough. They permit the defeated, Polybius tells us, to be, with their wives and children, sold into slavery. When Scipio, after a treacherous Carthaginian attack upon Roman envoys, declines to admit to mercy towns freely surrendering, and
Polyb. XV. 4. enslaves all the inhabitants, his conduct is in no way denounced. The deliberate cutting to pieces in the first moments of a successful storm of every living thing which comes in the path of the assailants, is merely noted as a Roman custom designed to strike terror
Polyb. X. 15. into the defenders.

There are none the less definite "laws of war."

In 218 B.C. Philip attacked the great Aetolian mart of

[1] The Achaeans authorised reprisals against the Aetolian raiders: τὸ λάφυρον ἐπεκήρυξαν κατὰ τῶν Αἰτωλῶν. The Eleutherans, suspecting that one of their male citizens had been put to death by the Rhodian admiral Polemocles, first proclaimed a state of reprisals and then declared open war upon Rhodes. Τὸ μὲν πρῶτον ῥύσια κατήγγειλαν τοῖς Ῥοδίοις, μετὰ δὲ ταῦτα πόλεμον ἐξήνεγκαν.

Thermus. The Macedonians, gorged with booty of all descriptions, selected the most portable part of it, and collecting the remainder in a heap burned it. Of the consecrated arms hanging in the porticoes, some they carried off, some they exchanged for their own, the rest they destroyed. In so doing, says Polybius, they acted rightly and justly in the exercise of "the laws of war" (*κατὰ τοὺς τοῦ πολέμου νόμους καλῶς καὶ δικαίως ἐπράττετο*).

But words fail to convey the denunciation which Polybius launches against the Aetolian commander, Scopas, who at Dium set fire to the colonnades round the temple, destroyed offerings and threw down the statues of kings, and against his colleague Dorimachus, who demolished utterly the temple of Dodona. They demonstrated, he declares, *μήτ' εἰρήνης ὅρον μήτε πολέμου πρὸς Αἰτωλοὺς ὑπάρχειν, ἀλλὰ ἐν ἀμφοτέραις ταῖς περιστάσεσι παρὰ τὰ κοινὰ τῶν ἀνθρώπων ἔθη καὶ νόμιμα χρῆσθαι ταῖς ἐπιβολαῖς.* And the plea of retaliation advanced by Polyb. iv. 67. Philip for similar conduct at Thermus is unhesitatingly rejected.

"He imagined that he was doing nothing wrong in "giving the rein to his anger, and retaliating upon the "impious acts of the Ætolians by similar impieties, and "'curing ill by ill;' and while he was always reproaching "Scopas and Dorimachus with depravity and abandoned "wickedness, on the grounds of their acts of impiety at "Dodona and Dium, he imagined that, while emulating "their crimes, he would leave quite a different impression "of his character in the minds of those to whom he spoke. "But the fact is, that whereas the taking and demolish-"ing an enemy's forts, harbours, cities, men, ships and "crops, and other such things, by which our enemy is "weakened, and our own interests and tactics supported, "are necessary acts according to the laws and rights of "war; to deface temples, statues, and such like erections in "pure wantonness, and without any prospect of strengthen-"ing oneself or weakening the enemy, must be regarded

Polybius v. 11. Trans. Shuckburgh.

Polyb. iv. 27.

xxiii. 15.

"as an act of blind passion and insanity. For the purpose "with which good men wage war is not the destruction "and annihilation of the wrongdoers, but the reformation "and alteration of the wrongful acts."

Treachery Polybius always sternly condemns. The cutting down of trees upon hostile land is in his opinion absolute folly.

(2) "the common laws of mankind."

Polyb. ii. 8, 58; iv. 6.

The "laws of war" of Polybius are clearly the *Jus Belli* of the Roman. The "common laws of mankind" (*οἱ κοινοὶ τῶν ἀνθρώπων νόμοι, τὰ κοινὰ τῶν ἀνθρώπων δίκαια*) and "the well-settled rules of human right" (*τὰ παρ' ἀνθρώποις ὡρισμένα δίκαια*) are in like fashion Roman *Jus Gentium* operating upon a wide international platform. "The common laws of mankind" protect ambassadors and temples, prohibit the plunder of the lands of a friend and ally, and condemn breach of faith. The conception is obviously that of universal rule observed by just and law-abiding men.

Jus Belli and *Jus Gentium*, in a word, represent conceptions common to the Roman and the Greek, and probably to the entire ancient civilised world, although in the international practice of different districts those conceptions may be set forth with some slight divergence of detail.

International attitude of the conquering Roman:—

(1) Roman cosmopolitanism,

Dion. Hal. ii. 16.

(2) Rome the metropolis.

§ 34. Two noteworthy features distinguished the international relations of Rome in the second stage in her history. As the area of Roman conquests extended and province was added to province, (1) the cosmopolitanism of the Republic became ever the more apparent, and (2) Rome became more and more the centre and metropolis of the civilised world. The Roman citizenship was extended to the free population of Italy, and even to favoured foreign cities, but it was still the Senate and People of the Romans, ruling on the Seven Hills, which gave the law to subjects and allies, and negotiated with or waged war upon the ever-decreasing number of independent states.

§ 35. Foreign conquest by no means improved the Roman national character. Deterioration in Roman international practice under the late Republic.

The Roman still continued to refer to the obligations of *Jus Gentium:* he still attached high importance to the sanctity of ambassadors. He still had recourse to the ornate ceremonial of *Jus Fetiale*, although the ancient rites had come to be little more than formal[1]. *Jus Gentium*, Polyb. xv. 4. *Jus Fetiale*,

He still recognised a certain "Law of War" which imposed some restrictions upon belligerent cruelty. The order given by Hannibal when passing through Umbria and Picenum that all adult natives encountered should be slaughtered was customary only in the storming of cities. The treatment of the Numidian town of Capsa by Marius was *contra jus belli*, the town itself having, after surrender without a struggle, been burned to ashes, its youths put to the sword, its inhabitants sold for slaves, and the plunder divided amongst the Roman soldiers. The destruction in Attica by Philip of Macedon of temples and images of the gods was a breach of "all law, human and divine." and *Jus Belli.* Polyb. III. 86. Sallust, *Jug.* 91. T. Liv. xxiv. 33; xxxi. 30; xxxvii. 21; xxxix. 4.

In the first and second Punic Wars the opposing Roman and Carthaginian generals exchanged prisoners, a fixed sum in gold being paid by the receiver of the greater number. The ransom of prisoners and even of lands against ravage, was not unknown at the same period. T. Liv. xxii. 23. T. Liv. xxii. 52, 58; xxii. 31; xxxviii. 14. Polyb. xxi. 15.

We may even detect a faint glimmering of respect for neutral rights[2] in the abstention from hostilities of Roman

[1] It having been resolved to despatch a herald to declare war on Philip of Macedon in 200 B.C. the Fetial, in reply to the consul Sulpicius, stated that the declaration would be rightly (*recte*) made whether delivered to the king in person or to the first garrison within his borders. T. Liv. xxxi. 8. In later days when distance forbade the despatch of the Fetial to the foreign frontier, the requirements of law were deemed sufficiently complied with by the hurling of the bloody javelin into a plot of ground specially designated for the purpose at Rome.

[2] At the close of the second Punic War Macedonian envoys advanced a claim which recalls the doctrine of "limited assistance" of the 17th and 18th centuries. A force of Macedonian mercenaries under their general Sopater having been made prisoners by the Romans when serving for hire in the army of Hannibal, their liberation was asked. The

T. Liv. xxviii. 17. and Carthaginian vessels which chanced to meet in the harbour of Syphax.

Appearance of treachery, But there were sure signs in the later days of the conquering Republic of a lowering of the Roman national tone.

The deterioration in Roman domestic manners which followed upon close intimacy with the lax morality of the Flor. ii. 19. Vell. Pater. ii. 1. East is remarked upon by all Roman historians. The same feature is very perceptible in the international field. Livy draws attention to the altered state of Roman feeling which, in spite of the protests of the older senators, secured popular approval for Roman consuls who boasted of having deliberately beguiled Philip of Macedon in negotiation with a view to gaining time for belligerent preparation. savage cruelty, It was in a Servile War that Perperna, in a contest with pirates that Caesar, crucified prisoners. It was in a Civil Flor. iii. 19. Vell. Pater. ii. 42. War[1] that Sulla put to death in cold blood in the Villa Publica thousands of unarmed Italians and massacred without exception the inhabitants of a town which had voluntarily surrendered. But the history of the wars in Spain and the East tells the same evil story. In the affair of the Numantine treaties the Roman Senate repeated the questionable conduct of the incident of the Flor. ii. 18. Vell. Pater. ii. 1. Flor. ii. 17. Caudine Forks. Viriathus was assassinated. Aquillius poisoned springs in order to bring about the surrender of Asiatic towns, "a most dishonourable proceeding," "contrary to the divine laws and the practice of our ancestors," Flor. ii. 20. and "a desecration of the Roman arms."

and wars of mere plunder. The wars of the decaying Republic were in well-nigh every instance wars of mere plunder, the credit at Rome of the triumphing consul being largely dependent upon the value of the treasure brought to the public chest by the pillage of conquered cities. Causes of the deterioration: The causes of the depreciation in the Roman code of honour, and particularly

Romans rejected the demand, remarking that the league between them and Philip was broken in fact by the grant on the part of the Macedonians to the Carthaginians of aid in the shape of auxiliaries and money. T. Liv. xxx. 42.

[1] The war-practice in the civil contests of the early Empire is remarked upon as peculiarly savage. Tac. *Hist.* ii. 44; iii. 33.

in his war practice, are easily assignable. Not only did the Roman fall a victim to the lust of wealth and the temptations of undisputed power, but he was ruined by evil associations. The Carthaginian war-practice was at all times more cruel than that of Rome. The *crudelitas* of Hannibal is frequently remarked upon. Hasdrubal, in the last defence of Carthage, subjected to horrible torture on the walls in the sight of the besiegers the Roman prisoners in his hands. The tale of Regulus, even although apocryphal, may be taken as representative of Punic manners. The thin veil of Syrian and Egyptian civilisation concealed peculiarly hateful treachery and the fiercest of human passions. Thus Ptolemy Lathyrus overrunning the villages of Judaea strangled Jewish women and children and boiled them in cauldrons to secure for his forces the terrifying reputation of cannibalism.

barbarous foes, Polyb. XVIII. 35.

T. Liv. XXI. 13, 14. Eutrop. III. 11.

Eutrop. II. 25.

Joseph. *Antiq.* XII. 10; XIII. 6.

Joseph. *Antiq.* XIII. 12.

Reprisals exercised upon savage foes degrade the more civilised belligerent, and the case becomes worse when barbarians are employed as auxiliaries or even as regular troops. The savage atrocities which distinguished the "truceless war" between Carthage and her mercenaries are expressly referred by Polybius to the character of her levies, which were mainly drawn from barbarous peoples, Iberians, Celts, Ligurians and Balearic islanders. When the Romans adopted the same evil practice, and filled the ranks of the legions with the rude vigour of Gaul, Illyria and Germany, it was inevitable that the Roman military temper should in some degree suffer. And Rome under the late Republic was not only an African, but an Asiatic, Power.

Flor. II. 4.

barbarous allies, and barbarian legionaries.

Polyb. I. 65, 67, 80—86.

§ 36. Philopoemen and his contemporaries clearly saw that the goal of Roman statecraft was no less than the dominion of the civilised earth. It was with the thought that to the victor would belong the undisputed lordship of the world that Scipio, according to Polybius, encouraged his legionaries before Zama, and the battle, the historian is careful to add, assigned universal dominion

International Law in the days of the Roman Empire.

(*a*) The *Great Empire* 31 B.C. —395 A.D.

The Empire in conception, Polyb. I. 2, 3; IX. 38.

Polyb. XV. 9.

Polyb. xv. 10, 15. to Rome. The victories of the younger Scipio, of Sulla, of Pompey and of Caesar completed the work of Africanus, and, when the Roman Republic became the Empire of Augustus, not only Roman poets, but the voices of all thinking men, hailed the Eternal City as the mistress of the navigable ocean and of every habitable land, the first and only state recorded in history which made east and west the boundaries of her empire.

Dion. Hal. I. 3. Joseph. *Antiq.* XII. 3. Amm. Marcell. XXIX. 5. Justin, XXIX. 2.

and in actual extent.

Facts, historical and geographical, sufficiently harmonised, although they failed at any time to accord to the full, with this magnificent conception.

Under Trajan (98–117 A.D.) the Roman Empire reached its furthest actual extent. Then from the Firth of Forth and St George's Channel to the Persian Gulf, from the Dnieper to the Numidian deserts, and from the mouth of the Rhone and the upper reaches of the Danube and Theiss to the cataracts of the Nile, all nations and languages obeyed a single ruler.

An International Law impossible in a World State,

§ 37. The rise of this vast political creation threatened to extinguish the possibility of any true International Law.

When Caracalla (211–217 A.D.) extended to all his free subjects the full rights of Roman citizenship, there was but one people in the Western world. Conquering, the Roman had divided his spoils with the conquered, and continually extending throughout his conquests the Roman suffrage, he had at last familiarised mankind with the conception of a World State, a vast congeries of provinces enjoying various forms of local government, the free inhabitants of which, however diverse in race and social characteristics, were all equally Roman citizens, and equally subjects of one Imperial ruler, whether Spaniard or Dacian, Briton or Numidian, who claimed a world's obedience. In a World State International Law must find its vanishing point. And in point of fact, a science of International Law in the Roman Empire had been little else than a science of a World Law enforced by the arbitrament of a

Dion. Hal. VI. 19. Tac. *Hist.* III. 47.

single supreme ruler amongst subject tribes, cities and vassal kings. "Hast thou appealed unto Caesar? To Caesar shalt thou go."

It was practically the whole known world which acknowledged the *Pax Romana*. That peace was undisturbed by other than civil strife save in the far East by the restless Parthian, and in the far North by the wild bands of the Teuton and of the yet more barbarous Pict and Scot.

but a Law Universal still applicable.

§ 38. But the very fact that the Roman of the Kingship and of the Republic failed to conceive of a veritable *International* Law would naturally preserve its substitute from expulsion from the stage of the all-absorbing Empire, even had German, Parthian, New Persian and Goth, pressing upon the frontier, failed to convince the Emperor that his rule was less than divine. Law Universal was as applicable to a world of provinces as to a world of independent states. So whilst *Jus Belli* and *Jus Fetiale* still found field for employment in petty frontier wars, *Jus Gentium* lived on within the Empire alike as the "Law of all Mankind[1]" and as Roman Equity, to be employed in the moulding by Grotius and his successors of the International Law of to-day. And not only so: the extension of the Roman citizenship throughout the limits of the Empire completed the familiarisation of the whole western world with the magnificent creation of the Roman Civil Code, and secured the easy incorporation into modern International Law of decision after decision of Roman municipal origin.

Jus Gentium, *Jus Belli* and *Jus Fetiale* within the Empire. Tac. *Ann.* I. 39. Justin, XXXVIII. 4.

The Roman was, to the last, although a stern soldier,

§ 39. The international practice of the Empire is, in general, in no way distinguishable from that of the late Republic.

The Roman remained to the last at once a stern soldier and a man of law.

[1] Civilis, according to Tacitus, seeking to justify his rebellion referred to his twenty-five years' service in the Roman legions rewarded by the death of his brother, his own imprisonment and the demand for his life. His answering demand for vengeance he based upon *jus gentium*, i.e. universal law. *Jure gentium poenas reposco*, Tac. *Hist.* IV. 32.

The patriot-king or gallant chieftain, who had held out to the last in his native fastness against the disciplined valour of the Imperial legionary, having feasted the eyes of a gloating Roman populace in the long procession through the streets of the city, was led aside like an ox to the shambles as the white steeds of his conqueror's chariot breasted the Capitoline hill; while the common herd of his captive followers were fortunate if spared the death of the gladiator[1] to spend a life of bondage among the labourers of the mines or in the slavegang of some Roman villa.

Eutrop. IV. 20, 27; x. 3. Tac. *Hist.* II. 61.

Slavery was expressly declared by the Roman lawyer a mitigation of strict right in respect of the surrendering enemy.

Inst. I. 3. 2 and 13.

Germanicus, no specially severe commander of the early Empire, attacking the Marsi, divided his legions into five columns, and ravaged a space of fifty miles with fire and sword. Neither sex nor age moved his compassion. Every building, sacred or profane, including the famous temple of Tamfana, was levelled to the ground. The soldiers, without receiving a wound, cut down half-asleep, unarmed, or straggling foes. Coming unexpectedly upon the Chatti, the Romans captured or slew on the first onset *all those helpless by sex or age.* In battle on the Aller Germanicus gave no quarter. Tacitus, the historian of the campaign, seems to betray a sense of the severity of this war-practice, but in no way questions its legality. Yet *Jus Belli* exists, and in some degree restrains. A weak Roman and allied force besieging Uspe in Pontus in the time of Claudius, the besieged offered to surrender, but, "as it would have "been inhuman to slay prisoners and very difficult to "keep them under guard, the conquerors rejected the "offer, preferring that they should perish by the just "doom of war." And when Adgandestrius, chief of the Chatti, offered by letter to the Senate to poison Arminius,

Tac. *Ann.* I. 51. Tac. *Ann.* I. 56. a man of law. Tac. *Ann.* XII. 17.

[1] Constantine exposed to wild beasts in the arena captive Frankish and Allemannian kings. Eutrop. x. 3.

the reply was made that it was not by secret treachery, but openly and by arms, that the people of Rome avenged themselves on their enemies. Tac. *Ann.* II. 88.

The legionaries of Julian in Germany nearly four centuries later followed in every particular the war-practice of Germanicus, wasting the country with fire and sword, and slaying like sheep male and female, without distinction of age. The Emperor Valentinian in like fashion, advancing into the territory of the Quadi, slew every human being whom his sudden inroad surprised straggling in the open field, and, having burned the whole country, retired without loss. Amm. Marcell. XVI. 11; XVII. 10; XVIII. 2. Amm. Marcell. XXX. 5.

But the conduct of the Romans in slaying by ambuscade marauding Saxons retiring to their homes under the sanction of a truce is by Ammianus Marcellinus pronounced "treacherous and disgraceful." Amm. Marcell. XXVIII. 5.

To put ambassadors to death was in the view of the Greek historian of the Augustan age, παρὰ τὸν ἁπάντων νόμον. So too thought Tacitus: *Sacrum etiam inter exteras legatorum jus.* In the days of Nero the Gods were still regarded as protectors of the faith of treaties. Dion. Hal. VI. 16. Tac. *Hist.* III. 80. Tac. *Hist.* IV. 57.

The Roman contrasts favourably with his contemporaries.

And, as in earlier days, the Roman contrasts favourably with his foes. The record of the discovery by Germanicus of skulls nailed to trees in the sacred groves in which the conquering warriors of Arminius had burned to death and otherwise barbarously slain the centurions and tribunes of the legions of Varus presents a remarkable picture of comparative civilisation. Tac. *Ann.* I. 61. Flor. IV. 12.

The Persian Sapor in 260 A.D. held a general massacre in Caesarea, and treated his captives with relentless cruelty. The skin of his prisoner, the Emperor Valerian, was preserved in a Persian temple. Gibbon, *Decline and Fall*, Chap. X.

Another Persian ruler in 359 A.D. crucified Roman prisoners and blinded, tortured and finally slew the Armenian king Arsaces, whom he had seized by treachery. Amm. Marcell. XIX. 9; XXVII. 12.

But the later Imperial armies were

The Roman war-practice of the third and fourth centuries was still that of the leaders of civilisation. It made up of Barbarian Mercenaries (*Fœderati*).

suffered when Roman legions, however recruited, were exchanged for armies of Gothic *Fœderati* led by their own elective chieftains.

(*b*) The *Divided Empire* 395—476 A.D.

The Barbarian Conquerors overrun the Roman Western provinces,

Tac. *Hist.* III. 46; IV. 59.

§ 40. A new epoch in international history opens with the Barbarian Conquest of the West.

From the very earliest days of the Great Empire the Teutons pressed hard upon the Northern frontier. Caesar had hurled back the Germans across the Rhine; Drusus and Germanicus avenged Varus, and Cerealis checked the imperial aspirations of Civilis; but from the day of Marcus Aurelius (161—180 A.D.) the Empire was constantly fighting a hard battle in defence of its Rhenish and Danubian provinces. Julian drove the Germans once again from Gaul, but under his successors, Decius, Tacitus and Valentinian, the struggle went ill. Under Decius (249—251) the Goths harried Dacia and Maesia; in 376 they were by the advance of the Hunnish hordes pushed forward *en masse* across the Danube; two years later they slew the Emperor Valens at Hadrianople, and obtained a firm footing on old Imperial soil. At last under Honorius (395—423 A.D.) and Arcadius (395—408 A.D.) the veteran planted barriers fairly yielded. Alaric, the West Gothic mercenary, cast off his allegiance and, roaming at large through devastated provinces, at length entered as conqueror through the gates of Rome (410 A.D.); across Gaul, through Spain, and over the Strait streamed the Barbarians in a succession of rolling waves, they poured over the Danube, they swept through the Alpine passes, and overran the whole astonished West. Under Athaulf, the successor of Alaric, the West Goths quitted Italy, traversed southern Gaul in masterful career, and, pressing upon the heels of the Vandals, Suevi and Alans, laid the foundations of a great kingdom which, penning the Suevi in Lusitania and Galicia, ultimately stretched from the Loire to the Straits of Gibraltar. On all hands such Teutonic kingdoms arose. The Vandals crossed the strait (429 A.D.), and occupied the Roman Africa, with the Balearic isles, Corsica and

Jordanes, *De Reb. Get.* XVIII., XXV., XXVI. Amm. Marcell. XXXI. 4.

Jordanes, *De Reb. Get.* XXIX. XXX.

Sardinia. The Burgundians established themselves in south-eastern, the Franks in northern, Gaul. The Gepidae pushed on behind the Ostro-Goths into Dacia. The Angles, Saxons and Jutes began the conquest of the deserted Roman province of Britain. At length in 476 A.D. Odoakar, the chieftain of a composite body of Turulingian, Scyrrian and Herulian auxiliaries, deposed Romulus Augustulus, the feeble successor of Honorius, and ruled in Italy in his room. Jordanes, *De Reb. Get.* XLVI.

but fail to destroy the Roman Empire.

In the first instance, strange as it seems, these events wrought no change in contemporary conceptions of Imperial rights. The Teuton had his own conception of the State, the conception of the masterless Tribe roving and warring under the leadership of elective kings or chieftains chosen by the host of free tribesmen from a certain heaven-born family. And the Teutonic victory over the legions seemed to announce the end of Roman dominion. But the Imperial Idea lived on, not only after the first Barbarian inrush, but until after the days of Barbarian regular settlement.

The explanation of the failure.

Diocletian had in 292 A.D. confessed the weakening of Imperial administrative power by associating in the government of the Empire four colleagues, two Augusti and two Caesars, ruling in four several districts. Reunited under Constantine (324 A.D.), the Imperial dominions were, after various shortlived partition arrangements, at length divided between Arcadius and Honorius, reigning respectively as Eastern and Western Emperor (395 A.D.). By these several divisions the Imperial Crown was placed in commission, but the unity of the Empire was deemed to be unaffected. Meantime the removal by Constantine of the seat of undivided Imperial rule to the shores of the Bosphorus made the Roman Empire independent of locality. Henceforward Rome followed the Emperor. Bryce, *Holy Roman Empire*, p. 9.

Three periods of Barbarian Conquest:—
1. The Barbarians are trespassers

When, therefore, the Barbarians overwhelmed the West, and entered old Rome as masters, they failed to destroy the Roman Empire. They were trespassers within, rather than new owners of, Imperial dominions. The within the Empire. The old Imperial claims asserted after the Barbarian victory by the Eastern Emperor, Jordanes, *De Reb. Get.* XXVIII. and at first admitted by the Western conquerors. 2. The Barbarians accept Roman commissions. Jordanes, *De Reb. Get.* LVII. Procop. *De Bello Goth.* I. Gregory of Tours, II. 38. 3. The Barbarians repudiate Imperial authority. Oman, *Dark Ages*, pp. 117, 137.

old Imperial claims were still asserted by the Emperor who ruled at Constantinople; the Barbarians themselves came under the glamour of the Roman name, and, invading Roman provinces *de facto* as conquerors, accepted from the successor of Arcadius the style and commission of Roman officials. It was under commission from the Emperor to restore the Roman province of Spain that Athaulf[1] marched towards the Pyrenees; when Odoakar extinguished in 476 the Empire of the West, he was content to rule in form as Patrician under grant from the Byzantine Zeno; Theodoric in 493 overthrew Odoakar, and established the great Italian kingdom of the Ostro-Goths, under authority derived from the same quarter; and the Frank Clovis, after the overthrow of Syagrius and the conquest of Aquitaine, accepted with joy from Anastasius I. the title of Roman Proconsul and Patrician, and was invested in the Cathedral of S. Martin at Tours with the purple tunic, the chlamys and the diadem. It was not until 539 A.D. that the Ripuarian Theudebert struck the first coin from which was omitted the head of the Eastern Emperor. The Visigoths retained the significant emblem until the reign of Leovigild (570—586 A.D.).

When the Barbarian Kings repudiate Imperial authority International Law reaches its nadir in the West. The savagery of the Barbarian conquerors. Mallet, *Northern Antiquities*, 145, 169, 178. Gregory of Tours II. 32; III. 7; IV. 48; VI. 31; VIII. Zosimus, V.

§ 41. In the Dark Ages, between 476 and 800 A.D., International Law reached its nadir in the West.

The war-practice of the Teutons stamps them as barbarians devoid of all conception of international right.

The Goths, Vandals, and Thuringians, like the Vikings of the North in later days, burned, pillaged and slew without mercy. They ravaged fields, uprooted vines, cut down olive trees, and burned without distinction all buildings, sacred or profane, leaving their track behind them in smouldering ruins. Valhalla, the Barbarian Heaven, was to be won by a violent death alone, and for Odin's worshippers accordingly life had no value. They

[1] For the story of Athaulf's deliberate resolution to maintain, rather than overthrow, the Roman Empire see Orosius VII. 43; Gibbon c. XXXI.

slew in attack alike priest and layman, man and woman, and put to death their prisoners in the most cruel fashion. Nor were they all, like the Saxon invaders of Britain, merely pitiless. The Alans, who fought side by side with the Vandals, like the ancient Scythians from whom they would appear to have descended, decked their war-horses with the scalps of slain enemies. The famous incident of the Lombard Alboin's drinking cup, fashioned out of the skull of his conquered father-in-law, the king of the Gepidae, merely stands out from many similar circumstances by reason of the singular vengeance which befell the fierce monarch.

Amm. Marcell. XXXI. 6. Jordanes, *De Reb. Get.* XLVIII. Gregory of Tours II. 27; III. 20. Chron. Saxon. *Anno* CCCCXC. Amm. Marcell. XXXI. 2. Paul Warnef. *De Gestis Lang.* II. 28.

Even after the formal adoption of Christianity the war-practice of the Barbarian Conquerors was more than brutal. The history of the wars of Clovis, the hero of the orthodox clergy, is the tale of savage murder and the most hateful treachery. The noble Ostro-Goth Totila, warring against Belisarius, restrained his troops from the plunder of captured cities, and on the fall of Rome (546 A.D.) sternly forbade murder, rape or other open violence; but Totila stands out a bright chivalrous knightly figure in an age of savagery. The Chagan of the Hunnish Avars in 599 A.D. put to death in cold blood 12,000 Roman prisoners, and the Frankish Chilperic conducted his wars with a cruelty well-nigh incredible. A peculiar faithlessness distinguished the Frank even amongst his treacherous Teutonic kinsmen.

Gregory of Tours II. 40, 42. Procop., *De Bello Goth.* III. Oman, *Dark Ages*, pp. 98, 100. Oman, *Dark Ages*, p. 153. Gregory of Tours IV. 48; VI. 31.

When Theudebert and Leovigild repudiated the formal semblance of Imperial authority, International Law was in all seeming overwhelmed in the West, submerged beneath the rolling waves of Barbarism. The Empire, and with it the sphere of International Law, was formally as well as actually cut short. The circle of Civilisation became narrowed to the Eastern seaboard of the Mediterranean, where the Byzantine Emperor held out at once against the Barbarians pressing upon his Danubian lands and against the great Persian kingdom of Kobad and Chosroes.

Zosimus VI. p. 112. Amm. Marcell. XXXI. 2. Oman, *Dark Ages*, p. 207.

The Church saves Civilisation in the West.

§ 42. At this crisis it was the Church, and the Church alone, which saved Civilisation in the West. Constantine had enlisted Christianity as the State Religion of the Empire, and when not only had Ostrogoth and Lombard cut short the Empire in old Rome, but Frank and Visigoth had in Gaul and Spain laid aside the last emblems of subjection to the Eastern Emperor, the World Church continued the idea of world unity in the spiritual field until the time came, when she could hand it back to a new Emperor crowned in the city of the Seven Hills, and the Frankish Karl, assuming the claims, not of Romulus Augustulus, but of Constantine I. and Constantine VI., gave form and life to the scattered bones. And not only so: spite the worldliness and unworthy lives of many of the prelates themselves, spite a weak obsequiousness or a native rudeness which made Christian bishops the courtiers of Clovis and Fredegunde, or mere privileged brawlers, the Church was in those dark days at once the sole refuge of the oppressed and an active civilising agent.

She (i) continues the idea of world unity,

Bryce, *Holy Roman Empire*, p. 63.

Gregory of Tours IV. 43; VII. 37.

and (ii) acts as a general civilising agent.

The very superstition of the time operated in the direction of improvement; for, although the sanctity commonly accorded by the little better than pagan Teutons to the shrines of particular saints protected numberless malefactors from a well merited doom, it preserved very many otherwise defenceless innocent refugees, and secured the presence of little oases of peace in the midst of the general turmoil[1]. And again and again the voice of a bold prelate stayed the sword of a Barbarian king as it threatened general massacre.

Gregory of Tours V. 14.

Gregory of Tours VII. 42; IX. 3.

Goths, Vandals and Franks bowed to the Church as they bowed to the majesty of the Roman name.

Alaric entering Rome issued orders that all refugees in sanctuaries, and particularly in the basilicas of S. Peter and S. Paul, should be spared, and slaughter elsewhere as far as possible avoided. The event merits all the

Orosius VII. c. 28. Jordanes, *De Reb. Get.* XXX. Isidore, *Goth. Chron.*

[1] The right of asylum (*jus asyli*) was in the East equally recognised as belonging to churches. Its occasional disregard was condemned even by pagan historians. Zosimus v. pp. 94, 95.

enthusiasm excited in S. Augustine. *Quod autem novo more factum est, quod inusitata rerum facie immanitas barbara tam mitis apparuit, ut amplissimae basilicae implendae populo cui parceretur eligerentur et decernerentur, ubi nemo feriretur, unde nemo raperetur, quo liberandi multi a miserantibus hostibus ducerentur, unde captivandi nulli nec a crudelibus hostibus abducerentur, hoc Christi nomini, hoc Christiano tempori tribuendum, quisquis non videt, caecus; quisquis videt nec laudat, ingratus: quisquis laudanti reluctatur, insanus est.* Augustine, *De Civ. Dei*, I. c. 7. Christianity had checked the hand of the Barbarian warrior. *Testantur hoc martyrum loca et basilicae Apostolorum, quae in illa vastatione urbis ad se confugientes suos alienosque receperunt. Huc usque cruentus saeviebat inimicus: ibi accipiebat limitem trucidatoris furor: illo ducebantur a miserantibus hostibus, quibus etiam extra illa loca pepercerant, ne in eos incurrerent, qui similem misericordiam non habebant. Qui tamen etiam ipsi alibi truces atque hostili more saevientes, posteaquam ad loca illa veniebant, ubi fuerat interdictum, quod alibi jure belli*[1] *licuisset, tota feriendi refraenabatur immanitas, et captivandi cupiditas frangebatur.* *De Civ. Dei*, I. c. 1.

An example so striking could not but bear fruit. The power which restrained Alaric affected Genseric the Vandal, and reached even Attila the Hun at the gate of the Imperial city. Jordanes, *De Reb. Get.* XLII. Gibbon, cc. 35, 36. Procop. *De Bello Goth.* III. It was by threats of the anger of Heaven that Totila held back his Gothic warriors from murder and rapine. In the midst of perpetual war and turmoil priests, like Gregory of Tours, cried aloud continually, and not without effect, against every form of cruelty. And just as it was the hand of Pope Leo III. which placed the crown of the restored Empire of the West upon the head of the Frankish Karl, called to the defence of Rome against the Lombard, so it was

[1] The account of the capture of Rome given by Jordanes is noteworthy as evidence of contemporary war-practice. *Ad postremum Romam ingressi, Alarico jubente, spoliant tantum: non autem,* UT SOLENT GENTES, *ignem supponunt, nec locis sanctorum in aliquo penitus injuriam irrogari patiuntur.* Jordanes, *De Reb. Get.* c. 30.

Christianity, preached by missionary bishops and monks[1] to Saxons and Frisians, Angles and Slavs, Scandinavians, Irish and Scots, which at length brought not only the Teutonic conquerors of Roman provinces, but the whole Barbarian West, within the pale of revived and extended International Law.

Justinian reconquers Italy, Africa and part of Spain (534—550),

§ 43. Under Justinian the Eastern Empire not only held its own, but, thanks to the prowess of Belisarius and Narses, showed itself a conquering power. The Persians were forced to accept terms of peace (531, 545); the Vandal kingdom in Africa (534) and the great islands (535) was brought to an end; the Ostro-Goths were, after a gallant struggle, driven from Italy (553); and even a portion of southern Spain was recovered from the possession of the Visi-Goths (550).

Paul Warnefr. *De Gestis Lang.* II.

but the Empire is again cut short by the Lombards, Visigoths, Slavs, Avars and Bulgarians,

But this blaze of glory was only evanescent. In 568 a new band of Barbarian invaders, the Lombards, quitting their seat in Pannonia, poured into Italy under their savage king Alboin[2], and in no long time were masters of all the peninsula save a few broken fragments round Rome, Naples and Ravenna, and in the extreme South. The Visigoths rapidly won back the recovered districts of Spain. Under the Emperor Heraclius in the early years of the seventh century, not only did the Slavs establish themselves south of the Danube, but the Persians, overrunning Syria and Asia Minor, laid siege to Chalkedon (617). In 626 the Avars attacked Constantinople. By a mighty effort the Empire rose superior to the peril. The Slavs were erected into an imperial bulwark. The Avars were shaken off, and Heraclius hurled Chosroes back to his Eastern lands (628). But a more terrible enemy appeared on the scene. Emerging from Arabia the Saracens tore from

and by the Saracens.

[1] St Columban, St Gall, St Fidian, St Willibrord, St Killian, St Boniface, St Ansgar.

[2] For Alboin's vow to put to the sword the entire population of Pavia and its miraculous enforced recall, see Paul Warnefr., *De Gestis Lang.*, II. 17. Compare *Ibid.* I. 27, II. 28; *Ante* p. 65.

the Empire all its Syrian possessions (632—639), overwhelmed the Persians (632—651), and, sweeping on in conquering career through the newly recovered Imperial provinces in Africa (647—711), passed the strait (711), chased the Visigoths into the mountains of Leon and Asturias, and, pushing across the Pyrenees, were only stayed at Poictiers (732) by the Frankish Karl Martel. In 717 the army of Moslemah besieged Constantinople by land and sea, and was only beaten off by the Greek fire of Leo the Isaurian and the barbarian forces of the Bulgarian Terbel (718).

Oman, *Dark Ages*, p. 302.

In 750 the Saracenic Empire stretched from Scinde to Galicia and the mouth of the Rhone. From that time forth Christianity and Mahometanism, West and East, battled for mastery round the Mediterranean shore.

Freeman, *Historical Geography*, p. 113.

(c) The *Eastern Empire*, 476—800. The final lesson of the Empire taught in the claims and practice of Justinian.

§ 44. It were an immense and scarcely remunerative labour to trace the course of international practice through the struggles of the Empire of the East from Zeno to Nicephorus I., through palace revolutions and religious feuds, through the contests of Blues and Greens, of Arians and Orthodox, and the desperate fight against Persian, Avar, Bulgarian and Saracen. For the historian of International Law the Roman Empire speaks its last word of practical instruction in the legislation and acts of Justinian.

Union of Greek, Roman and Oriental civilisation in the Pagan Empire.

Greek and Roman had met in Polybius. In the Pagan Empire were united the purest streams of Classical, African and Syrian civilisation. In the *Corpus Juris Civilis* of Justinian, and the record preserved in the pages of Cassiodorus and Procopius of his dealings with East and West, of the campaigns of Imperial generals, of the embassies of prelates and eunuchs, of popular faction fights and religious controversy, mutiny and intrigue, we see the composite product of the regular blending with Imperial Roman, Greek and Oriental, of Christian and Barbarian material.

In an Oriental Court, established in an old Greek

The Christian Justinian (i) asserts the claims of a *Universal Empire.*

colony and defended by Barbarian bands, Justinian, professing the Faith of the Galilaean Messiah, issues under the style of Augustus or Marcus Aurelius his Imperial mandate for the codification of the Roman Law. His conceptions of international right are those of old Rome coloured by Greek philosophy, and affected at the root by contact with Barbarians, transplanted to the shores of the Bosphorus, the meeting ground of Europe and Asia. The lines of the narrow International Circles traced by the exclusive hands of Greek, Jew and Egyptian have been effaced by the sceptre of the common ruler; Laws of the Hellenes and laws amongst kindred Tribes have alike sunk into insignificance before the Law of Mankind and the Roman Civil Law; and, in spite of the stern logic of facts, Justinian asserts as the setting forth of the Byzantine conception of the prevailing international system the claims of the World Empire. It is to recover, not to reconquer, that Belisarius goes forth to Carthage and to Italy; the kingdom of Theodoric is deemed by Imperial statesmen to have never been other than an Imperial province.

(ii) His International Law is Law Universal.

Tribonian and his colleagues in like fashion advance no other conception of International Right than that of the Romano-Hellenic Universal Law set out by Ulpian, Gaius and Hermogenianus.

They classify all law as *Public* or *Private.* Public law, which regards the government of the Roman Empire, regulates public worship and civil administration: Private Law which concerns the interests of individuals, comprises precepts belonging to *Jus Naturale, Jus Gentium* and *Jus Civile. Jus Naturale* is common to men and animals, *Jus Gentium* is the law of men only. *Jus Civile* is the law of a particular community: *Jus Gentium* is law common to the human race, the "common law of all "mankind[1]."

Dig. I. 1. *Inst.* I. 1 and 2.

[1] *Hujus studii duae sunt positiones, publicum et privatum. Publicum jus est quod ad statum rei Romanae spectat, privatum quod ad singulorum utilitatem: sunt enim quaedam publice utilia, quaedam privatim. Publicum*

The same conservatism is apparent in the actual practice of Justinian.

His International practice based on that of old Rome.

The Roman *Jus Legationis* and the Roman *Jus Belli* define in their several spheres for the ministers and generals of Justinian the requirements of International Law. When invading the Vandal kingdom as a province about to pass back to its rightful ruler, Belisarius deemed it politic to restrain his troops from pillage, and the account of his entry into Carthage is an anticipation of the history of that of Marshal Berwick into Barcelona in 1714. The inhabitants suffered no violence, even heard no threats; the artificers were not interfered with; the shops remained open; the soldiers were lodged in regularly assigned billets, and bought their supplies in the open market. But the orderly demeanour of the invaders is remarked upon with wonder by the eyewitness Procopius as altogether unusual in Roman practice and the direct result of the extraordinary discipline maintained by Belisarius. And Belisarius himself, in the speech with which he attempted in vain to induce the Neapolitans to avoid by surrender the horrors of a storm, bears witness in no uncertain fashion as to the character of general contemporary war-practice. *Vidi equidem saepe urbes expugnari et capi, et qualia a victoribus captae jam patiantur sat calleo. Nam et milites ipsi sine ullo aetatis respectu occidunt quos in eo furore offenderint, matres familiasque*

Procop. *De Bello Vand.* II. p. 230.

The war-practice of Belisarius.

Procop. *De Bello Vand.* I. p. 200.

Memoirs of Marshal Berwick, II. 175.

Procop. *De Bello Vand.* I. p. 205.

jus in sacris, in sacerdotibus, in magistratibus consistit. Privatum jus tripertitum est: collectum etenim est ex naturalibus praeceptis aut gentium aut civilibus. Jus Naturale est, quod natura omnia animalia docuit...Jus gentium est, quo gentes humanae utuntur. Quod a naturali recedere facile intellegere licet, quia illud omnibus animalibus, hoc solis hominibus inter se commune sit. Dig. I. 1.

Jus autem civile vel gentium ita dividitur: omnes populi, qui legibus et moribus reguntur, partim suo proprio, partim communi omnium jure utuntur; nam quod quisque populus ipse sibi jus constituit, id ipsius proprium civitatis est vocaturque jus civile, quasi jus proprium ipsius civitatis; quod vero naturalis ratio inter omnes homines constituit, id apud omnes populos peraeque custoditur vocaturque jus gentium, quasi quo jure omnes gentes utuntur. Et populus itaque Romanus partim suo proprio, partim communi omnium jure utitur. Inst. I. 2. 1.

tam foede afficiunt, ut mortem sibi efflagitantibus illaturos se negent. Nam dum ad injuriam ferendam trahuntur, et militum inservire coguntur libidini, indecora omnia tolerant, et admodum miseranda: puerique vix dum ablactati, ab his abducuntur in servitutem, quos omnium infensissimos habent, ut quorum manus paterno respersas sanguine conspicentur. Praetereo amantissime Stephane injectum per urbes ignem, et flagrantia tecta nunc meminisse, quo ut res caeterae deperduntur, ita et urbis nitor et pulchritudo dehonestatur.

Procop. *De Bello Goth.* I. 261. Hodgkin, *Italy and Her Invaders* IV. 62.

The subsequent fate of the unhappy city abundantly confirmed these warning words, the soldiers of the Imperial army, in spite of the strongest efforts of their commander, indulging in savage atrocities, the Huns in particular showing no regard even for the sanctity of churches.

Procop. *De Bello Goth.* I. 263.

Procop. *De Bello Goth.* II. p. 336. Hodgkin, *Italy and Her Invaders* IV. 365.

Belisarius, failing in the attempt to cut the aqueducts of besieged Osimo, did not hesitate to poison the well from which the garrison drew its water supply.

The hopeful feature in the international practice of Justinian:—the Barbarians are being gradually brought within the Circle.

There is, however, one noteworthy and hopeful feature in the international practice of the reign of Justinian. It is clear that the International Circle is widening. The influence of the Barbarian had in times past in some degree degraded, and still did tend to degrade, the Roman war-practice, but in the reign of Justinian the Teutonic conquerors of old Roman provinces, bowing their heads to Christianity, are likewise yielding to Roman higher civilisation, and advancing rapidly in the direction of humanity.

The victory won by Roman Civilisation and

The war-practice of the Christian Franks beyond the Alps is still savage in the extreme. The Vandal Gelimer offers a price for the head of every slain Roman. Even the Ostrogoths, under the noble Totila, at times wage war with ferocity. Upon the fall of Milan in 539 all the male inhabitants, to the number, according to Procopius, of three hundred thousand souls, are massacred by the Gothic conquerors. Totila on occasion mutilates prisoners and puts all the

Procop. *De Bello Vand.* I.

Hodgkin, *Italy and Her Invaders* IV. 334, 448, 452, 587.

inhabitants of captured cities to the sword. But the Ostrogoths in general display a temper contrasting brightly with that of the contemporary Moors and Slavonians or of the Persians of Chosroes, and Totila in his treatment of captive women stands forth as an early knight of chivalry. The cowardly Theodahad enters into argument with an envoy of Justinian as to the privilege of ambassadors in a fashion which demonstrates the acceptance of Roman teaching, whilst Totila declares that the Goths recognise *as strongly as do the Romans* the duty of showing respect to the legatine office.

Procop. *De Bello Vand.* II. Paul Warnef. IV. 42. Hodgkin, *Italy and Her Invaders* IV. 448.

Hodgkin, *Italy and Her Invaders* IV. 22, 527.

The armies led by Belisarius and Narses were composed wellnigh entirely of Barbarians, Huns, Herulians, Gepidae, Moors, Armenian and Isaurian mountaineers. From time to time in moments of excitement, as after the victory of Tricamaron or the storm of Naples, these rude bands broke free from control, but in general they yielded to the stern hand of Roman discipline. And international humanity gained by this schooling within the Empire of large bodies of men.

Procop. *De Bello Vand.* II. Hodgkin, *Italy and Her Invaders* III. 686; IV. 67.

by Christianity.

Meanwhile beyond the frontiers of the provinces which obeyed Justinian and his successors, Christianity operated, not only as a civilising force, but as a principle of attraction towards a common Light. Slowly but surely the Barbarian Darkness, which enshrouded the West, was dispelled, and at length in the grey Dawn a Frankish Emperor stood within the International Circle.

The Saracens establish a rival Empire built upon the foundation of Religion, 632–755.

§ 45. Seventy years after the death of Justinian the Saracen flood swept upon the Empire from deserts which had never owned allegiance to any ruler of old Rome.

A singular interest attaches to the international practice of the Saracens.

The place of the Saracen in the international field.

Their success represents no barbarian conquest. The Saracens, cutting short the provinces of the Byzantine Emperor in Asia and Africa, occupied with far more widely extended dominions and a far higher civilisation the international position belonging at various periods to the Persians and Parthians.

(i) The Saracenic conception of the State is founded on that of the Jew.

In his conception of the state the Arab was most nearly allied to the ancient Jew, with whom he claimed a common descent. He was a man of the Tribe and of long genealogy, for whom the sacred Mecca, on whose soil no enemy might be attacked[1], had for many generations occupied the place of Jerusalem. When he emerged from his deserts to the attack upon the Provinces of the East this conception had, however, developed into that of the People of God, whose religion claimed the obedience of the world, and the Caliph, the successor of Mahomet, was at once Pope and Emperor. The prophet proclaimed, and his successors carried on, a *Jehad* or Holy War which drew a clear line of separation between the Moslem and the Infidel; the conquered was admitted to equal rights with his conqueror by becoming a proselyte. The Caliphate was nothing less than a new World Empire built directly upon the foundation of religion.

The Caliph at once Pope and Emperor.

(ii) International practice of the Saracens.

In his international practice the Arab was far from the ruthless destroyer, the scourge of the world, offering the alternative of Islamism or death, whom Western Chroniclers describe. Edris, the founder (*circ.* 788) of the shortlived independent Caliphate of Fez, forced all Christians and Jews within his dominions to embrace Mahometanism on pain of death. The Saracens of Fez, however, in this as in other particulars displayed a barbarity not usual with their contemporary co-religionists.

Condé, *Arabs in Spain* II. 74, 77.

The Saracenic war-practice is modelled on the Mosaic Law;

The war-practice enjoined by Mahomet was modelled closely on the lines of the Mosaic Law. The Prophet commands the utter destruction of idolaters: to Jews

[1] The territory of Mecca was delimited by a line of small minarets constructed at the distance of seven or ten miles from the Kaaba. Within this radius it was held impious to assail an enemy. The Arabs, moreover, before the days of Islam set apart four months in the year as *dies nefasti* for the waging of war. Mahomet declared it legitimate to fight in any month against the Idolater. Ockley, *Life of Mahomet*, pp. 6, 9. *Koran*, c. IX.

and Christians are offered the alternatives of conversion, tribute or war. Should the choice of the Infidel fall upon war, all his males taken in arms may be put to death, his women and children become the captives of the conqueror. Jews and Christians have thus taken the place of peoples other than the Seven Nations.

Deut. vii., xii., xx. Koran, II. 187, 189, 190; VIII. 40; IX. 5, 9; XLVIII. 16.

These instructions were closely followed by the early Saracenic conquerors.

In civil and sectarian struggles the Saracenic like the Christian belligerent too often abused his victory.

Musab, the brother of Abdollah, the son of Zobeir, Anti-Caliph in Mecca, having in 686 A.D. defeated the hostile force of El Mukhtar, put to the sword seven thousand men who had surrendered, at discretion in the castle of Cufah. In the same year the Separatist sect of Azarakites overrunning Irak committed wild atrocities, and repeated their conduct in 691 A.D. The marauding bands of renegades and Saracens who from their nests in Crete and elsewhere for generations harried the coasts of the Eastern Empire, of Italy and even of the Teutonic North, were not specially careful exponents of the International Law of Islam. But, in general, the Saracen displayed a civilisation which compared favourably with that which descended from the Greek and the Roman.

Sédillot, *Hist. Gén. des Arabes*, I. 178, 182. Ockley, *History of the Saracens*, II. 264, 265, 282.

Finlay, *Byzantine Empire*, I.

The charge with which Abu Bekr, the first of the Caliphs succeeding Mahomet, sent forth his troops to the conquest of Syria, establishes at once the place of the Arab in the history of International Law. "When you "meet your enemies in the fight, comport yourselves as "befits good Moslemah; and remember to prove your-"selves the true descendants of Ishmael. In the order "and disposition of the host, and in all battles, be careful "to follow your banners boldly, and be ever obedient to "your leaders. Never yield to, or turn your backs on, "your enemies; it is for the cause of God that you fight. "You are incited by no less noble desire than His glory; "therefore fear not to enter into the fight, nor let the

It is that of a people in a state of advanced civilisation.

"number of your foes alarm you, even though excessive. "If God should give you the victory, do not abuse your "advantages, and beware how you stain your swords in "the blood of him who yields; neither touch ye the "children, the women, nor the infirm old men whom ye "may find among your enemies. In your progress through "the enemy's land, cut down no palms or other fruit "trees[1]; destroy not the products of the earth; ravage no "fields; burn no dwellings; from the stores of your "enemy take only what you need for your wants. Let "no destruction be made without necessity, but occupy "the cities of the enemy; and if there be any that may "serve as an asylum to your adversaries, them do you "destroy. Treat the prisoner and him who renders him- "self to your mercy with pity, as God shall do to you in "your need, but trample down the proud and rebellious, "nor fail to crush all who have broken the conditions "imposed on them. Let there be no perfidy nor falsehood "in your treaties with your enemies; be faithful in all "things, proving yourselves ever upright and noble, and "maintaining your word and promise truly. Do not "disturb the quiet of the monk or hermit, and destroy "not their abodes, but inflict the rigours of death upon "all who shall refuse the conditions you would impose on

Condé, *Arabs in Spain*, I. 3.

"them."

The charge of Abu Bekr was re-echoed by later Saracen

Condé, *Arabs in Spain*, II. 43. Ockley, *Hist. of Saracens*, I. 166.

generals. Tarik, the first Saracen invader of Spain, commanded that no offence should be offered to the peaceable and unarmed inhabitants, that those only should be

Protection of non-combatants,

attacked who bore or assisted those bearing arms, and that plunder should be confined to the field of battle and

Condé, *Arabs in Spain*, I. 11.

to towns carried by assault.

The early Saracen war-practice was by contrast with that of the contemporary Franks merciful in the highest degree.

Conquered monarchs, such as Cahina of Barbary or

[1] Compare Deut. xx. 19.

Dataro of Scinde, who obstinately refused to adopt the faith of Islam, were indeed put to death; rebels were cruelly handled, beheaded or impaled; the heads of slain Christian commanders were despatched to Caliph or Emir as trophies of victory; but such severities were commonly confined to important personages, the general mass of the people being usually treated by the Saracen invader with peculiar mildness. The Saracen general approaching a Christian city demanded submission and tribute. It was only after the refusal of these terms that the heavier "contribution of blood," or ransom from the sword, was exacted, and only actual forcible resistance that was followed by slaughter. The sword fell heavily upon all active combatants, and sometimes on all inhabitants, in a place carried by assault, but it was only on rare occasions, and then with the strong disapproval of all good Moslemah, that even in civil strife Saracen commanders ravaged fields, burned cities, slaughtered unarmed men and carried off into captivity the wives and children of the unresisting. Even spies were offered the alternative of Islamism or death. Ali, the cousin of Mohamet, forbade the Moslemah in their civil contests to slay a fugitive after he had escaped from the field of battle, to pursue him beyond a single *comarca*, or to continue a siege beyond a set period. To destroy crops, plunder open towns without mercy, burn houses and cut down trees, all proceedings characteristic of contemporary Frankish war-practice, was, in the view of early Arabian chroniclers, to be guilty of "barbarous extravagances altogether unknown to regular "warfare." The Northmen, who ravaged the coasts of Spain as they ravaged the coasts of France and England, were in the eyes of the Ommeyads little better than savages.

Condé, *Arabs in Spain*, I. 5, 7; II. 28, 32, 62. Ockley, *Hist. of Saracens*, I. 47.

Ockley, *Hist. of Saracens*, I. 182.

Condé, *Arabs in Spain*, I. 11, 16, 35; II. 27.

prohibition of devastation,

Ockley, *Hist. of Saracens*, I. 244.

Condé, *Arabs in Spain*, II. 70 n.

Condé, *Arabs in Spain*, I. 15, 22, 33; II. 2, 16, 20, 44, 49.

The Christian inhabitants of towns freely surrendering to the Saracen arms were regularly permitted to retire, should they elect to do so, subject to the condition of leaving behind their personal effects. Those who remained were protected in the enjoyment of their own laws and

toleration of religious opinion,

allowed the free exercise of their religion, except only in the matter of public processions, the ringing of bells, and in the erection of new churches. The Caliph Walid in 707 A.D., requiring the site of a Christian church in Damascus for the erection of a great Court-House offered payment therefor, and it was not until the offer was rejected that the church was forcibly razed. Cordova, Toledo and other great Saracen cities were full of Christian and Jewish merchants. Whilst Christian casuists laid down the doctrine that no faith need nor should be kept with the Infidel, the Saracen, obeying the express injunction of the Prophet[1], was particularly distinguished by his good faith and rigid adherence to treaties. Safe conducts were freely granted and commonly scrupulously observed.

Condé, *Arabs in Spain*, I. 7, 12, 13.

and good faith.

Koran, cc. III, V, VIII, XVII. Condé, *Arabs in Spain*, I. 15, 20, 24; II. 14, 67.

Constantine Copronymus in 769 A.D. concluded a convention with the Saracens under which prisoners were exchanged man for man, woman for woman and child for child. This arrangement materially mitigated the severity of the continued war of Caliph and Emperor, preserving, as it naturally did, numerous lives. By the end of the eighth century the campaigns of the generals of the Caliph of Bagdad had developed into slave-catching expeditions rather than efforts at territorial conquest, prisoners of lower rank being sold in slave markets, their superiors ransomed or exchanged. In 797 a new clause was introduced by Haroun el Raschid into the treaty with the Eastern Empire, whereby the contracting parties bound themselves to release in return for a fixed

Finlay, *Byzantine Empire*, I. 65.

Finlay, *Byzantine Empire*, I. 106.

[1] "Be faithful in the keeping of your contracts, for God will require "an account of such at your hands." *Koran* c. XVII. 36. The maxim was cited by El Hakem Ben Abdelrahman in 966 in reply to the demands of his cavaliers for a declaration of war upon the Christians of Galicia. Condé, *Arabs in Spain*, II. 90. Compare the Declaration of the Council of Constance concerning the safe conduct granted by Sigismund to Hus. *Cum dictus Johannes Hus fidem orthodoxam pertinaciter impugnans, se ab omni conductu et privilegio reddiderit alienum, nec aliqua sibi fides aut promissio de jure naturali, divino vel humano, fuerit in praejudicium catholicae fidei observanda.* Creighton, *History of the Papacy* I. 339.

payment per head the supernumerary prisoners remaining after an exchange.

The Saracens in Spain stood in the very forefront of Civilisation. The Arabs were a race of poets, of astronomers, of merchants and travellers. The schools and colleges founded by Abdelrahman Ben Moawiyah, his son Haschem the Just and their successors contained the first mathematicians, scientists and historians in the world. Hospitals, aqueducts, public baths, fountains for men and cattle, great roads, quays and palaces, all the creation of Saracenic architects, engineers and artists, more than recalled the glories of the old Roman province.

The Saracens in Spain.

Sédillot, *Hist. Gén. des Arabes*, I. 348.

§ 46. When in 755 Abdelrahman Ben Moawiyah, a refugee scion of the Ommeyad dynasty overthrown in the East, established at Cordova an independent state, which developed into a Western Caliphate[1], and forty-five years later the style of Emperor was assumed by Karl the Great, a new period in the history of international relations began.

III. International Law of the Middle Ages. 800 A.D.—1519 A.D.

i. The International System of the Middle Ages.

Under Leo the Isaurian (717—741), Constantine Copronymus (741—775) and Leo IV. (775—780) the Byzantine Empire battled up with some success against the Saracen. Leo the Isaurian, however, embarked in a crusade against the superstition of his subjects, and his Iconoclastic decree of 726 not only tore with new religious dissension the poor remains of the Eastern dominions of the Empire, but brought about a Schism between Rome and Constantinople. Pope Gregory II. took up the cause of the Image-Worshippers, and the struggle became embittered. The Empress Irene, ruling after 780 as Regent for her infant son, Constantine VI., restored the worship of images, but in 797 she alienated all but the most violent of men by deposing and blinding the young emperor.

The rival Empires and the rival Caliphates.

Pope and Emperor;

[1] Abdelrahman Anasir Ledinallah (912—961) was the first Saracen ruler of Cordova who claimed the style of Caliph by striking coins on which the title of "Prince of the Faith" was assumed (Condé).

Meanwhile in the West a close alliance had been contracted between the Papacy and the Franks.

Thanks mainly to the efforts of Gregory I. (590—604), of Gregory II. (715—731) and of Gregory III. (731—741) the Papacy became a power in Italy. In 727 Luitprand the Lombard (712—743) attacked and cut short the Exarchate, the main portion of the poor remnant of the Italian dominions of the Eastern Emperor; in 738 he threatened Rome itself, in consequence of the sanctuary afforded by the Pope to the rebel duke of Spoleto.

Pope and Lombard;

Pope and Frank.

North of the Alps all real power had passed from the descendants of Clovis to the strong hands of certain great Court officers, the Mayors of the Palace. After a fierce struggle Pippin the Younger, Mayor of the Palace of Austrasia, the land of the East Franks, overcame his rival of Neustria, and under the style of Mayor of the Palace of Austrasia, Neustria and Burgundy, ruled at Metz over all divisions of the Franks (688—714). In 717 he was succeeded by his son Karl Martel. It was Karl Martel, the conqueror of Frisians, Swabians, and other border peoples, who at Poictiers stayed the advance of the Saracen. And to Karl Martel Gregory III., despairing of assistance from the East, appealed for aid against the outraged Lombard. Karl was not at the moment prepared to give the assistance asked, but the application bore fruit. In 751 Karl's son, Pippin the Short, becoming tired of ruling as Mayor of the Palace of Neustria, was encouraged by the countenance of Pope Zacharias to depose the puppet ruler Childerich III., and, raised on the shield as King of the Franks, was consecrated by the hand of S. Boniface. When in the same year Aistolf, the successor of Luitprand, took Ravenna, and subsequently twice threatened Rome, Pope Stephen called upon Pippin for assistance, and twice Pippin descended from the Alps to the rescue. The grant to Stephen by the Frankish conqueror of the exarchate of Ravenna erected the Papacy into a new secular power. Pippin died in 768, but the alliance between the Frank and the Papacy continued. Hadrian I. (772—795), encouraged

Finlay, *Byzantine Empire*, I. 51.

by the success of his predecessor, having involved himself in a dispute with the Lombard King Desiderius, called into Italy Karl the Great, the son of Pippin, and in 774 the Frank was hailed King of the Lombards. Six years later "Because the name of Emperor had now ceased "amongst the Greeks, and their Empire was possessed by "a woman, it seemed both to Leo the Pope himself, and "to all the holy fathers who were present in the council "with him, as well as to the rest of the Christian people, "that they ought to take to be Emperor Charles, King of "the Franks, who held Rome herself, where the Caesars had "always been wonted to sit, and all the other regions "which he ruled through Italy and Gaul and Germany; "and inasmuch as God had given all these lands into his "hand, it seemed right that with the help of God and at "the prayer of the whole Christian people he should have "the name of Emperor also. Whose petition King Charles "willed not to refuse, but submitting himself with all "humility to God, and at the prayer of the priests and of "the whole Christian people, on the day of the nativity of "our Lord Jesus Christ he took on himself the name of "Emperor, being consecrated by the lord Pope Leo."

Eginhard, *Annales, ad ann.* 773.

The Coronation of Karl the Great.

Annals of Lauresheim. Bryce, *Holy Roman Empire*, p. 53. Oman, *Dark Ages*, p. 374.

In Karl the Great were thus restored the claims, not of the Western, but of the old undivided, Empire. So two rival Empires stood opposed to rival Saracen Powers, now two, now more in number, according as fortune dictated through a kaleidoscopic succession of dissolutions and reconquests. The rivalry was a sort of four-cornered duel, Western Emir or Caliph uniting with Greek Emperor against Holy Roman Emperor and Caliph of Bagdad.

Eginhard, *Vita Kar. Magni*, p. 20. Condé, *Arabs in Spain*, II. 39, 44.

§ 47. The Empire of Karl the Great differed strangely from that which it was held to succeed.

(a) *The Karling and Holy Roman Empire*, 800—1519.

The dominions of Karl, which stretched from the Baltic to the Ebro, from the Eider to Gaeta, and from the Theiss to the Atlantic, were the broadlands of a congeries of dominant Teutonic peoples, which admitted the political supremacy

The Empire of Karl the Great an Empire of a new type.

of, or were conquered by, the Franks, together with a fringe of territories won by Frankish rulers from the Saracen, the Slav, or the Avar. The Empire of Karl, whilst it did not extend to several old Roman provinces, included broadlands which had never formed part of the Empire of the Caesars.

Eginhard, *Vita Kar. Magni*, p. 18.

Moreover the authority exercised by Karl was of a new order. Karl the Great, King of the Franks and King of the Lombards, not only restored the name of the Empire in old Rome, but by his own strong hand and stark energy, and by the searching eye of his *missi dominici*, revived much of the reality of imperial control. But already under his sceptre Feudalism was nascent. The Empire of his descendants and of their successors down to the Peace of Westphalia was a Feudal Empire.

The origin and work of Feudalism.

§ 48. Feudalism, the form of society which was evolved in the West out of the intermingling of conquering Teuton and conquered Roman, fulfilled as a system a twofold function. It was a system of land-tenure and a system of government. As a system of land-tenure it was at once the composite product of barbarian and Roman materials, and a compromise between old free ownership and invading power. As a system of government it was a link, and a necessary link, between ancient and modern political unity, between the unity of the World Empire and the unity of the Nation. It was the temporary cement which was employed to bind together the disintegrated fragments, which constituted the society created by the barbarian irruption into the West, until new links could be forged, and man be bound to man, not by the force of fear, but by community of interest and the consequent community of feeling. "Feudalism was a *pis-aller*," and its work was done when it gave birth to Territorial Sovereignty. "Territorial Sovereignty was distinctly an "off-shoot, though a tardy one, of feudalism."

Guizot, *Civilisation in Europe*, Lect. IV.

Maine, *Ancient Law*, p. 106.

The Empire of Otto I. a makeshift

§ 49. Under the immediate successors of Karl the disintegrating forces of Feudalism ran wild and rank.

The dominions of Karl, partitioned amongst his three grandsons by the Treaty of Verdun (843 A.D.), were well-nigh all momentarily reunited under the sceptre of the incompetent Karl the Fat, but were finally dispersed into several hands upon his death in 888 A.D. In each of the divisions the chief ruler, whether King of the East or of the West Franks, King of Burgundy or King of Italy, had a hard fight to maintain himself against rebellious vassals, and the imperial title, bandied from kingdom to kingdom, secured for its holder no better fate. The military prowess and statesmanship of Henry the Fowler and his son Otto I. won back a share of real power for the German Kingship. Otto renewed the direct connection of Germany with Italy, won for himself the Lombard Crown, and in 962 was crowned as Emperor at Rome by the hands of John XII. But the revival of the Imperial idea in the Holy Roman Empire[1] did not bring back the old order. The Empire of Karl, it has been said, whilst it included territories upon which the Roman legionaries had never trod, did not extend to the bulk of the Roman Mediterranean and Eastern provinces; the Empire of Otto was an Italo-German state. England, Denmark, and the main portion of the Spanish peninsula never belonged to Karl; France broke off from Germany in 888. Kings of France, of England, of Denmark or of Aragon might from time to time formally acknowledge the precedence of the Holy Roman Emperor, but they were in fact independent; and, whilst a king of France might find himself confronted by a body of nominal vassals whose power individually often rivalled, sometimes exceeded, his own, the Emperor even in his own Germany was scarce more than the head of a loose federation of powerful princes. Everywhere Private War reigned; everywhere turbulent barons attempted to assert their local independence. In such a state of society the ground-plan of International Law was necessarily ill-defined. The times called for an interbaronial rather

until the rise of a New Order.

Bryce, *Holy Roman Empire*, ch. 12.

[1] Barbarossa seems to have been the first to attach the adjective "Holy" to the ancient title. Bryce, *Holy Roman Empire*, p. 199.

than for an international law. The old Order was overthrown. The Empire of Karl, of whose fallen stones Otto built up the smaller Holy Roman erection, with its high claims and actual narrow powers, was a makeshift until a new stable international system could arise in the West. Such as it was, however, around it centred the hopes of International Law.

The struggle for the New Order:—twofold struggle of Feudal Monarchy.

§ 50. The new Order arose by the positive and negative establishment of the authority of Feudal Monarchy; by the victory of that Monarchy in the struggle with baronial disorder, and by the defeat alike of Papacy and of Holy Roman Empire in the attempt to establish an effective World Sovereignty.

(a) The struggle of Monarchy against the Baronage.

§ 51. The first efforts of the Monarchy were directed towards the restraint of the all-prevalent Private War. So long as Private War remained unchecked there was small hope either for Monarchy or a general International Law.

Alliance of Monarchy and the Church in:—

(i) The attempt to restrain Private War.

And here the Catholic Church was the best ally of the Monarch, and did a great and noble work. For black and evident as may have been and were the faults of individual Churchmen, and great the sins chargeable to the account of high ecclesiastics, and even of the Holy Pontiff himself, sins of commission and of omission, ambition incompatible with the character of disciples of the lowly Jesus, and successors of the Galilaean fisherman, partiality and gross self-seeking, which not merely forgot the spiritual in the worldly, but set at nought the plainest dictates of morality and justice, these failings of the preachers of the gospel of peace must not blind us to the vast importance to the world at large of the preaching of mighty truths, though by imperfect agents. The conception of the Unity of the Church could not but produce a lasting influence despite the struggle of Papacy and Empire whereby that conception was sought to be realised. Nor could the proclamation of the blessedness of peace be wholly robbed of its efficacy by the exploits of such exponents of the practice of the Church Militant as a John XXIII. or a Julius II. And much could be pardoned in priests who secured the observance of a *Treuga Dei*, or Peace of God, although individual popes were skilful directors of sieges, and individual bishops were proficient at the dashing out of brains. The Truce of God anticipated the *Quarantaine du Roi*.

The Truce of God, and

Guicc. v. 145. Froissart, I. XXXIX., LX., CLXI

In 1027 a convention of local clergy and faithful laity met in the County of Roussillon, on the summons of their bishop, and agreed on the observance of certain rules as to the time and manner of making private war. *Constituerunt itaque praefati Episcopi simul cum omni Clero et fideli populo ut nemo in toto supradicto Comitatu vel Episcopatu habitans assalliret aliquem suum inimicum ab hora Sabbati nona usque in die Lunis hora prima, ut omnis homo persolvat debitum honorem diei dominico, neque ullo modo aliquis assalliret monachum cum clericum sine armis incedentem, neque aliquem hominem ad Ecclesiam cum Concilia euntem vel redeuntem, neque aliquem hominem cum sportella proficiscentem, neque aliquem hominem cum feminis euntem, neque aliquis auderet Ecclesiam vel domos in circuitu positas à XXX passibus violare aut assallire.*

Dumont, *Corps Diplomatique*, I. i. 43.

About the year 1045 the truce so instituted, and now styled *Treuga Domini*, was renewed by a larger assembly of prelates and magnates, under the presidency of the Archbishop of Narbonne, and its operation considerably extended, so as to cover the period from the sunset of Wednesday in each week to sunrise on Monday, and all the chief feasts, fasts and vigils of the Church year. In 1054 a yet more representative gathering, including many of the same active peacemakers, renewed the *Treuga Dei*, prohibiting all hostilities *ab occasu Solis quartae feriae usque secundae feriae illucescente Sole.* A decree of Calixtus II., in 1119, ordered the observance of the truce from Advent to the octave of Epiphany, from Quinquagesima to the octave of Pentecost, during the Ember Seasons, and on the vigils and feasts of the Saints.

Dumont, *Corps Diplomatique*, I. i. 45.

Dumont, I. i. 47.

Dumont, I. i. 65.

Beginning with a few bishops in a particular locality,

the system of the Truce of God thus became universal, whilst in see after see the prelate wielded his spiritual weapons for the suppression of war and feud.

The Truce of God established particular days and periods as *dies nefasti* for the carrying on of private war, ecclesiastical penalties being denounced against its in-fringers. The *Quarantaine du Roi* was instituted seemingly by Philip Augustus, but confirmed and made effective by Saint Louis. On the outbreak of a quarrel the relatives of the parties were forbidden to take up the dispute, and seek revenge by arms, until the lapse of forty days.

the *Quarantaine du Roi.*

Guizot, *Civilisation in France*, III. p. 251.

So Church and King united to pacify, to establish the King's Peace and the *Pax Ecclesiae.*

Ward, II. 15.

Prescott and Robertson's *Charles V.*, Section 1.

(ii) The Crusades.

And a yet mightier work the Church wrought for mankind, and all unconsciously for Feudal Monarchy, when she hurled united Christendom against the Saracen. The motive actuating an Urban II. might be by no means disinterested, might be the clearing of a new path to universal empire by turning to good account the enthusiasm aroused by a Peter the Hermit, and confounding the crosier of Rome with the Cross of the Crusade. But however diverse might be the inducements swaying the parties to the movement, inducements, according to the individual low and unworthy, or visionary and useless; although the Pope might be moved by self-interest, the king by king-craft, the knight by the sheer love of fighting, the desire for glory, or the desire to wipe out the stain of a crime, the great mass of the common herd by blind enthusiasm, or the desire to expiate a life of sin, with here and there a Godfrey of Bouillon, and here and there a Louis the Saint, pure-hearted heroes who accepted in simple faith the Divine call ("Deu le volt!") to the war for the Truth, the defence of the Pilgrim and the Holy Sepulchre; although, too, the practical outcome in the East itself was in no way proportionate to the exhausting expenditure of energy, of blood and of treasure; yet the direct gains to Europe and European civilisation were great and all-important.

Work of the

Europe was pacified by the turning of the stream

of superabundant baronial martial energy into foreign channels. The waste of vital force was immense indeed, but it was only when avarice and ambition craftily diverted crusading zeal to the attack upon Constantinople or upon the Albigenses that the internal peace of Christendom directly suffered.

Crusades:—
1. They find outlet for martial energy.

The Crusades wrought a social revolution. While the crusading baron wasted his strength and his substance in distant lands, the burghers of his domain were enabled by taking advantage of his necessities to purchase trading privileges, and some serfs, it may be, to buy their freedom.

2. Create great towns, centres of political power.

So great towns[1] arose, to be a check in the future upon the feudal baronage. The cities of Italy, Genoa, Florence, Pisa, Venice and the rest, through which flowed the tide of the movement eastward, sprang at once into importance, and the new commercial activity, reacting upon the towns of central and northern Europe, prepared the way for the operations of the Hanseatic and Low Country merchant-princes, and for the great Leagues of the Rhenish and Swabian cities.

New power passed to the hands of the Church, militant abroad but pacificatrix at home. For was not the Crusade the cause of God, the cause of His Church, the cause to which monk and secular alike urged on the layman who came under their influence? The crusading vow became a new religious penance, and the new military orders, the offspring of the Crusades, yet the more extended the influence of the Churchman. Knights Templars, Knights of St John, Teutonic Knights, and Knights of the Sword, various in origin, various in aim and various in fate, destined to martyrdom, or, outliving the spirit which gave them birth, to senile decay or to secularisation, all were at once Knights of the Church and new political powers[2].

3. Increase power of Church, which at home is a peacemaker.

[1] Henry the Fowler won fame as a town-builder in Germany, his design being the securing of the country from the attacks of the Hungarians. In later days the leagues of the towns played an important part in the pacification of the country.

[2] For the territorial acquisitions of the Teutonic Knights and Knights of the Sword, see Freeman, *Historical Geography*, pp. 512 et seqq.;

4. Familiarise the West with Saracenic civilisation.

Condé, *Arabs in Spain*, II. 173, 219; III. 5.

The Crusaders might even learn, and doubtless did learn, from the Saracens lessons in civilisation. It is rather amongst the dashing followers of the Prophet than in the woods of Germany that must be sought the real origin of Chivalry. The Arabs were early familiar with the institution of knighthood and with coats of arms. The Rabitos, a military Order professing great austerity of life and bound by vows to protect the Saracen frontier from the Christians, took a prominent part in the contests of the Caliph of Cordova with the kings of Afranc as early, at any rate, as the reign of Haschem el Motad Billah (1026—31 A.D.), thus preceding the Knights Templars and the Knights of St John.

Condé, *Arabs in Spain*, II. 119.

Ten qualities were by Arab historians remarked as distinguishing the noble and generous cavalier, viz., integrity, valour, knightly honour, gentle courtesy, poesy, eloquence, strength, skill in the use of the lance, readiness with the sword and dexterity in drawing the bow. These qualities were held to be combined in Said Ben Suleiman Ben Gudi, a cavalier of the close of the ninth century. It was not without reason that the Saracen exercised a singular fascination upon rulers like the brilliant Frederick II. The mail-clad warriors of the West were barbarians alike in their war-practice and in their social and literary education when compared with the chivalrous and poetic sons of the East. Saracenic toleration put to shame the persecution of the Roman and Eastern Church, even as Saracenic commercial greatness more than rivalled the efforts of the Italian, German and Flemish traders. The Seljukian Turks who followed the Arabs in the dominion of the East, and against whom, with the

Condé, *Arabs in Spain*, II. 63.

Schmauss, *Corpus Juris Gent. Academ.* II. p. 2162. The two Orders united in 1237, but were again separated in 1515. In 1525 the dominions of the Teutonic Order were secularised by Albert of Brandenburg, and became a Polish fief; the Livonian Order lost its independence in 1561, when the Grand Master, Gotthard Kettler, became a feudatory of Sigismund Augustus of Poland. Schmauss, I. pp. 212, 313. The Knights of St John, driven from Rhodes, were planted in Malta in 1522, where they remained till the days of Napoleon and English annexation.

Fatimites, the early Crusades were directed, were indeed Mahometans of a sterner mould, but it was not until the Seljuks, weakened by the Moguls, were succeeded by the Ottomans, that Western might definitely claim precedence of Eastern civilisation. The Crusader in Spain met no more barbarous antagonist than the Almohade.

The Crusades taught new ideas even to ignorant brawling barons: they taught the unity of Christendom: yet more, they taught the unity of nations. When French and German barons journeyed in company to the Crusade, they entered not merely upon a contest with the Saracen, but upon a mutual rivalry, a rivalry which showed itself in the extolling by each of the power and majesty of his own sovereign, Conrad III. or Louis VII., the symbol of his race. The lesson spread to the people at home, and kings, to whom the Crusades had brought new honour, found it so much the easier to overcome the strictly defended independence of vassal barons. Feudal power was in its essence territorial. The lord was lord of his castle, and within the limits of his own domain; and his vassals owed him service in respect of landholding. So, therefore, when the various barons bowed their heads to the central power, the sovereignty which resulted was not, as it had been in the old days, personal, the kingship of the race, but territorial, the kingship of the kingdom.

5. Teach ideas of unity of Christendom and

6. Unity of Nations.

Monarchy reaps the fruit.

Thus the Church as Peace Maker and as Crusader fought the battle of the Throne. And the Throne knew the value of its ally, and was fain to constitute itself the advocate and protector of the cause of Religion, to strike for Christianity against the Moor and the Albigensian, and for morality against English John, for orthodoxy against Saxon Harold or for papal suzerain rights against Conradin and Manfred, to pass a *Statutum de Comburendo* or burn a heretical Hus. But it did not at the same time neglect other strong auxiliaries.

Other allies and efforts of Monarchy.

Hemmed in and thwarted on every side, Monarchy caught at any chance prop capable of lending it support: it won over the lawyer by favour and promotion, and by

Alliance with towns and lawyers.

his love of the imperial principles of the Roman Civilians, until the royal courts, the royal parliaments, and the royal law became a power in the land: it allied itself with the burgher against the baron by the grant of privilege and charter, *hanshus* and market toll, and balanced the wealth of the trader against the wealth wrung from the free tenant or the serf: it watched quietly and astutely to profit by the penury of a Robert of Normandy or the rashness of a Charles the Bold: it matched with the heiress of broad domains, Eleanor of Poitou or Breton Anne, Burgundian Mary or Isabella of Castile: it studied economy, and saved money, and therewith bought a train of artillery, or took into pay a Free Company, or a Company of Ordonnance: and then it assumed a bold tone, it introduced a Star Chamber and a Statute of Liveries, it fined and attainted, escheated and judicially murdered: and it went on and prospered. And as the days of the 15th century closed in and mediaeval passed into modern, Monarchy might raise the paean, for the scale had finally turned and gone down, and Monarchy had triumphed over Feudalism.

Its growing power

and final triumph over Feudalism.

(β) The struggle of the Monarchy against the Empire.

§ 52. The work was perfected in the Reformation days. Then Feudal Monarchy flung off the control of Empire and Papacy, and Territorial Sovereignty revealed itself stark before the world.

The Emperor fails to constitute himself international arbiter and pacificator.

The Empire and the Pontiff had alike failed to fulfil their mission. The Emperor at no time fully responded to his call. Endowed with an unique style, held the natural protector and leader of Christendom, Divine Vicegerent in things temporal, the rightful source of the royal title[1], the convoker, at least concurrently with the Pope, of œcumenical councils, he failed to constitute himself international arbiter and *pacificator mundi*. Stronger Emperors did, indeed, in some degree maintain order in

Dumont, *Corps Diplomatique*, I. 1. 105, 173, 260, 355; II. 2. 282; III. 1. 118.

[1] For the grant reciting the Imperial right of the title of king by Frederick II. to Ottocar of Bohemia, see Dumont, *Corps Diplomatique*, I. 1. 144.

Germany, and less satisfactorily in Italy: even weak rulers arbitrated from time to time between quarrelling prelates and barons, issued the Imperial ban against a Galeazzo Visconti, or proclaimed a much needed *land-fried*. Otto I. convoked, and presided at, the Synod which deposed John XII. Otto III. nominated to the Papacy Gregory V. and Sylvester II.[1] Henry III. deposed three unworthy claimants to the Papal See, and appointed a well-qualified candidate.

Dumont, *Corps Diplomatique*, III. 1. 119, 256.

Dumont, I. 1. 83, 84; II. 1. 87, 210, 265; III. 1. 377, 433.

But, except in such comparatively unimportant ways, and in the single instance of the appearance of Sigismund as the convener of the Council of Constance, the imperial authority was never effectively exercised in the international field.

Bryce, *Holy Roman Empire*, p. 254.

The formation during the fourteenth century amongst the cities and princes of Germany of league after league for mutual defence was a practical indictment of the Emperor as guardian of the peace[2].

Dumont, II. 1. 159, 168, 192, 200; III. 1. 281, 316.

The Popes, more keen-sighted, exercise their powers with greater effect,

The Popes, more keen-sighted than the Emperors, recognised their powers, and on occasion exercised them with effect in the cause of peace and morality. Pippin, by the grant of the Exarchate of Ravenna, had established the Papacy as a lay Power. Otto III. and Henry III., in purifying the Papal Chair, erected the Pope into the rival

[1] The citizens of Rome conferred upon the Emperor in the person of Otto I. the right of veto upon Papal Elections, and this grant was confirmed by Leo VIII. A Roman Synod decreed to Henry III. the right of nomination. It was Nicholas II. in 1059 who, reserving the imperial rights, established a regular body of electors to the Papal See. Bryce, *Holy Roman Empire*, chap. x.

[2] The League of the Rhine arose about 1250, the Swabian League in 1376. Forty-one free and Imperial cities of the Circle of Swabia and the Rhine united in a three years' confederation for mutual defence in 1381. In the following year several princes acceded to the union. In 1385 fifty-five cities of the Circles of Franconia, Swabia, the Rhine and elsewhere united in a similar association. Wenceslaus placed such unions under the ban of the Empire. The Swiss mountaineers, drawing together first in 1291, vindicated the independence won at Morgarten (1315), against the Austrians at Sempach (1386), against Charles of Burgundy at Granson, Morat and Nancy (1476—7).

of the Emperor. The superbly imperial sentence of deposition pronounced by Gregory VII. in 1076 brought the Franconian Henry IV. upon his knees. "*Peccavimus*," wrote Henry, "*in Coelum et coram vobis, etiam digni non sumus vocatione vestrae filiationis*." And the world wondered at the humiliation of Canossa.

Dumont, *Corps Diplomatique*, I. 1. 53.

An authority so far-reaching was capable of boundless possibilities in the international field. Pontiffs of the school of Gregory did not fail to exercise it to the full.

Gregory not only, usurping imperial functions, conferred the royal title upon princes and dukes[1], but wielded the weapons of religion to maintain peace amongst kings[2].

Innocent III. followed in the same path. He threatened the penalty of excommunication against the Kings of Castile and Portugal, should the peace between them be broken. At the time of his death he was on his way to make peace between Pisa and Genoa. Peter of Aragon and John of England alike discovered the weight of his arm.

Schmauss, I. 7. Dumont, *Corps Diplomatique*, I. 1. 138, 146, 148.

Subsequent Popes bid fair to secure the general recognition of the occupant of the Chair of St Peter as international judge. The First Council of Lyons met in 1245, on the summons of Innocent IV., to consider the deposition of the Emperor Frederick II., whom Thaddeus of Suessa appeared to represent and defend. The sentence of dethronement pronounced by Innocent was generally accepted throughout Christendom. At the Second Council of Lyons, summoned by Gregory X. in 1274, the Hapsburger Rudolph was confirmed as Emperor, and judgment given in favour of Venice, on a formal complaint laid by Ancona, as to dues levied in the Adriatic. Boniface VIII. endeavoured, although with but indifferent success, to mediate a peace between Philip IV. of France and

Dumont, I. 1. 185. Ward, II. 59.

Hosack, p. 56. Dumont, I. 1. 286, 310, 332.

[1] Gregory, in 1075, conferred the crown of Russia upon the son of Demetrius and in 1076 raised the Duke of Croatia and Dalmatia to royal rank. Dumont, I. 1. 52, 53.

[2] In 1086 Gregory forbade Wezelin to invade Dalmatia. Dumont, I. 1. 57.

Edward I. of England. The claim of the Pope as Lord of the Isles of the Ocean, upon which Alexander VI. in 1493 based his bull dividing future maritime discoveries between the Spanish and Portuguese, had been accepted by Henry II. of England in 1155, at the hands of Hadrian IV., as a good title for the conquest of Ireland[1]. In 1454, Nicholas V. issued a bull conferring upon Alfonso of Portugal the Empire of Guinea, newly discovered by the Infant Henry, and forbidding all other peoples to voyage thither or supply arms to the natives without the permission of the Portuguese king.

Dumont, I. 1. 80. Ward, II. 109, 111. Schmauss, II. 2155.

Dumont, III. 1. 200. Schmauss, I. 112.

But the Popes missed the golden opportunity. With small prescience, they prostituted their power to the loftiness of personal pride or to the meanness of nepotism, and sacrificed the real in the vain pursuit of the shadowy. They abdicated the seat of the arbitrator in the attempt to possess the subject of judgment. The names of Gregory VII. and Boniface VIII., of Innocent III. and Julius II. recall, with a tale of magnificent claims, a tale of grasping worldly ambition.

but throw away their opportunity.

Alexander II. in 1062 claimed tribute from Sweyn of Denmark[2]. Gregory boldly claimed kingdom after kingdom. In 1073, asserting a title to Spain as an ancient possession of the Roman see, he granted to a nominee to be held as a fief of Rome such lands therein as he should be able to win from the Saracen. In 1079 he advanced a similar claim to Corsica. Innocent III. demanded tribute from Portugal and Aragon, and was ready, upon the surrender by John of his kingdoms of England and Ireland to be held as fiefs of the Holy See, to defend that worthless monarch against his barons, and quash the Charter of Liberties.

Dumont, I. 1. 50.

Dumont, I. 1. 51, 52, 55.

Dumont, I. 1. 123, 149, 155. Dumont, I. 1. 320.

[1] *Sane omnes insulas, quibus sol justitiae Christus illuxit, et quae documenta fidei Christianae susceperunt ad jus Sancti Petri, et Sacro Sanctae Romanae Ecclesiae (quod tua etiam nobilitas recognoscit) non est dubium pertinere.* Grant of Hadrian IV. to Hen. II. Dumont, I. 1. 80.

[2] A similar claim is ascribed by Dumont to Alexander III. under date 1159. Dumont, I. 1. 84. See also as to Portugal, Schmauss, I. 3.

Scotland was claimed by Boniface VIII. in 1299, *pleno jure et ab antiquis temporibus.*

Various popes granted Sicily, Apulia and Calabria to Norman dukes, erected them into a kingdom, declared their annexation to the Holy See, and offered them to successive princes as the reward of conquest. Petty additions to the estate of the Church attracted the frequent keen attention of papal statesmen.

And no tie of allegiance, sworn oath or treaty was permitted to tie the papal hand.

Dumont, II. 1. 168.

The double failure of Emperor and Pope as international arbitrators.

The Pope failed, as the Emperor failed, to constitute himself the universal pacificator and arbitrator. But the Emperor failed for lack of power, the Pope for lack of impartiality. The Sword was too heavy for the feeble arm which strove to wield it: the Keys lost their magic influence when its exercise was bought with a price. Empire and Papacy symbolised in outward form the majesty of one Law-giver and one Law; but they failed entirely as active international agents.

And perchance the world profited by the double failure. The realisation of the ideal of Hildebrand, the creation of a Church Militant of the peoples of Earth, fashioned after and corresponding to the Church Triumphant of the hosts of Heaven, might, like the realisation of the dreams of Karl and Otto, have satisfied the aspirations of theorists like Leibnitz, but would have bound mankind for ever in the choking fetters of hopeless slavery. The mind feeds and grows on liberty.

The World Empire and the World Church promised peace, but it was the peace of infallible, indisputable and irresponsible authority, the peace of a living death: the World chose independence, which offers peradventure the best gage for expansion and real life.

Empire and Papacy, advancing rival claims to a world sovereignty, wasted their powers in mutual strife, until at length the Emperor sank back into a mere German suzerain prince, indebted for his *de facto* force to his ancestral dominions, whilst the Pope was degraded to an intriguing Italian petty potentate, whose exorbitant temporal claims, veiled under a spiritual disguise, were repelled in more than one quarter of the Christian world. The imperial throne of Karl and Otto, the throne of the Hohenstaufen, became the heritage of the Habsburgs, dukes of the Austrian Marchland; Guelf and Ghibelin came to denominate mere Italian political parties; and good men deemed that they might yet be Christians, even though they denied the spiritual claims of an Alexander Borgia.

Alliance of Pope and Emperor in the Reformation struggle.

And when at length the spirit, which had burned in Wiclif and Hus and Savonarola, blazed out anew at the call of Luther in the Reformation movement, and the Emperor allied himself with the Pope to crush the rising revolt, the success of that movement was fatal to both, and territorial sovereignty declared itself in all its nakedness.

Civilisation is after 1000 A.D. extended to the Northmen,

§ 53. Whilst Territorial Sovereignty was developed in the West under the shadow of the Empire of Karl and Otto, advancing civilisation brought the barbarian peoples one by one within the pale of International Law.

The Roman province of Britain, overrun in the fifth and sixth centuries by the heathen Picts and English, and won back in the seventh to Christianity and civilisation by the preaching of Irish and Roman missionaries, was again overwhelmed in the ninth by the bands of the Northmen. But the Vikings firmly established under Æthelwulf and his elder sons (837—871) in Northumbria, East Anglia and Mercia, and regularly settled in the Danelagh by the treaty of Wedmore (878), speedily became Englishmen, and before Svend Cleftbeard and Knut set up in England a shortlived dynasty of Danish kings (1016—1042) Scandinavia had entered upon the road to civilisation. Whilst the Northmen settled around the Seine mouth under the treaty of Clair sur Epte (912) forthwith renounced their barbarism, and in the eleventh and twelfth centuries sent forth armies of polished French knights to the conquest of England, Apulia and Sicily,

Christian monks, the couriers of civilisation, were at work in Denmark, Norway and Sweden. Karl the Great by force of arms compelled the Saxons to adopt Christianity (772—785): his son Louis the Pious encouraged efforts for the evangelisation of Jutland and Schleswig; and, although the labours of Ansgar (827—865) were ineffectual in Denmark, they bore in Sweden lasting fruit. Christianity made some progress amongst the Danes under Gorm the Old (860—935), the first king of all Denmark: his son Harald Blaatand (935—985) himself accepted the Faith: under Knut the Great (1014—1035), who united for a moment the dominion of England, Denmark, Norway, Sweden and Scotland, the kingdoms of the Scandinavian North, sometimes obeying a single ruler, more often separate states, passed in halting fashion within the circle of civilised powers, although not until the lapse of more than another century did Paganism disappear north of the Baltic.

Eginhard, *Vita Kar. Magni*, p. 10.

Eginhard, *Annales, ad ann.* 23.

Hungarians, Bohemians,

Meanwhile the Hungarians[1] and Bohemians, repelled from Germany by Henry the Fowler (919—936) and Otto the Great (936—973), established settled states whose rulers did homage to the Empire; the Livonian knights rivalled the Danes in the forcible conversion of the Esthonians (1219), and the Teutonic knights offered civilisation to the Prussians at the point of the sword (1226—1283). When in 1492 Granada was won from the Arabs an unbroken line of Christian civilised states, some clustered round the Holy Roman Empire, others owning a doubtful allegiance or indisputably independent, stretched from Gibraltar and the southern coast of Sicily to the North Cape and to the plain of the Vistula and Niemen, where the Christian cavalier kingdom of the Poles and the little more than heathen Grand Duchy of Lithuania[2],

Wends, Poles, and Lithuanians.

[1] Christianity was introduced into Hungary by Duke Geisa and his son Stephan, who was crowned first king of Hungary in 1000 A.D.

[2] The Lithuanians were the last Aryans in Europe to lay aside Paganism. Their prince Jagello became a Christian on his marriage with the Queen of Poland in 1386.

united by several titles under the Jagellons, marched upon the Christian, but only semicivilised Muscovites, and the barbarian Tartars of Krim.

In the East, Imperialism fought another but still a losing fight.

(b) The Byzantine Empire, 800—1453.

§ 54. The loss of the West, betokened by the coronation of Karl in 800 A.D., only in part represented the perilous condition into which the operations of the Iconoclastic Emperors had brought the Byzantine Empire. In the early days of the ninth century the Eastern Empire was compelled to fight a hard battle for very existence. Whilst the Caliph Haroun el Raschid (786—809) overran in successive forays the provinces of Asia, and exacted tribute from the representative of Augustus and Constantine, the hordes of the Sclavonians and Bulgarians, barbarians who had long before found their way across the northern frontier, inundated the themes of the Hellenic mainland and swept down into Peloponnesus. Of the old Asiatic dominions of Rome there was left to the Byzantine Emperor only Asia Minor north of the Taurus; in Hellas there remained but the islands of the Archipelago and some extensive strips of coastland; in Italy, Sicily and a few scattered fragments, and for some time Sardinia, poorly attested to the valour of Belisarius and Narses. In 811 the Emperor Nicephorus I., who had in 802 succeeded the dethroned Irene, was slain in battle by the Bulgarian Crumn, and his skull became a drinking cup after the old barbaric fashion. The conquerors spread over Thrace, pillaging and burning. Michael Rhangabe (811—13), the feeble successor of Nicephorus, could offer no effective resistance. Crumn appeared before the walls of Constantinople, and it was not until death removed the vigorous barbarian that Leo the Armenian (813—20) was enabled by victory in a great battle at Mesembria to force the Bulgarians to a thirty years' truce. The Bulgarians were left in the secure possession of the frontiers of a strong independent kingdom planted upon Imperial soil.

Struggles of the Empire against the Bulgarians, Sclavonians and other Barbarians, and against the Saracens.

Procop. *De Bello Goth.* III. 29, 38.

Freeman *Historical Geography*, p. 386.

Finlay, *Byzantine Empire*, I. 127.

The Bulgarian Kingdom, 695—1018.

of Bari and Tarentum, but even of Beneventum, the armies of Basil pressed so hardly upon the Caliph of Bagdad that he was fain to commit the defence of Cilicia to Touloun of Egypt. Cyprus was temporarily recovered (881—88).

Finlay, *Byzantine Empire*, I. 294.

Troubles of his successors, (886—959).

Leo the Philosopher (886—912), Alexander (912—13), and Constantine VII. (913—59) failed to sustain the military fame of Basil. The Saracen corsairs ravaged the unprotected coasts and islands of the Archipelago, whilst town after town upon the mainland passed under the Crescent.

Successes of the Saracens,

Finlay, *Byzantine Empire*, I. 328.

and Bulgarians.

In 904 the great city of Thessalonica was looted by the corsair Leo of Tripolis, when over 20,000 prisoners, the survivors of a fearful massacre, were carried off to be sold in the slave marts of Crete and the Levant. Simeon the Bulgarian, routing the Byzantine troops in battle after battle, ravaging Thrace and Macedon, and sweeping up to the gates of the capital, emulated the exploits of his ancestor Crumn. Adrianople fell (914). The alliance of the Empire with the barbarian Patzinaks, who had established themselves upon the northern shores of the Pontus, brought no relief. The Emperor obtained rest only when in 923 Simeon dictated the terms of peace, and turned his conquering arms and barbarian cruelty upon his Croatian neighbours. But then the evil days of the Bagdad Caliphs became the Imperial opportunity, and under Nicephorus II. and John Zimiskes (969—76) the Christian frontiers again advanced. Crete was in 961 reconquered by Nicephorus, Cyprus in 965; Tarsus, Antioch and other great cities were regained. Zimiskes, extending the Imperial borders to the Danube at the expense of the Bulgarians, carried his arms to the Euphrates. His successor, Basil II. (976—1025), earned for himself the title of the Slayer of the Bulgarians by the campaigns by which he reduced to obedience the kingdom of Crumn and Simeon (1018). Thanks to the teaching of prisoners and the labours of devoted Greek missionaries the Bulgarian kingdom had already become a semicivilised

Finlay, *Byzantine Empire*, I. 341.

Reconquests of Nicephorus II. and John Zimiskes (959—76).

Basil II. subjugates the Bulgarians, 1018,

power[1]. Then once again the star of the Empire paled. In 1040 the Servians revolted against the fiscal oppression of the Byzantine officials, and under Stephen Bogoslav secured their independence. A party of Norman mercenaries, enlisted in the Byzantine service in Italy, turned upon their ungrateful employers, and by the conquest of Apulia (1040—43) laid the foundations of the future kingdom of Sicily. With the capture by Robert Guiscard of Bari disappeared practically the last vestige of Greek dominion west of the Adriatic. Constantine X., in 1064[2], brought to an end the independent kingdom of Armenia, only to find himself directly confronted, in room of the weak forces of the decaying Caliphate, with the virile strength of the Seljukian Turks, a pastoral people from beyond the Oxus, whose Sultan, Togrul Beg (1038—63), called after the conquest of Persia to the defence of the Caliph of Bagdad against his own rebellious subjects and the Fatimite Caliph, who had in 969 seized Egypt and Syria, overthrew the Bowides (1055), and ruled as temporal lieutenant of the Vicar of the Prophet. Alp Arslan (1063—73), the nephew and successor of Togrul, conquered Armenia and Georgia, ravaged Colonea, Cappadocia, and the Imperial districts of Asia Minor in a series of slave-hunting raids, and made prisoner the Emperor Romanus IV. himself (1071). Michael VII. (1071—78), in despair at the successive defeats inflicted upon his armies by Alp Arslan's son, Malek Shah (1073—92), the conqueror of Syria, ceded territory to Suleiman, cousin of the great Sultan, and so created (1074), in the heart of Asia Minor, the Seljukian Sultanate of Roum. The numerous rebels who rose against his successors, Nicephorus III. (1078—81) and Alexios I. (1081—1118), were equally ready to purchase the assistance of Turkish allies by cessions of Imperial districts. Alexios himself, a rebel whose reign was inaugurated by

but the Servians revolt, 1040;

the Normans conquer Apulia, 1040—3;

Freeman, *Historical Geography*, p. 383.

and the Empire is confronted by the Seljukian Turks, 1065.

Gibbon, *Decline and Fall*, c. LVII.

Establishment of the Sultanate of Roum, 1074.

[1] Bogoris, the Bulgarian king, accepted the faith and name of the Emperor Michael in 861.

[2] Kars was not annexed until 1064, in which year the Turks took Ani.

the plunder of Constantinople by Bulgarian and Sclavonian mercenaries, made extensive grants to Suleiman to secure assistance against Robert Guiscard, whose ambition, emulating the deeds of his brother Roger, the conqueror of Sicily from the Saracens (1060—91), carried him in 1081 across the Adriatic to the invasion of Greece. Turkish emirates arose in Cyzikus, Smyrna, Sinope, and other Imperial cities.

Cutting short of the Imperial provinces.

The advance of the Seljuks represents the first stage of that closing in of Barbarism upon Civilisation, which was to remove the holders of Asia Minor, Syria and Mediterranean Africa from the list of the peoples of the International Circle. A rude horde of Turkoman shepherds, their religion constituted well-nigh their sole likeness to the studious, polished, and chivalrous Arab. The deliberate policy of depopulation, which they adopted towards the lands in which they proposed to settle, marking them off from their Saracen predecessors, sufficiently denoted the character of their conquests.

With the advance of the Seljuks Barbarism begins to close in upon Civilisation in Asia.

Finlay, *Byzantine Empire*, II. 24, 33.

The Byzantine Empire was in but poor condition to resist their inroads. For centuries, despite misfortune after misfortune, Constantinople had continued to occupy the position of the metropolis of the leading Great Power of the civilised world. In its administrative organisation, in its legal code, and in the perfection of its justice, the Byzantine Empire represented for ages the nearest practical approach to the ideal of orderly government, whilst its material prosperity kept pace with its military glory. The commerce of the world centred in the Golden Horn. Silk and other manufactories sustained a wealthy middle class in Hellas; the possession of silver mines secured the abundant supply of one precious metal; the gold coinage of the Byzantine Emperors, known in the most distant lands, told of the large stores of a second, amassed by successive Caesars. Already under the Basilian dynasty, however, the Empire had begun to move down the path of decline. The Emperor had become a despot of the most absolute type. Eunuchs and slaves took the place

Decay of the Byzantine Empire.

Finlay, *Byzantine Empire*, I. 539.

of aristocrats as ministers of state. The fiscal oppression of Imperial officials combining with the ravages of barbarian invaders crushed agriculture in the provinces. The peasantry deserted their fields for the great towns, and their places were unwisely filled by colonies of barbarian settlers. The privileged Venetians began to monopolise the Greek markets. The Byzantine army, always largely composed of semi-barbarous mercenaries, became a strange conglomeration of Varangians, Normans, Patzinaks, Franks, Germans and Turks.

Alexios I. (1081—1118), asks the aid of the West against the Turks.

When the ambassadors of Alexios at the Council of Placentia (1095) asked the aid of the West against the Turks, and the answer was given in the form of the Crusades, all the unruly elements in the social system of Northern and Western Europe were suddenly let loose upon the provinces of the Eastern Empire. The Crusaders in their first onrush captured Nicæa (1097), cut short the dominions of the Sultan of Roum, and established various petty Christian principalities in Syria; Alexios, playing the jackal, was enabled to recover possession of Rhodes, Chios, Ephesus, and other coastland cities and districts; the early Crusaders did homage to the Greek Emperor for their Asiatic conquests; but the ruler of Constantinople speedily learned to regard the Champions of the Cross as allies more dangerous than the Turkish enemy, and it was the Crusades which finally determined the fate of the Eastern Empire. John II. (1118—43) and Manuel I. (1143—1180) won new military glory for Byzantium by the defeat of Patzinaks and Servians, Hungarians and Turks. But the wars of Manuel with the Norman Roger of Sicily, with the consequent sack of Corinth and Thebes (1146), materially weakened the Empire; the system of maritime defence was ruined by Manuel's centralisation of the Greek fleet; the Genoese and Pisans, encouraged by commercial treaties with the same monarch, rivalled the now independent Venetians in the attempt to drain away the Greek commerce; and, when at last in 1204 the Crusaders seized Constantinople, the Byzantine Empire,

The Crusaders temporarily win back some territories for Christendom, but finally ruin the Byzantine Empire.

Finlay, *Byzantine Empire*, II. 192.

partitioned into a group of petty Latin and Greek states, was offered by Western greed a prey to the Mussulman. The Bulgarians had already reestablished their independence (1187), and their ruler had sought the royal title at the hands of Innocent III. Cyprus had fallen away (1182), and become a crusading kingship (1191—1489). Now the Fleming Baldwin ruled in Constantinople as Emperor of Romania, the overlord of a disorderly body of Italian and French feudatories, Kings of Thessalonica, Despots of Romania, Dukes of Athens, and Princes of Achaia; the Venetians and Genoese seized upon the scattered islands; the Greek Michael, Despot of Epirus, disputed the title of Augustus with two scions of the house of Comnenus, the Emperor of Nicæa and the Duke of Trebizond; an Armenian king seated in Cilicia asserted his independence. It was a singular succession of surprising incidents which restored in less than sixty years a Greek Empire at Constantinople. Theodore of Epirus conquered the kingdom of Thessalonica (1222). John Vataces (1222—55), the son-in-law and successor of Laskaris, the first Emperor of Nicæa, annexed the territory of the Emperor of Romania upon the Asiatic mainland, reduced Chios, Lemnos and other islands, and united the kingdom of Thessalonica to the Empire of Nicæa. Michael Palaeologus (1260—82), with the assistance of Bulgarian and Coman allies, recovered Constantinople (1261). Once again a legitimate wearer of the purple ruled at Dyrrhachium, at the foot of Mount Haemus, and on both the Propontic shores. But the restored Byzantine Empire of the Palaeologi represents the last great effort of Roman Imperialism in the East. Barbarism closed in alike upon it and upon Saracenic civilisation. The power of the Seljukian Turks was shattered by the Moguls. When the common fate of all great Oriental monarchies overtook the mighty Empire of the Great Khan, and the hordes of the Tartar horsemen disappeared in the steppes of Central Asia, civilisation was left expiring in the wide Euphrates plain and amidst the ruins of the Seljukian

The Latin Empire of the East (1204—61).

The restored Byzantine Empire (1261—1453) the last effort of Roman Imperialism in the East cities. The World Empire of the Saracen had been extinguished at Bagdad, and the Byzantine Emperor, again seated in his ancient capital, was confronted by the squadrons of the Ottoman Turks, relics of the broken army of the Khorasmian Jelaleddin.

The conquest of the Byzantine Empire by the Ottoman Turks is the victory of Barbarism. Laurent, VIII. 122.

As the troops of Orchan (1326—60) and his successors swept over Bithynia (1326—39), and, crossing the Ægean, overwhelmed alike Servian and Bulgarian kingdoms and Roman themes, the boundaries of the International Circle were definitely and for centuries cut short in the lands of the Eastern Mediterranean. The Ottomans were still less advanced in civilisation than their Seljukian predecessors. The Seljuks had in the course of years profited by contact with more polished peoples. The Ottomans, with Hungarian, Vlach and Albanian neighbours in their immediate front, were pressed in the rear by the Tartars of Timour. The shadow of the Roman Empire of the East hovered for fifty years over the Golden Horn and a narrow headland, to disappear on the capture by Mahomet II. of the capital of Constantine (1453). Then a semicivilised Mahometan Sultan ruled from the outskirts of Belgrade to the outskirts of Iconium, and prepared to annex as subject or vassal states the dominions of a long series of coreligionists as little or scarcely more advanced, who possessed the entire Asiatic and African Mediterranean seaboard.

The end of the Roman Empire of the East, 1453.

§ 55. Imperialism was not more fortunate amongst the Saracens than amongst the Christians. The Caliph combining with the claims of the World Empire those of a World Religion was exposed to the assault not only of ...y rebellion but of religious schism, and within thirty ...ars of the death of the Prophet sectarian divisions ...eared within the Mahometan fold. Moawiyah, the ... of the family of the Ommiyah, set himself up in ...scus in opposition to Ali, the fourth of the successors[1]

[1] ... Bekr, 632—634, Omar, 634—644, Othman, 644—655, Ali, 655—

of Mahomet, and, although the assassination of Ali in 660 secured for the Ommiyah for ninety years the possession of the Caliphate, it laid the foundation of an abiding schism between the Sonnite upholders of the Caliphs of Damascus or Bagdad[1] and the Shiite supporters of the claims of Ali, Hassan and Hosein.

Overthrow of the Ommeyads at Damascus, 752. Sédillot, *Hist. Gén. des Arabes*, liv. IV. c. 1.

In 752 the Ommeyad Caliph Merwan was overthrown and his family well-nigh annihilated by the Abbasside Abul Abbas el Saffah. Forthwith the cutting short of the dominions of the Caliph began. Scinde had been lost in 750. In 755 the Ommeyad Abdelrahman, who had escaped to Africa from the massacre which overtook his relations, laid the foundation of the rival Caliphate of Cordova. The example thus set was speedily imitated. The Caliphs of Bagdad surrendering themselves to luxury and the enervating delights of an Oriental court, distant provinces were induced by ambitious Emirs or by successive Imams, who offered themselves as Mahdis or Guides of the Faithful, to repudiate their allegiance. The Caliphs themselves assisted in the work of disruption by the ample commissions conferred upon their more vigorous lieutenants. So the Aglabites under licence from Haroun el Raschid established themselves at Kairwan (800), and maintained themselves until succeeded by the Fatimites (907), who extended their power to Egypt and Syria (969–1071); the Edrisites ruled in Maghreb el Aksa ([788] 803–949); the Taherites became (814) in virtue of a lieutenant's commission granted by El Mamun the first of a long succession of practically independent rulers in Khorasan.

Loss of Spain and other distant provinces, 755, 800, 814.

Sédillot, *Hist. Gén. des Arabes*, I. pp. 233, 249, 300.

The Empire of the Saracens already early in the ninth century had become a congeries of Mahometan states of the tribal or ruling race model, some of which acknowledged, whilst others repudiated, the spiritual headship of the Prince of the Faithful at Bagdad. A hundred years later there were three, if not four, rival Caliphates.

The rival Caliphates of the 10th Century.

[1] The seat of the Caliphate was transferred from Damascus to his new foundation of Bagdad by the second Abbasside El Mansur in 762.

Alike as a subject of the undivided or of the partitioned Caliphate the Arab belongs to the circle of Civilised Powers.

Murphy, *Mahometan Empire in Spain*, 1, Part II. Sédillot, *Hist. Gén. des Arabes*, liv. IV. c. 2. Bargès, *Hist. des Beni Zeiyan*, 22, 47, 78. Sédillot, *Hist. Gén. des Arabes*, I. 241. Eginhard, *Vita Karoli Magni*, p. 20.

Alike, however, in Asia, Africa, and Spain the Arab claimed a place within the International Pale. Bagdad competed with Cordova as a centre of literature, the arts, commerce, and all that appertains to civilisation; the sovereigns of Cairo, Kairwan, Fez and Tlemcen strove to rival the glories of the enlightened rule of the Caliphs of the older dynasties. Haroun el Raschid corresponded on equal terms not only with the Byzantine Emperor, but with Karl the Great; Saladin more than emulated the chivalry of Richard Cœur de Lion; the ruler of Tunis was a worthy opponent of Guiscard or Saint Louis; the court of Granada compelled the admiration of all Western Europe.

(i) The Saracens in the East. The Abbasside Caliphate, 752—1258. Wars of Haroun el Raschid and his successors with the Byzantine Empire, 786—847.

Sédillot, *Hist. Gén. des Arabes*, liv. IV. c. 2.

§ 56. The glory of the Abbasside Caliphs culminated in Haroun el Raschid (786–807) and his son El Mamun (813–833). The Empire of Haroun at the close of the eighth century extended from Morocco to Scinde and Samarcand, and from the range of Taurus and the hills of Armenia to Aden and Muskat. In eight successive campaigns Haroun overran the Roman Asiatic Themes. Irene purchased peace by the payment of tribute (802–811), and when Nicephorus I. ventured to withhold it, he was speedily compelled by another invasion of Asia Minor and the conquest of Tyana and Ancyra to agree to a new treaty on similar disgraceful terms (806 A.D.). The death of Haroun (809 A.D.) and the civil wars arising amongst his sons relieved the Empire from further immediate danger. Haroun had found himself compelled to entrust the government of Tunis to the Aglabites. His sons lost both Morocco and Khorasan. The Emperor Theophilus (829–842) endeavoured to strengthen himself against the Caliph by an alliance with the Khazars, but in 831 the Caliph El Mamun (813–833) invaded the Empire, and, although Theophilus secured a victory in the field, Cappadocia was ravaged and Heracleia lost. On the death of El Mamun, Theophilus, encouraged by the troubles occasioned to the Caliphate by Persian rebels

(833-841) ravaged Commagene and took Zapetra, but the Caliph El Motassem retaliated by the capture of Amorium (838). Then evil days came for the Caliphate. El Motassem had surrounded himself with a guard of upwards of fifty thousand Turks from beyond the Oxus. His younger son, El Motawukel (847-61), a cruel and sanguinary ruler, was murdered by these Prætorians, by whom a succession of Caliphs were set up and deposed. Between 861 and 871 there were five Princes of the Faithful in Bagdad. A natural consequence was the loss of further outlying provinces. The Toulonides and subsequently the Ischkides (936-969) established their independence in Syria and Egypt (877-905), the Samanides beyond the Oxus (874-999), the Hamadanites in Mesopotamia (892-1001); the Soffarides succeeded the Taherites in Khorasan (873-902); the Karmathians, a heretical sect, which, arising in the neighbourhood of Cufah, had conquered the province of Bahrein, attacked in 930 Mecca itself, and, entering the sacred city upon the occasion of a festival, put to the sword some thousands of inhabitants and pilgrims, polluted the Kaaba and carried off the black stone. The dominions of the Saracen World Emperor were reduced to the proportions of a narrow strip of territory around Bagdad, and the Prince of the Faithful became a mere shadow, whose name served to authorise the proceedings of a Mayor of the Palace in the form of a Turkish Emir el Omra. In 945 Bagdad was taken by the Persian Bowides, who, expelling the Turks, ruled as Emirs el Omra until 1055. A succession of able Emperors of the Basilian dynasty pressed hard upon the Saracen frontiers and reconquered wide territories. In 969 the Fatimite Caliph from Kairwan extended his rule to Egypt and Syria. At length (1055) the Caliph of Bagdad, threatened at once by rebellious viziers, by the Emirs of Syria and the Fatimites of Egypt, called in the Seljukian Turks, who had seventeen years before proved their prowess by the rout of the Sultan of Ghazna and the conquest of Persia. Togrul

El Motassem introduces Turkish guards.

Decay of the Caliphate, 861—1055.

Sédillot, *Hist. Gén. des Arabes*, I. 247.

Sédillot, *Hist Gén. des Arabes*, I. 249, 261.

Sédillot, *Hist. Gén. des Arabes*, I. 258.

The Caliph calls in the Seljukian Turks, 1055.

The Seljukian Sultans, 1038—1258.

Beg (1038–63), his nephew Alp Arslan (1063–73), and his grandnephew Malek Shah (1073–92), invested with the temporal functions of the Prince of the Faithful, overthrew the Bowides, swept the Fatimites out of Syria, and won wide tracts of territory from the Eastern Emperor. Once again a single Mahometan Empire stretched from the Oxus to the frontiers of Egypt (1076). Suleiman, the cousin and lieutenant of Malek Shah, established a Seljukian Sultanate of Roum in the heart of Asia Minor, with Nicæa as his capital (1074). When, upon the death of Malek Shah, his government was partitioned amongst his sons, a wide-reaching group of Sultanates continued to own the spiritual headship of the Caliph of Bagdad. Zenghis, the Atabek governing in Mosul and Aleppo (1122–46), recovered the Crusading principality of Edessa.

Extinction of the Fatimite rival Caliphate, 1171. The Ayoubite Sultans, 1171—1250.

Sédillot, *Hist. Gén. des Arabes*, I. 284.

His son Noureddin (1146–78) extended his sway to Damascus and the banks of the Nile, and brought to an end the Fatimite Caliphate (1171). Saladin, the son of Ayoub, the nephew of Noureddin's Kurdish lieutenant in Egypt, becoming Grand Vizier of the Caliph on the death of his uncle, not only established himself as independent (1171–93), but overthrew the Atabeks, took Jerusalem from the Christians (1187), and added to his lordship Mecca, Medina and Yemen. His descendants ruled in Egypt and Syria until 1250, when the last Ayoubite Sultan

The Mamalukes in Egypt and Syria, 1250—1517.

was murdered by the Prætorian Mamalukes, Circassian slaves, whose nominees thereupon reigned in his room (1250–1517). The Seljukian Sultan of Roum extended his borders at the expense of the Byzantine Empire; the Mamalukes drove the Crusaders from their last hold in

Sédillot, *Hist. Gén. des Arabes*, I. 280.

Syria (1291). But before the fall of Acre the Arab Empire of the East was no more. The Caliphs of Bagdad

Advance of the Moguls and extinction of the Caliphate of Bagdad, 1258.

had recovered something of their ancient authority. In 1258 their line came to an end. The Moguls had swept from the Chinese seas to the Caspian and the borders of Germany. Driving before them the Khorasmians and other wild peoples, they burst upon Western Asia, overthrew in unchecked career all the Mahometan rulers east of the

Euphrates, whose dominions, virtually if not nominally independent, had been carved out of the territories of the old Caliphates, dashed to pieces the power of the Seljuks, and slew Mostasem, the last Caliph of Bagdad, in his pillaged capital.

The Ottoman conquest successively removes Asia Minor, Greece and Syria from the International Pale.

Sédillot, *Hist. Gén. des Arabes*, I. 279, 291.

The World Empire of the Saracen was extinguished, whatever the efforts to restore in Africa the spiritual claims of the Caliph, and with it the bulk of Western Asia was rent from civilisation. The barbarian Seljuks had in the course of two centuries assimilated something of the civilisation of the Arab. The Moguls were barbarians of more irreclaimable type, and when, on the disruption of their vast Empire, the Ottomans established their supremacy in Asia Minor and gradually extended it through Syria into Egypt, Progress retreated across the Mediterranean. The conquest of Constantinople was delayed for half-a-century by the overthrow of Bajazet (1402) by the savage Timour, but the Ottomans were well avenged. When Charles V. in 1519 was elected to the Empire of the West, the sovereignty or the suzerainty of the Porte was acknowledged from the frontiers of Hungary to the frontiers of Tunis and Tlemcen.

The Ottoman suzerainty extended to Egypt and Algiers, 1517, 1518.

(ii) The Saracens in Spain, 800—1492. The Ommeyads at Cordova, 755—1028.

§ 57. The Saracens in Spain as subjects of the undivided Caliphate, and until the fall of the Ommeyads in 1028, stood, it has been said, in the very forefront of civilisation. Amongst the Ommeyads themselves, or amongst the petty Emirs whose principalities rose upon the ruins of the Ommeyad Caliphate of Cordova, there appeared from time to time tyrants like the hardhearted El Hakem, "the Father of Cruelty," or the savage Muhamad El Moatahad of Seville (1043), who preserved in his palace a collection of cups made out of the skulls of foes slain by himself or by his father; but it was not until the peril of Islam brought over from beyond the strait the bands of the Moorish deserts that the Spanish Saracens in general began to recede from their place of honour.

Condé, *Arabs in Spain*, II. 30, 31, 36, 153; III. 2.

The dominions of the Ommeyad Caliphs of Cordova

included the whole of Spain with the exception of the old Suevic country of Galicia and the hill districts of Asturias and the Western Pyrenees, where the fugitive Goths held out against the invader, and whence they descended from time to time to raid, and later to reconquer, the lands of which they had been dispossessed. In the course of time a number of petty Christian principalities arose. The union of Asturias and Cantabria made up first the kingdom of Oviedo and then that of Leon. Sancho the Great of Navarre (1000–35) secured the dominion of extensive territories at the foot of the Pyrenees, which upon his death split up into the four kingdoms of Navarre, Castile, Aragon and Sobrarbe. Sobrarbe was soon absorbed in Aragon (1040), which, uniting temporarily with Navarre (1076–1134), annexed the country of Barcelona (1162). Castille and Leon, united between 1037 and 1157, separated in the latter year to come finally together in 1230. Portugal appearing as a county in 1094, developed into a kingdom in 1139. These various Christian states, individually or in combination, waged—except in the intervals of brief truces and short-lived alliances, the fruit of minorities or civil contests—a running war upon the Saracens upon whom their borders marched.

Disruption of the Caliphate of Cordova, 1028.

When in 1028, after some years of internecine war, the Ommeyad line was extinguished at Cordova, and the Cordovan dominions were partitioned into a number of petty Saracen kingdoms and emirates, the Christian rulers obtained a decided advantage. Alfonso VI. of Castile and Leon conquered Toledo (1085). The Arabian powers were only saved (1086) by the advance across the strait under their Emir, Jusef Ben Taxfin, the founder of Morocco, of the Almoravides, a hardy people from the Western Sahara, who had overrun El Maghreb. The Almoravides extended their rule to all Saracen Spain except Saragossa. When in the early years of the following century, on the overthrow of the Almoravide dynasty (1010), the Christians again made head, the hard-pressed

The Almoravides in Spain, 1086—1110.

Saracens called in the Almohades, a sect of Berber origin and more than doubtful orthodoxy, who, uniting the territory of the Edrisites to that of the Aglabites, passed over into Spain, and routed the Castilians in the great battle of Alarcos (1195). The power of the Almohades was, however, as short-lived as that of their Almoravide predecessors. In 1212 they were totally defeated on the plains of Tolosa. Twenty years later they were expelled from Spain, to experience in their African dominions the regular fate of Oriental dynasties. The World Empire of the Arab was no more in West, as in East. Long after Holagou had put to death the last Abbasside Caliph of Bagdad the title of Commander of the Faithful was bandied about amongst the various petty dynasties which arose in El Maghreb, but already in 1258 the Saracen power was reduced in Spain to the narrow boundaries of the kingdom of Granada, across the strait to the principalities of Fez, Tlemcen and Tunis. The flag of the Prophet floated for two hundred years longer upon the walls of Granada, but at length the end came. Ferdinand of Aragon had in 1469 married Isabella of Castile. The troops of the two sovereigns advanced upon the Arab kingdom, which was torn by civil strife. Abdallah el Zaghir, the last Moorish ruler, in vain preached the Jehad. In 1491 Granada itself was driven to capitulate, and the first days of 1492 saw the last Saracen cavalier quit the Andalusian shore. Portuguese troops had already preceded him and conquered the Kingdom of Algarve beyond Sea (1415–71); Portuguese discoverers were already carrying the fame of their sovereign along the coasts of Africa and across the Western Ocean.

The Almohades in Spain, 1146—1232.

End of the World Empire of the Saracen in the West, 1232—1492.

§ 58. The Saracens of Northern Africa played a by no means inconspicuous *rôle* amongst the civilised peoples of the Middle Ages. Separated from Egypt by sandy deserts El Maghreb and Ifrikijiah, the Arabian provinces which corresponded to the old Vandal kingdom of Africa, necessarily took up, even before repudiating allegiance to

(iii) The Saracens in Africa, 800—1519. Their relation with the Caliphates of Bagdad and Cordova and with the Caliphates of Fez (803—949) and the Fatimites (907—1171).

They are always in close intercourse with barbarous races.

Condé, *Arabs in Spain*, III. 248.

They remain for a moment, the wreckage of the Saracenic World Empire,

but finally fall under Ottoman supremacy (1517—72) or are left behind in the march of Civilisation.

Sédillot, *Hist. Gén. des Arabes*, I. 389. Guicc. VII. 95.

the Caliph of Bagdad, a position of practical independence. Divided under the Aglabites and Edrisites but reunited under the Almohades, they were in whole or part at times variously connected with the Abbasside Caliphs, with the Caliphs of Cordova and with the rival Caliphates of Fez (803–949) and the Fatimites (907–1171). Repeatedly recruited from the virile force of the borderland deserts, they sent forth successive bands of conquerors to Sicily and Southern Italy, to Egypt and to Spain. The source of their strength was, however, a source of danger. The chief warriors of the Almoravides were the tribesmen of Lamtuna from the Sahara beyond Sûs. The squadrons of the Almohade invaders of Spain were mainly drawn from peoples described by Andalusian historians as "in a state of barbarism." When in 1492 Abdallah el Zaghir retired from Spain the states of Northern Africa, Morocco, Tlemcen, Algiers, Tunis and Tripoli, non-progressive and bordering upon savage negro races, were by the combined Christian and Ottoman advance left, with the Mamalukes of Egypt, to represent the last relics of Saracenic civilisation. In 1509 the Spaniards took Oran. In 1510 Peter of Navarre imposed tribute on Tunis. The Sultan of Algiers in alarm called to his aid Horoudj, a famous corsair of Mitylene (1516). Horoudj slew his master and established himself in his room. His brother and successor Barbarossa in 1518 submitted himself to rule as lieutenant of the Ottoman Sultan, and it was as capitan-pacha of Suleiman that he conquered Tlemcen and Tunis. The Mamalukes had already yielded to the all-absorbing power (1517). So Barbarism laid a firm grip upon the old Vandal lands. Charles V. might momentarily win back Tunis for a vassal Arabian prince (1535); the Knights of St John might maintain the old Crusading fight yet a few years longer in Tripoli (1551); Morocco might continue to assert her independence of the Turk; but all the states of the African Mediterranean shore had already in the last days of Ferdinand the Catholic began to lag behind the leading states of Christendom in point of social advance, and, receding more and more as civilisation extended throughout the West and North, they, as at best semicivilised communities, had by the beginning of the seventeenth century passed beyond the pale of International Law; and the treaties made with the Barbary Powers of the eighteenth century by various Christian states present a curious picture of the survival of mediæval practice at the very gates of modern civilised Europe.

ii. International Practice in the Middle Ages. The conception of Territorial Jurisdiction subordinated to that of the Empire and of the Tribe, alike in the municipal and international administration of justice.

§ 59. The laws of the mediæval ruler inevitably reflected the character of his claims. Monarchs who claimed the allegiance of the world and monarchs who were proud to be styled the kings of particular races alike paid small heed to land limits as the bounds of jurisdiction. The municipal laws of mediæval Europe were imperial or tribal laws; the laws of the Saracen states were found in the Koran and in the codes and customs of the subject peoples who were permitted to retain their own magistrates. Side by side in the same state men obeyed the *Laws of the Burgundians*, the *Laws of the Visigoths*, and the Roman *Jus Civile*, the law of Islam and the law of the Christian. Even the usages which were in name, like the *Customs of Normandy*, the laws of particular districts were rather the laws of a people than the laws of a locality. Rulers fought incessantly for lands and tribute, but territoriality was in the administration of civil justice subordinated to the consideration of the person. So the International Law of the Middle Ages was not first and foremost an inter-territorial law.

1. *The Law of Peace.* (α) Contempt of modern notions both on part of and in dealing with foreign sovereigns within local bounds.

§ 60. The little prominence of the territorial conception in the Middle Ages was directly shown in the frequent mediæval failure to recognise even in time of peace local sovereign claims. On the one hand, a feudal sovereign, passing through the territory of his neighbour with a sufficient guard, would not hesitate to exercise therein the functions of sovereignty, at least over his own subjects; on the other hand, the local ruler was ever ready, in contempt of modern notions of the claims of courtesy, to lay hands upon a foreign sovereign, who came within his reach without passport and unaccompanied by force to protect himself.

Richard Cœur de Lion on his way to the Crusades hanged thieves and robbers on gibbets, which he erected outside the camp at the rendezvous at Messina, dealing, in the words of the applauding chronicler, equal *justice to the stranger and the native.* And the French Courts after solemn debate assigned to Edward I. of England during a stay in Paris the jurisdiction over a thief, seemingly a native Frenchman, taken within his *hôtel.*

Richard of Devizes, s. 20.

4 Rep. 15.

On the other hand, Cœur de Lion himself, on his journey home from Palestine, was seized by his enemy Leopold of Austria, and retained in close imprisonment by the Emperor Henry VII., and it was not recognition of wrong-doing in the seizure of a reigning sovereign, but the indignation of Christendom at the imprisonment of her hero, reinforced by an actual ransom, which secured to the captive his liberty.

Condé, *Arabs in Spain*, III. 286.

Abu Said of Granada was in 1363, with his suite of Moorish cavaliers, treacherously murdered at Seville by Pedro of Castile, in violation of the usages of hospitality.

The detention of Prince James of Scotland by Henry IV. of England (1405) and of the Archduke Philip by Henry VII. (1505) might be cited as other examples of similar unchivalrous conduct towards nominal friends.

(β) Ambassadors, their treatment in the West, at the Saracen courts,

Eginhard, *Vita Karoli Magni*, 20.

§ 61. When the monarchs of Christendom had overcome their first horror of the Arab, and the Emperor at Constantinople had so far condoned the assumption of the imperial title by the Frank as to seek his assistance and alliance, a regular diplomatic correspondence was opened up between the East and West. The system of resident ministers was not introduced until the close of the Middle Ages, but embassies passed at no infrequent intervals between the Courts of Bagdad and Aachen, Byzantium and Cordova. Bulgarian and Danish envoys appeared in the audience chamber of Karl the Great. In the

Eginhard, *Ann.*, *in var. loc.*

fourteenth and fifteenth centuries in the confused maze of Italian politics diplomacy became an art. Throughout the whole course of the Middle Ages *Jus Legationis* retained its place of importance.

Ambassadors of foreign powers were courteously treated alike by the Saracen and the Christian. Chivalrous sovereigns received with honour and dismissed with gifts even the herald who brought a formal declaration of war. Safe conducts were, nevertheless, wont to be asked for the protection of negotiators, and not a few tragedies accentuated the need for such caution.

Condé, *Arabs in Spain*, II. 71. Oakley, *Hist. of Saracens*, I. 203.

Dumont, *Corps Dipl.*, III. 1. 459.

The envoys of Barbarossa were seized and imprisoned at Constantinople by the Greek Emperor in 1187, to the no small indignation of Vinsauf, who stigmatises the transaction as contrary to the rules which usage and honour had sanctified from all antiquity, even amongst Barbarians. And it remained for Constantinople in later centuries to enjoy an evil preeminence in the matter of the treatment of ambassadors. The Ottomans were accustomed in the sixteenth century, according to Busbecq, to imprison and otherwise misuse the foreign envoys accredited to them, with a view to extracting an immediate disclosure of the terms of their instructions. The ambassador of the great Charles V. was imprisoned at Constantinople for eighteen months, and the colleagues of Busbecq for three years. Busbecq himself spent the major portion of his many years' residence in Turkey in a species of honourable captivity[1]. It was by conduct such as this that the Turk excluded himself from the pale of civilised powers.

and at Constantinople.

Geoff. de Vinsauf, c. 21.

Epistles of A. G. Busbequius, Ep. I. p. 5; II. p. 126; III. p. 216.

§ 62. The private individual travelling abroad was

(γ) The foreign private individual.

[1] So late as 1806 the Turks proposed to seize as hostages on the outbreak of war the British Minister and other residents at Constantinople, and Arbuthnot found it necessary to withdraw by stealth to avoid the torture and death which Turkish traditions rendered imminent. Lord Howick to the Admiralty, Nov. 21, 1806. Orders to Sir J. Duckworth, Jan. 13, 1807. Rt Hon. C. Arbuthnot to Lord Howick, Feb. 3, 1807. *Papers relating to the Expedition to the Dardanelles*, 1807.

during the greater part of the Middle Ages more assured of protection in the dominions of the Saracen than in the Christian West.

The great extent of mediæval commerce demonstrated by maritime codes and trading leagues.

The very great expansion of mediæval commerce is demonstrated legally by the *Basilika*, by the *Assises of Jerusalem*, and by the Maritime Codes of various dates from the end of the eleventh to the beginning of the sixteenth century. The earliest of these last, the *Rooles* or *Jugemens d'Oléron*, was adopted successively by the merchants of France, of England and of Spain. The so-called *Jugemens de Damme* or *Lois de Westcapelle* and the *Droit Maritime de Wisby* were nothing more than later reissues of the same rules for the use of the shipmen of the Low Countries and the Baltic. (Pardessus, *Us et Coûtumes de la Mer*, I.) The *Consolato del Mare*, a more detailed and extensive collection made, seemingly, at Barcelona about the middle of the fourteenth century, was accepted by all the chief traders of the Mediterranean Northern sea-board. (Pardessus, II. c. 12.) Originating in the practice of merchants and seamen, sanctioned by gradually extending usage, and dealing with the mutual rights under the various chances of maritime adventure of owners and freighters, masters and mariners, with pilots and deserters, with jettison and collisions, loss by pirates, by the detention of princes, and by the act of God, these codes at once set out a veritable common law of the sea and furnish an eminently instructive illustration of the method of evolution of all International Law. Incidentally they tell of the existence already in the thirteenth and fourteenth centuries of a vast carrying trade around the entire coast of Europe from the Bosphorus to the Baltic and with the Saracen ports of the Levant, Barbary and Spain. (*Consolato del Mare*, CCXXIX., CCXXX. (cc. 274, 275). Pardessus, II. 299.) The Pisans, Venetians and Genoese, in fact, emulating and outstripping the men of Amalphi, who had obtained from Saracen rulers special quarters and immunities in the cities of Sicily, Egypt and the Asiatic sea-board, established their factories throughout the East, so laying the foundations of still existing consular privileges. (Hallam, *Middle Ages*, II. 392. Pardessus, I. 143.) The Hanseatic League, commencing with the union (circ. 1260) of a number of Baltic towns, extended in the course of a century to upwards of eighty cities, whose great depôts at Bruges, London, Bergen and Novgorod spread a trading network throughout all the lands of the North. The League of the Rhine (circ. 1250) and the Swabian League (1376) linked the Baltic Confederacy with the Mediterranean traffickers. At Bruges, at London, and in the Italian cities the woollen manufactures of Flanders were exchanged for the wines of Southern France and the silks of Sicily and Greece; at Novgorod and Constantinople the western dealers met the vendors of furs and spices from the distant East. The business of maritime insurance proper, as distinct from mutual sharing of risk, was regularly carried on amongst the Italians at the end of the fifteenth century, and afforded the chief material for the French *Guidon de la Mer* of a century later. The institution of Consuls, in the character of magistrates who accompanied vessels upon their voyages, is recognised by the *Consolato*[1], and was probably general as early at least as 1279.

Pardessus, II. c. 14.

Hallam, *Middle Ages*, II. 388.

Pardessus, II. 370, 377.

Consolato del Mare, LXXIV. (c. 119). Pardessus, II. 119.

The mediæval traveller and his foes;

In spite, however, of the seeming prosperity of commerce and consequent frequency of international communication the traveller or merchant of the Middle Ages had need of a stout heart, strong hand and good arms to guard his head. Christianity dictated care for the stranger, and the capitularies of successive Emperors provided for the protection of the foreign wayfarer; but such laws were of little avail when kings were weak and the alien perchance more frequently experienced the need, than secured the attention, of the good Samaritan. In Crusading days the wandering palmer was fairly secure of a kindly reception in any Christian land, but the packhorse or the vessel of the trader was for long a favourite prey. The baronial castle, perched upon the hill-top commanding the German Imperial ford, was only too apt to be the

the baronial robber,

[1] In the numbering of the Chapters of the *Consolato* the Arabic numerals represent the usual but incorrect method of citation. See Pardessus, ii. 49.

stronghold of a robber-band, preying upon the passing merchant.

the pirate, In like fashion, in accordance with the principles of the Roman Civil Law, which constituted the basis of Imperial legislation alike in West and East, the navigation of the high sea was open to all, and the shore to high-water mark was the subject of common user, but piracy was until a late period well-nigh universally prevalent. In the ninth century the pirates of the northern seas made a voyage to England dangerous, even for a legate of Karl. A regular piratical republic flourished at Jomsburg until 1043. A marauding association known as the *Vitallien Brothers* distressed the Hanseatic merchants in the Baltic in 1418. The men of Monaco in the sixteenth century carried on the same trade as the Saracens of Crete or Fraxinent[1] of earlier days or as their contemporaries the infidels of Tunis and Algiers. Dunkirk pirates preyed upon the Dutch, and the Venetian merchant was defied and robbed at his very door and in his own Adriatic by daring plunderers, who found a ready shelter in the Archduke's borders. The mediæval claim to ocean lordship was based upon the benefits conferred by the maintenance of the police of the sea.

Dig. 1. 8. 2. 1; 50. 16. 112. *Basilika*, XLVI. 3, 2.

Recés de la Ligue Anséatique, 1412, 1417, 1418, 1432. Pardessus, I. 141; II. 461, 531. Eginhard, *Ann.*, *ad An.* 809.

Pardessus, II. 466.

Guicc. IV. 56.

Grotius, *Hist.*, 4, 419.

Nani, *Histoire de la Rep. de Venise*, Lib. I.

and the wrecker. The prevalence for many centuries of wrecking has been referred with great probability to the fact that in early ages every sea rover was practically a pirate. The Cypriotes in the days of Cœur de Lion were practised wreckers, and their prince took his share in the spoil. Travellers, cast ashore by storms in Cyprus, were, if wealthy, held to ransom, if poor enslaved. Richard's pious chronicler applauds the justice of the chastisement inflicted by his hero upon the Cypriot tyrant, but a very similar practice had been the custom of Richard's Norman duchy a short century before. Harold Godwinson, being cast by storm on the coast of Ponthieu, was seized and

Pardessus, I. 315.

Richard of Devizes, s. 60.

Geoff. de Vinsauf, c. 29.

[1] Fraxinent, upon the coast of Provence, was a Saracen pirate-nest from 888 to 975.

imprisoned by the lord of the district[1], and did not escape from the hand of the over-lord, Norman William, until he had given his famous pledge. Condemned by Emperor and by Council, by Assises of Jerusalem and Capitularies of French Kings, the wrecker continued his barbarous trade from century to century, and defied alike the excommunication of Papal Bulls and the rising voice of humanity. So late as the time of Elizabeth the institution flourished in the light of day. A vessel conveying a present of 8000 crowns in gold from the Pope to Mary, Queen of Scots, having the misfortune to be cast away upon the English coast, the Earl of Northumberland, as lord of the territory, claimed the gold under some "just law," which he caused to be read in the old Norman tongue[2] to Melvil, who was sent to demand restitution of the money.

Dig. 47, 9; 11, 5. Pardessus, I. 142, 177, 316, 346. *Mare Clausum*, pp. 153, 154.

The treatment of the alien resident varied in the Middle Ages with the various countries and the varieties of policy.

The mediæval alien resident.

In some states the stranger was protected in life and limb, and allowed to sue and be sued in the ordinary courts; sometimes he was placed under the care of a special host, or he was even, as a suitor, granted the privilege of a jury *de medietate linguæ*: he was a "man of the Emperor," or a Hanseatic merchant, and the king received him gladly, though native traders might growl their hate, and native apprentices while away a happy holiday in sacking his well-stored steelyard. Or again, while defended by the local ruler from the attacks of others, he was taxed and pillaged by that ruler himself in every conceivable fashion, and on every conceivable pretext: he came to claim the heritage of a deceased ancestor, and he was fined by the monarch in virtue of a *droit de détraction*; he was a Jew or a Lombard, and

Stat. 5 Hen. 4, c. 9. Stat. 28 Edw. 3, c. 13. Stat. 33 and 34 Edw. 3, c. 14, s. 5.

Droit de détraction, Vattel, II. 8, § 113.

[1] For the punishment under the Rooles d'Oléron of a seigneur who is the confederate of wreckers see Pardessus, i. 349.

[2] Which, says Melvil, neither he nor the Earl understood. Melvil, *Memoirs*, p. 58.

he became the royal sponge, paying for the privilege of extracting usury of the people, by the privilege of providing for the extravagance of the king: he resided in his special Jewry and his Lombard Street, and his money bags furnished the bankrupt local royal exchequer under the telling inducements of the hangman's whip or the niceties of torture; he might be at any time expelled *droit d'émigration,* by the tyrant, but if, his wrath provoked by some unusual outrage, he strove to withdraw, he might find himself obliged to purchase permission so to remove with his Vattel, I. 19, § 220. goods by the payment of a *gabelle* (*droit d'émigration*); and, should he at last die a stranger in a strange land, it and *droit d'aubaine.* commonly happened that the vultures of the Crown Vattel, II. 8, § 112. Grotius, *De Jure Belli ac Pacis*, II. 7, 14. swooped down once more, and robbed the alien heir under the name of the *droit d'aubaine.*

English mediæval practice as to the alien resident.

In England the merchant stranger was always encouraged, and statutes without number were passed from time to time for his comfort and protection. He was permitted to enter the country and leave it without let or hindrance, except in time of war[1]; he might buy and sell within the realm without disturbance[2]; special facilities were given him for the recovery of his debts[3]; and, should he require the assistance of a court, or be put upon his trial[4], he was granted the advantage of a jury partly composed of his fellow-countrymen. Sometimes it was sought to regulate his traffic and turn it into particular channels, and anon the attempt was made to compel him to spend his gains in the land where they were secured[5], but, in general, his lot was cast in pleasant places. Foreign craftsmen were induced to settle by the offer of liberties, and skilled workmen like

[1] Stat. 9 Hen. III. st. 1, c. 30.

[2] Stat. 9 Edw. III. st. 1, c. 1. Stat. 25 Edw. III. st. 4, c. 2. Stat. 2 Rich. II. st. 1, c. 1. Stat. 11 Rich. II. c. 7. Stat. 16 Rich. II. c. 1. Stat. 2 Edw. III. c. 9. Stat. 14 Edw. III. st. 2, c. 2. Stat. 27 Edw. III. st. 2, c. 2. Stat. 3 Car. I. c. 4.

[3] *Statutum de Mercatoribus*, 11 or 13 Edw. I.

[4] Stat. 27 Edw. III. st. 2, c. 24. Stat. 28 Edw. III. c. 13.

[5] Stat. 5 Hen. IV. c. 9.

the Flemish clothworker enjoyed peculiar favour[1], albeit it was not till later that full rights of citizenship were, in return for particular services, or in pursuance of a particular policy, conferred upon whole classes of persons[2]. In one particular alone was the English law strict against the alien. He might hold and acquire personal property within the realm, and maintain a personal action[3]; but he was forbidden property in real estate[4].

In most states the condition of the alien was one of progressive improvement.

Liability of the alien sojourner to the exercise of reprisals

Hallam, *M. A.*, II. 399. Rymer, I. 839; II. 891.

Amongst the special risks of his trading the merchant stranger of the Middle Ages numbered the liability to attachment in person or property in respect of the debts of a defaulting fellow-countryman, and the liability to the exercise of reprisals. Accordingly, by a statute of Edw. III., it was enacted that a Lombard company should be responsible for the debts of any of its merchants left unpaid within the realm, " o that any merchant, "which is not of the company, should not be thereby "grieved or impeached." And the grant of special reprisals, being the formal authorisation by his sovereign of a person judging himself wronged by a foreign power to indemnify himself by the seizure of property belonging to any subject of that power, was no uncommon occurrence[5].

Stat. 25 Edw. 3, st. 5, c. 23. Stat. 2 Hen. 4, c. 16.

Pardessus, II. 410. Hallam, *M. A.*, II. 398. P. de Commines, p. 21.

[1] Stat. 11 Edw. III. c. 5.

[2] Stat. 15 Car. II. c. 15. Stat. 6 Anne, c. 37, s. 20. Stat. 7 Anne, c. 5. Stat. 13 Geo. II. c. 7. Stat. 2 Geo. III. c. 25.

[3] Co. Lit. 129 *b*.

[4] Stat. 17 Edw. II. c. 12. Stat. 32 Hen. III. c. 16. Progers v. Arthur, 3 Salk. 28. Jevens *v*. Harridge, 1 Saund. 7. Sir Upwell Caroon's Case, Cro. Car. 8. Hyde *v*. Hill, Cro. Eliz. 3. Bacon *v*. Bacon, Cro. Car. 601. R. *v*. Boys, 3 Dy. 283 b.

[5] "Lettres de marque ou represailles se concedent par le roy, prince, potentats, ou seigneurs souverains, en leurs terres, quand, hors le fait de la guerre, les sujets de diverses obeyssances ont pillé, ravagé les uns sur les autres, et que par voye de justice ordinaire droit n'est rendu aux interessez, ou que par temporisation ou delais justice leur est deniée. Car, comme le seigneur souverain, irrité contre autre prince son voisin,

and to embargo. Pardessus, II. 409.

The fear of reprisals, whether in the shape of retorsion or of an answering act of violence of another species, constituted in fact the chief check upon the arbitrary action of the mediæval sovereign for whom the goods of the passing foreigner would otherwise have furnished a too ready temptation. Bolder potentates not infrequently relieved their pressing necessities by the imposition of an embargo upon the ships or merchandise of friendly traders.

2. *The Law of War.*

§ 63. Perhaps the darkest feature in the international history of the Middle Ages is the savagery of the prevailing war-practice.

Savagery of the war-practice of the early Middle Ages. Civilised belligerents emulate the Barbarians in cruelty.

The Northmen, who in the ninth and tenth centuries harried the shores and river courses of all Western Europe, were, like the earlier barbarian conquerors, rude and merciless. They sacked and burned towns, wasted lands and put their prisoners to death. The Magyars, in like fashion, on their first appearance upon the Danube at the end of the ninth century (896) and for many years longer, burned, plundered and slew in defenceless open villages.

par son heraut ou ambassadeur, demande satisfaction de tout ce qu'il pretend luy avoir esté fait, si l'offence n'est amandée il procede par voye d'armes, aussi à leurs sujets plaintifs, si justice n'a esté administrée, font leurs griefs, mandent leurs ambassadeurs qui resident en cour vers leur majestez, leur donnent temps pour aviser leurs maistres. Si par aprés restitution et satisfaction n'est faite par droit commun à toutes nations, de leur plein pouvoir et propre mouvement concedent lettres de marque, contenant permission d'apprehender, saisir par force ou autrement, les biens et marchandises des sujets de celuy qui a toleré ou passé sous silence le premier tort ; et comme ce droit est de puissance absolue, aussi il ne se communique ny delegue aux gouverneurs des provinces, villes et citez, amiraux, vice-amiraux, ou autres magistrats.

"Elles se concedent aux naturels sujets et regnicoles pour chose pillée, depredée, retenue ou arrestée par force à eux appartenant, mesme par benefice du prince aux estrangers naturalisez, ou à ceux qui ont droit de bourgeoisie pour pareilles causes que dessus.

"Le plus frequent usage se pratique pour les marchands depredez sur mer, trafiquans en estrange pays, lesquels, en vertu d'icelle, trouvent par mer aucuns navires des sujets de celuy qui a toleré la premiere prise, l'abordant, s'ils sont les plus forts, mettent en effet leurs represailles." *Le Guidon de la Mer*, c. 10. Pardessus, II. 410.

The Bulgarians of the same century were accustomed to ransom at the end of each campaign the greater number of their prisoners, the remainder being sold as slaves or killed. The Bulgarian Simeon, warring against the Croats, systematically depopulated their territory, murdering the inhabitants and leaving the land waste and desolate. Defeating the Byzantine troops in the open field, he cut off the noses of his prisoners. The contemporary Muscovites not only massacred their foes by thousands in captured cities, but crucified, burned alive and otherwise tortured their captives. Three centuries later a Bulgarian monarch, Kalo-John, a Christian and a member of the Roman communion, could employ the arms of barbarous heathen Comans for wholesale massacre in the cities of Romania and Thessalonica, the Emperor Baldwin himself and a large number of Latin knights perishing in his dungeons or under the strokes of his headsman. The Saracen corsairs who raided the coasts of Italy and the Greek Empire murdered prisoners whom they found themselves unable to carry off to Eastern slave-marts, and at times vented their fury in general slaughter. Timour the Tartar (1402) not only put to the sword every living thing in captured cities, but buried alive a garrison of four thousand Armenians who unsuccessfully resisted his assault.

Finlay, *Byzantine Empire*, I. 131.

Finlay, *Byzantine Empire*, I. 334, 368, 369.

Finlay, *Byzantine Empire*, I. 404, 405, 409.

Villehardouin, cc. 182, 185, 216, 219, 220, 231.

Finlay, *Byzantine Empire*, I. 328.

Gibbon, *Decline and Fall*, VI. 344.

These rivals in cruelty were barbarians, peoples on the verge of civilisation or irresponsible irregulars, but the foremost leaders of early mediæval civilisation exhibited on occasion similar belligerent ferocity.

The four thousand five hundred Saxons whom Karl the Great slew in cold blood were rebels, who had provoked his anger by repeated breaches of faith, but the wars of Karl and his son Lewis the Pious were regularly wars of fire and sword. The German Arnulf, storming Bergamo (894), hanged the governor and massacred the entire garrison. Raymond of Toulouse, being attacked on his way to the first Crusade by the inhabitants of Dalmatia, cut off the noses and hands and put out the eyes of his

Eginhard, *Vita Kar. Mag.* 9. *Ann. ad ann.* 782 *et in al. mult.*

Oman, *Dark Ages*, p. 464.

Finlay, *Byzantine Empire*, II. 125.

prisoners. Richard Cœur de Lion not only slew thousands of Saracen prisoners and cut open their bodies, but blinded captive French knights, an example which Philip Augustus only too promptly imitated. The Eastern Emperor Theophilus put all the men in Zapetra to the sword and reduced the women and children to slavery (840). The execution of prisoners was at Constantinople a common event. When Basil II (1014) could blind fifteen thousand Bulgarians, leaving an eye to the leader of every hundred, it ceases to be matter of surprise that Saracen marauders should thirty years later be impaled by Byzantine officials, that the Greeks of Adramyttium in the time of Malek Shah (1106–16) should drown Turkish children in boiling water, that the Emperor Nicephorus (961) should cast from catapults into a Cretan city the heads of Saracens slain in the attempt to raise the siege, or that a crusading Prince of Antioch (1097) should cook human bodies on spits to earn for his men the terrifying reputation of cannibalism.

Richard of Devizes, ss. 21, 68. 69. Finlay, *Byzantine Empire*, I. 445 n. Sédillot, *Hist. Gén. des Arabes*, I. 232. Finlay, *Byzantine Empire*, I. 405; II. 35. Finlay, *Byzantine Empire*, I. 445, 487; II. 151. Gibbon, *Decline and Fall*, c. 58.

Work of the Church, Mahomet and Chivalry in ameliorating war-practice.

§ 64. The world owed its rescue from the continued reign of savagery in the main to the Church, to Mahomet and to Chivalry.

All these in their several spheres did something to limit the frequency and much to limit the horrors of war.

(*a*) The Church.

§ 65. Of the work of the Church as pacificator we have already spoken.

War-practice of the Crusades severe,

The practice of the Crusaders, the warriors of the Church, was singularly cruel. In Religion's name they mangled prisoners in barbarous fashion, and beheaded shipwrecked Saracens with wild shouts of mockery. The career of Montfort in Languedoc was one long chapter of savage and relentless butchery. When Jerusalem fell before the Crusaders (1099) seventy thousand Mahometans and Jews perished in a promiscuous three days' massacre. The good Louis the Saint himself lost his habitual mildness when dealing with the Paynim. It was

Geoff. de Vins. cc. 34, 56, 61. Condé, *Arabs in Spain*, II. 96. Richard of Devizes, ss. 21, 68, 69. Sismondi, *Hist. des Francais*, VI. Chaps. 24, 26—28.

Frederick Barbarossa, Crusader and hero of legend, who besieging Crema, exposed captives on his battering-rams to the fire of their fellow-townsmen, an example which another crusading Emperor, the gifted and unfortunate Frederick II., was not ashamed to imitate. And it was a Crusading Churchman who, when Beziers fell, and they hesitated to immolate the orthodox with the heretical, cried, "Slay them all! The Lord will know his own." But though the Churchman himself, in spite of Canon and Council, was at times hardly distinguishable from the knight, in general he preached peace; and, though his zeal on occasion carried him to the wildest excesses, in his services and in his common practices he taught the blessedness of the merciful. The organisation which could marshal Christendom to the contest for the Holy Land and secure some reverence for a Truce of God did not despise the pettier task of watching over the agents of war[1]. And they were theologians of the Catholic Church who, as the Middle Ages closed, first entered upon the formal discussion of the right of conquest, the rights of discoverers and the obligation of treaties, and so prepared the way for Gentilis and Grotius.

but the Church, in general, preaches mercy.

§ 66. It is a relief to turn from the rude warfare of the Christian West to the belligerent doings of the Arab. Not only did the Koran furnish a new Code of the Laws of War, but the war-practice of the conquering Saracen supplied an object-lesson for the whole civilised world.

(b) Mahomet. The Koran contains a new Code of the Laws of War, and the Arab war-practice, in general, compares favourably with the Frankish. Comparison in Spain:—

Fanatical Moslem warriors in Spain called for perpetual warfare and war with fire and sword against the Infidel, and inveighed against monarchs like the Ommeyad Abdallah Ben Muhamad (886–911) who made treaties of peace with the Visigothic kings. On occasion, by way of reprisals or under stress of necessity, the Spanish Emirs

Condé, *Arabs in Spain*, II. 65, 67, 97.

[1] Thus the Second Lateran Council (1139) forbade the use of the cross-bow; which was, however, reintroduced by Richard Cœur de Lion, whose death before Chaluz was held up as a Divine judgment. Finlay, *Byzantine Empire*, II. 123 n.

Condé, *Arabs in Spain*, II. 73, 80, 82.

had recourse to measures of terrible severity. But, in general, alike in his faithful adherence to engagements and in the method of his war-waging the Arab contrasted brightly with his Visigothic and Frankish opponents.

the practice of the Christians (1211—1492)

In the later wars of the Saracens and Christians in Spain the Christians displayed a most determined ferocity. At the battle of Tolosa (1211) the Christian cavaliers gave no quarter: in Ubeda and other towns subsequently stormed they slew every Moslem "great or small." The entrance of Ferdinand of Castile into Balma (1232) was marked by "unusual circumstances of cruelty," all the inhabitants being put to death without distinction of age or sex. Before the battle of Guadalete the Christians put to the sword in cold blood a large number of Moslem prisoners. In the matter of the devastation of raided territory the Castilians and Aragonese rivalled the Almohades in every particular. The destruction condemned by the early Mahometan teachers was by the Arabian victims of the Christian war-practice of the fifteenth century enumerated amongst the ordinary calamities of war.

Condé, *Arabs in Spain*, III. 74, 80, 118, 119, 258.

Condé, *Arabs in Spain*, III. 182, 212, 258, 335, 346, 380, 388.

and the instructions of El Hakem (963).

On the other hand, the instructions given in 963 by King El Hakem Ben Abderahman as to the duties of Moslemah when going forth to the Sacred War reflect the ancient spirit of the Prophet of Arabia:—

"It is the duty of every good Mosleman to undertake "willingly the Algihad or Holy War against the Infidels, "the enemies of our Law. The Christian is to be required "to embrace Islam, except when, as now, the invasion has "been commenced by the Moslemah; but in every other "case the proposal to become a Believer is to be made, "and if refused, the Infidel is then to pay such an "amount of tribute as hath been settled and arranged "for the Christians living under our lordship.

"If the Enemies of the Law be not twice as numerous "as the Moslemah, then he who turns his back upon them "in the battle hath proved himself to be a vile coward; "he sinneth against the law and hath offended our honour.

"When taking possession of a city, let no man slay "women, children, or old men past power of resistance; "neither shall any man attack monks vowed to a life of "solitude, save in the cases where these latter are making "a defence injurious to the Moslemah cause. Do violence "to none to whom you have once given promises of "security, but be careful to keep all engagements and "fulfil all contracts.

"The safe conducts granted by the Generals shall be "respected by all; none shall disturb or offend any who "have obtained such." Condé, *Arabs in Spain*, II. 89.

The Hagib El Mansur, a stout Moslem, who to the delight of fanatics declared perpetual war on the Christian and repudiated the treaties made by El Hakem, adopted a by no means lenient war-practice, but he too forbade violence to pacific and unarmed populations. The Cordovan historians never fail to denounce deliberate and superfluous cruelty whether on the part of Franks, of negroes of Sûs, or of Saracen princes. The Arab ruler who cut to pieces every Christian in a captured city and allowed slaughter to continue long after victory was achieved was "hardhearted," the "Father of Cruelty" and guilty of "atrocious carnage." When a band of Northmen, landing on the coast of Portugal (843), plundered towns, massacred all who fell into their hands, burned or pulled down buildings and destroyed growing crops, they proved themselves "savages" and "enemies of the whole human race." Condé, *Arabs in Spain*, II. 96. Condé, *Arabs in Spain*, II. 31, 36, 73, 108, 112. Condé, *Arabs in Spain*, II. 30, 31, 36. Condé, *Arabs in Spain*, II. 45.

The war-practice of the Almoravides

The warfare of the Saracen against the Christian assumed a sterner appearance in the hands of the Almoravides, who prided themselves upon their close adherence to the traditions of Islam as to the burdens imposed upon the Infidel. Jusef Ben Taxfin offered the old alternatives of Islam, Tribute or War. He chivalrously fixed a day for battle with Alfonso VI., and it was the Christian king who, in order to secure, if possible, a tactical advantage, began hostilities before the stated period. But the troops of Jusef destroyed gardens, Condé, *Arabs in Spain*, II. 214, 278. Condé, *Arabs in Spain*, II. 279.

devastated fields, burned villages and slaughtered unarmed people in countless numbers in contempt of earlier Saracenic models. In captured towns he slew without mercy immense multitudes. The Almohades failed to attain ever to the Almoravide standard. Upon Christian Spain they burst like a storm; they destroyed towns burned open villages, laid waste the fields, cut up olive-gardens and vineyards and spoiled seed-corn, uniting armed and unarmed inhabitants in promiscuous slaughter. Impaling and burying alive were numbered amongst their regular methods of execution. But these cruelties did not pass unnoticed by the Spanish Arabs. The treachery and ill-faith displayed by the generals of Jusef were denounced by contemporary Cordovan writers as "ferocious" and "violations of all justice and of compact." The Almohades, recruited from the rudest tribes of Barbary, rough mountaineers emerging from rock-hewn holds, were unhesitatingly classed as mere Barbarians. The war-practice of the Almoravides and Almohades was in fact that of the semi-civilised African.

Condé, *Arabs in Spain*, II. 219, 225, 296, 302, 315.

and the Almohades

Condé, *Arabs in Spain*, II. 385, 481; III. 27, 39, 54.

condemned by the Spanish Arabs.

Condé, *Arabs in Spain*, II. 422, 428, 441; III. 248.

Condé, *Arabs in Spain*, II. 444, 454. Bargès, *Hist. des Beni Zeiyan*, 29.

Comparison in the East:—

In the East the Arab to the last showed himself a relatively merciful belligerent. His war-practice indeed enslaved, the raids of Haroun el Raschid and his successors upon the provinces of the Byzantine Empire wearing the character rather of slave-catching expeditions than of invasions with a view to conquest. On occasion the Caliph or the Emir, like the Byzantine Emperor or the Crusading Prince, denied quarter in stormed towns or put important prisoners to the sword. The Kurd Saladin beheaded the faithless Reginald of Chatillon and two hundred and thirty Knights of St John taken at Tiberias. His descendant, Touran Shah, the last Ayoubite Sultan of Egypt, put to death large numbers of French prisoners (1249–50). But Saladin, in bright contrast to the proceedings of Godfrey of Bouillon and his companions, or to that of Cœur de Lion, permitted such of the Christian prisoners taken in Jerusalem as were able to pay a ransom to purchase their freedom from the slavery which befell

Saladin and Richard.

Gibbon, *Decline and Fall*, c. 59. Sédillot, *Hist. Gén. des Arabes*, I. 287.

Geoff. de Vins., c. 9.

their poorer brethren, and treated the majority of the captives of Tiberias with marked kindness. The conduct of Touran Shah had some show of justification in the immense numbers of the captives, and his fierce and arbitrary temper led to his speedy murder by his own Mamalukes. Saracen corsairs angered by repeated defeats carried off monks from the island of Patelaria and sold them in Spain *contra omnem justitiam*. But it remained Eginhard, *Ann. ad ann.* 807.
for the Ottoman, the Mogul and the Tartar of Tamerlane to refuse quarter in the open field and offer a price for the heads of slain enemies. The Algerines did not sink to the level of lawless scourges of the human race till the day of the Turkish pirate Barbarossa.

§ 67. Chivalry, if not a creation of, was extended (*c*) Chivalry.
and glorified by, the Crusades. The German youth in the days of old had been on coming to man's estate Chivalry enforces the code of Honour,
solemnly invested with spear and shield in the presence of the assembled host. The mediæval ceremony of knighthood raised the aspirant to warrior's fame to membership of an order independent of birth and country, sworn to the honour of woman and the protection of the distressed.

The vows of knighthood could not but react upon the manner of warfare. The code of Honour, the watchword Villehardouin, c. 112.
of Chivalry, commanded the formal defiance of the foe preparatory to attack, and the employment of only knightly methods of combat: it protected the herald, sanctified the pledged word, and in some sort alleviated the horrors of war. When Henry I. introduced tournaments into Germany it was ordained that no one should be permitted to take part who did not profess Christianity, or who had been known to be guilty of perjury, treason, sacrilege or dishonour of woman. Ward, II. 161.

Courtesy and liberality were marked characteristics of the perfect knight. The Edward the Thirds and the Du Guesclins, the Chandoses and the Talbots gave formal Froissart, I. XXXIV., XXXV., XXXVIII., XL., CXLIV.
notice to their enemies before making their attack, and

Villehardouin, c. 112.

at times fixed beforehand by mutual agreement the place and day of battle.

But the code was the code of equals.

But Chivalry, like the Church, failed to exercise a perfect restraining influence upon even the most knightly combatant. The code of Chivalry in fact laid down the law for equals only, and the rascal rout, the man-at-arms, the archer, and the common footman, met with small kindness in the time of defeat, while the peasant and the townsman were ridden down without mercy. The history which tells of Barbarossa at Crema (1159 A.D.) and his grandson at Brescia (1238 A.D.), of Edward III. at Calais and of Henry V. at Harfleur, of Charles of Burgundy at Nesle and Nancy, the history of almost every prolonged siege, reveals with abundant clearness how little Chivalry sufficed, even in its brightest ornaments, to restrain the storms of passion and expel the lust of cruelty.

Philip de Commines, p. 95. Ph. de C. pp. 150, 157. Cf. Ph. de C. pp. 40, 69.

War-practice of the Golden Age of Chivalry.

§ 68. The tale of the war-practice of the Golden Age of Chivalry is the tale of tinsel splendour and cold-blooded brutality.

Distinction of German, Spanish, Anglo-French and Italian practice.

Practice indeed was not uniform. The war-practice of Spain and of Germany in the days of Froissart was regarded with disfavour by the knighthood of France and England as in some points unduly severe. On the other hand, the Italians of 1494 A.D. were astounded at the severity of the war-practice of the invading French.

Froissart, I. CCXCII., CCCVII.

The mild practice of Italy:—

The war-practice of Italy seems to have been unusually mild, a fact which recalls the opposition of the civilised Roman to the invading Barbarian of the North. The mercenary generals of mediæval Italy, the Hawkwoods, the Landos, the Barbianos and the Sforzas avoided bloody battles; they killed no one in fight, contenting themselves with making prisoners, and dismissed one another on capture without hurt or ransom. Their forces charged squadron against squadron, as in the lists of the tournament, so that a battle very commonly lasted a whole day without any great slaughter or decisive result.

bloodless battles;

Machiavelli, *The Prince*, ch. XII.

The Battle of Fornova (1495) was long remembered as being the first after a long series of years fought in Italy which was attended with slaughter and bloodshed. The Italian "Law of Arms" enjoined the release of all ordinary prisoners at the price of an absolute stripping. The Italians were filled with amazement and terror at a war-practice which sacked the stormed city and put to the sword its defenders. The Spaniards were the first in Italy to maintain themselves upon the substance of the inhabitants, their conduct being the result of bad pay. In one particular, however, the war-practice of Italy enjoyed an evil fame. The "villainous practice" of poisoning, which was almost unknown to the nations beyond the Alps, was common in many parts of Italy. The Venetians brought a charge of poisoning cisterns against Alphonso of Calabria, and Commines held it a sign of the special Divine Grace attending the French that the Italian country people did not poison the victuals supplied by them to the invading army of Charles VIII., or the wells in the line of march. "If they had minded," says he in his quaint simplicity, "to have poisoned them, they would sure have done it; "but because they did it not, it is to be thought that our "Saviour and Redeemer Jesus Christ took from them all "desire to do it."

Guicc. I. 339. stripping of prisoners; Guicc. II. 337, 389; III. 137, 159, 270, 291, 372; IV. p. 261. P. de Commines, p. 255. humanity after storming; Guicc. I. 167, 175; II. 328; IV. 257. Froissart, I. CCLXXXVIII., CCXC. absence of 'free quarters'; Guicc. III. 325. but use of poison. Guicc. I. 163, 278. P. de Commines, p. 252. P. de Commines, p. 311.

The war-practice of the Trans-Alpines may be traced in the history of the Hundred Years' War.

The Anglo-French practice:—

Edward III. invading France pillaged, burned and destroyed without distinction fortified towns, defenceless villages and quiet country houses. Descending upon Normandy before Crecy he found himself in a peaceful province, populous and wealthy, altogether unaccustomed to war, with barns full of corn, and towns, whose inhabitants fled at the very sight of the English archers, overflowing with merchandise. Edward marched through the country plundering on all hands, after the manner of the old Vikings, the booty being carried off to the English ships; a truly pitiful warfare. It is made a merit in

pillage and destruction; Froissart, I. XXXIX., XLV., XCIV. Froissart, I. CXXI.—CXXIV.

Edward that he had strictly charged that no church should be violated nor monastery set on fire.

ransom and exchange of prisoners;

The practice of permitting captured foes to ransom themselves became general in the later days of chivalry; indeed the prospect of revenue from this source was the main incentive of many famous knights of adventure[1]. Sometimes an exchange of prisoners took the place of ransom, and, as early at all events as the beginning of the Hundred Years' War, distinguished captives were on occasion released upon their parole. But from time to time recourse was had to the old stricter war-practice. Until a late period the soldier of the common herd was cut down without mercy in the hour of defeat, and too often deliberately butchered after his surrender. The like fate on occasion befell nobler captives, although not always without expostulation. Froissart treats the slaughter of the whole loyal garrison of a stormed citadel as a matter of ordinary occurrence.

Geoff. de Vins. c. 15.

Froissart, I. XXXI. P. de Commines, p. 305.

Froissart, I. XLVI., LVIII., LXXXVII.

slaughter after storm;

hanging of resisting commandants and garrisons;

Nothing was more common in the age of Chivalry than the hanging of the commandant of a captured town. The famous incident of the cruel designs of Edward III. against the leading citizens of Calais was distinguished from many like occurrences solely by the ultimate romantic escape of the fated victims. Henry V., who enjoyed the reputation of a mild-mannered soldier, hanged in chains Alain Blanchard, the gallant defender of Rouen. At Rougemont he drowned a party of sixty Dauphinois in the Loire. Louis XII., in 1509, taking Peschiera by storm, put to the sword the Venetian garrison of five hundred men, and hanged the governor, a Venetian nobleman, together with his son, on the battlements, in order to strike terror into the breasts of the besieged garrison of the castle of Cremona. The biographer of Bayard held this conduct on the part of the French king great cruelty. But Bayard himself procured

Froissart, I. CXLV.

Monstrelet, V. 16, 65, 75.

Guicc. IV. 257.

History of Bayard, II. XIX.

[1] The Germans and Spaniards according to Froissart fettered their prisoners in order to extract a higher ransom, a practice which the chronicler strongly deprecates.

the surrender of the Castle of Bassano by threatening the immediate execution before its gate of two prisoners of rank, one being the uncle of the commandant, and to such brutal devices the besiegers of Chivalry had habitual recourse.

History of Bayard, II. XXV. Vattel, III. 8, § 143 n.

The gallants of knighthood murmured when ignorant burghers put to death a promising young squire for the sake of his splendid armour, but it was not only Spanish princes schooled in Moorish warfare who allowed themselves at times to play the wholesale butcher. The English gave no quarter at Crecy, a resolution which proved fatal to John of Bohemia and a host of gallant knights. The Black Prince massacred in cold blood the three thousand inhabitants of the conquered Limoges. A false alarm after Agincourt caused the issue of orders for a general slaughter of prisoners.

Froissart, I. XLVI.

denial of quarter, and wholesale execution of prisoners.

P. de Commines, 40, 69, 95, 139, 293. Guicc. I. 167, 175, 323; II. 370; IV. p. 66. Froissart, I. LX., CXXIII. *History of Bayard*, II. XXVIII., XXIX., XXXVII. Froissart, I. CXXIX., CCXC.

§ 69. The state of the war-practice of the leading states of civilisation in the last half of the fifteenth, and the early days of the sixteenth, century is mirrored in every page of Philip de Commines, and of Guicciardini, the historian of the Italian Wars.

War-practice in the 15th and 16th centuries:—

Spending a long life in the personal service of Philip the Good (1419–67) and his headlong son, of Lewis XI. (1461–83) and Charles VIII. (1483–98), Commines was directly in touch with the prevailing spirit of his time. The picture which he draws of his masters, their contemporaries and their doings, is one to excite mixed feelings. We seem with him to breathe the air of the camp and the closet, of the tented field of the reckless swordsman Charles the Bold and the secret chamber of the false and scheming Lewis. It is an age of haughty cruelty and savage vengeance, of plot and treason, treachery and lack of faith, of contempt of law and slight of honour. In a word, it is the age of "The Prince" of Machiavelli. And yet, withal, it is an age of hope, of progress made, and of good to come.

The war-practice of Charles the Bold was, according

to Commines, in common mild. In his younger days of foreign foray he held back his men from plunder, and paid for all he took; but he burnt houses and mills of rebels, and, invading Vermandois, he made "foul and cruel war contrary to his accustomed manner." When the Liégois broke their treaty, the hostages in his hands were, after deliberate counsel, dismissed, subject to condition of death if found in arms[1]. But it was for little mercy that that town might look which fell before Charles of Burgundy. Eight hundred prisoners taken in the stormed Dinant were drowned in cold blood. With this butchery vengeance had to do, but the like cruelty was enacted at Liège, and the men of Nesle expiated the slaughter of a herald and of a couple of Burgundians in time of truce by pitiless hanging and lopping of hands. The humanity of centuries later could not protect in the hour of storm the defenders of a captured city, a Ciudad Rodrigo or a Badajoz. Charles the Bold could put to death by the hundred the Swiss garrison of Granson surrendering to his mercy, and the express terms of capitulation did not prevent Swiss in their turn from the sack and firing of Pontremoli and the slaughter to a man of its hapless defenders. The members of a party captured in the attempt to relieve besieged Nancy were put to death by the Duke of Burgundy in accordance with his view of "the Law of Arms."

ravage; P. de Commines, pp. 7, 70, 95. slaughter of hostages; P. de Commines, p. 43. slaughter after storm; P. de Commines, pp. 40, 69, 95. P. de Commines, pp. 139, 293. contempt of capitulations; slaughter of prisoners; P. de Commines, p. 150.

The French invaders of Italy showed small mercy to their foes. When Castelforte was taken by assault, all within were put to the sword, and a similar fate awaited Mon San Giovanni. On the men of the days of Lewis XI. and Charles VIII. Chivalry seemed to have lost its hold. Small reliance was to be placed in the pledged word, and negotiation was not merely difficult but dangerous. The safe conduct and the legatine character afforded a scanty protection, and the assassination of John, Duke of Burgundy, in the presence of Charles VII. stood out from

P. de Commines, p. 272. treachery and faithlessness; Guicc. I. 288. contempt of safe conducts; assassinations.

[1] The rigour of the Laws of War would, according to Guicciardini, permit a monarch to put to death hostages on a breach of faith by their giver. Guicc. I. 376.

many like incidents in nothing save the rank of the parties engaged, and the extent of its effects. P. de Commines, pp. 53, 136, 267, 268.

Yet the outlook has its brighter side. Commines and Guicciardini never hesitate to condemn cruelty and breach of faith. No Western Sovereign would have dared like Sultan Mahomet Othman not only to refuse quarter, but to offer a price for the head of every slaughtered foe. The ravages committed by papal troops in Venetian territory in 1513 were, in Guicciardini's opinion, unpardonable in Italians. P. de Commines, p. 296. Guicc. VI. 188–9.

3. *The Law of Neutrality.* Absence of recognition of Neutrality.

§ 70. Yet one more characteristic of mediæval international practice is specially noteworthy, the seemingly total absence alike in practice and conception of the idea of Neutrality. There was in fact in the mediæval international system no room for Neutrality. Whilst no member of the World Empire could be other than directly interested in the internecine strife which interfered with the harmony of the association, no Christian could be indifferent as to the struggles of the World Church, could stand neuter in the battle of orthodoxy against heresy or of Christendom against the Saracen. The Crusader might for special reason make a *truce* with the Saracen, but for a true Christian there might, it was deemed, be no *peace* with the Infidel. Machiavelli condemned neutrality on another ground. It was, he said, more profitable to declare for the one or the other. And Machiavelli's contemporaries did not fail to appreciate his teaching. The Borgias, hesitating as to their side in the Franco-Spanish struggle, gave leave to both parties to enlist levies in Rome. And this was the utmost extension of neutral care for which the belligerent of the age might reasonably look. Foreign assistance was always freely forthcoming for the belligerent of the Middle Ages. Not merely were private adventurers ever ready for foreign warfare; not merely did penniless knights-errant and needy squires in time of domestic peace wander abroad, like the ancient Vikings, in search of honour and of profit; Brabançons and Genoese

Conception of Neutrality opposed to theory of World Empire and World Church.

7 Rep. 17. 4 Inst. 155.

Neutrality condemned by politicians, *The Prince*, c. 21.

Guicc. III. 223.

and in practice non-existent.

i. Assistance of Belligerents:— "Free Companies"; levies for foreign belligerent service; Dumont, *Corps Dipl.* III. I. 465, 520. and auxiliary regiments.

cross-bowmen took service in troops with the monarchs of England and France; skilled commanders like Hawkwood and Bertrand du Guesclin led well-trained and organised armies under the name of "Free Companies" to the banners of prince after prince; and princes and kings themselves not only permitted recruiting within their borders for foreign warfare, but despatched, and even in person led, auxiliary regiments to the assistance of one or the other belligerent, while claiming to be on terms of undiminished general friendship with the assailed opponent. On the other hand sovereigns declined to

ii. Oppression of neutral merchants.

distinguish between the military and merely mercantile assistance of their foes, and the foreign trader who carried on his accustomed commerce with a belligerent was apt to be roughly handled by the enemy. So Edward I. attempted to induce the Flemings to cease their commercial dealings

Rymer, *Foedera*, I. 2, p. 821. Hallam, *M. A.*, II. 384 n. Rymer, II. 2, 747. Jenkinson, *Discourse*, pp. 26—29.

with Scotland, and in 1295 compelled the masters of neutral vessels lying in English ports to give security not to trade with France. Granting a charter to foreign merchants, he reserved the right to prevent any trading

iii. Violation of neutral territory.

with his enemies. Small regard was paid by belligerents pursuing or marching against their foes to the sanctity of intervening foreign territory, whilst early practice dis-

Guicc. VII. 265.

played little trace of any particular care for the comfort of

iv. Disregard of the neutral flag on the high seas.

the neutral carrier. The Venetians and Genoese when at war searched the ships of the neutral Greeks and made prisoners of the subjects of their opponents found hidden

Grotius, *De Jure Belli ac Pacis*, III. 6, 6 *note*. Jenkinson, pp. 23—4.

on board. The framers of the *Consolato del Mare*, following the terms of various treaties[1] of the thirteenth and fourteenth centuries, adopted in respect of property found upon the high seas the simple rule, "Confiscate the goods of your enemy; respect the property of your friend." They declared for the condemnation of an enemy's goods found under the neutral flag and for the release of neutral property laden on board a captured belligerent vessel,

Consolato del Mare, CCXXI. (c. 273).

regulating equitably in either case the question of freight.

[1] Pisa and Arles, 1221; England with Biscay and Castile, 1351; England and Portugal, 1353. Pardessus, II. 303. Rymer, III. 1. 71, 88.

There are not wanting suggestions of a more severe practice which confiscated the friendly vessel laden with hostile goods. The neutral vessel whose master refused to carry belligerent goods to the port designated by the captor might, according to the rule of the *Consolato*, be sent to the bottom without any compensation to its owner.

De Jure Belli ac Pacis, I. 5, note 4; III. 6, 6 *note*.

CHAPTER II.

THE EVOLUTION OF INTERNATIONAL LAW—BIRTH OF TERRITORIALITY.

IV. International Law in the Age of the Reformation (1519—1648). (1) The International System of the Age. Beginning of the Age:— 1. The Circle is Christian.

§ 71. A NEW era in international history opens with the election as Emperor of Charles V.

Civilisation, retreating before the Ottoman, had rallied upon and disseminated its influence through the peoples of the West and North: its bounds had come to be practically conterminous with the Christian states of Europe west of the Theiss, of the great Polish watershed and of the Baltic; the Universal Empire of the Byzantine and the Universal Empire of the Saracen had alike disappeared; and in an International Circle which was exclusively Christian a single lay and a single spiritual ruler claimed to represent the majesty of Imperial Rome.

2. The Holy Roman Emperor is a German *primus* amongst *de facto* independent states,

The title of the Holy Roman Emperor to actual World Supremacy had long since been successfully challenged in the field of practical politics. Jurists like Bartolus, steeped in the legal lore of the old jurisconsults, united with political enthusiasts like Dante, whose poetic souls were afire with glorious memories of the deathless Republic, in ascribing to Frederick Barbarossa and Henry of Luxemburg the boundless powers of Justinian and Constantine, but, in point of fact, the Roman Empire of Karl had already under the Ottos shrunk to the proportions of an Italo-German state, and under the Hohenstaufen

Bryce, *Holy Roman Empire*, Chap. xv.

and their successors, the field of its obedience, broken in upon by the partitioning influences of Feudalism and of Nationality, was yet more curtailed. Hungary, Denmark and Poland successively withdrew from their temporary allegiance; England under Edward II. and Edward III. repudiated in the clearest fashion the suggestion of Imperial Supremacy, to which the oath of Cœur de Lion had lent some tinge of colour; Burgundy was in great part annexed by Louis XII.; and Italy, already beginning to escape from control before by the Peace of Constance (1183) Barbarossa admitted defeat at the hands of the Free Cities, saw her lands dispersed amongst a group of royal, ducal, ecclesiastical and republican states, confessedly independent or owning a dubious subjection. Frederick III. (1440–93) was the last Emperor who was crowned at Rome. Maximilian I. (1493–1519) was content to rule as King of the Romans and Emperor Elect. Germany itself, the Holy Imperial heart, displayed in miniature the same picture of decentralisation. Spending his strength in the contest with the Popes for the fleeting shadow of Universal Dominion and its ancient historic foundation, the command of Rome and Italy, the Emperor lost to the German princes the authority of the Feudal Monarch. The Golden Bull of Charles IV. (1347–78) only confessed and legalised a condition of things already existing (1356). Titular chief of all the rulers of Christendom, the Emperor was in fact now no more than the President of a German Confederation, the members of which, ecclesiastical and lay principalities and free cities, remitting to their elected head the issuing and execution of decrees of common concern, were in domestic matters practically independent. Maximilian magnified his office in no inconsiderable degree by the institution of the Imperial Chamber (1495) and the Aulic Council (1512), but the crown-lands and regalian rights had been sold by or wrested from penurious or weak Emperors, and when, on June 28, 1519, the choice of the seven princes representing

Conringius, *De Finibus Imp. Germanici*, I. 14, 17, 18.

Bryce, *Holy Roman Empire*, p. 187.

Conringius, *De Finibus*, II. 22, 23.

Bryce, *Holy Roman Empire*, p. 225.

Robertson, *History of the Reign of Charles V.*, I. 387.

Wicquefort, *Election of the Emperor*, Chap. VII.

old German officials, into whose hands the Golden Bull of the Bohemian Charles IV. had committed the election of his successors, fell upon his Habsburg namesake, the ministers of the successful candidate found that he had for the support of his dignity "not a hazel-nut's worth out of the Empire," that as Emperor he possessed not a foot of soil.

Granvella to the Diet of Spires. Bryce, *Holy Roman Empire*, p. 224 n. Wicquefort, *Election of the Emperor*, Chap. XVIII.

The practice established first in the person of Charles V. by which the Electors exacted as the price of their voices the signature of a Capitulation still further reduced the Imperial authority.

but his precedence is nevertheless admitted by all the states of the International Circle. Laurent, VIII. 58.

Sentiment nevertheless is power. Whilst the Archbishop of Mayence, presiding at the election of Charles, did not hesitate to describe the assembly of the Electors as "the Supreme Council of the Universe" summoned "to deliberate for the well-being of the human race,' contemporary historians hailed the fortunate Habsburger as "the highest Magistrate of the whole universal world." Even Francis I. attached to the Imperial office the formal headship of Christendom claimed for it by the Golden Bull. No one of the remaining monarchs of the West and North, who, by the combination of courage, fortune and dexterity, had prevailed or were prevailing against the centrifugal force of their great feudatories in the building up of solid ring-fence kingdoms, ever ventured, even when stoutly repudiating the supremacy, to dispute the precedence of the Holy Roman Emperor. It was not until after the lapse of more than a century that men seriously denied the claim of the elected of the German princes to a Roman genealogy, and then the denial came from the mouths of Protestants. The force of historic sentiment was, in fact, only overmastered by the superior strength of religious conviction.

Sleidan, II. 25.

Conringius, *De Finibus Imp. Germanici*, Lib. I. c. 1. Bryce, *Holy Roman Empire*, p. 341.

Transition in political thought during the Reformation Age.

§ 72. The Age inaugurated by the election of Charles V. was an age of transition in political thought.

Charles himself was of all living princes the best calculated to lend majesty to the Empire. Grasping in the right of one parent the sceptres of Isabella and Ferdinand the Catholic and securing through the other the heritage of Mary of Burgundy and the headship of the House of Austria, he was, before his assumption of the Imperial dignity, King of all Spain from Gibraltar to the Pyrenees, of Sardinia, of Sicily and of Naples, Count of Burgundy and Charolois, and lord under various titles of the whole Netherlands, of Oran in Africa and of lands of indefinite extent in the newly discovered American Continent. By force of arms he added to these immense possessions Milan and Tunis. By common consent of contemporaries the most powerful Emperor since the day of Karl the Great, he was vehemently accused of aspiring to *Universal Monarchy*. And in point of fact he would appear to have been inspired rather by the Mediæval Conception of his office than by ideas more in harmony with the actual situation of the Empire of his time. But the unity of the World Empire was when he set his hand to the Electoral Capitulation already yielding before the unity of the Nation; his strength was that of the Austro-Spaniard not of the Holy Roman Emperor; his rivalry with Francis I., spite of the charge and countercharge with which each of the duellists sought to embarrass his opponent, was a mere contest for *political predominance*; contemporary statesmen discovered the fatal term "the Balance of Power"; and keen-sighted Venetian ambassadors saw that it was the concentrated might of France rather than the scattered forces of the Hapsburgs which really threatened the liberties of Europe.

Sleidan, Preface and Book I.

Laurent, VIII. 54. Ribier, *Lettres et Mém. d'État*, I. 451; II. 47, 340.

Laurent, VIII. 58.

The conception of World Unity superseded by that of the Nation, the conception of World Empire by that of the Balance of Power.

Granvella, *Papiers d'État*, IV. 121. Tomaseo, *Relations des Ambassadeurs Vénitiens*, II. 16. 546, in Laurent, VIII. 65.

§ 73. The resolutions of the world of politics were finally determined by a spiritual revolt.

3. The authority of the World Father challenged by Luther.

The accession of Charles V. synchronised with the formal challenge by Luther of the authority of the Pope.

The Renaissance paves the way for the Reformation.

As the years of the fifteenth century closed in and the sixteenth opened Europe awoke as to a new Day Dawn. Not Barbarossa and his knights came forth from the cavern of the Untersberg but the Spirit of Learning, scared by the cannon and the tambours of the conquering Mahomet, fled from fallen Constantinople to Italy and the furthest West. Little groups of Greek exiles, received and welcomed by the Medici, became for Roman Christendom messengers from the sages of antiquity. Inquiry quickened in one branch of knowledge spread into other fields. Whilst Copernicus taught men the secrets of the Universe, Columbus gave them a New World, and Vasco de Gama opened a new way round the Cape to the treasure-house of the East. The invention of printing at once extended the sphere of influence and increased tenfold the forces of the Revival. The Light came not alone for scholars but for the people. The New Learning paved the way for the Reformation. The Greek tutors came from lands which had for centuries down to the mock reconciliation of Florence rejected in bitter scorn the supremacy of the Pope. Men in the West cast off under their instruction the fetters of the schoolmen, and, so doing, loosed the links which bound them to Rome. Rome, whether by instinct or by strange lack of insight, threw herself into opposition to the Humanists at a time when the Monastic Orders, ceasing to be popular teachers, had sunk into sloth and sensuality, and the Bishop was a great temporal Prince. The same school which had sent forth Reuchlin and Erasmus produced Luther and Melancthon.

The Reformation in its political and international aspect:

§ 74. When Luther first appeared and prepared to defend before Legate and Diet the famous propositions nailed to the old kirk-door of Wittenberg, Charles V. thought to find in him a new pawn in the long drawn-out game of the Empire against the Papacy. But when it became clear that there was more involved in Luther's teaching than academic theses, that Luther was not to be an Imperial puppet, but the preacher of a purer faith, Charles stood aside from his cause, and the friends of the prisoner of the Wartburg (1521) recalled the days of Hus and the plighted word of Sigismund. But while the Emperor hung back, the people gathered round the champion of Reform, and leading German princes were found to lend him countenance and protection. So the movement in origin essentially a spiritual revolt took on in its course a political character; Holy Roman Emperor took his side with Roman Holy Father, his colleague in "the chief magistracy of Christendom"; and the struggle which ensued became the death grapple of Roman World Sovereignty whether under lay or ecclesiastical disguise.

a struggle against World Sovereignty in its last defences.

§ 75. The contest was long.

The Reformation Struggle. The struggle in Germany down to the Peace of Augsburg, 1555.

The premature action of knights errant like Franz von Sickingen and Ulrich von Hutten (1522–3) injured the cause of Reform. The Peasants' Revolt (1525) and the enormities of the fanatics of Münster, vigorously condemned though they were by Luther, lent a handle to his enemies. The German princely supporters of the Reformed doctrines united in the League of Schmalkalden (1531), but hesitated and wavered, and at length the Imperial victory of Mühlberg (1547) seemed to ring the death-knell of their hopes. Then, however, Maurice of Saxony, cool-headed and scheming, threw off the mask, and the flight of the Emperor through the Innsbruck pass with the subsequent Treaty of Passau (1552) proclaimed the forceful revival of the Lutheran cause. The Peace of Augsburg (1555) confirmed the terms of the Passau settlement. Charles was compelled to yield to the Princes the religious freedom for which they had wrestled, and German Protestant Independence secured a legal foothold before the face of Imperial and Papal Supremacy.

§ 76. The struggle which thus seemed over had in reality but just begun.

With the abdication of Charles V. (1556) the centre of gravity of European politics shifts to Spain.

With the abdication of Charles V. the centre of gravity of European politics shifted from Germany to Spain. Ferdinand I. (1556–64) added to the ancestral Hapsburg territories, and so restored to the central European system, the kingdoms of Bohemia and Hungary. But Ferdinand

and his son, the mild and just Maximilian II. (1564–76), followed the path of peace, and the continuation of the work of Charles V. fell to Philip II. (1556–98). The possession by Philip of the Netherlands, Sardinia, Sicily and Milan secured for the sovereign of Spain and America the predominance in Italy and on the Rhine. By his marriage with Mary Tudor Philip threatened to reduce England to a Spanish province. In later days he annexed by force of arms the neighbouring Portuguese state. The kingdom of France alone, with her feeble Scottish ally, opposed the ambition of Philip II. when he renewed that close alliance with the power of Rome which might carry him to the overlordship of the entire West.

Philip II. (1556—98) initiates a Crusade against Protestantism and Popular Liberty.

§ 77. In Philip II. was born again and intensified all the ancient religious zeal of the House of Ferdinand the Catholic. Throughout the length and breadth of his scattered lands Philip renewed, with more than the ardour of the ancient Crusader, the failing fight of the Roman Church. In Spain the Inquisitors passed on their iron way, the dread of the trembling nation, and in the flames of the *autos da fé* expired alike every trace of Spanish heresy and the last bulwarks of Spanish liberty. The same system extended to the Netherlands produced results widely different. The Low Countries became the battle-ground of Europe in a giant struggle at once for religious and civil liberty. The Netherlanders combined in defence of their time-honoured privileges. In vain the Bloody Council did its awful work. In vain the noblest Netherlanders, men who had gloriously upheld the honour of Spain on the hard fought field of St Quentin, were hurried one after another to the traitor's block. In vain were crowds of humbler victims burned, immured in loathsome dungeons or driven into exile. In vain the licentious Spanish soldiery were let loose on the flourishing Low Country cities. The Union of Utrecht (1579) marked the beginning of the end. The assassin's bullet of Gerard of Franche Comté laid William the Taciturn

The rebellion of the Netherlanders.

Schmauss, I. 391. Bentivoglio, *Wars in Flanders*, Pt. II. Bks 4, 6, 7.

low in the Banqueting Hall at Delft; but in Maurice was found a worthy successor. England, which had under Elizabeth (1558—1603) passed over to the side of Protestantism, was drawn into the struggle, and Leicester's army faced the troops of Spain (1585). Philip turned in fury on the English Queen, but the same winds of Heaven which saved England assured the independence of the Hollanders. The contest indeed dragged wearily on, but the event was decided when the Invincible Armada (1588) drove helplessly towards the Orkneys. Catholic Flanders fell back to her old allegiance to pass with the daughter of Philip to an Austrian Cardinal Infant; but the truce of 1609, mediated by Henry IV. of France, secured the freedom, political and religious, of the Seven Dutch United Provinces and rent the first fragment from the overgrown empire of Spain, although not until the Peace of Westphalia did the Spaniard finally confess his defeat.

Grotius, *History of the Low Countries*, Bk I. Bentivoglio, *Relation of the Treaty of the Truce of Flanders*, II.

The Seven United Provinces secure their independence, 1609 (1648).

§ 78. The struggle in the Netherlands might have had another end had not foreign powers recognised in the belligerents opposing brigades in a general European contest.

France leads the resistance to Philip.

France was the inevitable leader in the resistance of the nations to the ambitious designs of Philip. But France was in the latter half of the sixteenth century herself the prey of religious divisions. Whilst all the neighbouring states were ablaze with the strife-fires kindled by the Reformation torch, it was impossible that she should escape every falling spark. Francis I., the ally of the German Protestant princes in their struggle with Charles V., burned heretics at Paris, and Henry II. (1547—59) was no friend of reform. French refugees sheltering in Geneva returned to carry the doctrines of Calvin throughout the cities of Southern France, and their adherents increased in numbers every day. When under Francis II. (1559—60) and Charles IX. (1560—74) Condé and Coligni allied themselves with the Huguenots against the all-powerful Guises a long succes-

The religious struggle in France, 1519—98.

Sleidan, IX. 118. Laurent, VIII. 69.

sion of cruel wars tore France from end to end. For one brief moment the noble efforts of Coligni and the nuptials of Margaret of Valois with Henry of Navarre, the youthful hope of the Protestants, seemed to promise peace, but the bloody Massacre of St Bartholomew aroused to fever heat the slumbering passions of the opposing parties. Charles IX. died, and his brother Henry fled from his uncongenial Polish kingdom to assume the fairer crown of France. The weakness of the unstable voluptuary Henry III. (1574—89) called into being (1576) and encouraged the encroachments of the Holy League. The proud Henry of Guise even dared to aspire to the throne. His assassination and that of his brother (1588) goaded the Papists into fury. The King in self-defence was forced into alliance with the Huguenots. His death by the hand of a fanatic left Henry of Navarre heir to the throne, but face to face with the League led by Mayenne and supported by Philip II. of Spain. Henry IV. (1589—1610), spite his stoutest efforts, made small progress towards securing the obedience of France until he made his peace with the old Church; then Paris submitted (1594), the leaders of the League negotiated, and the harried land found rest in the Edict of Nantes (1598).

Henry IV., victorious at home, designs a combination against the Habsburgs.

§ 79. Elizabeth, the Dutch, and the German Protestant princes had sent succours to the Huguenots; the powers of Roman Catholicism had aided the Guises. Philip II. in particular had actively interfered. He had dispatched Walloon foot and Flemish lances against the German allies of the Huguenots (1569); he had taken the League under his special protection; he had sent Egmont to the succour of Mayenne at Ivry (1590), and Alexander of Parma to compel Henry IV. to quit the siege of Paris. On the extinction of the line of Valois in Henry III. he had, in default of hopes of personal success, offered his daughter in candidature for the French throne, and had bitterly complained of the reconciliation of Rome with the Bourbon proselyte. When Henry IV., having made

Dumont, *Corps Dipl.* v. 1, 481.

Davila, *Civil Wars of France*, pp. 146, 227, 441, 470.

Bentivoglio, *Wars in Flanders*, Pt. II. 5, 6; III. 1.

peace with his domestic enemies, declared open war upon Philip (1595), he recalled France to her natural national policy. Henry II. had gained Metz, Toul and Verdun by his alliance with Maurice of Saxony; Charles IX. had assisted the revolted Netherlanders; and Henry III. had permitted his brother to accept the proffered governorship of the United Provinces. Henry IV., satisfying his resentment by pitting himself against Philip, continued in the course of his predecessors. But Henry went further. Giving repose to France by the Edict of Nantes he determined by a coalition of the lesser states to break for ever the chain of Austro-Spanish supremacy. The truce of 1609 marked the first victory of the new French statesmanship. The dagger of Ravaillac cut short the victor in the hour of his triumph, but his mantle fell upon Richelieu. Richelieu, Cardinal of the Church and Minister of the Most Christian King, suppressing the Huguenots of Rochelle with iron hand, flung the sword of his Catholic master into the scale of German Protestantism, and the fruits of his labours were reaped in the Peace of Westphalia.

Mémoires de Sully, I. 388.

Mémoires de Sully, III. 137, 417.

Richelieu continues Henry's policy.

§ 80. Meanwhile in England, in Scotland, in Scandinavia, and in the valleys of Switzerland Protestantism in various forms wrestled and won the victory.

The victory of Protestantism in England, Scotland, Scandinavia, and part of Switzerland.

§ 81. The struggle fitly, and perchance necessarily, terminated upon the scene of its beginning in the great shock of the Thirty Years' War.

The Thirty Years' War (1618—48) the last rally of World Sovereignty.

Important in many respects, political, moral and historical, that war worked decisive consequences in the field of International Law. In its inception a war of Bohemian rebels against the Habsburger Ferdinand, it became the giant fight of Protestantism and Roman Catholicism, of Territorial Independence and Imperialism, the last vain rally of World Sovereignty.

The Peace of Westphalia proclaims the defeat of Pope and Emperor.

The Peace of Westphalia proclaimed the victory of Protestantism and Territoriality. The exiled princes came back to their ancient dominions or to indemnities.

Roman Catholic Bavaria retained the Upper Palatinate and the electoral title, but Charles Louis, the son of "the Winter-King," was restored to the ancestral Lower Palatinate with the dignity of an eighth elector. Switzerland and the United Provinces were formally acknowledged as independent, while France and Sweden obtained territories within the bounds of Germany itself. The toleration of Passau and Augsburg was confirmed and extended; the prince lost the *jus reformandi*; the New Year of 1624 was chosen to usher in a new departure, and to its *uti possidetis* were referred the conflicting temporal claims of the Church and the sectaries. In the spiritual field Schism obtained an authoritative establishment; in the political Territorial Sovereignty stood confessed. The Pope saw princes who repudiated not only his temporal lordship but his spiritual sovereignty secured in the settled possession of their lands; whilst his own dominion, confined in Italy to the limits of a petty principality, was in the rest of Papal Europe remitted to things spiritual and subordinated to the will of the local ruler. The Holy Roman Empire as a political institution was reduced to the Austrian headship of a loose German confederation. The representatives of civilised Europe united to formally proclaim the erection upon the ruins of World Sovereignty of an international system of states, unequal indeed in power, but claiming each to be independent and each to exercise an exclusive jurisdiction within definite territorial limits.

A system of Territorial States takes the place of the World Empire.

(2) International Legal Theory of the Age. Writers of the Reformation Age assert with increasing confidence the independence of kings and free States:

§ 82. Such a settlement as that of the Peace of Westphalia would have been impossible had it not been preceded by a great change in general political thought.

The territorial state had long existed in point of fact, but, whilst each royal, ducal, or republican ruler of provinces had failed to recognise in his frontiers the precise limits of his jurisdiction, the sense of national independence had been held down in pupilage by the awe-inspiring shadow of a majestic common superior.

As, however, the years of the sixteenth century went on, no longer here and there a heretic or a solitary daring political thinker, but a long succession of jurists and orthodox theologians, questioned with ever-increasing boldness the claim of any single potentate, whether Pope or Emperor, to be *totius orbis dominus*. In 1548 Conradus Brunus in his treatise *De Legationibus*, after referring to the weakness of the Merovingian monarchs, remarked in half-doubting fashion, *Hodie autem tanta est Regum Franciae authoritas, ut multi eosdem a jurisdictione Romani Imperii exemptos esse contendunt.* It was no part of the policy of Philip II. either to allow the precedence of France or to admit the superiority of any lay ruler. It constitutes accordingly no matter of surprise that Spanish scholars should have stood forth not only to claim for Philip II. the independence noted by Brunus as preferred on behalf of France, but to extend the claim to all kings and free states. In 1557[1], the Navarrese Franciscus a Victoria, whilst recognising the fullest power of the Pope *in ordine ad finem spiritualem*, unhesitatingly denied the title of the Holy Father as *orbis dominus* in things temporal or to exercise a temporal jurisdiction above princes. Seven years later his fellow-countryman Fernando Vasquez (1509–1566) roundly declared that neither Christ Himself, Pope, Emperor, nor any single man since Adam was ever in temporal things even *de jure* lord of the whole earth. Contemporary orthodox Churchmen were more careful in the handling of Papal than of Imperial claims, but in 1629 an eminent Spanish jurist, who occupied high office in the New World, wrote at Madrid: *Princeps nullus, etiam Papa et Imperator, in alienis Regnis temporalem jurisdictionem exercere potest....Jurisdictionem nemo habet extra territorium.*

Conradus Brunus, 1548; C. Brunus, *De Legationibus*, Lib. v. c. 19.

Franciscus a Victoria, 1557; Victoria, *Relectiones Theologicae*, I. II.

F. Vasquez, 1564; Vasquius, *Illustr. Controv.* I. cc. 20—22.

Soto, *De Justitia et Jure*, IV. 1, 2.
Ayala, *De Jure et Officiis Bellicis*, c. II.

J. de Solorzano, 1629.
Solorzano, *De Indiarum Jure*, II. c. 14. 7, 11.

The declaration of Solorzano recalls a familiar principle of Canon Law definitive of the jurisdiction of diocesans. "No bishop may exercise jurisdiction out of his own

They apply herein a maxim of Canon Law.

[1] Franciscus a Victoria died in 1549. His collected *Relectiones Theologicae* were published in 1557. See Chap. III.

diocese; for jurisdiction coheres with territory." The legists of the seventeenth century merely extended the principle of the canonists to all temporal rulers, and likened principalities to lay dioceses without a Metropolitan, but the extension is characteristic of the teaching of the Reformation Age.

A revised theory of the Law of Nations becomes necessary.

§ 83. When such declarations were possible, it was inevitable that amongst jurists and political philosophers some one should sooner or later arise, who should recognise the need of a revised theory of the Law of Nations.

Materials available:

§ 84. In the Age of the Reformation men still recognised the obligatory force, together with the injunctions of national Statute and Common Law and with the precepts of Revealed Religion, of the Roman and the Canon Law.

Roman Law;

The Roman Law survived the wreck of the old Roman Empire. In the East, codified by Justinian, it spoke with full coercive civil authority in the *Basilika* (circ. 900 A.D.) until the capture of Constantinople by Mahomet II. In the West, percolating through Barbarian codes and continued in the common usage of the Roman population, it was raised to new eminence in the mediæval Law Schools which sprang up under the shadow of the Holy Roman Empire. Irnerius lecturing at Bologna (circ. 1120 A.D.) found imitators at Padua, at Oxford, and at others of the great Universities, which came into being during the twelfth, thirteenth, and fourteenth centuries. The earlier professors of the glossing school (the *Glossatores*), who confined themselves to the closest running commentary upon ancient texts, were succeeded by scholastic lawyers like Bartolus and Baldus (the *Bartolists*), who adopted a freer method, but the foundation of the teaching of each was the *Corpus Juris Civilis*. In the Courts of Justice the Civil Law had to contend with local custom founded upon Keltic or Teutonic ideas and with the rooted animosity of the Common Lawyer, but in the Law Schools it secured and held for centuries an undisputed

Muirhead, *Roman Law*, Part v.

predominance. The atmosphere of legal science in the Age of the Reformation was an atmosphere of Roman Law.

Side by side with that of the Civilians sprang up in the mediæval University the faculty of Canon Law. Canon Law;

In 1144, Gratian, a Benedictine monk, published at Rome his famous *Decretum*. A digest of canons of councils, universal and provincial, of decrees of Popes, whether *proprio motu* or by way of rescript (*epistolæ decretales*), of extracts from the writings of early Fathers, ecclesiastical historians and other worthies of the Church, and of citations from the *Corpus Juris Civilis* and from later Imperial Constitutions, this compilation, prepared at Bologna in direct emulation of the classic work of Justinian, became the *Pandects* of the Canon Law of Western Christendom, speedily superseding various less systematic earlier collections. In 1234, Raymond de Pennaforte issued by the authority of Gregory IX. a digest of the decretals of the preceding ninety years. Pope Boniface in 1298 added a sixth (*Liber Sextus*) to the five books of Raymond. Clement V. (1313) and John XXIII. (1317) having contributed new material (*Clementinae, Extravagantes Joannis XXIII.*), it remained for Gregory XIII. (1580) to reissue the whole with the formal authority of a *Corpus Juris Canonici*. *Encyclo. Britan.* Art. "Canon Law." See the preface to the *Corpus Juris Canonici, Gregorius XIII. ad futuram rei memoriam.*

Meanwhile the Schools of Divinity had claimed their part in the determination of the touchstones of moral obligation, not only by the systematic study of pure Theology but by the careful elaboration of logical forms. Peter Lombard, who at Paris by the publication of his *Sententiæ* (circ. 1160) may be said to have performed for pure Theology the service which Gratian at Bologna had rendered to Canon Law, did not want for able successors. The mediæval divine who was attracted to philosophical studies was well-nigh inevitably drawn into the endless word-strife of the Realists and Nominalists, but in the Age of the Reformation the Aristotelian Schoolmen had been succeeded by the Moral Theologians, whose elaborate discussions of cases of conscience, degraded in the hands of the Jesuits to the subtlest of perilous casuistry, were Pure Theology; Moral Theology.

destined to prepare the way amongst Protestant teachers for a new science of Moral Philosophy.

To these several instructors men in the sixteenth century would naturally look for any such learning in legal science as that involved in the formal setting forth of a theory of the mutual Right of Nations.

The mediæval Civilians adopt the Roman Classical distribution of *Jus Naturale*, being rule dictated by Right Reason, *Jus Gentium*, rule universally observed, and *Jus Civile*, the law of a particular people.

§ 85. The most advanced Roman conception of Public Law was represented by that idea of *Law Universal* which was evolved out of the meeting of the old Roman *Jus Gentium* with the Greek *Jus Naturale*. The Prætor in old Rome administered, it has been seen, under the name of *Jus Gentium* a system of Private International Law, which, whether as composed of rules common to Romans and *Peregrini* or as pure Equity, was clearly distinguished from *Jus Civile*, which was the Municipal Law of the pure Roman citizen. Roman historians and orators referred furthermore to *Jus Gentium* as applicable to particular cases of public international dealing. Contact with Greek philosophy familiarised the Roman jurist with the conception of *Jus Naturale*, being rule recognised by all law-abiding men by virtue of their rational nature. The two conceptions, Roman and Greek, covering in the main the same ground and at first glance easily confused, were seen on closer examination not to be absolutely coincident. Slavery was permitted by *Jus Gentium*, but the most thoroughgoing lawyer hesitated to admit its agreement with *Jus Naturale*. *Jus Naturale* and *Jus Gentium*, in fact, alike represented *Universal Law*, but whereas *Jus Naturale* was held to be derivable directly from the operation of Natural Reason, *Jus Gentium* was extracted primarily from actual practice, although ultimately referred to the same root. Ulpian having ventured upon a new delimitation, and endeavoured to distinguish between *Jus Naturale* as common to all animals and *Jus Gentium* as common to all peoples[1], Justinian attempted to incorporate this unfortunate effort with the older

[1] *Jus naturale est quod natura omnia animalia docuit; jus gentium est quo gentes humanae utuntur.*

definitions. Dividing Private Law into *Jus Naturale*, *Jus Gentium*, and *Jus Civile*, and accepting *Jus Naturale* as common to men and animals, he described *Jus Gentium* as the product of Right Reason observed by all peoples alike[1].

Isidore, Bishop of Seville, writing before the revival in the West of the special study of the work of Justinian and when the chief authority upon the Civil Law amongst Western lawyers was doubtless the Romano-Barbarian *Breviarium Alaricianum*, defined *Jus Gentium* by reference to its subject-matter, and so employed language which might be well applied to the International Law of modern times[2]. He displayed, however, no trace of any recognition of *Jus Gentium* as *jus inter gentes*. The mediæval lawyers in general, commenting upon Justinian, fell back upon the older classical jurists. Rejecting the classification of Ulpian, they commonly adopted the ancient distribution: *Jus Naturale* was again the dictate of Right Reason, *Jus Civile* the law of a particular people, and *Jus Gentium* law universally observed. The value attached by the mediæval civilians to the letter of written text would have effectually prevented their wide deviation from the lines of their predecessors, even had they been able to shake off entirely the influence of the Imperial theory. Their Public Law continued Law Universal; if they stumbled it was only fortuitously upon *Jus Gentium* as

[1] *Quod vero naturalis ratio inter omnes homines constituit, id apud omnes populos peraeque custoditur vocaturque jus gentium quasi quo jure omnes gentes utuntur.*

[2] *Jus Naturale est aut civile aut gentium. Jus naturale est commune omnium nationum, eo quod ubique instinctu naturae, non constitutione aliqua habeatur: ut viri et foeminae conjunctio: liberorum successio et educatio: communis omnium possessio; et omnium una libertas, acquisitio eorum, quae coelo, terra, marique capiuntur. Item depositae rei vel commendatae pecuniae restitutio: violentiae per vim repulsio. Nam hoc aut si quid simile est, nunquam injustum, sed naturale aequumque habetur. Jus civile est quod quisque populus vel civitas sibi proprium, humana divinaque causa constituit. Jus gentium est sedium occupatio, aedificatio, munitio, bella, captivitates, servitutes, postliminia, foedera pacis, induciae, legatorum non violandorum religio, connubia inter alienigenas prohibita, et inde jus gentium, quod eo jure omnes fere gentes utuntur. Isidori Hispalensis Episcopi Originum sive Etymologiarum Lib.* v. Compare Professor Westlake, *International Law*, p. 24.

international law. When John Oldendorp, Professor at Marburg, issued in the first half of the sixteenth century a handbook for the use of students under the title *Juris Naturalis Gentium et Civilis εἰσαγωγή*, he followed exactly in classification and understanding the regular mediæval model[1].

The Canonists and Theologians recognise *Jus Naturale*, *Jus Divinum*, and *Jus Humanum* (including *Jus Civile* and *Jus Gentium*). Cf. p. 78 note.

§ 86. Meanwhile the conceptions of *Jus Naturale*, *Jus Gentium*, and *Jus Civile* had passed to the schools of the canonists and theologians. These distributed law under the several heads of *Jus Naturale*, *Jus Divinum*, and *Jus Humanum*. Under the head of *Jus Humanum* they placed *Jus Civile*, and, in part at any rate, *Jus Gentium*. The Moral Theologians, probing to the bottom the founts of moral obligation, were naturally led to the most minute differentiations. Amongst these writers accordingly we find that *Jus Gentium* is subdivided as *Jus Gentium Primaevum* and *Jus Gentium Secundarium*. The ground of this distinction is clearly set out by Vasquez:—*Jus gentium primaevum, quod jus recte appellatur naturale, quia simul cum ipso genere humano proditum fuit, et jus gentium secundarium, quod postea coepit—quod non simul cum ipso genere humano proditum fuit, sed labentibus temporibus a plerisque earum gentium, quae moribus et legibus reguntur nec ritu aut more ferarum sylvestrem vitam agunt, receptum reperitur.*

Moral Theologians distinguish between *Jus Gentium Primaevum* and *Jus Gentium Secundarium* (between *Jus Naturae* and *Jus Positivum*).

Cf. Paulus in *Dig. De adquir. rer. domino.*

F. Vasquius, *Illustr. Controv.* I. c. 10, ss. 17, 18; c. 41, s. 30.

The principle of differentiation here adopted is identical with that of the mediæval civilians, being the opposition of rule determined by Natural Reason and rule determined by Common Usage[2], but in its new application *Jus Gentium* no longer represents the second narrower product, but becomes the common name for a body of rules proceeding

[1] Oldendorp's *Isagoge* was, according to Ompteda (*Litteratur*, p. 163), first published at Cologne in 1539. Antonius Garius published with the sanction of the author a second edition in the same year at Antwerp, in which he claims to have corrected numerous typographical errors appearing in the former issue. The work has in itself no claim whatever to be included in the literature of International Law.

[2] The same distinction is covered by the opposition of *Jus Naturae* and *Jus Positivum* which appears in the pages of Brunus, *De Legationibus*, II. c. 9; Oldendorp, *Isagoge*, IV., and elsewhere.

from a dual source. Elsewhere Vasquez fell back upon the older terminology, but at the same time employed language in which it is difficult not to see an anticipation of the system of Grotius and Puffendorf. *Principes inter se vel populi liberi inter se semper et sunt et esse videntur ac fuisse...ut inter eos jus solum naturale et gentium non etiam civile in consideratione sit.* Casting to the winds the claims of World Emperor and World Father with the blunt denial that any one man ever was or will be lord of all the earth, this subject of Philip II. conceived of a group of free states with rights *inter se* regulated by *Jus Naturale et Gentium*, in which we may obviously identify a composite International Law.

Vasquez, 1564, points out the place of International Law (*jus inter principes vel populos liberos*), and fills it with *Jus Naturale et Gentium*.

Vasquius, *Illustr. Controv.* II. c. 51, s. 30.
Illustr. Controv. I. c. 21.

Francis Suarez (1548–1617), Professor of Theology at Coimbra, a prolific writer, who has been styled "the last of the Schoolmen," in his *Tractatus de Legibus ac Deo Legislatore*, published at Coimbra in 1612[1], not only in like fashion represented *Jus Gentium* as law *between* rather than law *common* to all nations, a law *quod omnes populi et gentes variae inter se servare debent*, and applied to the law so conceived of the distinction between law natural and law positive, but he insisted on the necessary existence of such a law and of its dual source as founded in the necessary association of states. *Ratio hujus juris est, quia humanum genus, quantumvis in varios populos et regna divisum, semper habeat aliquam unitatem, non solum specificam, set etiam quasi politicam et moralem, quam indicat naturale praeceptum mutui amoris et misericordiae, quod ad omnes extenditur, etiam extraneos et cujuscunque nationis. Quapropter licet unaquaeque civitas perfecta, respublica aut regnum, sit in se communitas perfecta et suis membris constans, nihilo minus quaelibet illarum est etiam membrum aliquo modo hujus universi, prout ad genus humanum spectat. Nunquam enim illae communitates adeo sunt sibi sufficienter*

Suarez, 1612, advances a complete philosophic theory of International Law.

Tractatus de Legibus ac Deo Legislatore, II. c. 19, n. 8.

[1] A small folio. Another edition (large folio) was published at Antwerp in 1613–4 from the press of Joannes Keerbergius; a third at Mayence in 1619. A London edition appeared in 1679.

sigillatim, quin indigeant aliquo mutuo juvamine et societate ac communicatione, interdum ad melius esse majoremque utilitatem, interdum vero etiam ob moralem necessitatem et indigentiam, ut ex ipso usu constat. Hac ergo ratione indigent aliquo jure, quo dirigantur et recte ordinentur in hoc genere communicationis et societatis. Et quamvis magna ex parte hoc fiat per rationem naturalem, non tamen sufficienter et immediate quoad omnia: ideoque aliqua specialia jura potuerunt usu earundem gentium introduci.

Suarez, *Tractatus de Legibus ac Deo Legislatore*, II. c. 19, n. 19. Ompteda. *Litteratur des Völkerrechts*, p. 167.

In these words of Suarez we may recognise the conception not only of independence, but of interdependence, not only of states, but of a real *society* of states, and in the yet clearer and more philosophic delineation of the *jus inter principes vel populos liberos* of Vasquez we may hail a complete theory of International Law. It remained but to apply these conceptions in detail in the field of practical politics to obtain a *Corpus Juris Naturae et Gentium* at once consistent with the needs of the present and flexible in view of the demands of the future.

It remained but to apply the theory in practice to obtain a *corpus* of International Law,

and to this end storehouses of systematic legal principle were to hand in (1) the Canon Law, and (2) the Roman Law.

§ 87. In this further extensive task it was natural that men should draw upon existing storehouses of accepted and systematized legal principles. When Mary Queen of Scots asked her judges in 1586 whether they proposed to proceed by the Canon or the Civil Law she revealed the manner of the international legal thought of her day. The Canon Law contended, as the law of the Universal Church, for the allegiance of all Western Christendom; the *Corpus Juris Civilis* of the Romans supplying distinctions for students of jurisprudence and arguments for lawyers peculiarly prone to the worship of *litera scripta*, was regarded as directly and particularly applicable to disputes between princes[1]. The most cursory examination of the

[1] The famous Chancellor de l'Hôpital, advising the French Royal Council to reject the demand of the English for the surrender of Calais at the expiration of the eight years' period stipulated for its restoration by the Treaty of Cateau Cambrésis, referred unhesitatingly to pure Roman *Jus Civile*. "The prescription of time, which they allege, taketh no place among Princes, but the right ever prevaileth, and according to the Twelve Tables the authority against the enemy is perpetual."

legal literature of the Age of the Reformation will suffice to prove that not only the foundation-stone, but the material for all the lower tiers, of the Grotian system was furnished by the labours of the canonist theologians of the Middle Ages and the classical jurists of the Roman Empire.

(3) International Practice of the Age. It reflects the transition in political thought. The growth of *National Consciousness*

§ 88. The international legal practice of the Reformation Age, reflecting its political thought, tells the same tale of transition.

In Italy, Germany, and elsewhere in Europe men were fated to grope and struggle for centuries yet after that form of political combination which should apparently give fullest play to racial and other common sympathetic facts, but already at the beginning of the age Frenchmen and Spaniards, Englishmen and Scotchmen, Portuguese, Danes, and Swedes were distinguished as particular peoples at once politically and sentimentally united. As the age went on it was characterised by *growing national consciousness.* The Reformation contest broke rudely in upon the national sentiment. Christendom mobilised under opposing flags, and the barriers between people and people and the ties of national allegiance were in the first instance forgotten in the fervour of religious opinion. When, however, the course of the struggle made it evident that the two great hostile armies must be finally content to partition the field of battle, and a clear rule of distribution was looked for, Nationality stepped from behind Religion and asserted effectually the claims, which, voiced by Shakspeare's King John and "old John of Gaunt," had been heard speaking in tones of resolute protest in more than one

King John, Act v. Sc. vi., l. 112. *King Richard II.*, Act II. Sc. i., l. 40.

Camden, *Eliz.* I. 98. The five English civilians to whom the legitimacy of the punishment of Leslie, Bishop of Ross, was referred by Elizabeth's Council, advised, that "an Embassador procuringe an insurrection, or rebellion, in the Prince's country towards whom he is Embassador, ought not *Jure gentium et Civile Romanorum*, to enjoye the privilege otherwise dew to an Embassador; but that he may notwithstandinge, be punished for the same." The diplomatists of the period habitually strengthened their contentions by citations of the Civil Law.

famous international controversy of the day of Elizabeth. The *Nation* stood forth the ripened product of the work of centuries.

is accompanied by a clearer understanding of the attributes of the State.

§ 89. The comprehension of National Unity involves the understanding of the conception of the *State.*

In the Middle Ages Europe was long acquainted with Patrimonial States. Marquisates, duchies, kingdoms, and even empires were sold from hand to hand, mortgaged, bequeathed or transferred by deed of gift[1]. The English, however, already in the thirteenth century had secured a very full measure of constitutional government; in subsequent generations the peasants of the Swiss Cantons, the burghers of the Low Countries, the citizens of various German free towns and Italian merchant republics, and even the Cortes of Castile and Aragon familiarised mankind with popular political liberty; whilst the Hanseatic League, composed in part of cities which individually owned subjection to different princes, presented the spectacle of an artificial Power, which negotiated, made war, and otherwise demeaned itself after the manner of an independent state. The learning of the political thinkers of Greece and Rome was applied to these new creations, and in the Age of the Reformation not only was the conception of the State (*respublica, civitas*) well understood, but Sovereignty (*summa potestas*) was clearly distinguished from its forms. The international character was assigned to republics like Venice and Genoa equally with despotic monarchs. Ayala had no difficulty in ruling that a treaty made by a prince binds his successor, since the prince contracts for the commonwealth (*respublica*), and *that*

Ayala, *Lib.* I. c. 7, 10.

[1] The Landgrave of Thuringia in 1301 sold the Marquisate of Lusatia to Burchard, Archbishop of Magdeburg, *insuper cum ministerialibus, vasallis et mancipiis, et aliis hominibus cujuscunque conditionis in jam dicta terra commorantibus.* Robert of Normandy, as is well known, mortgaged his duchy to his brother William Rufus. The successive adoptions of heirs by Joanna of Naples were the prolific source of serious trouble. Charles VIII. of France in 1494 bought the Empire of Constantinople from the titular Eastern ruler, Andrew Palæologus. Ward, II. c. 15; Dumont, *Corps Dipl.* I. 330, II. 155.

remains although *he* be removed. The *Free State* was realised, and with it forms of *Government*.

(a) *The Law of Peace.*
(I.) The State is recognised as self-constituent.

§ 90. The foregoing positions, to be established by reference to the literature of the Age, are equally capable of illustration from State Papers and judgments.

The Law Courts of the Reformation Age asserted the self-constituent right of every state.

Local statute or custom had already in early mediæval days been called upon to determine the conditions for the acquisition of local citizenship. Two main principles contended for favour. The lawyers of most Western lands, familiar with the sight of peoples of different race dwelling intermixed, commonly followed the ancient Roman rule and assigned the condition of the child by reference to that of one or other of the parents. The English practice was formed upon a conception of allegiance which, combining personal obligation with considerations of territorial lordship, is probably traceable to feudal influences. English citizenship was acquired by birth "within the allegiance" of the British Crown, the tie thus created being indissoluble at the option of the subject[1]. The pursuit of different principles by neighbouring States naturally led to frequent interesting conflicts of judgment. The consequent evolution in the municipal courts of each state of a special quasi-International Law[2] in itself amounted to the assertion of self-constituent power.

[1] Dr John Story, an English Papist, who acted as searcher for prohibited English merchandise under Alva, was in 1569 kidnapped by the captain of an English vessel, and brought over to England. Being arraigned in respect of treason committed in the Netherlands by taking part in schemes for the invasion of England, he refused to plead, on the ground that he was not a sworn subject of the Queen of England but of the King of Spain. The Court held that "no man can shake off his country wherein hee is borne, nor abjure his native soyle, or his prince at his pleasure," and Story was condemned and executed. Camden, *Eliz.* I. 123, II. 30. The carelessness of territorial rights involved in Story's seizure can only be dismissed as characteristic of a day of religious fanaticism.

[2] Private International Law, considered in respect of its imposer, its court, and its sanction, is but a particular species of municipal law.

(II.) The boundaries of State control are defined. The foundation of international dominion is brought into discussion by geographical discoveries. i. Land Dominion.

§ 91. The great geographical discoveries of the Age brought under formal review the whole subject of international ownership.

Title by discovery is alleged, *Dig.* 41, 1 and 2.

as also Papal Grant.

When the navigators of England began to follow those of Portugal and Spain in the field of distant exploration, the necessity for a universally recognised list of international titles to lands was urgently felt. The earlier explorers displayed a not unnatural disposition to attach the highest value to the fact of first discovery. Jurists when appealed to had recourse to the Roman Law. It was, however, impossible for men familiar with the language of the Roman texts or of mediæval commentators as to the establishment by occupation of proprietorship in *res nullius* to contend that the mere finding (*inventio*) of unoccupied or heathen lands constituted an absolute proprietary right in the state of the finder. The Spaniards and Portuguese accordingly turned from the Lawyer to the Churchman, fell back upon the claims of the mediæval Papacy, and sought to close the seas of the New World and the East against the shipmen of the rest of Europe by virtue of bulls procured from Alexander VI. and other Roman Fathers. The orthodox seamen of the Peninsula went forth to Western and Eastern annexation under cover of the conversion of the native inhabitants. The Indians, who by Spanish jurists were held barbarians incapable of legal rights, were by Spanish theologians pitied as heathen whom charity called Christian kings to bring under Christian government, or as infidels denuded by their infidelity of the right of ownership, and Rome conferred her formal sanction upon a Hispano-Lusitanian missionary monopoly. But whilst amongst the Spaniards themselves there arose just men like Las Casas who raised their voices in protest upon behalf of the oppressed Indians, Englishmen and Hollanders, and subsequently Frenchmen, denied the virtue of the grant of Alexander and his predecessors.

Solorzano, *De Indiarum Jure*, II. cc. 9, 10.

Molina, *De Justitia et Jure*, II. 105. Solorzano, *De Indiarum Jure*, II. cc. 1, 6, 7, 8.

When Don Bernardin de Mendoza, the Spanish ambassador, demanded of Elizabeth the restoration of the plunder taken by Drake in his famous voyage to the Pacific, he received the answer: "That the Spaniards by "their hard dealing against the English, whom they had "prohibited Commerce contrary to the Law of Nations, "had drawne these mischiefes upon themselves. That "Drake should be forthcoming to answer in Law and right, "if he might be convict by any certaine evidence and "testimonie to have committed anything against Law "and right. That those goods were layed up to that "purpose, that satisfaction might be made to the Spaniard, "though the Queene had spent a greater summe of money "than Drake had brought in against the Rebels, whom "the Spaniard had excited in Ireland and England. "Moreover, she understood not, why hers and other "Princes subjects should be barred from the Indies, which "she could not perswade herselfe the Spaniard had any "rightfull title to by the Byshop of Rome's donation, in "whom she acknowledged no prerogative, much less "authority in such causes, that he should bind Princes "which owe him no obedience, or infeoffe as it were the "Spaniard in that New World and invest him with the "possession thereof: nor yet by any other title then that "the Spaniards had arrived here and there, built Cottages "and given names to a River or a Cape; which things "cannot purchase any proprietie. So as this donation of "that which is anothers, which in right is nothing worth, "and this imaginary property, cannot let, but that other "Princes may trade in those Countries, and without breach "of the Law of Nations, transport Colonies thither, where "the Spaniards inhabite not, for as much as prescription "without possession is little worth; and may also freely "navigate that vast Ocean, seeing the use of the Sea "and Ayre is common to all. Neither can any title to "the Ocean belong to any people, or private man; foras- "much as neither Nature, nor regard of the publike use, "permitteth any possession thereof."

Elizabeth, no less than Grotius, insists on the necessity of actual occupation.

Camden, *Elizabeth*, II. 116.

Hawkins, Granville and Raleigh and the great company of the Buccaneers backed up with the pike the arguments of Elizabeth, which, recapitulated by Grotius in his *Mare Liberum*[1], were in truth but the echo of the opinions held by the majority of mediæval civilians. The appearance in North America of French, English, Dutch, and Swedish settlements warned the Spaniard to yield to the stern logic of facts, and, although prior discovery still continued to be employed as the proverbial "any stick" in international discussions, the world began to feel towards a more generally satisfactory rule of territorial delimitation. Whilst title by occupation progressed in favour at the expense of title by mere finding, the term "occupation" began to assume a precise and stricter meaning, and the possible field of operation of the international occupier was threatened with curtailment by the recognition of differences of class amongst native peoples corresponding to their varying stages of advance towards the civilisation of Europe.

Title by occupation ousts other titles,

and is gradually defined.

Solorzano, *De Indiarum Jure*, II. c. 9, s. 8.

ii. Maritime Dominion. Claims to ocean lordship, admitted during the Middle Ages,

§ 92. In the Middle Ages claims were advanced by various peoples to sovereignty over portions of the open sea. The Venetians claimed the dominion of the Adriatic, the Genoese of the Ligurian Gulf, the Danes, Swedes and Poles of various parts of the Baltic, the English not only of the narrow seas but of the ocean from the North Cape to Cape Finisterre. These and similar pretensions in other

[1] Grotius struck at the foundation of the Hispano-Lusitanian claim by emphasizing the position that to constitute title by discovery (*inventio*) there must be actual apprehension (*occupatio*). *Invenire enim non illud est oculis usurpare, sed apprehendere, ut Gordiani epistola ostenditur: unde Grammatici invenire et occupare pro verbis ponunt idem significantibus.* In general territories were, he admitted, acquired by the occupation of people as private property by the occupation of individuals. *Territoria sunt ex occupationibus populorum, ut privata dominia ex occupationibus singulorum.* In the case of the Indies, however, title by occupation could not be alleged by Europeans, since lands already possessed by peoples in a condition of civilisation so advanced as were the Orientals were not *res nullius*. *Invenire nihil juris tribuit, nisi in ea quae ante inventionem nullius fuerunt.* And *Occupatio in mobilibus est apprehensio, in immobilibus instructio aut limitatio. Mare Liberum*, cc. 2, 5.

quarters were at once in no way inconsistent with the dicta of leading mediæval lawyers[1] and regularly admitted by neighbouring states. Julius II. had recourse to treaty with Venice to secure for the subjects of the Church the right of free navigation in the Adriatic, the privilege stipulated for including exemption from customs and the freedom of foreign merchandise upon the Papal shipping. The pretensions of England were equally publicly acknowledged. From the days of Norman John to those of Scottish James the omission on the part of a foreigner to "vail," that is, to strike his flag and lower his topsail, on meeting a British man-of-war in the *Quatuor Maria* or "four British seas" would have infallibly been deemed an act of war or of piracy.

Guicc. IV. 376.

Wynne, *Life of Jenkins*, XCV.

The dominion thus claimed was no empty honorary sovereignty. It was not, as a modern inquirer might be tempted to think, a mere jurisdiction over individuals or shipping using the affected waters. The claim of the ocean lord as asserted by its thoroughgoing exponents amounted to nothing short of absolute proprietorship (*dominium*): the power to prohibit navigation, or in the alternative to exact customs from passing vessels, to interdict fishing and issue fishing licences, was regarded as belonging to his supremacy. To him, too, it belonged to forbid all hostilities[2]. So the Venetians prohibited the entry of any armed ship into the Adriatic, and in 1478 and 1479 the Emperor Frederick III. was compelled

Burgus, *De Dominio Gen.* Lib. I. c. 16. Selden, *Mare Clausum*, Lib. I. c. 16. Borough, *Sovraigntie of the Sea*, p. 62.

[1] Mediæval civilians laid down various canons for the determination of the ocean expanse over which a maritime state might legally exercise control. By some the boundary was fixed at one hundred miles from shore, by others at a less or greater distance. Bodin, in the days of Elizabeth, asserted, following Baldus, that by a kind of common right of all princes of maritime nations the dominion of the sovereign of the coast extended to the distance of sixty miles therefrom. Alb. Gentilis, *Hispan. Adv.* I. c. 8. Selden, *Mare Clausum*, I. c. 22. Solorzano, *De Indiarum Jure*, III. c. 3, s. 41. Bodinus, *De Repub.* Lib. I. c. 10, p. 170.

[2] The English, whilst insisting on the "vail," made no attempt to prevent hostilities on the part of foreign powers in the British seas.

to ask the permission of the Doge for the transportation of corn from Apulia through the gulf.

continue to be asserted in the Reformation Age.

These claims were in the Age of the Reformation still stoutly maintained. Philip II. was fired upon by an English commander when he flew his Spanish flag in "the British seas" upon coming to marry Mary Tudor. Catharine de Medici applied to Elizabeth for a safe conduct through the same seas for her son Henry of Anjou upon his voyage to his Polish kingdom (1573). The English sloop, upon which Rosny had embarked on his mission (1603) to the court of James I., fired into the French Vice-Admiral when, by way of compliment to the ambassador, he hoisted the French flag to his masthead upon quitting his anchorage at Dover. In 1606 the King of Denmark, when off the mouth of the Thames on his return from a visit to London, was forced by an English captain to strike his Danish flag.

Camden, *Hist. of Eliz.* II. 50.

Mémoires de Sully, III. 314.

Hall, *Int. Law*, II. c. 2.

The practical justification of the claims.

These high pretensions were generally tolerated from considerations grounded on the general benefit to navigation resulting from the maintenance of an effective police of the sea. The claims of the Venetians were directly rested upon an asserted Papal grant[1] made in respect of their valour and expenditure in ridding the gulf of pirates, and the rights of other ocean lords were founded upon similar practical services[2]. The wide ocean was, doubtless, in the earliest days of antiquity open to the vessels of all who were daring enough to adventure themselves thereon; but the primæval sailor had in his composition more of

Guicc. IV. 360. Burgus, *De Dominio Genuensis Reip.* Lib. II.

[1] Variously assigned to Alexander III. and to Alexander IV. Solorzano, *De Indiarum Jure*, III. c. 3, 34; Selden, *Mare Clausum*, I. c. 16; Guicc. IV. 360.

[2] The English merchants in 1582 complained through Peregrine Bertie, Lord Willoughby d'Eresby, who was sent on special mission to the King of Denmark, "that the customes were too much increased, whereas in times past they payed in passing the Danish straight or Sound, but for every shippe a Rose noble, that is, the fourth part of an ownce of gold, and as much for their lading or merchandises, with some small moneyes towards fires by night to direct their course, and barrells to shew the shelfes and rockes." Camden, *Eliz.* III. 4.

the robber than of the fisher or the pushing trader. Piratical leagues flourished for ages in every corner of the Mediterranean, and even the merchant-princes of Tyre and Sidon were not too proud to blend a little piracy with more legitimate operations. The first lord of the sea was the man of the strong hand who earned his lordship by clearing the ocean of its plundering pests, a task wherein the mythical Minos anticipated the historic Pompey. So the English mediæval merchant looked to his king for the "keeping" of the British seas. There was no more persistent complaint in the days of weaker English monarchs than that of the Commons that the seas were not kept. Chaucer's *Merchant*,

Thuc. I. 488. Wynne, *Life of Sir L. Jenkins*, xc.

> "Would the sea were kept for anything
> Betwixen Middleburgh and Orewell."

Canterbury Tales Prol

Ocean dominion was in fact founded in police, and neither in the Middle Ages nor in the Age of the Reformation was the police of the sea, where effective, any light duty. Every sea had its pirate's nest, and the privateers, the *escumeurs ou gens labourans sur la guerre* of late fifteenth and early sixteenth century treaties, were the plague of peaceful commerce. The narrow seas were not too safe in the days of Elizabeth when Dunkirk pirates could take thirty-five Dutch vessels at a single swoop and hold the masters to ransom, nor yet in the following century when Turkish corsairs kept the Irish coast-towns in a state of perpetual alarm. Wentworth on his way to assume the duties of Lord Deputy in Ireland was robbed of his baggage by the "picking thieves" of St George's Channel. Cottington and other British statesmen of the reign of James I. complained of the extraordinary strength and boldness of the Mediterranean pirates. The Dutch, who were accused by Englishmen of making a rod for themselves by the supply to the Algerines of powder and other warlike material, were reduced to negotiating with the Dey for the exemption of their vessels from attack. Blake in

Grotius, *Hist.* IV. 419. Stat. 22 and 23 Car. 2, c. 11.

Cabala, p. 206. *Carleton's Letters*, pp. 126, 135, 232.

Carleton's Letters, pp. 381, 493.

1655 avenged the unsuccessful attack made upon Algiers in 1621 by Sir Robert Mansel, but in 1664 a Spanish Viceroy of the New World bound from Cadiz to his government was taken by Turkish pirates.

Fanshaw's Letters, p. 105.

When Spain and Portugal advance new claims the Dutch, English and French resist.

When, upon the discovery of the New World and of the route round the Cape, the Spaniards and Portuguese strove, in pursuance of the bulls of Nicholas, Sixtus and Alexander, varied by treaty between the two states, to exclude all other civilized powers not only from any share in the newly revealed lands but from the profitable navigation of the Eastern and Western oceans, England united with the revolted Dutch in determined opposition to the claim, and Catholic France backed their combined resistance. Elizabeth declared the Spanish exclusion of foreign merchants from Indian commerce to be contrary to the Law of Nations. The Dutch, negotiating for the truce of 1609, contended that the navigation to the Indies was "by the laws of nature and the right of nations" open to all mankind, and secured under the treaty the recognition of their vested interests. Sully denied the right of Spain to interdict the Indies to other Europeans, and Louis XIII. in 1634 granted powers of reprisal against Spanish and Portuguese who should interfere with French navigators to the west of the first meridian or to the south of the Tropic of Cancer.

Camden, *Hist. of Eliz.* II. 116. Ward, II. 471.

Bentivoglio, *Relation of the Treaty of Flanders*, Bk. II.

Mém. de Sully, III. 423.

Schmauss, I. 505.

The discussion leads to the review of the older claims.

Grotius in his *Mare Liberum* (1609), defending against Spain the cause of his countrymen, was led to do so upon grounds which could not but reflect upon older pretensions. Citing in support of his position well-known dicta of Ulpian and other classic jurists, he contended that nature and public utility alike forbade the existence of private property in the sea. Proprietorship began in occupation. All things being by nature common, certain objects were capable of appropriation, but such things as air, the flowing stream, and the wide sea, which might be enjoyed by one individual without the necessary exclusion of another, must be regarded as naturally, inherently, and for ever subject to common use.

Mare Liberum, c. 5. *De Jure Belli ac Pacis*, II. 2, 2 and 3.

In *Mare Liberum* spoke the voice not only of a famous theologian, civilian and philosopher but of a pensionary of Rotterdam and a leading Dutch statesman.

The Dutch begin to resist the British claims.

The enterprising fishermen of the United Provinces had taken advantage of the alliance between the revolted States and Elizabeth and of English indolence or English eagerness after more distant gains, to establish during the course of the last half of the sixteenth century an immense fishing industry on the British coasts. The armed ships which had fought against Spain accompanied their fishing smacks to the Orkneys for their protection against pirates or other rovers, and soon in the pride of their newly won independence Dutch captains began not only to resist the payment of duties levied without question for generations within the British seas, but to refuse the honours of the "vail" to the English flag.

Carleton's Letter pp. 38, 327.

In 1609 James I. announced by proclamation that no person, not being a natural born subject of the British realm, would be permitted to fish upon any of the coasts or seas of Great Britain and Ireland without a license obtained from the Royal Commissioners at London or Edinburgh.

A Proclamation touching Fishing, May 6, 1609. Selden, *Mare Clausum*, Translation of 1663, p. 464.

The proclamation failed of the effect designed by its author.

In 1617 John Browne, an officer of the Admiral of Scotland, upon going on board a Dutch vessel engaged in fishing upon the Scotch coast to demand the ancient duty known as the *size herring*, was not only refused payment, but arrested and carried off as prisoner to Holland by the commanders of two Dutch convoying ships. This proceeding aroused to striking point even the sluggish James. Reprisals were immediately ordered upon Dutchmen in London, and Sir Dudley Carleton, the English Minister to the Provinces, was instructed to demand signal satisfaction in the instant release of the prisoner and the exemplary punishment of his captors. The States-General[1],

They refuse the "size-herring,"

[1] Grotius was employed as the mouthpiece of the States-General on this occasion.

the States of Holland and the Brotherhood of the Pescherie found it politic successively to disavow the action of the two commanders as being "neither authorised beforehand nor approved *post factum*," and the States of Holland finally yielded to the demand of James based upon "the laws of all nations both ancient and modern" that the delinquents should be sent over to England to make submission for their offence. Offended English honour was thus satisfied, but the Dutch statesmen showed during the course of the incident the strongest desire to bring into question the initial claim, their Commissioners in England not hesitating to set up a right under the law of nations based upon immemorial possession.

Carleton's Letters, pp. 156, 170, 179, 186, 192, 193, 240.

Carleton's Letters, p. 327. Sec. Naunton to Sir D. Carleton, Dec. 21, 1618.

In 1618 James was stirred by "new and fresh com-"plaints of his marriners and fishers upon the coasts of "Scotland, that, within these four or five last years, the "Low-Country fishers have taken so great advantages "of his Majesties toleration, that they have grown nearer "and nearer upon his Majesties Coasts year by year than "they did in preceding times, without leaving any bounds "for the country-people and natives to fish upon their "Prince's coasts, and oppressed some of his subjects of "intent to continue their pretended possession; and "driven some of their great vessels through their nets to "deter others by fear of the like violence from fishing "near them." In consequence of these representations James requested the States to forbid by proclamation any other subjects to fish within fourteen miles of the British coast until a final settlement could be arrived at. It was not without cause that Lord Carleton, with his experience of the dilatory and evasive methods of Dutch negotiation, recommended his master to begin with the fishers themselves by announcing the distance at which he would permit them to ply their industry.

Secretary Naunton to Lord Carleton, Jan. 21, 1618.

Lord Carleton to James I., Feb. 6, 1618.

In 1636 Charles I. renewed the proclamation of 1609 and announced his resolution to keep such a competent strength of shipping upon the seas as should be sufficient both to hinder further encroachment on his regalities, and to assist and protect good friends and allies who should thenceforward take the benefit of British royal licenses for fishing upon the British coasts. The declaration was backed by the preparation of a considerable fleet. The misfortunes of Charles were, however, as fatal to British interests as the pompous futility of James, and the Dutch were enabled to retain the position which they had gained. *A Proclamation for restraint of Fishing upon His Majesties Seas and Coasts without Licence,* May 12, 1636.

The honours of the flag were at first more covertly but none the less eagerly contested. Here, however, the slumbering British spirit woke from sleep. The weakness of the first two Stuart kings encouraged the Dutch to assert their new pretensions in the light of day[1], but the valour of Blake and the firmness of Oliver won back the emblems of lost supremacy from Van Tromp and Ruyter. In treaties of 1645, 1654, 1662, 1674, and 1684 the Dutch were obliged formally to admit the ancient right between Cape Finisterre in Spain and Stadland in Norway. In British Admiralty charges the pretension was strongly insisted upon, and so late as the present century[2] it was, and the "vail." Wynne, *Life of Jenkins,* LXXXVIII., XCV.

[1] "The other Embassadour sent to the Arch-Duke was the old Earle of Hertford, who was conveyed over in one of the King's Ships, by Sir William Munson (*sic*), in whose passage a Dutch Man of Warre comming by that ship, would not vaile, as the manner was, acknowledging by that our Soveraignty over the Sea, Sir William Munson gave him a shot to instruct him in manners, but instead of learning, he taught him, by returning another, he acknowledged no such Soveraignty; this was the very first indignity and affront ever offered to the Royale Ships of England, which since have beene most frequent; Sir William Monson desired my Lord of Hertford to goe into the Hold, and hee would instruct him by stripes, that refused to be taught by faire meanes; but the Earl charged him on his Allegiance first to land him, on whom he was appointed to attend; so to his great regret he was forced to endure that indignity, for which I have often heard him wish to have been hanged rather than lived that unfortunate Commander of a King's Ship to be Chronicled for the first that ever endured that affront, although it was not in his power to have helped it." *Court of King James*, p. 44.

[2] Lord St Vincent in 1803 proposed to insert in an Anglo-American regulation, forbidding the taking by the armed forces of each power of any person from under the flag of the other on the high seas, a proviso excepting the Narrow Seas, they having, he said, been immemorially considered to be within the dominion of Great Britain (*British and*

though not enforced, as carefully maintained as in the days when the broom at Van Tromp's masthead challenged the lordship of the Channel.

(III.) The rights of the representatives of national dignity are discussed. *a.* Sovereigns. The case of Mary, Queen of Scots, 1568—87.

§ 93. In 1567–8 Mary, the deposed Queen of Scots, after escaping from custody to make at Langside a last bid for the recovery of her throne, fled across the Solway to English soil. The consequent political embarrassment of Elizabeth and the nineteen years' detention and final execution of Mary are amongst the most familiar facts in English history. The interest of the incident in international legal history is less generally appreciated.

Camden, *Eliz.* I. 97.

1. The difficulty as to her detention, 1568—9.

Elizabeth, unwilling to admit the right of subjects to depose their ruler, had forbidden her ambassador, Throckmorton, to be present at the coronation of James VI., lest the deposition of Mary might be taken as having her approval. Upon the appearance of Mary in England the English Council, equally afraid to restore the fugitive to her native country, to permit her to proceed to France, or to allow her to remain at liberty within English territories, determined after mature deliberation that she should be detained "as taken by right of warre, and not to be "delivered, till she gave satisfaction for usurping the "Title of England, and answered for the death of Lord "Darly (*sic*) her husband, who was a native subject of "England." This palpable subterfuge reveals the straits of the English Queen. Mary insisted on her rights as a sovereign. An English Commission having been appointed to investigate the complaints of her subjects against her, her delegates appearing at York protested

Camden, *Eliz.* I. 111.

Foreign State Papers, I. p. 1404). In 1805 the Admiralty instructed its officers that: "when any of His Majesty's ships shall meet with the "ships of any foreign power within His Majesty's seas (which extend to "Cape Finisterre) it is expected that the said foreign ships do strike their "topsail and take in their flag, in acknowledgment of His Majesty's "sovereignty in those seas; and if any do resist, all flag officers and com- "manders are to use their utmost endeavours to compel them thereto, "and not to suffer any dishonour to be done to His Majesty." Hall, II. 2, § 40 n.

that they did not thereby acknowledge their mistress to be under the sovereign command of anyone, she being a free princess and under the authority and vassalage of none. The Commissioners replied by a counter protest saving the title claimed by the Kings of England as superior lords of the kingdom of Scotland. Apart from the recognition of the legality of Mary's deposition, there was in fact but one possible justification for her imprisonment. "To speake the truth," said Elizabeth at last, when rejecting the intercession of the French ambassador on behalf of the captive, "I for my part do detaine the "Queene of Scots in honourable custody for the safeguard "of England and mine own security; and that by the "example of the French, which shut up Chilferic in a "monastery; Charles of Lorraine in a deepe dungeon; "and Ludovic Sfortza, Duke of Millan, into an yron Grate, "to secure their own estates....Such great examples as "these doe always draw with them some kind of injustice."

Camden, *Eliz.* I. 113.

Elizabeth's justification of Mary's detention.

Camden, *Eliz.* II. 46.

2. The question as to her liability for offences against the local law, 1586.

In 1586 the detection of Mary in complicity in Babington's Plot directly raised the question of her liability in respect of a breach of local territorial law. It was proposed to bring her to trial under an Act of 1584 passed for the protection of the life of Elizabeth. The procedure followed is in itself noteworthy. It was not deemed proper to proceed in the ordinary course by jury or by trial before the House of Lords. A special body of Commissioners was appointed *ad hoc*. The fact lends additional point to Mary's query whether they proposed to proceed by Civil or by Canon Law. The Commissioners declared that they proceeded neither by the Civil nor by the Canon Law but by the Common Law of England. Mary maintained her old position. Her appearance before the tribunal seems to have been the result less of Hatton's arguments that in the case of such a crime as that charged "the royal dignity is not exempted from answering, neither by the Civil, nor Canon Law, nor by the Law of Nations, nor of Nature," than of the feeling that a refusal would be deemed a confession of guilt or at least unworthy of innocence. Appearing she declared that "she was no subject of the Queene but "had beene and was a free and absolute Queene, and not "to be constrained to appear before Commissioners, or "any other Judge whatsoever, for any cause whatsoever, "save before God alone the highest Judge, least she should "prejudice her owne Royal Majesty, the King of Scottes "her Sonne, her Successors, or other absolute Princes. "But that she now appeared personally to the end to "refute the crimes objected against her." The Lord Chancellor in reply urged that "whosoever (of what place "and degree soever he were) should offend against the "Lawes of England, in England, was subject unto the "same Lawes and by the late Act might be examined "and tryed." The Commissioners admitted the protest and the answer alike to record.

The subsequent sentence was hotly discussed even in England.

Elizabeth's defence of her proceedings.

Elizabeth was driven to her strongest line of defence. In the course of a long and considered reply to renewed French intercessions on behalf of Mary she urged:

(1) "That the English which in England did ac-"knowledge the Souvraigne authority of Queene Elizabeth "only, could not acknowledge two supreme, free, and "absolute Princes in England at once; or any other "whomsoever to be equall unto her in England as long as "she lived. Neither indeed did they see, how the Queene "of Scottes, and her Sonne at that daie reigning, could "bee holden both at one time to bee supreme and Absolute "Princes."

(2) "That no man was ignorant of that saying of "the lawyers, A man offending in another's territory, and "there found, is punished in the place of his offence, "without regard of his dignity, honor, or priviledge. And "that this was both lawfull by the Lawes of England, and "apparent by the example of Licinius, Robert King of "Sicily, Bernard King of Italy, Conradine, Elizabeth "Queene of Hungary, Joane Queene of Naples, and

"Deiotarus, for whom Tully pleading said, It was no "unjust thing for a king to be guilty and put to death "for a capitall crime, though not usuall."

(3) "That howsoever the Guises the Queene of Scottes "kinsmen tooke the matter, yet it maynly concerned "the Queene to regard rather the safety of herselfe, the "Nobility and people of England (upon whose love shee "wholly depended) than the displeasure of any whosever. "That the matter was now come to that passe, as that old "saying concerning the two Princes Conradine of Sicily, "and Charles of Anjou, might now be taken up of the "two Queenes, and it might now be truly said, The death "of Mary is the life of Elizabeth, and the life of Mary is "the death of Elizabeth." Camden, *Eliz. Ann.* 1586.

Principles recognised in the course of the discussion.

Here we may see the clear recognition of the negative and positive attributes of the Territorial State: (*a*) exclusive jurisdiction within certain definite territorial limits, and (*b*) independence of external control. But with this recognition comes the admission of a duty and a complementary right, equally necessary in practice to friendly international intercourse, viz., (1) the duty of the fullest possible international courtesy towards the representative of national dignity, and (2) the right of self-preservation as the overriding condition of all law.

β. Public Agents. Appearance of Resident Ministers.

§ 94. The necessities of closer international intercourse brought about in the Age of the Reformation a distinction amongst Public Agents.

The Public Agent of the Middle Ages, despatched for a special temporary purpose to a foreign Court, survived in the Extraordinary Ambassador, whose functions were commonly those of the bearer of particular compliments, but all the chief Courts of the West now despatched and entertained as Ambassadors in Ordinary ministers regularly resident with the sovereigns to whom they were accredited. Popular adages current in the sixteenth century, which assigned to such residents the character of public spies, explains the contention of Grotius that an Ambassador in

Grotius, *De Jure Belli ac Pacis*, Lib. II. c. 18, 3. Wicquefort, *The Embassador and his Functions*, p. 6.

Ordinary may well be refused reception as unnecessary and as the product of an upstart custom unknown to former times[1]. The Poles so late as the end of the seventeenth century still looked upon a foreign resident agent with open disfavour. But Charles V., his leading contemporaries, and their successors found it desirable to retain regular representatives even with the Sultan, who himself disdained to employ the services of any other than a *chiaus* or messenger. An inevitable consequence was the swift appearance of a crop of questions of disputed precedence and the necessity for the re-examination and definition in numerous particulars of the rights and obligations of the legatine office.

A science of International Etiquette founded.

§ 95. State etiquette became the subject of a regular science, and the diplomatic history of the period furnished rich material for such masters of ceremony as Finett and Wicquefort[2].

Three main rules as to the determination of precedence seem to have been generally admitted:

(1) The Pope's ambassadors, known as Nuncios, were, in the Courts in which they were received, allowed precedence of the representatives of all lay rulers.

(2) The ambassador of the Emperor was allowed precedence of the representatives of all other lay rulers.

(3) The representative of monarchs regularly claimed and commonly secured precedence of the ministers of republics. Venice, however, as the holder of the kingdom of Cyprus was admitted to rank with crowned heads, and her representative followed immediately after those of kings. The representatives of the United Provinces succeeded in obtaining at Munster the right to rank with those of

[1] Henry VII. of England refused to receive Lieger (i.e. Resident) Ambassadors: Coke, *Inst.* 4. 155.

[2] *Finetti Philoxenis: some choice Observations of Sir John Finett, Knight and Master of Ceremonies to the two last Kings:* London, 1656. The classical work of Abraham Wicquefort (1598–1682), "L'Ambassadeur et ses Fonctions," appeared at Cologne in 1679.

Venice, and the power of England under the Commonwealth was too great to permit her relegation to a lower place.

Ward, *Law of Nations*, II. 384–452.

Beyond the limits of these general rules there were frequent fierce disputes.

Disputes as to precedence amongst Public Agents.

Upon the abdication of Charles V. Philip II. was unwilling to accord to France the place of honour after the Emperor which had hitherto been universally allowed to belong to the Most Christian as against the Most Catholic King. The pretension found vent in a great contest between the ambassadors of the rival sovereigns which disturbed for more than a century the peace of every Court in Europe, and led from time to time to scenes of disorderly and excited brawling. Similar controversies were contemporaneously waged between the representatives of other Powers. The negotiations at Boulogne in 1599–1600 between England and Philip III. mediated by Henry IV. were broken off at the outset in consequence of a lively dispute between the negotiators arising out of the claims advanced by the English, on the ground of ancient practice with regard to Castile, to precedence of the Spaniards. The Swedes refusing to yield place to the French at the Congress of Westphalia, separate sessions were, to avoid a rupture between the two allies, held at Munster and Osnaburg.

Dumont, *Supplément aux Corps Diplomatique*, V. 2. 203.
Wicquefort, *The Embassador and his Functions*, pp. 209, 220.

Mém. de Sully, II. 402.
Bentivoglio, *Wars in Flanders*, p. 391.
Camden, *Eliz. Ann.* 1600.

See Ompteda, *Litteratur*, pp. 491, 493, 494.

These contests, which afforded material for a war of pamphlets, were the direct outcome and formal expression of the quickening of the conception of national sovereignty, a consideration which lends importance to many otherwise miserable legatine disputes concerning "the arm-chair," "the hand," "the door," and the right "to cover." Public Agents were classified in accordance with the terms of the credentials with which they were furnished as being representative or non-representative. When the representative character of the minister was recognised the regulation of etiquette between the agents of states claiming equal rank was no longer a trivial thing.

Public Agents classified as representative and non-representative.

A consequence of the recognition of the representative character of a Public Agent: the right to send an Agent scrutinised. Wicquefort, *The Embassador*, p. 11. Finett, *Observations*, p. 19.

§ 96. Under the same circumstances the reception or recognition of a minister was seen to involve the most far-reaching consequences, affecting as it clearly might the claim of the sender to sovereignty. So, until the formal recognition of the independence of the United Provinces by the Peace of Westphalia, Spanish ambassadors were accustomed to protest against the presence at the state ceremonial of the courts to which they were accredited of the representatives of the Dutch.

The rights and duties of Public Agents in course of definition. C. Brunus, *De Legationibus*, Lib IV. cc. 1—5.

Grotius, *De Jure Belli ac Pacis*, Lib. II. c. 18. 4.

§ 97. The general protection afforded by mediæval practice to international public agents was freely extended to their successors of the following age, and the "Laws of Nations" were regularly invoked in support of their sacred character, but in many important respects practice with respect to legatine privileges had not yet hardened into definite universally accepted principle.

(*a*) The limits of the personal exemption of the ambassador from the criminal law reviewed.

§ 98. (*a*) The limits of the personal exemption of the ambassador himself from the operation of the criminal law of the state to which he was accredited were not finally ascertained.

Merveille's case, 1533.

Sforza, Duke of Milan, in 1533, tried and beheaded Merveille, the French envoy at his Court, after decoying him into a duel in which the Frenchman killed his antagonist. The justification offered on behalf of the Duke, which was grounded upon the fact that Merveille was only a secret agent, was by subsequent generations deemed insufficient.

The case of Leslie, Bishop of Ross, 1571.

In 1568 John Leslie, Bishop of Ross, a prelate of no small learning, appeared at York as one of the six delegates appointed by Mary Queen of Scots, then a refugee detained at Carlisle, to represent her cause before the Commission nominated by Elizabeth to investigate the complaints of the deposed Queen against her victorious rebellious subjects. He subsequently remained in London in the character of ambassador of Mary. Having repeatedly engaged in intrigues for the release of his mistress, he was at length detected (1571) as a prime mover in the famous plot which brought the Duke of Norfolk to the scaffold. The sequel is related by Camden. "But whereas by all the confessions of them all, yea and "of the Duke himselfe, the Bishop of Rosse was charged "as the plotter of the matter, it was seriously consulted "what should bee done with him, who was an Embassadour. "For whilest hee (as the manner of that sort of men is,) "thought it was lawfull for him to advance by any meanes "the affayres of his Prince, and that by the sacred and "inviolable priviledge of Embassadour hee was not to be "subjected to a forraine jurisdiction, he had now a good "while done many things turbulently, by giving fire to "rebellion, and holding nightly counsayles with the Earle "of Southampton and others, and now lastly with the "English fugitives in the Netherlands, the Duke of Alva, "the Spaniard, and the Bishop of Rome, for invading of "England: It was therefore propounded to David Lewis, "Valentine Dale, William Drury, William Aubrey, and "Henry Jones, most learned Civil Lawyers.

"First, *Whether an Embassadour which rayseth rebellion "against the Prince to whom he is sent, may enjoy the "priviledges of an Embassadour, and be not subject to "punishment as an enemy.* They answered, that such an "Embassadour hath by the Law of Nations, and by the "Civil Law of the Romans, forfeited all the priviledges "of an Embassadour, and is to be subjected to punish-"ment.

"Secondly, *Whether the Minister or Procurator of a "Prince which is deposed from his publique authority, "and in whose place another is inaugurate, may enjoy the "priviledges of an Embassadour.*

"They answer, If such a Prince have been lawfully "deposed, his procurator cannot challenge the priviledges "of an Embassadour, for as much as none but absolute "Princes, and such as have the prerogatives of Majesty, "can constitute Embassadours.

"Thirdly, *Whether a Prince which hath come into "another Prince his kingdom, and is kept under custody,* "*may have his Procurator: and whether he may be holden* "*for an Embassadour.*

"They answered, if such a Prince have not forfeyted "his Principality, he may have a Procurator: but whether "that Procurator may be reputed for an Embassadour, "that depended upon the authority of his Delegation.

"Fourthly, *Whether if a Prince doe denounce to such a* "*Procurator and Prince under custody, that the sayd* "*Procurator shall from thenceforth be no longer holden* "*for an Embassadour, whether the sayd Procurator may* "*by Law challenge the priviledges of an Embassadour.*

"They answered, that the Prince may prohibite the "Embassadour that he enter not into his kingdome, and "may command him to depart out of his kingdome, if "hee containe not himself within the bounds prescribed "to an Embassadour: yet in the mean time he may "enjoy the priviledges of an Embassadour according to "the authority to him delegated.

"According to these answers of the learned Lawyers, "Rosse being called back from the Isle of Ely[1], and "sharply rebuked, it was denounced unto him by the "Councell, that hee should no longer be acknowledged "for an Embassadour, but severely punished as one that "had well deserved it. He answered, *That hee was an* "*Embassadour of an absolute Queene, and of one that was* "*unjustly deposed, and had according to his duty, carefully* "*sought the delivery of his Princesse, and the safety of* "*both kingdomes: That hee came into England with most* "*ample authority of an Embassadour, and that, upon* "*publike warrandies or safe conduct, which he had ex-* "*hibited: and that the sacred priviledges of Embassadours* "*are by no meanes to be violated.* Burghley most gravely "shewed him, that neither the priviledges of an Em- "bassage, nor letters of publike warrandies can protect "Embassadors which offend against the publique Majesty, "but they are lyable to penall action: otherwise, lewd

[1] He had been apprehended and committed to the custody of the Bishop of Ely.

"Embassadours might assayle the life of Princes without "punishment. He to the contrary obstinately maintayned, "that the priviledges of Embassadours have never beene "violated (to use his owne words,) *Via juris*, that is, By "way of *Right*, but *Via facti*, that is, By way of *Fact*; "and pleasantly wished them that hee might bee no "sharplier dealt withall, then were the English Em- "bassadours Throkmorton in France, and Randolph and "Tamworth in Scotland, who had raysed rebellions, and "openly fostered them, and yet they endured no heavier "matter, but that they were commanded to depart within "certaine dayes prefixed." Camden, *Hist. of Eliz.* II. 26.

After this interview with the Council the Bishop was conveyed to the Tower of London, where being kept in close custody, he answered all questions put to him, but was ultimately merely ordered to quit the kingdom, whilst the Duke of Norfolk and other conspirators suffered death. Camden, *Hist. of Eliz.* II. 62.

Henry IV.'s opinion in Bruneau's case, 1605.

The English Civilians were by no means alone in their view of the rights belonging by strict law to the local sovereign. "The ambassadors," said Henry IV. of France in 1605, when announcing his resolution in Bruneau's case, "are sacred by the right of nations: now they first "break them (*sic*), when they contrive any treason against "the State, or against the Prince to whom their Master "sent them; and therefore by consequence this right "ought not to secure them from being sought out and "punished. Moreover, it is not to be presumed that they "are either ambassadors, or that they represent the "Sovereign who sends them, when they commit those "treacheries and infidelities which their Masters would "neither act nor avow. However, there is more generosity "in not using in this part the utmost rigour, but reserving "the advantage to chastise them without doing it." *History of Henry the Great*, p. 318.

Coke upon the personal privilege of the ambassador.

Chief Justice Coke shared the opinion of Henry, and held that a foreign minister who should commit any crime in England, which might be termed *contra jus gentium* "as treason, felony, adultery", would thereby lose his privilege and render himself liable to punishment like

Co. 4 *Inst.* 153. any private alien. And in the case of *R. v. Owen* in 1615 the King's Attorney laid it down that by the law of nations an ambassador, who compassed the death of the king in whose land he was, could be condemned and executed for treason, although it was otherwise in the case of any other species of treason, it being incumbent in these to send him home for trial.

R. v. Owen, 1 Rolle, 185.

Mendoza's case, 1584.

In 1584, however, Gentilis and Hottoman, on consultation by Elizabeth's council as to the propriety of bringing to justice Mendoza, the Spanish ambassador, who had been detected in a conspiracy for the dethronement of the Queen, advised that an ambassador was not punishable with death under the English law, but must be referred for punishment to his own sovereign. Mendoza was accordingly merely dismissed from the country[1]. The like forbearance was shown by the Venetian Government in 1618 towards the Spanish ambassador, the Marquis de Bedmar, and practice from this time forward finally set in the direction of the fullest personal exemption of the ambassador from the local jurisdiction of the land to which he was accredited, the trend of events being powerfully assisted by the popularisation of the fiction of Exterritoriality, which was advanced by Grotius[2] as

Ward, *Law of Nations*, II. 522.

Bedmar's case, 1618.

Martens, *Causes Célèbres*, I. 471. Walker, *Manual of Public Int. Law*, p. 72.

[1] Philip's resentment in respect of this dismissal (Camden, *Eliz.*, *Anno* 1584) hardly accords with the sentiments which he expressed on another occasion. A criminal took refuge from justice in the house of Bodoaro, the Venetian ambassador at Madrid. An officer of justice invited by the ambassador, speaking from a window, to enter the house was assaulted and driven out by servants of the Embassy. The police authorities returning in force found the ambassador and his suite prepared for resistance, but contrived to seize without violence several offenders. One of the prisoners, a relative of the ambassador, was condemned to be beheaded, and several subordinates were hanged or flogged. Philip wrote to Venice and other powers expressing his desire that when his ambassadors committed any crime unworthy of their station they should be stripped of their privileges and judged by the laws of the kingdom where they resided. (Ward, II. 553: De Callières, *Manière de Négocier*, II. 294.) Whatever may be thought of Philip II.'s good faith in the matter, the incident clearly belongs to a period before the privileges of the *suite* of an ambassador were acknowledged.

[2] *Quare omnino ita censeo, placuisse gentibus ut communis mos qui*

the philosophic support of the most extensive legatine privilege.

(b) The privileges of the ambassador's *Hôtel* reviewed.

§ 99 (*b*). When doubts were yet expressed in authoritative quarters concerning the personal inviolability of the ambassador himself, it was natural that the privileges of his residence should still be deemed to afford matter for discussion. A fracas having arisen at Valladolid in 1601 between some Spaniards and a party of bathers belonging to the French embassy, the Frenchmen killed two of their assailants. Thereupon the house of the French ambassador, the Count de la Rochepot, was forced, and a number of the members of his suite, including his nephew, were carried off to prison[1]. The ambassador vehemently protesting, the difference was only settled by the intervention of the Pope, who obtained the delivery of the prisoners to himself at Rome, when they were handed over to Bethune, the French ambassador there resident.

The Count de la Rochepot's case, 1601.

History of Henry the Great, III. p. 259.

The right to conduct worship in the ambassador's *Hôtel* admitted.

In general, however, the sanctity of the ambassador's *hôtel*, otherwise than as a sanctuary for native criminals[2], was at once theoretically recognised and in practice respected. The right of the ambassador to conduct within the walls of his residence public service according to the

quemvis in alieno territorio existentem ejus loci territorio subjicit, exceptionem pateretur in legatis, ut qui sicut fictione quadam habentur pro personis mittentium (*Senatus faciem secum attulerat, auctoritatem reipublicae, ait de legato quodam M. Tullius*) *ita etiam fictione simili constituerentur quasi extra territorium. Unde et civili jure populi apud quem vivunt non tenentur; De Jure Belli ac Pacis*, Lib. II. c. 18. s. 4. Grotius admits an exception in the case of extreme necessity and rules that "to prevent any imminent danger an ambassador may be both "imprisoned and examined." Ward points out that the ambiguity of the word *legatus* (as applied to a public *ambassador* and to a Roman *legate*) had, when Roman Law was still freely cited, an important effect in restricting the advance of conceptions as to the rights of ambassadors. (Ward, *Law of Nations*, II. 520.)

[1] Compare Bodoaro's case. The coincidence affords strong proof of the Spanish legal view.

[2] For the denial of the existence of any *jus asyli* under International Law see Grotius, *De jure Belli ac Pacis*, Lib. II. c. 18. s. 8.

ritual of his own communion was denied by Philip II. to Mann, the representative of Elizabeth (1568), but this highly valued privilege was even by his contemporaries generally admitted, although subject to the limitation that domestics only should be allowed to attend.

Camden, *Hist. of Eliz.* I. 102, 108; Wicquefort, *The Embassador and his Functions*, p. 267.

(c) The privileges of the ambassador's suite reviewed. Contemporary opinion as to the case of the Count de la Rochepot's servants, 1601.

§ 100 (c). The general consensus of contemporary opinion as expressed in the no little discussion provoked by the Valladolid incident seems, according to the Bishop of Rodez, to have been adverse to other than the narrowest interpretation of the privileges of the suite of an ambassador. "It is true, said they, that an Ambassador "hath alone right of Sovereign Justice in his Palace; but "the people of his train are subject to the Justice of the "estate in which they are, for those faults they commit "out of his palace; and so if they be taken out of it, their "Process may be made: and though it be known that "this rigour is not generally observed, and that the respect "born to the Ambassador's person extends to all those "that follow him; yet however this is a courtesie, and "not a right. But notwithstanding it is not permitted to "go seek the Criminal in the Palace of the Ambassador, "which is a sacred place, and a certain Sanctuary for his "people; yet ought it not however to be abused or made "a retreat for wicked persons, nor give Sanctuary to the "Subjects of a Prince against the Laws and Justice of his "Realm; for in such cases, on complaint to his Master, he "is obliged to do reason."

History of Henry the Great, p. 259.

Bruneau's case, 1605.

In 1605 the privileges of the ambassador's suite in respect of the local criminal law came up for examination at the Court of France. Bruneau, the Secretary of Don Balthazar y Zuniga, the Spanish ambassador in Paris, was detected in an intrigue with Mairargues, a Provençal gentleman, for the betrayal by the latter to the Spaniards of the city of Marseilles. Mairargues was, under sentence of the Parliament of Paris, beheaded and quartered as a traitor. The Secretary was arrested, but the ambassador hotly complained of his incarceration as a violation of the *droit des gens*, and process against the culprit was stayed by direct command of the French king.

Flassan, *Diplomatie Française*, II. 232.

The case of the servants of the Count du Fargis, 1621.

The Spaniards were in 1621 less courteous to the French. Two alguazils having been killed by servants of the French ambassador, the Count du Fargis, in the course of a contest arising out of a dispute as to the legal possession of a house at Madrid, the King of Spain ordered that, whilst the person of the ambassador himself should be respected, any of his servants found otherwise than in their master's presence should be seized and imprisoned. The individuals arrested were not released until the arrival at the Spanish Court of a French Extraordinary Ambassador, the Marshal de Bassompierre.

Flassan, *Dipl. Française*, II. 346. *Ambassade du Mareschal de Bassompierre en Espagne*, p. 42.

The jurisdiction enjoyed by an ambassador over his servants brought in question.

Sully, who denounces as a flagrant breach of the *droit des gens* the conduct of the Spaniards in the matter of the Count de la Rochepot's servants, was himself two years later the hero of an incident which raised the question of the jurisdiction over the members of an ambassador's suite in another aspect.

Mém. de Sully, III. 123.

Combaut's case, 1603.

Combaut, a member of the suite which accompanied Sully, then the Marquis de Rosny, upon his famous embassy to James I., having killed an Englishman in a disgraceful brawl in a London brothel, the ambassador caused the culprit to be forthwith tried and condemned to death by a council of members of the embassy sitting within the walls of the ambassador's *hôtel*. To the representations of the Mayor of London, to whom he applied for the execution of the sentence, Sully answered by handing over the prisoner to be dealt with according to English law. James therefore exercising in favour of the prisoner the prerogative of pardon, the Frenchmen complained of the proceeding as an infringement of the rights of their own monarch. On the other hand, the judicial proceedings within the walls of the embassy were as little conformable with the opinion of Grotius[1] and with later international practice.

Mém. de Sully, III. 325.

[1] *Ipse autem legatus an jurisdictionem habeat in familiam suam, etiam jus asyli in domo sua pro quibusvis eo confugientibus, ex concessione pendet*

Ambassadors at Munster surrender the jurisdiction.
Wicquefort, *The Embassador and his Functions*, p. 271.

The ambassadors negotiating at Munster voluntarily surrendered the jurisdiction over their servants to the magistrates of the town.

(*d*) The civil privileges of the ambassador and his suite not yet precisely defined.
Brunus, *De Legationibus*, Lib. IV. c. 5.

§ 101 (*d*). The privileges of the ambassador and his suite in respect of the local civil jurisdiction remained ill-defined. Brunus, whilst ascribing to the public agent a special privilege in respect of suits upon home debts contracted before his appointment, seems to admit a very limited exemption with regard to liabilities contracted or attaching during the course of the embassy. Grotius recognises the complete exemption of the ambassador from civil coercion either in person or property, but in an apologetic fashion which appears to cover a personal opinion rather than an acknowledged usage.

Grotius, *De Jure Belli ac Pacis*, Lib. II. c. 18. s. 9.

(*e*) The local character of legatine privileges recognised.
Case of Rinçon and Fregoze.

§ 102 (*e*). The local character of legatine privileges seems to have been generally recognised during the sixteenth century. The murder upon the Po by contrivance of the Imperial governor of the Milanese of Rinçon and Fregoze, the envoys of Francis I. to the Sultan, excited much adverse comment, but Grotius laid it down without hesitation that the law dictating the inviolability of public agents "doth not oblige those through whose territories "ambassadors presume to pass without their permission "(*venia*)." The Queen of Hungary endeavoured to intercept Henry II.'s ambassador, the Mareschal St André, upon his return from a mission to Edward VI. of England. The ambassador of Selim II. to France was arrested at Venice, and the proceeding was justified on the ground that "a sovereign power need not recognise a public Minister "as such, unless it is to him that his credentials are "addressed."

De Jure Belli ac Pacis, Lib. II. c. 18.

Ward, II. 561.
Wicquefort, I. 177.

(iv) The law-regarding spirit appears in the treat-

§ 103. The limited admission of the exterritorial rights of sovereigns and public agents implies the recognition in the local sovereign of very full authority to deal

ejus apud quem agit. Istud enim juris gentium non est. De Jure Belli ac Pacis, Lib. II. c. 18. s. 8.

with the ordinary passing or resident foreigner. Such authority was in fact habitually exercised in the Reformation Age.

ment by States of the foreign sojourner.

In this particular, however, States had come to recognise the need for careful regard of legal principles. The fact finds interesting illustration in the attitude taken up by Spain towards the English plunderers of Philip II.'s American possessions. The famous John Oxenham having in 1578 fallen into Spanish hands was, when tried at Lima, asked whether he had his Queen's authority for entering the King of Spain's dominions, and on the non-production of any commission was put to death as "a pirate and common enemy of "mankind." The question, coupled with the action of the Spaniards in other instances where the royal commission was forthcoming, proves the advised regularity of the proceedings of the Spanish judges.

Oxenham's case, 1578.

Camden, *Eliz.* II. 111.

When in 1664 the English Court of Queen's Bench directly ruled that a foreigner coming into Great Britain and remaining under the protection of the British Crown was a British subject, the judgment merely declared old standing well recognised international practice.

The Quaker's case, 1664. Kelynge, 38.

§ 104. One marked feature which characterised the international relations of the Reformation Age cannot be overlooked. When the perfidious assassination of opponents was lauded as an act of heroism alike by Catholic and Protestant divines, it was little wonder that amongst laymen treachery everywhere prevailed. William the Silent, Henry III. and Henry IV. were but more conspicuous victims of a state of opinion which enabled Philip II. of Spain to approve in his State despatches plots against the life of Elizabeth and to offer a public reward for the murder of Orange[1]; which permitted

(v) The anti-social characteristic of Faithlessness distinguishes the international dealings of the Age. Justification of Assassination. Laurent, x. 440.

[1] For the Proclamation of Philip and the reply of Orange see the interesting tract, *Apologia Illustrissimi Principis Willelmi Dei Gratia Principis Auraicae. Apud Car. Sylvium, Typographum Ordinum Hollandiae*, MDLXXXI.

Dumont, *Corps Dipl.* v. 1. 368. Grotius, *Hist.* III. 340, 341. Laurent, x. 170.

Gregory XIII. to sing a *Te Deum* for the Massacre of St Bartholomew.

Louis XIII. in 1624, enraged at a sentence of outlawry pronounced by the Genoese upon Claude Marini, a Genoese who had entered his service, not only ordered the seizure of the property of all Genoese merchants found within French dominions, but offered by public ordinance a reward of 60,000 francs to any person who should prove that he had killed any one of those who took part in pronouncing sentence upon Marini.

Flassan, *Dipl. Française*, II. 363.

Decay of Chivalry.

Francis I. affected amongst monarchs to represent the ideas of Chivalry. If Francis "lost all but honour" at Pavia, honest men of to-day must hold that he lost honour itself at Madrid, when he swore in most solemn fashion to observe the terms of a treaty which he had already deliberately resolved to repudiate upon securing the liberation from captivity, which was the price of its acceptance. A contemporary soldier could see that, if Francis was unable on recovering his freedom to carry out the terms of the stipulation whereby he had obtained his release, he was in honour bound to return to his confinement. But the Pope himself, the titular guardian of the world's morality, approved the proceedings of Francis by promptly absolving him from the observance of his oath; and the action of the French king only too well accorded with the regular practice of the age. The successors of Edward III. and Bertrand had become pupils in the school of Machiavelli. Subsequent Popes imitated the conduct of Clement in dissolving the bonds of faith solemnly pledged. Charles V. claimed for the Emperor a like authority, and annulled the bond granted by Maurice and the Elector of Brandenburg to the Landgrave of Hesse. Here and there the voice of a Bodin, a Montaigne, a Tavannes or a Sully might be raised in protest, but the great body of the statesmen of the period confessed and acted upon the opinion that nothing which profits is unjust. When Charles V. in 1539 accepted the invitation of Francis to pass through French territory on his way

Laurent, x. 332. Dumont, *Corps Dipl.* IV. 1. 412.

Mém. de Tavannes cited by Laurent, x. 333.

Robertson, *Hist. of Charles V.*, III. 366.

Robertson, *Hist. of Charles V.*, III. 203.

Laurent, x. 340. *Mém. de Sully*, II. 42, 167.

from Spain to the Netherlands, Triboulet, the Court fool of Francis, wrote on his master's tablets, "Charles is a greater fool than I am." "How so," queried Francis, "if I let him travel in safety through my dominions?" "In that case," came the ready reply, "I will put out the name of Charles, and put in that of Francis." They were not all titular fools who at the French Court held and expressed the like opinion.

Bradford, *Correspondence of Charles V.*, p. 230. Flassan, *Dipl. Française*, II. 4.

Low tone of Diplomacy.

The diplomacy of the age of Elizabeth covering an organised system of corruption, espionage and petty deceit lent force to Wotton's subsequent famous definition of an ambassador as "a good man sent abroad to lie on behalf of his country."

(vi) Frequency of recourse to Reprisals,

§ 105. Under these circumstances surprise is not excited by the large part played in the age by the rude method of Reprisals.

as a measure of protection

In many instances the grant took the protective form. In 1563 Philip II. seized English merchant ships in Andalusia in reprisals for the capture of Spanish vessels by the English when pursuing the French. In 1568 a number of Spanish ships carrying a large sum of money to the Netherlands having been driven into Plymouth, Falmouth and Southampton by French privateers, Elizabeth detained the money. Her object was doubtless to hamper the action of the Duke of Alva by the cutting off of his pecuniary supplies, but Elizabeth sought to justify her conduct on the ground that the money was the property of Genoese and other Italian merchants from whom she thought proper to borrow it, and as a matter of fact it was in the long run repaid to these proprietors. Alva, however, took up the matter hotly, confiscated all English goods and made prisoners all Englishmen in the Netherlands. Similar action was taken in the ports of Spain. Elizabeth replied by attacking the goods and persons of Netherlanders in England. In 1573 on the settlement of the dispute Elizabeth restored to Alva the property of the

Camden, *Eliz.* I. 68.

Camden, *Eliz.* I. 121, 123.

Netherlanders after satisfaction of the damages of English merchants.

Camden, *Eliz.* II. 55.

These were but two amongst many such incidents occurring in time of nominal peace.

and as a form of limited warfare.

On occasion the issue of reprisals assumed a more directly warlike guise.

Thus in 1563 "By publicke Proclamation liberty was "given to all Frenchmen to invade all Englishmen, take, "and rob them, as long as they should hold Newhaven. "The same liberty the Queene of England likewise "graunted to the English, that they might hold all "Frenchmen (except those that dwelt in London) for "enemies, as long as they should detaine Calice." This proceeding occasioned the appearance on the seas of a great fleet of English privateers, which pushed their "piratical insolency" even against the Spaniards.

Camden, *Hist. of Eliz.* I. 65.

(β) *The Law of War.* The Age of the Reformation an age of War, and of wars of singular atrocity.

A legacy of the Crusades.

Sleidan, III. 28. *Commentaries of Montluc*, I. p. 33. Laurent, VIII. 116.

§ 106. The Age of the Reformation was an age of war and of wars of particular atrocity. The very religious fervour, which had in mediæval days enlisted united Christendom in crusading warfare, worked, when union no longer existed, havoc in international practice. The old time fury against the Paynim had expired in Saint Louis. It left its traces merely in the old time memories which were invoked in vain to induce common Christian action against the ever present Turkish Terror, in the exclamations of the orthodox when the galleys of Barbarossa appeared at Nice to support Francis I. against the Most Catholic Monarch, and in the ardour which waned slowly out in expeditions to Tunis and Algiers and the struggles of the Knights of St John. The Holy Father still banned with heretics traders who sold arms to Turks and Saracens, but the ambassadors of Charles, Ferdinand and the Venetians followed at no long distance those of Francis to the Porte. Henry IV. made it a point of policy to secure by capitulation with the Sultan special advantages for the French flag. And every day more surely the Turk became a factor merely political in European counsels. The zeal of the crusader remained, however, although diverted to other objects. The Papacy had failed in practice to realise the ideal of the one World Judge, but the Crusades, the World Church's handiwork, handed down a legacy of fighting faith, whether to John Knox or to Ignatius Loyola. Men fought for the Pope or for Reform, and they fought as they thought, sullenly or passionately, but always fiercely.

The lingering influence of the Age of Chivalry seen in (1) the employment of heralds,

§ 107. In the war practice of the struggle between Francis I. and Charles V. and their immediate successors we may trace the lingering influences of the ideas of the Age of Chivalry.

Heralds were still commonly employed to declare war. In 1555 Norris as the herald of Mary of England declared war on Henry II. of France. In 1595 heralds proclaimed Henry IV.'s declaration of war against Philip II. at the Spanish frontiers[1]. Francis I. in 1528 sent a herald to carry to Charles a cartel of personal defiance. In 1537 a herald summoned Charles in the character of Count of Artois and Flanders to appear as recalcitrant vassal at Paris.

Wicquefort, *The Embassador and his Functions*, p. 23. Davila, *Civil Wars of France*, p. 694. Dumont, *Corps Dipl.* IV. 1. 502. Alb. Gentilis, *De Legationibus*, I. 19. Robertson, *History of Charles V.*, II. 301, 302, 406; III. 90.

and other privileged agents,

For purposes of necessary temporary intercourse between belligerents the trumpeter and drummer had succeeded to the privileges of the herald.

Wicquefort, *The Embassador*, p. 23.

(2) the treatment of prisoners,

Men of all ranks, like their mediæval ancestors, looked to the capture and ransom of prisoners as to the chief source of profit of a campaign. Noble commanders, however, held the view of Marshal Montluc that "It is a "great baseness to flea men to the bones, when they are "persons of honour and bear arms; especially in a war "betwixt Prince and Prince, which is rather out of sport "than unkindness to one another." Prisoners too poor to

Montluc, *Commentaries*, p. 177.

[1] In 1583, the semi-barbarous ruler of Muscovy "would not heare" from Sir Jerome Bowes, the British Special Ambassador, "that it was "not the part of a Christian, nor allowable by the law of Nations to "exercise hostility without warre denounced, and to make warre before "such time as hee from whom the injury began, bee warned to recom-"pence the wrong, and to abstaine therefrom." Camden, *Eliz.* III. 24.

ransom themselves were by virtue of this order unconditionally released, being simply turned adrift without any provision for their subsistence. Liberation under parole was a well recognised institution. It is further noteworthy that Montluc, although he regularly employed the arm, shared the prejudice of Bayard against the harquebuz[1].

Montluc, *Commentaries*, p. 14. Laurent, x. 386. Castelnau, *Memoirs*, p. 413.

(3) the unpopularity of certain weapons, Montluc, *Commentaries*, p. 9.

Ill faith between belligerents was by combatants of the Reformation Age generally condemned as unworthy of a great prince or a gentleman. The "Law of Arms," which protected the messenger sent to parley, also enforced the terms of capitulation[2]. And "good" was opposed to "evil" war (*la bonne guerre, la mauvaise guerre*).

(4) the praise of good faith between belligerents, *Mém. de Sully*, I. 125. Guicc. VII. 28. Sleidan, v. 57.

(5) the opposition of *la bonne guerre* and *la mauvaise guerre*. Laurent, x. 385.

But the ideas of the Captal de Buch and of Bayard struggled in singular fashion in the sixteenth century with conceptions of other ages.

Combination of modern humanitarian ideas

A striking incident from time to time suggests the existence in germ of modern humanitarian influences. Thus the Duke of Guise reaped particular glory by his kindly treatment of frost-bitten Imperialist wounded left behind upon the raising of the siege of Metz (1552). So too in 1521 it was, upon the intervention of Cardinal Wolsey, agreed by a remarkable treaty between Charles V. and Francis that the subjects of either prince who should be engaged in fishing upon the sea should until the end of January 1522 be free from any molestation. And this instance of international care for a poor and deserving class of men does not stand alone[3].

Robertson, *History of Charles V.*, III. 274.

Dumont, *Corps Dipl.* IV. 1. 352.

with the worst mediæval belligerent precedents.

But, on the other hand, feature after feature of the war-practice of the period recalls the worst mediæval precedents.

[1] Bayard, when lying mortally wounded by a harquebuz shot, thanked God that he had never shown mercy to a musketeer. With Montluc the harquebuz was "the devil's invention."

[2] Thus Dutch troops surrendering in Hoy were protected by the Spanish commanders by force against their allies, the Liègeois. Grotius, *Hist.* IV. 364.

[3] Drake, however, when "singeing the King of Spain's beard" in 1571, burned fisherman's boats and nets all along the Spanish coast. Camden, *Eliz.* Anno 1587.

The utmost severity was shown by besiegers of fortified places. So countrymen bringing provisions for the relief of the besieged were hanged without mercy, whilst "useless mouths" expelled by their fellow townsmen perished miserably between the walls and the lines of the enemy. To rashly resist the fire of cannon was, according to the general view of the "law of arms," to expose all the inhabitants of the town to death.

1. Strictness of the law of sieges.

Montluc, *Commentaries*, pp. 129, 147. Montluc, *Commentaries*, p. 368. De Thou XIII. Montaigne, *Essays*, I. c. 12. *Mém. de Sully*, III. 69.

In 1580 the fort of Smerwick held by a combined force of Spaniards and revolted Irish surrendered at discretion to Lord A. Grey. A council of English officers overruled the objections of their chief; the Irish prisoners were hanged and the Spaniards were put promiscuously to the sword, the captains only being saved. This proceeding was specially justified on the ground that, whilst the numbers of the prisoners equalled those of the captors, the English were destitute of victuals, and a strong force of rebels was in the immediate neighbourhood. Apart, however, from this excuse, the butchery was by no means unique in its day.

Camden, *Eliz.* Ann. 1580.

Stormed cities were regularly the scenes of wild carnage. The cruelty of belligerents in this respect was often deliberate. Montluc unhesitatingly justified his proceedings upon the assault of Capistrano and Rabasteins, where all within the walls, save a few women, were "to strike terror into the country" put to the sword[1]. Upon the capture of Rome by the troops of Bourbon (1527) neither age, character nor sex protected from injury, and for several months the insolence of the soldiery remained unabated. Upon the capture of Düren the Emperor indeed gave orders that the assailants should, on pain of death, spare all the women and children, and these were recommended to take refuge in the church, but the place was given over to pillage and burnt, and the general body of the inhabitants perished.

2. Deliberate savagery in places carried by storm.

Montluc, *Commentaries*, pp. 16, 368.

Robertson, *History of Charles V.*, II. 286. Sleidan, VI. 74.

Correspondence of Charles V., p. 539. Robertson, *History of Charles V.*, III. 15.

A single sentence, in fine, sufficiently describes the

[1] The Spaniards at Smerwick were slaughtered "for a terror."

3. Absence of distinction between combatants and non-combatants. character of the war-practice of the age: *the distinction between combatants and non-combatants remained to be drawn.* When Marshal de Brissac negotiated in 1552 with the Spanish opposing generals for the exemption of peasants from the scourge of hostile operations he could only appeal for a precedent to the conduct of Xenophon's ideal Cyrus. Sully himself wrote of *la sexe qui sont les malheureux droits de la guerre.*

Laurent, x. 388. *Mém. de Sully*, I. 124.

Special savagery of the Civil Wars of the period.

§ 108. The generals of the Reformation Age justified special severity in the waging of Civil War. "It is not," said Montluc, "in this case as in a foreign war, when men "fight for love and honour; but in a Civil War, we must "either be master or man, being we live as it were all "under a roof; and that's the reason why we must "proceed with rigour and cruelty."

Montluc, *Commentaries*, p. 241.

The French Wars of Religion.

Where religious fanaticism reinforced political resentment there was no limit to the barbarity of the rough soldiery. Castelnau, Sully and other eye-witnesses draw a tragic picture of the scenes enacted during the struggle with the Huguenots. Nothing was sacred from the hands of the plunderer, not even the sepulchres of the dead. The Huguenot leader Piles wasted Périgord with fire and sword in revenge, as he said, for the death of certain of his co-religionists, who had fallen in open battle. When Rouen fell (1562) before the forces of the Crown, the captured city was, in defiance of the plighted word of the king, and of the strenuous exertions of Guise, submitted during eight days to a wild and indiscriminate sack; the very courtiers shared in the pillage, and a price was set on the heads of the hapless inhabitants. Catholics and Huguenots alike looted the towns and villages of Normandy, and drove the wretched natives to live like wild beasts in caves and savage fastnesses. The Baron of Adrets took Mornas under capitulation, but nevertheless ordered the garrison of the castle to be thrown from the walls; when some miserable wretches seized in their agony upon the bars of the windows from which they

Mémoires de Sully, I. 87, 405. Castelnau, *Memoirs*, p. 248.

Castelnau, *Memoirs*, p. 370.

Castelnau, *Memoirs*, pp. 175, 177. Davila, *Civil Wars of France*, p. 75.

Castelnau, *Memoirs*, pp. 216, 217. Davila, *Civil Wars of France*, p. 86.

were hurled, their hands were lopped off by their merciless tormentors. Fifty persons met the same fate at Montbrison[1]. Condé himself was shot at Jarnac after giving up his sword as a prisoner of war. Montluc, carrying Montségur and other places by assault, hanged the survivors of the storm, and put to death prisoners who, as at Larochechalais, had surrendered at discretion. It is characteristic of the period that the relentlessness of the Marshal excited the special commendation of the Holy Father Gregory. Both parties shamefully violated their publicly pledged faith.

Castelnau, *Memoirs*, pp. 184–186.
Ibid. p. 377.
Montluc, *Commentaries*, pp. 247, 250, 257, 317, 339.
Castelnau, *Memoirs*, pp. 347, 398.

So, too, in the Low Country Wars the fight was to the death. In the days of Alva the Spaniard used but little mercy. Pillage and devastation reigned in the open field; and siege after siege terminated in a scene of wild licence and savage butchery. When Zutphen fell before the son of Alva in 1572, no distinction of sex or age stayed the hands of slaughter, and similar deeds of horror were enacted at Rotterdam, at Maestricht, and at Antwerp. The body of the Dutch leader, Schenck, fallen in an attack on Nymwegen, was exposed to popular insult, and left unburied for two years. Acts like these provoked reprisals. Captives from Nymwegen suffered for the contumely offered to Schenck, and the Dutch were soon little behind in the ways of cruelty. Spanish discipline, relaxed among the unpaid troops of Alva, perished altogether with the Duke of Parma in 1592. His successor had a strange experience. "He began," writes Grotius, "to abolish all the customs of war." Count Mansfeld, thereupon, "made it a law, that all prisoners taken in "war should be condemned to some corporal punishment, "and so should all that assisted the enemy, by pay-"ment of contribution." The consequences were notable. Prisoners taken by both sides being forthwith hanged, the soldiery deserted in crowds, or fled at the first onset. A natural revulsion of feeling ensued. "These things

"The Low-Country Wars."
Grotius, *Annals*, IV. 169; V. 187. *History*, II. 255, 261, 275; III. 327; IV. 361; XIV. 834. Bentivoglio, *Wars in Flanders*, pp. 93, 94, 147.
Grotius, *Annals*, II. 65.
Bentivoglio, *Wars in Flanders*, p. 186.
Grotius, *Annals*, II. 61, 73, 83.
Bentivoglio, *Wars in Flanders*, p. 102.
Grotius, *Hist.* I. 235.
Bentivoglio, *Wars in Flanders*, pp. 108, 119, 298.
Grotius, *Hist.* II. 301.

[1] In each instance cruelties practised upon Huguenots were urged to excuse these acts of cruelty.

"made them admire Antiquity, in the obedience of the "present times, and at last made them return to their "old customs, to redeem their lands with tribute, to make "exchange of prisoners; and that he who ransom'd himself, "should, for the same, give a month's pay." And "the Laws of Arms" were reestablished. Spanish discipline was restored by Spinola in 1604 by a system of exact reward and severe punishment. But the unhappy Netherlands in the interim had suffered hardly. Prince Maurice did all in his power to restrain his men, and sometimes with success, but from time to time they broke free from control, and pillaged and wasted with fire and sword. The troops of Mansfield spoiled and plundered, and used every kind of licentiousness, while the Holland horsemen carried their infamy far into the neutral German land. Grotius marks it as a display of singular continence that reinforcements, recovering a town from the hands of plunderers, should restore to its original owners the booty taken from the townsmen. On occasion the honour of Spanish commanders protected from insult a capitulating garrison; but a Spanish archduke hanged twelve sick Dutch soldiers made prisoners on a stranded vessel, alleging the pitiful plea that they were taken at sea, where there were no *laws of arms* to be observed. This last proceeding called down, as was to be expected, the prompt reprisals of Maurice; but within a little interval the Dutch themselves instructed their admiral to drown without pity all Spanish prisoners made at sea, an instruction only too faithfully followed.

Grotius, *Hist.* II. 305.

Ibid. XIV. 800. Bentivoglio, *Relation of Flanders*, I. c. 6.

Grotius, *Hist.* I. 238.

Ibid. II. 261.

Ibid. III. 349; XVII. 949.

Ibid. IV. 398. *Ibid.* IV. 364.

Ibid. XIV. 756.

Ibid. XIV. 793.

A struggle on these terms worked its natural end. Men grew sick by force of very satiety, and, wearied to sheer exhaustion, the combatants at last laid down their arms (1609).

Ferocity of the combatants in the Thirty Years' War.

The story of the Thirty Years' War will live for ever as a tale of horror. Twelve hours after the fall of Magdeburg 20,000 men, women, and children lay charred and blackened corpses amidst the ashes of the hapless city. The Walloons gave little quarter, and their Croatian allies none. A few hundred women and children of all Magdeburg were preserved in a single church to receive their lives from Tilly. Magdeburg was not alone in the fierceness of her visitation. During the siege of Leipsic Tilly's soldiery exercised the wildest licentiousness and cruelty in the surrounding towns: men and women were stripped, scourged, cropped, yoked, and submitted to such freaks of unrestrained barbarity as sicken the heart by their bare recital. The Imperialists under Colonel Gotze wreaked a frightful revenge for the reception of a few Swedish horse in some Pomeranian villages; men were tortured, women outraged, the very children smothered in their refuges in the cellars with burning straw, until at last the smoke of universal conflagration in mercy covered the scene.

Swedish Intelligencer, pp. 112–115. *Ibid.* p. 25. *Ibid.* p. 120. *Ibid.* p. 59.

Tilly and the Imperialists enjoyed no monopoly of cruelty. Gustavus himself was mild and humane, but after his fall at Lützen the Swedish commanders soon came little behind their opponents in the ingenuity of unchecked devilry.

Ibid. p. 100.

There was need indeed for the voice of a Grotius to call men back to *temperamenta juris belli.*

(γ) *The Law of Neutrality.* 1. Neutrality as the condition of particular areas early recognised.

§ 109. In the Middle Ages, Neutrality had in name as in fact been practically unknown. During the greater part of the sixteenth century the conception was hardly more familiar. Neutrality indeed as the condition of particular territory specifically exempted from the operations of war was as well recognised by the negotiators of Charles V. and Francis I. as by Maurice and Spinola; but down to the close of the century the subjects of states not directly engaged in any existing war were *non-hostes* or *medii in bello*[1], and Grotius could sum up in one short chapter their admitted rights and obligations.

Dumont, IV. 1. 378; 2. 137. *Correspondence of Charles V.*, p. 155. *Carleton's Letters*, p. 12. Grotius, *De Jure Belli ac Pacis*, III. 17.

[1] In the Act given by Francis I. in 1536 for the protection of the territories of the Duke of Lorraine the lands in question are designated as "neutres." Dumont, IV. 2. 137. The treaty of 1522 between Francis I.

2. The character of the wars of the period militate against the rapid spread of strict views as to neutral *duty*.

§ 110. The character of the wars of the period militated against any rapid advance of opinion as to neutral duty. Not merely did Christendom recognise no obligation on the part of any prince to stand neuter in the great contest of religious parties, but the active assistance of belligerents of his own communion was popularly deemed a duty incumbent on every Christian prince, and amongst sovereigns only an irresolute Scottish James had real qualms of conscience concerning the morality of interference between a subject and his king. Englishmen cried shame when Charles I. lent men-of-war to his French brother-in-law for the subjection of the Huguenots, but they thought it no harm that regiment after regiment of their fellow-countrymen was enlisted by the royal authority, or at least by the royal permission, for the service of the Dutch against the Spaniards, with whom England was nominally at peace; that Elizabeth received Havre as the price of assistance granted to the revolted French Protestants; or that six thousand Scots under the Marquis of Hamilton fought for German Protestantism against the Emperor.

Welwood, *Memoirs*, p. 255.

Rushworth, *Historical Collection*, pp. 313—339 (Ed. 1659).

In 1587 an army of 40,000 men raised by the Protestant princes of Germany for the support of the Huguenots was commanded by the Emperor Rudolph to disband, as having been levied without licence. The Lieutenant-General to Prince Casimir answered in writing that, the enterprise being neither his, against the Empire, nor against the Kingdom of France, but for the relief of the oppressed confederates of the Protestant Princes, and *the German nation having ever had liberty to enter themselves into pay under whom they pleased*, provided that it were not against the Emperor nor his jurisdiction, he neither thought himself obliged to desist nor to disband the army, but would continue the business begun under commission from his prince. The Emperor took no further action, and the expedition proceeded.

Davila, *Civil Wars in France*, p. 313.

and the Archduchess Margaret reveals a fair conception of Neutrality as the condition of abstention from warlike operations. For similar later agreements see Dumont, v. 1. 517, 527.

Grotius upon *medii in bello.*

Grotius lays it down that, "It is the duty of those "that are not engaged in the war to sit still and do "nothing that may strengthen him that prosecutes an *ill* "*cause*, or hinder the motions of him that hath justice on "his side....But in a dubious cause to behave themselves "alike to both parties; as in suffering them to pass "through their country, to supply them with provisions, "and not to relieve the besieged." The calls of religious partisanship were regularly offered as a sufficient excuse for intervention, and, in fine, the grant of assistance limited in amount was generally, if not universally, deemed in no way incompatible with the maintenance of the peace-footing between the auxiliary sovereign and the ruler against whom his forces were directed. France was not drawn directly into war with Spain when the Duke of Anjou accepted the governorship of the revolted Netherlands. It was not until 1595, when he had for three years been fighting against Spanish troops in alliance with the League, that Henry IV. declared war on Philip II. James I. gave in 1603 permission to the Dutch to raise forces in Scotland; and in 1620 the streets of London were placarded with proclamations setting out the royal licence given to "the Winter King," seemingly under prior treaty, to enlist troops to a limited number in the dominions of the English Crown.

Grotius, *De Jure ac Pacis*, III. 17. 3.

The prevalent looseness of thought as to neutral duty seen in the general attitude towards: i. Limited assistance.

Bentivoglio, *Wars in Flanders*, III. 2. p. 316.

ii. The permission of Foreign Enlistment.

Dumont, *Corps Dipl.* V. II. 333. Manning, *Law of Nations*, p. 236. Cf. *Carleton's Letters*, pp. 115, 122.

It may be that the doctrine concerning limited assistance prepared the way for stricter views, but, distinguishing between actual belligerency and active sympathy, it represents the very antithesis of the modern conception of Neutrality.

3. Neutral *rights* equally crudely conceived of.

§ 111. Neutral rights were as crudely conceived of as were neutral obligations.

(i) Neutral territory affords little protection.

The English, whilst insisting on the right of the "vail," made no attempt to prevent hostilities between belligerents in the British seas; and in 1521 Cardinal Wolsey would appear to have judged an express undertaking on the part of the Imperial and French belligerents necessary for the

Wolsey's Franco-Imperial treaty, 1521.

preservation of the peace even in English harbours. By the treaty contracted upon the intervention of Henry VIII. between Charles V. and Francis I.: *Conventum et conclusum est, quod, dicto Bello durante, nullus subditus principum praedictorum, intra Portus et Sinus Maris quoscumque, Flumina, Ostia Fluminum, Gurgites, Aquas dulces, stationes Navium, et praesertim stationem vulgariter vocatam,* LES DUNES, *aut alia Loca Maritima quaecumque Jurisdictioni dicti Regis Angliae subjecta, aliquam Navem Mercatoriam, onerariam, armatam vel non armatam, onustam seu vacuam, cujuscumque quantitatis aut oneris fuerit, de quacumque Natione eadem Navis extiterit, capere, spoliare, diripere, seu Merces, Victualia, aut armamenta quaecumque, ab eisdem Navibus, aut earundem Nautis auferre, nec eisdem vim, violentiam, aut molestationem aliquam inferre possit, aut debeat; sed quod liceat Navibus et Nautis quibuscumque, circa Loca supradicta, tutè, liberè, et securè morari, manere, et ad ancoram stare, absque cujuscumque alterius Navis armatae dictorum Principum, aut alicujus eorundem Subditi, violentia, infestatione, aut molestia.* In the same spirit it was further stipulated that no incursion, depredation, burning, or other hostile operation should take place within the limits, bounds, territory, or jurisdiction of the King of England beyond sea, and that victuals on the way to, or persons trading with, Calais should not be intercepted.

Dumont, *Corps Dipl.* IV. 1. 352.

Elizabeth Tudor's view of the sanctity of neutral territory.

The conceptions of neutral rights actuating Elizabeth Tudor, if indeed her words may be taken as representing her real opinions, seem to have been little, if any, more advanced.

In September, 1588, France and Spain were formally at peace. Elizabeth nevertheless instructed her ambassador to complain to Henry III. of France of the conduct of certain French officials in preventing the capture by her ships of Spanish property in waters which were obviously French. "Her Majesty's pleasure is," writes Walsingham, "you shall first make mention of the galeasses, which, "being entered and won by her subjects, with the loss of "their blood, and divers of their lives, she cannot but "think it a very hard point, that the strictness of law "should so far prevail against good debts, and the respect "of professed friendship and good neighbourhood, as that "restitution of the ordnance of the same should be made "unto the enemy because the said galleasse ran on ground "within gunshot of Calais. Adding thereto also, the "strange demeanour towards her, of his subjects of "Newhaven, in the road whereof, one of the enemy's "vessels of the number of her fleet, being assailed by one "of her ships, the Lieutenant of the Town, as her Majesty "is informed, making himself in a manner a party against "her with the enemy, planted his ordnance upon the sands "and discharged the same upon her said ship."

Sir F. Walsingham to Sir E. Stafford, Sep. 8, 1588. *State Papers from* 1501 *to* 1726, I. 362.

(ii) Neutral merchants forbidden to trade with belligerents. Elizabeth and neutral trade with Spain, 1588—97.

In October, 1588, upon the rumour of a scarcity in Spain, Elizabeth called upon the King of France to prevent the exportation of corn from France to Spanish ports, announcing her intention, in case the request were not complied with, to instruct the commanders of her ships lying upon the Spanish coast to "impeach" all Spain-bound vessels found laden with grain or any other kind of victual "of what nation soever they be." Notice had already been given to the Hanseatic merchants that, in the event of the finding upon the seas of any of their vessels laden with corn, munition or other warlike furniture for Spain, they would be held good prize. The King of France returned an answer with which Elizabeth was "very greatly contented." The Hanseatic merchants were more refractory. When in 1589 Drake captured in the Tagus sixty of their vessels laden with wheat and naval stores designed to furnish a new Armada, they complained loudly of the seizure as a breach of their ancient privileges. Elizabeth, however, defended Drake's proceeding, declaring that their merchandise had been often stayed and detained, for that in the heat of war they had supplied provision to the French, and this, not only by the English, but also for the same cause by Charles V., the Kings of Sweden, Denmark and Poland, and by the Prince of Orange. "And

Sir F. Walsingham to Sir E. Stafford, Oct. 20, 1588. *State Papers from* 1510 *to* 1726 I. p. 367.

Ibid. I. p. 370.

"that by the Law of Nations....The right of Neutrality "is in such sort to bee used, that while wee helpe the "one, wee hurt not the other."

Camden, *Eliz. Ann.* 1589. See also *Ann.* 1595.

To a Polish ambassador, who was sent in 1597 to complain of her interference with the traffic of Polish and Prussian vessels with the Peninsula, Elizabeth replied in the same strain with the uncompromising declaration, that "in the time of warre betwixt Kings it is lawful for the "one party to intercept the ayds or succours sent to the "other, and to provide that no damage may grow thereby "to himselfe." This was, she said, agreeable to Nature and to the Law of Nations, and had been often practised, not by her alone, but also by the kings of Poland and Sweden in their wars with the Muscovite.

Camden, *Eliz. Ann.* 1597. Wicquefort, II. c. 7.

The Dutch adopt similar views.

The Dutch, who were in the course of the next century to become the stoutest and most persistent advocates of the claims of the neutral trader, adopted in their War of Liberation the attitude of Elizabeth. In the like spirit the Venetians in 1617 compelled English merchantmen to unlade their cargoes and serve in war against the Duke of Ossuna.

(iii) Neutral shipping forcibly enlisted in belligerent service.

Carleton's Letters, p. 223.

More precise notions as to Neutrality appear at the end of the 16th century.

§ 112. As the years of the sixteenth century closed in more precise notions began to prevail as to the legal situation of sovereigns and subjects who were *medii in bello*.

Neutral territorial rights asserted by German States, 1598,

Bentivoglio, *Wars in Flanders*, III. p. 375.

When in the winter of 1598 the unpaid Spanish troops from the Netherlands quartered themselves in Cleves and Westphalia, the deputies of the aggrieved provinces, meeting at Coblenz to concert measures of redress, complained of the proceeding as "breaking all laws, both "of particular neutrality and common justice." Neutrality was in fact becoming a well-recognised state, and the opinion of leading thinkers clarified alike as to the rights and the duties of the neutral condition. Here amongst sovereigns a foremost place was taken by James Stuart.

and vindicated by James I., 1604.

Mém. de Sully, III. 366, 393.

Neutrality was a familiar term at the Court of that over-cautious monarch.

The proclamation of James I. as to the "King's Chambers."

In 1604, in view of the contest between the United Provinces and Spain, James issued a proclamation, whereby he forbade the exercise of any act of belligerency within certain prescribed limits, and extended his protection to all merchants and others endangered by the action of men-of-war hovering with a view to offering violence in the adjacent open sea. "Our pleasure is," he declared, "that within our Ports, Havens, Roads, Creeks, "or other places of our Dominions, or so near to any of "our said Ports and Havens, as may bee reasonably con-"strued to bee within that title, limit, or precinct, there "shall bee no force, violence, or offence suffer'd to bee done, "either from man of war to man of war, or man of war to "merchant, or merchant to merchant of either partie. "But that all of what Nation soever, so long as they shall "bee within those our Ports and Places of our Jurisdiction, "or where our Officers may prohibit violence, shall bee "understood to bee under our protection, to bee ordered by "cours of Justice, and bee at peace each with other."

Mare Clausum, p. 364. Vattel, I. 23, § 288.

He defines the neutral zone by the headland line.

The neutral territorial zone prescribed by James was defined as fixed by "a straight line drawn from one point "to another about the realm of England.[1]" The areas shut within these bounds, and styled "the King's Chambers," were in some cases of considerable extent[2].

The instant necessity for such action.

The proclamation was at the moment more necessary than effectual. In the following year the Dutch and Spanish fleets fought furiously in the very harbour of Dover, and it was only when, on the second day, the victory had declared for the Dutch, and, in obedience to

[1] The definition was arrived at by a jury of twelve sworn for the purpose, and their finding was presented to Sir Julius Cæsar, Judge of the Admiralty, on March 4, 1604. The headlands selected were Holy Island, Souter Pt., Whitby, Flamborough Head, Spurn Head, Cromer, Winterton-Ness, Caistor-Ness, Lowestoft, Easton-Ness, Orford-Ness, North Foreland, South Foreland, Dungeness, Beachy Head, Dunnose, Portland Bill, Start Pt., Rame Head, Dodman Pt., the Lizard, Land's End, Milford, St David's Head, Bardsey, Holyhead, Man.

[2] The longest headland line was that from Land's End to Milford, which represents a sea expanse of upwards of 95 miles.

the savage instructions of the States, the Spanish prisoners, tied two and two, were thrown into the sea, that the indignant English of the castle battery began a tardy fire upon their late allies. At a subsequent period, however, the English displayed greater energy in the execution of the royal decree. In 1624, a Dutch vessel having attacked a Dunkirker as she was leaving an English port, a "King's "ship came in to part them, and letting fly equally at "them both, with blows of cannon equally distributed, "persuaded them to peace."

Grotius, *Hist.* XIV. p. 794.

State Papers from 1501 *to* 1726, I. p. 534.

CHAPTER III.

THE EVOLUTION OF INTERNATIONAL LAW.—THE FORE-RUNNERS AND THE PROPHET OF INTERNATIONAL LAW.

§ 113. In the age of the Reformation we encounter for the first time a real literature of the Law of Nations[1]. The thought of one generation is, however, in the main but the extension or expansion of that of generations preceding; ideas like men have their natural parentage. The work of the so-called "Father of International Law" was but the product of long centuries of slow evolution.

Appearance of a real literature of the Law of Nations.

It represents a gradual evolution.

§ 114. Throughout the Middle Ages writers of legal bent had, following classical models, continued the discussion of the relations of *Jus Naturale, Jus Gentium*, and *Jus Civile*, and the handling and illustration of those branches of *Jus Gentium* in which the Roman jurists had attained to their furthest advance.

(*a*) Mediæval writers expand Roman legal learning concerning *Jus Naturale* and *Jus Gentium*.

In these labours the foremost place was naturally taken by the Civilians. Irnerius, Bartolus, and Baldus[2]

(1) Incidental discussions.

[1] In *Les Origines de Droit International*, by Professor E. Nys, the student will find a rich mine of mediæval bibliography. To this and other works by the same author every future historian of International Law must be profoundly indebted. Reference should also be made to Professor Holland's lecture upon the Early Literature of the Law of War: see *Studies on International Law*, II. To this last I owe more than one helpful suggestion.

[2] Irnerius, known as the Father of the Glossators, was born at Bologna in the second half of the eleventh century. He would appear to have derived his knowledge of Roman Law from study at Constantinople. Teaching both at Ravenna and Bologna, it was to him that the latter

1. The Civilians touch incidentally upon topics of international interest.

were succeeded by a great galaxy of emulators, amongst whom in the age of the Reformation Andrea Alciati[1], Francis Hotoman, and Jacques Cujas[2] shone preeminent. In their incidental comments upon Roman texts concerning the rights accruing by war, concerning booty, *postliminium*, prescription, and a hundred matters more must be recognised the first contributory spring of the seventeenth century *Jus Belli ac Pacis*.

2. The Canonists discuss similar questions in the light of Christian morality.

§ 115. But the Civilians did not work alone. Long before the time of Justinian the conceptions of moral and legal obligation current under the Pagan Empire had come necessarily under review in the light of Christianity.

Tertullian and other Fathers discuss the legitimacy of War.

Tertullian, *De Corona*, c. II., *De Idol.* c. 19.

The opinion of S. Augustine (354–430 A.D.).

Already at the end of the second century the fiery African Tertullian questioned the legitimacy of war for a Christian man. His opinions were echoed by more than one early Father. Augustine (354–430 A.D.), who was destined to exercise a predominant influence in the West, adopted more practical counsels. In a famous letter to

University owed the beginnings of its legal renown. Bartolus de Saxoferrato (1313–59) lectured first upon the Civil Law at Pisa in 1339, passing thence to Perugia and Bologna. His equally famous pupil, Baldus de Ubaldis (1327–1400), lectured *in utroque* at Bologna, and taught at various times at Perugia, Pisa, Florence, Padua, and Pavia. Amongst his scholars he numbered Pope Gregory XI.

[1] Andrea Alciati (1492–1550), after studying at Milan, Pavia, and Bologna, was at various periods between 1521 and the date of his death Professor at Avignon, Milan, Bourges, Pavia, Bologna, and Ferrara. He was a prolific writer of varied talents. Editions of his collected works were published at Lyons in 1560, at Basle in 1571, at Strasburg in 1616, and at Frankfurt in 1617.

[2] Francis Hotman or Hotoman (1524–90), a brilliant *alumnus* of Orleans, closed at Basle a chequered professorial career, which included sojourns at Paris, Lyons, Geneva, Lausanne, Strasburg, Valence, and Bourges. His son John followed in his footsteps with no inconsiderable success, and was with Gentilis consulted by Elizabeth's Council in the case of Mendoza. He was the author of a work *L'Ambassadeur*, which was published at Paris in 1603.

Jacques Cujas or Cujacius (1520–90) was successively Professor at Cahors, Bourges, Valence, Turin, and his native Toulouse. Editions of his much-esteemed works appeared at Paris in 1584 and 1658.

Count Boniface he expressed his disagreement with the view that no active soldiers could find favour with God. It was not, he conceived, for the citizen of the Kingdom of Heaven to separate himself entirely from the world of the present. *Hoc ergo primum cogito quando armaris ad pugnam, quia virtus tua etiam ipsa corporalis donum Dei est. Sic enim cogitabis de dono Dei non facere contra Deum, fides enim quando promittitur, etiam hosti servanda est contra quem bellum geritur, quanto magis amico pro quo pugnatur? Pacem habere debet voluntas, bellum necessitas, ut liberet Deus a necessitate et conservet in pace. Non enim pax quæritur ut bellum excitetur, sed bellum geritur ut pax acquiratur. Esto ergo etiam bellando pacificus, ut eos quos expugnas, ad pacis utilitatem vincendo perducas. Beati enim pacifici, ait Dominus, quoniam ipsi filii Dei vocabuntur. Si autem pax humana tam dulcis est pro temporali salute mortalium, quanto est dulcior pax divina pro æterna salute angelorum? Itaque hostem pugnantem necessitas perimat, non voluntas. Sicut rebellanti et resistenti violentia redditur, ita victo vel capto misericordia jam debetur, maxime in quo pacis perturbatio non timetur.* Augustinus, *Ad Bonifacium, Epist.* 205.

Elsewhere Augustine pointed out, on the one hand, the occasions which might render war just, and, on the other hand, the vices by which warfare might be tarnished and become immoral. Augustinus, *Contra Faustum Manichæum*, Lib. 22. cc. 71–8.

In the first days of the seventh century Isidore, bishop of Seville[1], to whose definition of *jus gentium* reference has already been made[2], attempted a classification of wars, and advanced under cover of the great name of Cicero a Isidore of Seville, A.D. 600, classifies Wars, and defines *bellum justum*,

[1] Isidore became Bishop of Seville in 601 A.D. and died in 636 A.D. In 633 he presided at the Œcumenical Council of Toledo. His *Etymologiæ*, a complete Encyclopædia of mediæval science, in twenty books, is included in the collection entitled *Auctores Latinæ linguæ in Unum Redacti Corpus*, published by Guill. Leimarius in 1585. The *editio princeps* of the works of Isidore was printed at Paris in 1580. Other editions appeared at Madrid in 1599 and at Paris in 1601: *Nouvelle Biograph. Universelle.*

[2] *Isidori Etymolog.* Lib. v. c. 6. *Ante*, p. 153, and Professor Westlake's *Chapters on International Law*, p. 24.

definition of *bellum justum*. *Quatuor autem sunt genera bellorum, id est justum, injustum, civile et plusquam civile. Justum bellum est, quod ex prædicto geritur de rebus repetitis, aut propulsandorum hostium causa. Injustum bellum est, quod de furore, non de legitima ratione initur. De quo in republica dicit Cicero: Illa injusta bella sunt, quæ sunt sine causa suscepta. Nam extra ulciscendi aut propulsandorum hostium causam, bellum justum geri nullum potest. Et hoc idem Tullius parvis interjectis subdidit: Nullum bellum justum habetur nisi denuntiatum, nisi indictum, nisi de repetitis rebus. Civile bellum est inter cives orta seditio et concitatio tumultus, sicut inter Syllam et Marium, qui bellum civile invicem in una gente gesserunt. Plusquam civile est, ubi non solum cives concertant, sed et cognati: quale actum est inter Cæsarem et* Isidore, *Etymolog.* Lib. XVIII. c. 1. *Pompeium, quando gener et socer invicem dimicaverunt.*

and *jus militare.* Proceeding in like fashion to the definition of *jus militare* Isidore was betrayed into what to a modern eye Holland, *Studies*, p. 55. is a singular combination of heterogeneous matters. *Jus militare est belli inferendi solennitas, fœderis faciendi nexus, signo dato congressio in hostem, vel commissio. Item signo dato receptio: item flagitii militaris disciplina, si locus deseratur: item stipendiorum modus; dignitatum gradus; præmiorum honor, veluti cum corona, vel torques donatur. Item prædæ decisio; et pro personarum quali-* Isidore, *Etymolog.* Lib. v. c. 7. *tatibus et laboribus justa divisio ac principis portio.*

His definitions are incorporated into the *Decretum Gratiani,* Whatever, however, the merits of the definitions of Isidore, they found their way side by side with the moral precepts of Augustine into the great compilation of Gratian. The definition of *jus gentium* and *jus militare* are incorporated without change[1] into the first *Distinctio* of *Decretum* I., D. I. cc. 9, 10. the First Part of the *Decretum*. In *Causa XXIII.* of the Second Part of the *Decretum* (*De re militari et de bello*) Gratian puts forward the several questions: (1) *An militare peccatum sit?* (2) *Quod bellum sit justum, et*

[1] *Fœdera pacis, induciæ* of the text of Leimarius (p. 153) appears in the *Decretum* as *fœdera, paces, induciæ.*

quo modo a filiis Israel justa bella gerebantur? (3) *An injuria sociorum armis sit propulsanda?* (4) *An vindicta sit inferenda?* (5) *An sit peccatum Judici, vel ministro reos occidere?* (6) *An mali sint cogendi ad bonum?* (7) *An hæretici suis, et Ecclesiæ rebus sint expoliandi, et qui possidet ab hæreticis ablata, an dicatur possidere aliena?* (8) *An Episcopis, vel quibuslibet Clericis sua liceat auctoritate, vel Apostolici, vel Imperatoris præcepto arma movere?*

Premising with Isidore that recourse to arms is only justifiable by way either of repelling injury or of exacting vengeance, both of which proceedings are seemingly prohibited by positive Gospel texts, Gratian notes that the bearing of arms may well appear to be sinful. He concludes, however, that the Gospel exhortations to patience were directed not to the outward show of the body but to the inward condition of the heart. If all wars had been incompatible with Christianity, centurions and soldiers who sought Christ would, he concludes with Augustine, have been positively commanded to relinquish their profession.

together with the moral precepts of Augustine.

Quæstio 1. *An militare peccatum sit?*

August. *Ad Bonifacium Epist.* 205.

In the succeeding *capitula* Gratian draws freely from the writings of the great Father. So we find it laid down on the support of the epistle to Boniface, that in the bearing of arms soldiers may acquit themselves well towards God; that valour itself is a gift of God to be used in accordance with His Will; that faith when pledged is to be kept even with the enemy against whom war is waged; that war is to be waged that peace may ensue. Another citation of Augustine denotes the nature of those belligerent proceedings which are to be reprehended. *Nocendi cupiditas, ulciscendi crudelitas, impacatus atque implacabilis animus, feritas rebellandi, libido dominandi, et si qua similia, hæc sunt, quæ in bellis jure culpantur*[1]. Yet a third dictum attributed to the same source brands motives which may render war unjust. *Militare non est*

Quæstio 1, c. 3.

Ibid. c. 4.

[1] Augustine, *Contra Faustum Manichæum*, Lib. 22, c. 74.

delictum, sed propter prædam militare peccatum est, nec rempublicam gerere criminosum est. Sed ideo gerere rempublicam, ut rem familiarem potius augeas, videtur esse damnabile. Propterea enim providentia quadam militantibus sunt stipendia constituta, ne dum sumptus quæritur, *Quæstio* 1, c. 5. *prædo grassetur*[1].

For the definition of "just war" Gratian falls back *Quæstio* 2, *Quod bellum sit justum?* once more upon Isidore: "A war is just when waged by command (*ex edicto*[2]) for the recovery of property or the repelling of enemies." Augustine's authority decides that as far as justice is concerned it matters not whether a war *Quaestio* 2, c. 2. be waged by open force or by stratagem[3]. A war may be justly waged upon a people or state which has neglected to punish the offences of its subjects or to restore property unjustly carried off. And wars may undoubtedly be waged with justice by command of God. The Israelites justly made war upon the Amorites when they were refused the *transitus innoxius, qui jure humanæ societatis* *Quæstio* 3, *An injuria sociorum armis sit propulsanda?* *æquissimo patere debebat.* Arms may properly be taken up in defence of allies: so Augustine, Ambrose, various Popes and the Council of Carthage. He, who being able to check a wrong-doer fails so to do, is a fautor of impiety. Vengeance is not to be sought. The evil are to be borne with, provided that there be no consent to their works, and this for the sake of the Church's peace: so again *Quæstio* 4, *An vindicta sit inferenda?* Augustine[4]. But discipline is necessary to the Church's weal, and, when offences are incompatible with the peace of the Church, their punishment is called for. Correction is dictated by charity towards the very offender. And the Church looks to rulers for aid against her enemies. God is provoked if enormous offences against Him are permitted to remain unpunished. *Mali sunt prohibendi a malo et cogendi ad bonum*[5].

[1] This passage does not appear in Augustine's nineteenth discourse, *De Verbis Domini*, to which it is referred.

[2] *Ex edicto* is substituted by Gratian for the Isidorian *ex prædicto.*

[3] Augustin. *Quæstionum* 6. 40. q. 10.

[4] Augustin. *De Verbis Domini*, 18.

[5] Augustin. *Ad Donatum*, Epist. 204.

The Church shields fugitive man-slayers, lest she should be a participator in the shedding of blood, and a private person may not slay either another or himself. But it is lawful to slay in a war waged by command of God, or in the exercise of public authority. Military discipline belongs to the king, and to the secular power is properly referred the punishment of various high crimes: so Ambrose and Cyprian. Schismatics and heretics should be restrained by the secular arm: so Pope Pelagius. They are not guilty of homicide who take up arms against the excommunicate: so Pope Urban II. Paul was compelled of Christ. In the compelling of evildoers to righteousness the Church imitates her Lord[1].

Quæstio 5. An sit peccatum judici, vel ministro reos occidere?

Quæstio 6. An mali sint cogendi ad bonum?

Earthly property is held either by Divine or human law. Ecclesiastical property held by heretics is but unjustly possessed, and may be justly taken away by Catholics. Finally, the personal bearing of arms by a Churchman is a notorious breach of Canon Law, but he may exhort others to take arms for the defence of the oppressed or for battle against the enemies of God. Thus have various Popes called men to arms against Langobards and Saracens.

Quæstio 7. An hæretici suis et Ecclesiæ rebus sint expoliandi?

Quæstio 8. An Episcopis, vel quibuslibet Clericis sua liceat auctoritate, vel Apostolici vel Imperatoris præcepto arma movere?

§ 116. The later Papal contributors to the *Corpus Juris Canonici* made, beyond the banning of the supply to Saracens of arms and other warlike necessaries and of the use of some particular weapons[2], few, if any, direct

Succeeding Canonists subjoin further matter by way of

[1] Augustin. *Ad Bonifacium*, Epist. 50.

[2] The Decretals of Gregory IX. included two canons issued by the Lateran Council of 1139 A.D. *Ita quorundam animos occupavit saeva cupiditas, ut qui gloriantur nomine Christiano Sarracenis arma, ferrum et ligamina deferant galearum, et pares aut etiam superiores in malitia fiant illis, dum ad impugnandos Christianos arma eis et necessaria subministrant. Sunt etiam, qui pro cupiditate sua in galeis et piraticis Sarracenorum navibus regimen et curam gubernationis exerceant. Tales igitur, ab ecclesiastica communione praecisos, et excommunicationi pro sua iniquitate subjectos, et rerum suarum per principes saeculi catholicos et consules civitatum privatione mulctari, et capientium fieri servos, si capti fuerint, censemus. Praecipimus etiam, ut per ecclesias maritimarum*

interpretation and illation. *Decret. Greg. IX.* II. 24; v. 12. *Sext. Decret.* II. 11; v. 4.

additions to the literature of *Jus Belli.* Important general principles were, however, embedded in the Titles *de Jurejurando* and *de Homicidio* of the Decretals of Gregory IX. and *Liber Sextus* and other scattered texts, and around these, as around *Decretum* II. c. 23, there sprang up under the hands of successive canonists a rich crop of commentative interpretation.

Holland, *Studies*, p. 44.

Henry of Segusia, circ. 1265, classifies Truces

Amongst the earlier of these commentators special mention may be made of Henry of Segusia, a prelate whose peculiar eminence in Civil and Canonical legal learning won for him the special favour of Popes Innocent IV. and Alexander IV. He published for the use of candidates *in utroque jure* a general compendium which became famous as the *Summa Hostiensis*[1]. In the 34th Rubric of his first Book, *De Treuga et Pace,* he defines and classifies the species of truce, peace and just war. Distinguishing between conventional and canonical truces, he recognises amongst canonical truces two varieties, the one perpetually enjoyed by individuals belonging to particular classes, the other temporarily enjoyed by all persons without distinction. *Perpetuam habent clerici, monachi, conversi, peregrini et rustici cum animalibus et ministris omnibus rusticanis, dum sunt in agricultura, et redeunt, et vadunt....Et sic legati gaudent privilegio, dum in legatione consistunt....Temporalem vero habent omnes communiter, et durat a quarta feria post occasum solis, usque ad secundam feriam ante ortum solis, feria quinta, propter Ascensionem Domini, feria sexta propter Domini passionem, die Sabbati, quia dies est requiei, die Dominica, propter Resurrectionem. Item ab*

urbium crebra et solennis in eos excommunicatio proferatur. Decretal. Greg. IX. Lib. v. *Tit.* VI. c. 6. (Ed. Richter.)

Artem autem illam mortiferam et Deo odibilem ballistariorum et sagittariorum adversus Christianos et catholicos exerceri de cetero sub anathemate prohibemus. Lib. v. *Tit.* XV. c. 1.

John XXII. added an extravagant specially prohibiting the lending of assistance to the Saracens of Granada. *Extravag. Joannis XXII. Tit.* VIII.

[1] The author was Archbishop of Embrun and Cardinal of Ostia. He appears to have died in 1271. Holland, *Studies*, p. 56.

adventu Domini usque ad octavas Epiphaniae, et a Septuagesima usque ad octavas Paschae. Referring to the 23rd Causa of Gratian and to Isidore's definition of *justum bellum*, Hostiensis distinguishes seven species of war, four just and three unjust. These are: (1) *Romanum*, being war waged between believers and infidels; (2) *judiciale*, waged between believers fighting under the authority of a judge; (3) *presumptuosum*, waged by believers in contempt of judicial authority; (4) *licitum*, waged by believers by authority of law; (5) *temerarium*, waged by believers against legal authority; (6) *voluntarium*, waged by believers by virtue of their own authority, they attacking others; (7) *necessarium*, waged by believers fighting unwillingly in self-defence.

and distinguishes seven species of War.

Summa Hostiensis, Lib. I. *De Treuga et Pace*, Rub. 39.

§ 117. Contemporary pure theologians did not fail to share in these discussions of canonists and jurists.

3. The Pure Theologians.

Thomas Aquinas (1224–74), the Angelical Doctor, whose influence upon the Church in the West was destined to be second only to that of Augustine, in his famous *Secunda Secundae* not merely classifies *jus* as *jus naturale* and *jus positivum*, subdividing the latter into *jus humanum* and *jus divinum*, and distinguishing between *jus naturale* and *jus gentium* after the fashion of Ulpian, but dedicates four articles to the discussion of moral problems connected with the subject of war. He decides, mainly on the authority of Augustine, that war may be just, provided it comply with three requisites, viz. that it be waged (*a*) by authority of a prince to whom belongs the conduct of war; (*b*) for just cause (*causa justa*), e.g. when they upon whom it is made deserve assault by reason of some fault; (*c*) in virtue of right actuating motive (*recta intentio*), e.g. the desire that good may be advanced or evil avoided. Turning to the question whether the bearing of arms be legitimate for a Churchman, he concludes that war-waging is prohibited for the clergy, not as in itself sin, but as being incongruous with the character of the clerical profession. The problem *Utrum sit licitum in bellis uti*

S. Thomas Aquinas (1224–74) on *Jus Gentium* and on War.

T. Aquinas, *Sec. Secund. Quæst.* 57.

Quæstio 40. War may be just.

Art. 1. *Utrum bellum sit semper peccatum.*

The bearing of arms is incompatible with the clerical profession.

Art. 2. *Utrum clericis et episcopis sit licitum pugnare.*

Stratagem is legitimate,

but not perfidy. *Art.* 3. *Utrum sit licitum in bellis uti insidiis.*

insidiis Aquinas meets by a distinction between deception by word and deception by act. No one, he rules, may deceive an enemy by direct false statement or by the non-fulfilment of a promise. *Sunt enim quaedam jura bellorum et foedera etiam inter ipsos hostis servanda, ut Ambros. dicit in lib. de officiis.* But deception by the non-disclosure of purpose or mind is in war in no way illegitimate. Aquinas concludes by admitting the plea of necessity in justification of combat on holy days. *Pro tuitione reipublicae fidelium licitum et justa bella exercere diebus festis: si tamen hoc necessitas exposcat. Hoc enim esset tentare Deum, si quis imminente tali necessitate vellet a bello abstinere. Sed necessitate cessante non est licitum bellare in diebus festis propter rationes inductas.*

Ambros. *De Officiis*, I. c. 29, III. c. 10.

Necessity may justify belligerent action on holy days.

(2) In the 14th and 15th centuries special pamphlets are written on War, Reprisals and kindred subjects by both divines and professors of law.

Nys, *Les Origines*, p. 68.

Joannes de Lignano, circ. 1360.

§ 118. In the 14th and 15th centuries divines and professors of law alike dealt in special pamphlets with the legitimacy of war and reprisals. A large collection of legal tracts reprinted at Lyons in 1549 included no fewer than six treatises *De Bello* or *De Duello*[1].

Of these the earliest was the brochure of Joannes de Lignano written in 1360. The author, as Professor of Civil and Canon Law at Bologna, was a colleague of Baldus, in conjunction with whom he was consulted by Pope Gregory XI. in 1380. His work *De Bello de represaliis et de duello* does not appear to have been published until 1477. Together with the well-worn question of the legitimacy of war, it touches upon the topics of the authority by which war may be entered upon, the treatment of prisoners, booty and *postliminium*. Except in respect of its historic interest, the book seems to deserve hardly more than the passing mention which is accorded by Grotius[2] to the name of its author. And the same

Holland, *Studies*, p. 45.

[1] *Tractatus Tractatuum ex variis interpretibus collectorum.* Lugd. 1549. See vol. XII. *Bellum* and *duellum* were identified by many mediaeval etymologists.

[2] *Vidi et speciales libros de belli jure partim a Theologis scriptos, ut a Francisco Victoria, Henrico Gorichemo, Wilhelmo Matthaei, partim a*

may be said of similar treatises by Martinus Laudensis, Joannes Lupus, Franciscus Arias, Jacobus de Castillo, Andrea Alciati, Henry of Gorcum, and a large proportion of those long-forgotten others who have been now rescued from oblivion by the indefatigable research of Professor Nys[1].

E. Nys, *Les Origines de Droit International*, c. 6.

(3) The area of discussion extends.

Some of these pamphleteers extended the area of their discussion to the obligation to keep faith with an enemy, to the binding quality of truces, and various other allied subjects. Writing, however, under the shadow of the Holy Roman Empire and of the still majestic Papacy, none of these early literary skiffmen had the hardihood to venture far from the ancient moorings.

Ompteda, *Litteratur*, 610, 637, 648. Von Kaltenborn, *Die Vorläufer des Hugo Grotius*, 181.

(β) The Moral Theologians of Spain in the Age of the Reformation embark upon extended discussions of current topics of practical interest.

§ 119. It fell to the Moral Theologians of the Reformation days to make the next new conquest. Here the lead was taken by the Scholars of Spain, who united to the solid learning of the Christian West a remarkable share of the brilliancy and independence of thought which had characterised those Saracen predecessors, upon the ruins of whose academies their own Universities had risen in new-born glory. Combining with the denial of the

doctoribus juris, ut Joanne Lupo, Francisco Ario, Joanne de Lignano, Martino Laudensi; sed hi omnes de uberrimo argumento paucissima dixerunt, et ita plerique ut sine ordine quae naturalis sunt juris, quae divini, quae gentium, quae civilis, quae ex canonibus veniunt, permiscerent atque confunderent. De Jure Belli ac Pacis, Proleg. 37. Martin Gariat of Lodi was Professor of Law at Siena and Pavia. His treatise *De Bello et ejus effectu* is reprinted in the *Tractatus Tractatuum*, together with *De Bello et bellatoribus* by Joannes Lupus, *De Bello et ejus justitia* by F. Arias, and two several treatises *De Duello* by Jacobus de Castillo and Alciati. The tractate by Arias appeared in 1533. Lupus, a Spaniard and a Canon of Segovia, died at Rome in 1496. Henry of Gorcum, Professor of Divinity at Cologne, published a volume of *Sententiae*, an edition of which was issued at Basle in 1498. Amongst other matters he wrote *De Bello justo*. Compare Holland, *Studies on International Law*, Essay II. Wilhelmus Mathiae seems to have been the author of a certain *Libellus de bello justo et licito*, published at Antwerp in 1514; Nys, *Les Origines*, p. 120.

[1] An exception must be made in favour of the *Arbre des Batailles* of Honoré Bonet which was edited by Professor Nys in 1883.

Universal sovereignty of the Emperor and the more daring rejection of the Universal temporal lordship of the Pope, the acceptance of those conceptions of Nature and Universal Law with which ancient Roman and mediaeval civilians had made the world familiar, the Spanish divines represented Christendom as a society of independent princes and free commonwealths with rights *inter se*, defined by *Jus Naturale et Gentium*, and so advanced a new theory of International Law. And not only so, but, ranging the field of practical life in pursuit of cases of conscience, they stumbled again and again upon questions of international conduct, and, resolving these by reference to the received canons of Divine, Human, and Natural Law, they gradually built up a *corpus* of well-recognised rule.

Franciscus a Victoria (1480–1549), a representative Moral Theologian,

§ 120. Amongst these philosophers of the Church a foremost place belongs to Franciscus a Victoria[1]. Deriving his name from the town in Navarre where he was born in 1480, before Ferdinand of Aragon had annexed the southern portion of that petty kingdom to his already wide dominions, Victoria was educated at Paris, whence he returned to the Peninsula a member of the Dominican Order, to acquire a high reputation as Professor of Theology at Salamanca. It may be that his cosmopolitan training exercised a special influence alike upon the subjects of his study and upon the width of his view. Certain it is, at all events, that, now well-nigh forgotten, a collection of thirteen *Relectiones* upon various topics of theological interest, first published at Lyons in 1557[2],

Moreri, *Grand Dictionnaire Historique.*

[1] For Victoria's pupil Soto (1494–1560) and J. de Covarruvias (1512–77) see Holland, *Studies*, pp. 52–3. For a full account of the combatants in the prolonged controversy concerning the legitimacy of war upon infidels and heretics see Nys, *Les Origines*, chap. 7.

[2] I have only seen the fourth edition, which bears the title *Relectiones Theologicae Tredecim Partibus per varias sectiones in duos libros divisae. Authore R. P. F. Francisco a Victoria ordinis Praedicatorum S.S. Theologiae Salmanticensis Academiae in primaria quondam cathedra professore eximio et incomparabili. Lugd.* MDLXXXVI. A second edition was published in 1565 at Salamanca, a third at Ingoldstadt.

Ompteda's brief account of Victoria (*Litteratur des Völkerrechts*, p. 169)

some years after the death of their author, establishes the claim of this learned Navarrese to rank among the foremost of the forerunners of Grotius.

a worthy forerunner of Grotius.

§ 121. Dealing in his first and second lecture[1] with the Ecclesiastical Power, Victoria rejects the claim of the Pope to be *Orbis Dominus* in things temporal, or to have a temporal jurisdiction above all princes. The church must necessarily wield, he says, some temporal authority, and the Pope possesses over all princes, kings and even over the Emperor the fullest temporal authority *in ordine ad finem spiritualem*, but the Civil Power, although it may be in a certain sense subject to the spiritual, is not subject to the temporal power of the Pope. Hence it follows that it does not belong to the Pope to judge in the ordinary way in the causes of princes concerning questions of subjection and titles to kingdoms, nor does an appeal lie to him in civil cases from the decision of the prince. The Pope has no *temporal* power to depose a prince even for just cause.

Examination of Victoria's *Relectiones Theologicæ*. *Relectiones* I., II. The Pope is not *orbis dominus* in things temporal. *Rel.* I. sec. 6.

§ 122. In the succeeding *Relectio*[2] Victoria glances with equal freedom at the proceedings of lay potentates. No war is just, if it be waged to the injury more than to the good and utility of the commonwealth, although there be otherwise sound title and reason for a just war. *Probatur, Quia si Respublica non habet potestatem inferendi bellum, nisi ad tuendum se, resque suas atque se protegendum: ergo ubi ipso bello attenuatur potius atque atteritur quam augetur, bellum erit injustum, sive a rege inferatur, sive a Republica. Imo cum una Respublica sit pars totius orbis, et maxime Christiana provincia pars totius Reip. si bellum utile sit uni provinciae aut Reipublicae*

Relectio III. War may justly be waged only for the good and utility of the common-wealth.

is in several particulars inaccurate. According to Professor Holland, Victoria died in 1546. Older authorities ascribe his death to 1549.

[1] *De Potestate Ecclesiae, super locum illum: Tibi dabo claves regni coelorum.*

[2] *Relectio* III. deals with the Civil Power; *Relectio* IV. with the Power of Pope and Council.

cum damno orbis aut Christianitatis, puto eo ipso bellum esse injustum. Ut si bellum Hispaniarum esset adversus Gallos, alias ex caussis justis susceptum, et alioquin regno Hispaniarum utile: tamen cum majori malo et jactura geritur Christianitatis (puta Turcae occupant interim provincias Christianorum) cessandum esset a tali bello.

Relectiones v., vi. *De Indis.* What rights have the Spaniards in the Indies?

§ 123. In the fifth and sixth *Relectiones*, in which he discusses at length the foundation and extent of the authority of the Spaniards in the newly discovered West, Victoria displays to the full the erudition, thoroughness of method, clearness of thought and sound independence of judgment which characterised the Moral Theologians of the first rank. Citing as his text the words of the Divine Commission, "Teach all nations, baptizing them in the name of the Father and of the Son and of the Holy Ghost," Victoria sets out the field of his inquiry as comprised under three heads: (α) By what right did the Barbarians come under Spanish subjection? (β) What power have the princes of the Spaniards over the Barbarians in temporal and civil matters? (γ) What power have those princes or has the Church over the Barbarians in spiritual matters? Justifying his own entrance upon the field on the ground that the rights of the Barbarians pertain to the sphere of authority not of jurisconsults alone but of theologians, he raises the initial question:— Were the Barbarians veritable owners (*veri domini*), private and public, before the appearance of the Spaniards? In its handling he draws freely upon all the main recognised sources of moral obligation, upon the text of Scripture and upon Fathers, upon Schoolmen and upon Councils, upon Civilians and the learned in Canon Law. Slaves are, he argues, incapable of holding property, and Barbarians are, it may be alleged, upon the authority of Aristotle, naturally slaves. The Indians, however, were at the advent of the Spaniards in peaceful possession of property alike privately and publicly. If they were not veritable owners, they must have lost the right of veritable ownership.

Rel. v. sec. 1.

The Indians were veritable owners, private and public, of lands and goods before the advent of the Spaniards.

This they might have conceivably done (i) as sinners, (ii) as infidels, (iii) as idiots, or (iv) as madmen. But (i) the doctrine that ownership is founded in grace is heretical. It is the error of the Waldenses and of Wiclif, and was repelled by the Council of Constance, which decreed that "Mortal sin does not impede civil and veritable dominion." (ii) Infidelity is not inconsistent with veritable ownership. So S. Thomas Aquinas, and likewise Scripture, which recognises the kingship of infidels, *e.g.* Sennacherib, Pharaoh. Paul commands Christians to be subject to the powers that be. Moreover, infidelity is less heinous than active sin. Heretics may indeed be deprived of property rights, but that by *Jus Humanum*[1], and not before condemnation. (iii) Granted that irrational creatures are incapable of holding property, the Barbarians were not irrational. The conclusion is clear. *Restat ergo ex omnibus dictis; quod, sine dubio barbari erant et publice et privatim ita veri domini sicut Christiani: nec hoc titulo potuerunt spoliari aut principes aut privati rebus suis, quod non essent veri domini. Et grave esset negari illis, qui nihil injuriæ unquam fecerunt, quod concedimus Saracenis et Judæis, perpetuis hostibus religionis Christianæ: quos non negamus habere vera dominia rerum suarum si alias non occupaverunt terras Christianorum.*

Titles alleged for the subjection of the Barbarians to the Spaniards examined. Sec. 2.

In the same judicial spirit Victoria next proceeds to examine various titles alleged for the subjection of the Barbarians of the New World to the Spaniards. Amongst these he classes seven as being inapplicable or insufficient (*non idonei nec legitimi*). Such are titles founded in:—

Seven bad titles:— (i) The World Lordship of the Emperor;

(i) *The World Lordship of the Emperor*. The Emperor is not lord of all the world. By *Jus Naturale* all men are free; by *Jus Divinum* the Emperors before the day of Christ were not lords of all the world, nor was seemingly Christ Himself according to the flesh lord in things temporal; by *Jus Humanum* the Emperor has no world title. And even if the Emperor were lord of the earth, he would

[1] Here Victoria distributes Law according to the mediaeval theological model as *Jus Divinum*, *Jus Naturale* and *Jus Humanum*.

not therefore be entitled to occupy the provinces of the Barbarians and to constitute new lords or to impose taxes. Mere jurisdiction, such as is claimed for the Emperor, confers no such power.

(ii) The World Lordship of the Pope;

(ii) *The World Lordship of the Pope.* Assuming, says Victoria, the Pope to possess the authority claimed for him by certain jurists,—that he possesses full jurisdiction in temporal matters in the whole earth, and that secular power is derived from him,—the Pope could certainly as supreme temporal lord constitute the King of Spain prince of the Barbarians, and, should the Barbarians refuse to admit the temporal lordship of the Holy Father, war might justly be made and princes imposed upon them. But (1) the Pope is not civil or temporal lord of the whole world, in respect of ownership (*dominium*) and civil power. Christ had, as already stated, no such power, and the Vicar is not greater than his Lord. (2) Granted that the Pope possessed secular power over the earth, he could not confer it upon secular princes: it would be a right annexed to the Papacy of which no Pope might deprive his successors. (3) The Pope has indeed temporal power *in ordine ad spiritualia,* and in the exercise of that power he may, with a view to avoiding the spiritual ills ensuing upon a war between Christian princes, arbitrate in the quarrels of, and even depose and set up rulers. Still (4) the Pope has no temporal power over the barbarous Indians or other infidels, since he has not over them that spiritual power which is the necessary basis of his temporal authority. It follows that, should the Barbarians refuse to recognise the lordship of the Pope, war cannot be on that account justly waged upon them and their goods occupied. The Spaniards, therefore, when first they sailed to the lands of the Barbarians, carried with them no right to occupy those lands.

(iii) Discovery;

(iii) *Discovery.* Did the Spaniards acquire any title to the lands of the Barbarians by their discovery? *Jus gentium est ut quod in nullius bonis est occupanti conceditur.* But the property of the Barbarians, they being, as already proved, *veri domini*, was not *res nullius*. The Spaniards acquired by their discovery no further title to the lands of the Barbarians than would have accrued to the Barbarians had they discovered Spain.

(iv) *The rejection by the Indians of the Christian Faith proclaimed and powerfully urged upon them.* The author's estimate of title so founded is unflinching. (1) They who have never heard the Word are in invincible ignorance, and therefore commit no sin: sin involves some species of negligence. (2) The Barbarians are not so bound to accept the first simple preaching of the Word without miracles or some other proof that they sin mortally by failing to believe. By the Barbarians' rejection of such preaching, the Spaniards acquire no right to wage or assert the rights of war against them. The Barbarians are innocent in this particular, and they have therein done no injury to the Spaniards. A *just cause* is required for the waging of a just war. (3) If the Barbarians called and warned to listen peaceably to the Word refuse, they are not excused from mortal sin. (4) If the Faith be preached to the Barbarians *probabiliter id est cum argumentis probabilibus et rationalibus et cum vita honesta et secundum legem naturæ studiosa, quæ magnum est argumentum ad confirmandum veritatem, et hoc non semel et perfunctorie, sed diligenter et studiose,* they are bound to receive the Faith under pain of mortal sin. (5) It does not sufficiently appear whether the Christian Faith has been yet so set forth and proclaimed to the Barbarians that they are bound upon pain of sin to believe. The author hears not of miracles, or signs, or of the example of religious life; on the contrary, *multa scandala seu facinora et multas impietates.* (6) Even though the Word have been proclaimed to the Barbarians in a convincing and sufficient fashion and by them rejected, it is not for this cause lawful to make war upon and spoil them. So Aquinas and the general conclusion of Doctors in both Canon and Civil Law. Acceptance of the Faith should be voluntary. War is no argument of the truth of the

(iv) The rejection by the Indians of the Christian Faith preached to them;

Sec. 2, 11.

Christian Faith. Compulsion produces not conviction but pretence.

(v) The sins of the Indians;

(v) *The sins of the Barbarians.* Christian princes, even by authority from the Pope, have no power to forcibly restrain Barbarians from sins against Nature or to punish them by reason of those sins. The Pope has, as before stated, no jurisdiction over the Barbarians.

(vi) Voluntary election by the Indians;

(vi) *Voluntary Election.* The Barbarians might doubtless adopt the lordship of the King of Spain, but fear and ignorance vitiate freedom of choice, and if the Barbarians elected the King of Spain as their lord, it was in ignorance of what they did and in the presence of armed force.

(vii) The Special Gift of God.

(vii) *The Special Gift of God.* It may be that God has condemned the Barbarians to destruction on account of their abominations. It does not follow that they who destroy them are without fault.

Good titles:—

In his third section Victoria sets out the titles by which he deems the Indians might legitimately come under the rule of the Spaniards. The first of these is rooted in *Natural Society and Communication.*

Title 1.

The Natural Right of Society and Communication gives to the Spaniards the right (i) of journeying to and remaining in the Indian lands,

(i) The Spaniards have the right of journeying to and remaining in the provinces of the Barbarians, provided it be without injury to the Barbarians, and this right the Barbarians may not deny them.

Probatur primo ex jure gentium, quod vel est jus naturale, vel derivatur ex jure naturali. Inst. de jure naturali et gent. *quod naturalis ratio inter omnes gentes constituit, vocatur jus gentium. Sic enim apud omnes nationes habetur inhumanum, sine aliqua speciali caussa hospites et peregrinos male accipere: e contrario autem humanum et officiosum, se habere bene erga hospites: quod non esset, si peregrini male facerent, accedentes in alienas nationes. Secundo, A principio orbis (cum omnia essent communia) licebat unicuique in quamque regionem vellet, intendere et peregrinari. Non autem videtur hoc demptum per rerum divisionem: nunquam enim fuit intentio gentium per illam divisionem tollere hominum invicem communicationem: et certe temporibus Noe fuisset inhumanum. Tertio, Omnia licent, quæ non sunt prohibita, aut alias sunt in injuriam aut detrimentum aliorum. Sed (ut supponimus) talis peregrinatio Hispanorum est sine injuria aut damno barbarorum: ergo est licita. Quarto, Non liceret Gallis prohibere Hispanos a peregrinatione Galliæ, vel etiam habitatione, aut e contrario, si nullo modo cederet in damnum illorum, nec facerent injuriam: ergo nec barbaris. Item quinto, Exilium est pœna etiam inter capitales: ergo non licet relegare hospites sine culpa. Item sexto, Hæc est una pars belli, prohibere aliquos tanquam hostes a civitate, vel provincia, vel expellere jam existentes. Cum ergo barbari non habeant justum bellum contra Hispanos, supposito quod sint innoxii: ergo non licet illis prohibere Hispanos a patria. Item septimo facit illud Poëtae:*

> *Quod genus hoc hominum, quaeve hunc tam barbara morem*
> *Permittit patria? hospitio prohibemur arenæ.*

Item octavo, Omne animal diligit sibi simile. Ecclesiast. 13. *Ergo videtur quod amicitia inter homines sit de jure naturali: et contra naturam est vitare consortium hominum innoxiorum. Item nono facit illud* Matt. 25, *Hospes eram et non collegistis me. Unde cum ex jure naturali videatur esse, recipere hospites, illud Christi judicium statuetur cum omnibus. Decimo, jure naturali communia sunt omnium, et aqua profluens, et mare, item flumina et portus, atque naves jure gentium undecunque licet applicare.* Instit. de rerum divis. *Et eadem ratione videntur publica: ergo neminem licet ab illis prohibere: ex quo sequitur, quod barbari injuriam facerent Hispanis, si prohiberent illos a suis regionibus. Item undecimo, ipsi admittunt omnes alios barbaros undecunque: ergo facerent injuriam non admittentes Hispanos. Item duodecimo. Quia si Hispanis non liceret peregrinari apud illos, vel hoc esset jure naturali, aut divino, aut humano: naturali et divino certe licet: si autem lex humana esset, quæ prohiberet sine aliqua caussa a jure naturali, et divino, esset inhumana, nec esset rationabilis, et per consequens non haberet vim legis. Decimo tertio, Vel Hispani sunt subditi illorum vel non. Si non subditi: ergo non possunt eos prohibere. Si sunt subditi, ergo debent eos bene tractare. Item decimo quarto, Hispani sunt proximi barbarorum, ut patet ex Evangelio* Luc. 10 *de Samaritano. Sed tenentur diligere proximos,* Matt. 22, *sicut seipsos: ergo non licet prohibere illos a patria sua sine caussa.* August. de doctrina Christiana, *Cum dicitur, Diliges proximum tuum, manifestum est omnem hominem proximum esse.*

(2) of trading with the Indians,

(2) It is lawful for the Spaniards to trade with the Barbarians, provided it be without injury to the country, whether by importing goods which the Barbarians lack, or exporting gold or silver or other objects in which they abound. Their princes may not impede their subjects from the exercise of commerce with the Spaniards, nor may the Spanish princes prohibit commerce with them. *Probatur ex prima. Primo, quia etiam hoc videtur jus gentium, ut sine detrimento civium peregrini commercia exerceant. Item secundo eodem modo probatur. Cum hoc liceat jure divino: ergo lex quæ prohiberet, sine dubio non esset rationabilis. Item tertio, Princeps tenetur diligere Hispanos jure naturali: ergo non licet eis si potest fieri sine detrimento illorum, prohibere illos a commodis suis sine caussa. Quarto, Quia videntur facere contra illud proverbium, Non facies alteri, quod tibi fieri non vis. Et in summa certum est quod non plus possunt barbari prohibere Hispanos a commercio suo, quam Christiani possunt prohibere alios Christianos. Clarum est autem, quod si Hispani prohiberent Gallos a commercio Hispaniorum, non propter bonum Hispaniæ, sed ne Galli participent aliquam utilitatem, lex esset iniqua, et contra charitatem: si autem hoc lege caveri juste non potest, nec etiam facto fieri (quia lex non est iniqua, nisi propter executionem legis, et ut dicitur* § de justi. et jure, *velut vim inter homines cognationem quandam natura constituit) unde contra jus naturale est, ut homo hominem sine aliqua caussa aversetur. Non enim homini homo lupus est, ut ait Ovidius, sed homo.*

(3) If there be amongst the Barbarians anything common to citizens and guests, it were unlawful for the Barbarians to differentiate against the Spaniards by excluding them from communication and participation. In the proof of this position Victoria incidentally sets out once again his view as to the origin and obligation of the "Law of Nations." *Exempli gratia, Si licet aliis peregrinis vel effodere aurum in agro communi, vel ex fluminibus, vel piscari margaritas in mari, vel in flumine: non possunt barbari prohibere Hispanos, sed eo modo duntaxat, quo aliis licet, dummodo cives, et naturales incolæ non graventur. Hæc probatur ex prima, et secunda. Nam si licet Hispanis peregrinari et negotiari apud eos: ergo licet eis uti legibus et commodis omnium peregrinorum. Secundo, Quia quæ in nullius bonis sunt, jure gentium sunt occupantis.* Instit. de rerum divi. § *ferae bestiae. Ergo si aurum in agro, vel margaritæ in mari; aut aliud quodcunque in fluminibus non est appropriatum, jure gentium erit occupantis, sicut et pisces in mari. Et quidem multa hic videntur procedere ex jure gentium, quæ quia derivantur sufficienter ex jure naturali, manifestam vim habent, ad dandum jus et obligandum. Et dato quod non semper deriventur ex jure naturali, satis videtur esse consensus majoris partis totius orbis, maxime pro bono communi omnium. Si enim post prima tempora creati orbis, aut reparati post diluvium, major pars hominum constituerit, ut legati ubique essent inviolabiles, ut mare esset commune, ut bello capti essent servi, et hoc ita expediret ut hospites non exigerentur, certe hoc haberet vim, etiam aliis repugnantibus.*

(3) of enjoying benefits common to Indians and strangers.

(4) The children born amongst Barbarians to domiciled Spaniards cannot justly be excluded from the rights of local citizens. *Quia hoc videtur esse de jure gentium, ut civis dicatur, et fit, qui natus est in civitate.* The subsequent stages in the argument are easy.

(4) Children born to Spaniards in Indian lands are entitled to all the rights of Indian citizens.

(5) If the Barbarians display a desire to hinder the Spaniards in the exercise of the rights thus belonging to them by *Jus Gentium*, the Spaniards should first have

(5) If the Indians endeavour to

deprive the Spaniards of these rights, the Spaniards may have recourse to reason and persuasion, and in necessary self-defence to acts of force; so

recourse to reason and persuasion. If the Barbarians resort to force, the Spaniards may adopt similar measures in self-defence, and may build forts to defend themselves in the possession of their rights. Even although the Barbarians are excited to the use of force by the appearance of armed men, the justice of the contest is not affected. A war is on both sides just, where right is with one and invincible ignorance with the other.

(6) to the occupation of Indian lands

(6) If the Spaniards, having tried all other means, cannot obtain security without occupying the states of the Barbarians and subjecting them to their rule, they may justly proceed thus far. And

(7) and all the rights of the Conqueror.

(7) If the Barbarians persist in their evil ways in spite of all the efforts of the Spaniards to shew their peaceable intention, the Spaniards have against them all the rights of war. So we reach the first title by which the Spaniards may justly occupy the provinces and states of the Barbarians, viz. *the title of war for the just cause of the refusal of natural rights.*

Title 2. The Propagation of the Christian Religion.

The second legitimate title which may be alleged in support of Spanish occupation of Barbarian lands connects itself with *the propagation of the Christian Religion.* Proceeding in the same syllogistic manner, and referring step by step to *Jus Divinum*, *Jus Naturale*, and *Jus Gentium* and to conclusions already established, Victoria seeks to demonstrate, (1) that Christians have the right of preaching and proclaiming the Word in the provinces of the Barbarians; (2) that the Pope may, in the exercise of his temporal power *in ordine ad spiritualia,* commit the work of evangelisation to the Spaniards, interdicting all others from the work, or even from commerce with the Barbarians, should the interest of the Christian mission demand it; (3) that if the Indians permit the Spaniards freely and without hindrance to preach the Gospel, it is not, whether they receive the Word or not, lawful on the plea of evangelisation to make war on them or to occupy their lands; (4) that should the Indians, on the other hand, hinder the preaching of the Gospel, the Spaniards

(1) Christians have the right to preach to the Indians. (2) The Pope may commit the work to the Spaniards. (3) If the Indians hinder the preachers all necessary means may be employed to carry on the work; so the Indian lands may be occupied.

may employ the means necessary for their conversion, and, should they be otherwise unable to effect that conversion, may proceed to occupy the lands and provinces of the recalcitrants, to erect new lords and depose old, and to prosecute the rights of war. Victoria closes this argument with a characteristic warning. *Sed considerandum valde est quod Paul. dicit,* 1 ad Cor. 6. *Omnia mihi licent, sed non omnia expediunt. Hæc enim omnia quæ dicta sunt, intelliguntur per se loquendo. Fieri enim potest, ut per hæc bella, cædes et spolia, potius impediretur conversio barbarorum, quam quæreretur et propagaretur. Et ideo hoc in primis cavendum est, ne offendiculum ponatur Evangelio. Si enim ponatur, cessandum esset ab hac ratione Evangelizandi, et alia quærenda esset.*

Title 3. Defence of Indian converts.

Title 4. Papal appointment of Christian prince upon petition of Christian converts.

Title 5. Protection against tyranny.

Title 6. True and voluntary election.

Title 7. Conquest in assistance of Indian allies.

The remaining legitimate titles may be shortly dismissed. Victoria is satisfied, that (*Title* 3) it is lawful for the Spaniards to take up the defence of Indian converts whom their rulers are seeking to bring back to idolatry; (*Title* 4), that the Pope may for sufficient cause or upon their petition give a Christian prince to Christian converts; (*Title* 5), that the Spaniards may interfere to protect innocent men from the tyranny of their barbarous rulers; (*Title* 6), that by true and voluntary election the Barbarians may accept the king of Spain as their prince; and (*Title* 7), that the Spaniards may legitimately acquire provinces by right of war in a contest waged on the request of Barbarian allies against their assailants. He suggests as matter of debate whether a title could not be founded upon the incompetence of the Barbarians for the constitution and administration of a legitimate republic, even within human and civil bounds.

Relectio VI. The Law of War.

§ 124. Led on by the preceding discussion, Victoria in his sixth *Relectio* treats of the Law of War. He advances four general questions:—(1) Is it lawful for Christians to make war at all? (2) With whom lies the

[1] *Reverendi Patris Fratris Francisci a Victoria De Indis sive de jure belli Hispanorum in barbaros, Relectio Posterior.*

power to wage or declare war? (3) What can and ought to be a cause of just war? (4) What may be done in a just war, and how far may one proceed against enemies? In Victoria's treatment of these problems, the reader, who is unprepared for the surprises of the literature of the Reformation Age, will be astonished to discover the setting forth of principles which the historian of international practice is wont to represent as entirely modern, and to connect with the wars of Marlborough and Villars rather than with the furious contests of the sixteenth century and the era of the Thirty Years' War.

(1) Is it lawful for Christians to make war?

§ 125. (1) It is lawful, rules Victoria, for Christians to wage war alike in offence and defence. He so concludes on the authority of arguments grounded in the opinion of Augustine, in Reason, in the Law of Nature, in the written Law of the Old Testament, uncontradicted in the New, and in the usage of good men in the past.

(2) With whom lies the power to declare or wage war?

(2) Who then may authorise the making of war? In self-defence even a private person may take up arms and wage war. In general any commonwealth (*respublica*) has power to declare and wage war. So a prince who wields the authority of a commonwealth may declare and make war. But what is a commonwealth? *Est perfecta Respublica, aut communitas quæ est per se totum, id est, quæ non est alterius Resp. pars, sed quæ habet proprias leges, proprium consilium, et proprios magistratus, quale est regnum Castellæ et Aragoniæ, principatus Venetorum, et alii similes.* Such a commonwealth, or prince, and such only, has the right, save under particular custom, to declare war.

(3) What are causes of just war?

(3) With respect to causes of just war, (i) *Caussa justi belli non est diversitas religionis.* So St Thomas Aquinas and the great Doctors. (ii) *Non est justa caussa belli, amplificatio imperii.* (iii) *Nec est justa caussa belli, aut gloria propria, aut aliud commodum principis.* War is to be waged for the good of the commonwealth, not for the private advantage of the prince. To act

otherwise is to accord to a people the position of slaves. (iv) *Unica est et sola caussa justa inferendi bellum, injuria accepta*, and (v) *Injuria quælibet et quantavis non sufficit ad bellum inferendum.*

(4) What measure of force is allowable in war? (i) *In bello licet omnia facere quæ necessaria sunt ad defensionem boni publici.* (ii) *Licet recuperare omnes res perditas et illarum præcipium.* (iii) *Licet occupare ex bonis hostium impensam belli et omnia damna ab hostibus injuste illata.* (iv) *Ulterius etiam progredi potest princeps justi belli, quantum scilicet necesse est ad parandam pacem et securitatem ab hostibus.* (v) *Nec tantum hoc licet, sed etiam parta victoria, recuperatis rebus, et pace etiam et securitate habita, licet vindicare injuriam ab hostibus acceptam, et animadvertere in hostes, et punire illos pro injuriis illatis.* **(4) What measure of force is allowable in war?**

Numerous doubtful cases are noted by Victoria as arising out of these considerations. Is it sufficient for a just war that the prince believes his cause to be just? Are subjects bound to examine the causes of war, or may they wage war on the mere command of their prince? What is to be done when the justice of the case is doubtful, each side having apparent and probable reasons? Is one who wages a war in ignorance of its injustice bound to make restitution on becoming convinced of that injustice? In the handling of these and other similar problems, Victoria consistently adopts the stricter view. His attitude becomes of peculiar interest when he approaches the examination of the limits of belligerent legal force in respect of particular classes of persons.

(*a*) Is it lawful, asks Victoria, in any case to slay in war the guiltless (*innocentes*)? His reply would win the approval of a Benjamin Franklin. It may be argued, he says, that since the slaughter of such is mentioned with commendation in the Old Testament, and "all Scripture is written for our learning," that, if it be lawful to make war at all, it is lawful to slay such persons. The correct conclusion, however, is clear. *Nunquam licet per* **(*a*) Is it lawful to slay *innocentes*?**

se et ex intentione interficere innocentes. It is not lawful to kill women and children even in war against the Turks. *Imo idem videtur judicium de innoxiis agricolis apud Christianos, imo de alia gente togata et pacifica, quia omnes præsumuntur innocentes nisi contrarium constaret. Hac etiam ratione sequitur, quod nec licet interficere nec peregrinos nec hospites qui versantur apud hostes, quia præsumuntur innocentes nec re vera sunt hostes. Eadem ratione nec clericos, nec religiosos, quia præsumuntur innocentes in bello, nisi constet de contrario,*
Rel. VI. 36. *ut cum actualiter pugnant.* Incidentally guiltless persons may be slain even knowingly, as when a town is besieged and fired upon, but only when the war cannot be otherwise carried on; when, for example, the town *must* be taken.

(*b*) Is it lawful to despoil *innocentes?*

(*b*) Is it lawful to spoil the guiltless? Yes, says Victoria, if the war cannot be otherwise sufficiently effectively waged. The wealth of the guiltless enriches the enemy: their money may accordingly be taken, their food destroyed, their horses killed. If war can be effectively (*satis commode*) carried on without the spoiling of peasants and other innoxious persons, they ought not to be
s. 40. spoiled: *bellum fundatur in injuria.* If, nevertheless, enemies are unwilling to restore property wrongfully taken, and the injured individual cannot otherwise secure redress, he may under *literæ marcharum aut repræsalium* take satisfaction where he can, at the expense of guiltless and guilty alike.

(*c*) May captives be enslaved?

(*c*) Furthermore boys and other harmless individuals may be made captive to be held to ransom, but slavery, although a legitimate consequence of capture in a war with Saracens, is not a lawful result of capture *jure gentium inter Christianos.*

(*d*) May hostages be put to death?

(*d*) Hostages may not be put to death upon a breach of faith by the enemy, unless they belong to the arm-bearing class.

(*e*) Is it lawful to slay all active enemies?

(*e*) Is it lawful to slay in war all the noxious?

It is lawful, says Victoria, (i) to slay in actual fight all who resist *quamdiu res est in periculo.* It is even lawful

(ii) to slay noxious enemies after victory has been secured and the issue is no longer doubtful: so *Deut.* xx. But such slaughter, being grounded in punishment, is only legitimate where it is proportioned to the offence, and when peace and security are otherwise unobtainable. Slaughter of prisoners by way of punishment is not in itself unjust, *sed quia in bello multa jure gentium constituta sunt, videtur receptum consuetudine et usu belli, ut captivi parta victoria (nisi forte sunt profugæ) et periculo transeunte non interficiantur, et servandum est jus gentium, eo modo, quo inter bonos viros servari consuetum est.* ss. 48, 49.

(*f*) Is it lawful to give up a state to plunder? Things captured in war justly belong to the taker to the extent of satisfaction for property wrongfully carried off, and even of expenses; and all movables, although they exceed the measure of compensation for loss, belong to the occupier *jure gentium. Sed ex hac determinatione sequitur dubium. An liceat permittere militibus civitatem in prædam. Respondetur, ... Hoc per se non est illicitum, si necessarium est ad bellum gerendum, vel deterrendos hostes, vel ad accendendum militum animos. Ita Sylvester* ver. *bellum* § 10. *Sicut etiam licet incendere civitatem ex rationabili caussa. Sed tamen quia ex hujus modi permissionibus sequuntur multa sæva, crudelia præter omnem humanitatem, quæ a barbaris militibus committuntur innocentum cædes; et cruciatus, virginum raptus, matronarum stupra, templorum spolia: ideo sine dubio, sine magna necessitate et caussa maxima civitatem Christianam prædæ tradere periniquum est. Sed si ita necessitas belli exigat, non est illicitum, etiam si credibile sit, quod milites aliqua hujus modi fœda et illicita patrent, quæ tamen duces et interdicere et quam possunt prohibere tenentur.*

(*f*) Is it lawful to give up the hostile state to plunder?

Victoria, *Relectiones Theologicæ*, VI. 52.

(*g*) Concluding with a discussion of the circumstances under which hostile territory may be occupied, tribute imposed on conquered enemies, and defeated monarchs deposed, Victoria finally lays down three general canons

(*g*) What are the rights of the conqueror in hostile territory?

for the guidance of belligerents:—(I) A prince, who possesses the power to wage, ought not to seek occasion and causes of, war. (II) Having a good cause, he ought not to wage war for the destruction of the people against whom the war is made, but for the obtaining of his rights, the defence of his country and state, and the obtaining of peace and security. (III) Having won the victory and brought the war to a close, he ought to conduct himself moderately, and use his triumph with Christian modesty, comporting himself as just arbiter between the belligerent commonwealths.

(γ) The Politicians and Political Philosophers.

§ 126. Side by side with Victoria and the scholars of whom he may be taken as representative, we may recognise another class of contributories to the swelling current of international legal thought. Of historians, memoir writers and poets, it is impossible to speak in detail, albeit these exercised no unimportant influence in the generation and popularisation of those ideas which govern the progress of civilisation. But it were unjust to pass over without particular reference the work of a succession of labourers in the allied fields of politics and political philosophy. In the thirteenth, fourteenth and fifteenth centuries Occam, Marsiglio of Padua, Dante, and other bold spirits, defending or challenging the respective claims of Emperor or Pope, prepared the way for a better understanding of the foundations of sovereignty[1]. In the

In the 13th, 14th and 15th centuries Occam, Marsiglio of Padua, Dante and others

[1] For an account of the work of William of Occam, Marsiglio of Padua, and other early challengers of the overweening claims of the Papacy, see Nys, *Les Origines du Droit International*, Chap. 2. A collection of mediæval tractates written in support of the rights of the Emperor, including Occam's *Disputatio inter Clericum et Militem*, Dante's *De Monarchia*, the *Tractatus de Potestate Regia et Papali* of John of Paris (1305), and the *De Ortu et Authoritate Imperii Romani* of Æneas Sylvius Piccolomini (afterwards Pope Pius II.), was made by Simon Schard, under the title of *Sylloge Historico-Politico-Ecclesiastica*. Another large collection, including the *Octo quæstiones super Potestate ac Dignitate Papali* (1336) and other works of Occam, the *Epistolæ de Juribus Imperii Romani* of Petrarch (1360), and the *Tractatus de Translatione Imperii* (1313) and *Defensor Pacis* (1324) of Marsiglio of Padua,

sixteenth, whilst Macchiavelli discoursed of the policy of rulers in the light of his peculiar experience of Italian statecraft, Sir Thomas More fell back upon Plato and Xenophon, and depicted the institutions of the ideal commonwealth, and Jean Bodin defined and elaborated the conceptions of the being and functions of the State.

dispute concerning the respective claims of Pope and Emperor.

§ 127. Nicolo Macchiavelli (1469–1527), secretary to the Ten of Florence, and as such engaged actively for fourteen years in the troubled field of Italian diplomacy, wrote, amongst other historical and political essays, a short treatise which made his name a by-word to subsequent generations. This was the famous *Il Principe*, which was published in 1532, after the author's death, under the sanction of Pope Clement VII. (Giulio de Medici). Destined to earn the favour of the new ducal rulers of Florence, by whom as a member of the republican party the author had been banished, imprisoned and put to the rack, and dedicated to Lorenzo de Medici, to whom as to "a new prince" is held up for imitation the political conduct of Cæsar Borgia[1], it is no marvel that the book contains propositions at which posterity looked askance. "A Prince is to have no "other design, nor thought, nor study, but War, and the "Arts and Disciplines of it; for indeed that is the only "profession worthy of a Prince, and is of so much more "importance that it not only preserves those who are born "Princes in their patrimonies, but advances men of private "condition to that Honorable degree." "A Prince that "is wise and prudent cannot, nor ought not to keep his "*parole*, when the keeping of it is to his prejudice, and "the causes for which he promised removed." "A Prince "is likewise much esteemed when he shows himself a "sincere friend or a generous Enemy, That is when without "any hesitation he declares himself in favour of one

Nicolo Macchiavelli (1469—1527), discourses of the policy of rulers.

Rose, *New Biographical Dict.* Art. "Macchiavelli."

"The Prince" throws a lurid light on contemporary Italian politics.

The Prince, c. 14.

Ibid. c. 18.

was published at Frankfurt by N. Hoffmann, in 1614: see *Monarchia S. Romani Imperii*.

[1] Macchiavelli had spent three months in the camp of Cæsar Borgia as Florentine envoy. *The Prince* was probably written about 1513.

"against another, which as it is more frank and Princely, "so it is more profitable than to stand neuter; for if two "of your potent Neighbors be at Wars, they are either of "such condition that you are to be afraid of the Victor or "not: In either of which cases it will be always more for "your benefit to discover yourself freely, and make a "fair War.......Those Princes who are ill advised, to avoid "some present danger follow the Neutral way, are most "commonly ruin'd." These and other like maxims throw a lurid light upon the state of contemporary political thought in Italy and even in the vestibules of Popes.

The Prince, c. 21.

Sir Thomas More (1478—1535) depicts the ideal common-wealth. The *Utopia*, 1516.

§ 128. A work of a very different order was the *Utopia* of Sir Thomas More (1478–1535), which first appeared at Louvain in 1516[1].

Under cover of a sketch of the distant republic of "Nowhere" the author reflects upon the political and social condition of the states of his day and in particular of his own England. Amidst the flashing play of wit from merry laughter to keenest irony, it is by no means easy to determine how far each and every institution ascribed to the Utopians conformed to More's serious ideals. It may be doubted, for example, whether More seriously intended to commend to the imitation of contemporary belligerents certain of the customs in war-waging which were practised by the men of "Nowhere." "Theyre chyefe and princypall purpose in warre ys to "obteyne that thynge, whyche yf they had before obteyned, "they wolde not have moved battayle. But if that be "not possible, they take so cruell vengeaunce of them "whych be in the fault, that ever after they be aferde to "doo the lyke. Thys ys theyre cheyffe and pryncypall "intente, whyche they immedyatelye and fyrste of all

More makes some suggestions which run counter even to contemporary notions as to legitimate belligerency;

[1] The work was written in Latin. Other editions in the same language were issued at Paris in 1517, at Basle by Froben in 1518, at Venice in 1519, at Louvain in 1548, 1565, and 1566, at Cologne in 1555, at Basle in 1563, at Wittenberg in 1591. The first English translation was that of Ralph Robynson, published in 1551. See the Rev. J. H. Lupton's Introduction to his Oxford edition of 1895.

"prosequute and sette forwarde; but yet so, that they "be more cyrcumspecte in avoydynge and eschewynge "jeopardyes, then they be desyerous of prayse and re-"nowne. Therfore immediatly after that warre is ones "solemply denounced, they procure manye proclamations, "signed with their owne commen seale, to be sette up "preuilie at one time in their ennemyes lande, in places "mooste frequented. In thyes proclamations they pro-"mysse greate rewardes to hym that will kyll their "enemies prince; and sumwhat lesse gyftes, but them "verye greate also, for everye heade of them, whose names "be in the sayde proclamation conteined. They be those "whome they count their chieffe adversaries, next unto "the prince . . . . Thys custome of byinge and sellynge "adversaryes amonge other people ys dysallowed, as a "cruell acte of a basse and a cowardyshe mynde. But "they in thys behalfe thynke themselfes muche prayse "woorthye, as who lyke wyse men by thys meanes dyspatche "greate warres wyth oute annye battell or skyrnyshe. "Yea, they cownte yt also a dede of pyty and mercye, "because that by the deathe of a few offenders the lyves "of a great numbre of ynnocentes, as well of their own "men as also of their enemies, be raunsomed and saved, "which in fighting shoulde have bene slaine. For they "doo no lesse pytye the basse and commen sorte of theyre "enemyes people, then they doo theyre owne; knowynge "that they be dryven to warre agaynste theyre wylles by "the furyous madnes of theyre prynces and heades."

Utopia, ii. c. 8. Robynson's translation, ed. J. H. Lupton, p. 248.

he elsewhere denounces unnecessary war

However uncertain in the foregoing passage may be the proportion of earnest and grim jest, there can be no hesitation as to the character of the sentiments covered by other portions of the same chapter, "Of Warfare" (*De Re Militari*). "Warre or battle as a thinge very "beastelye[1], and yet to no kynde of beastes in so muche "use as it is to man, they do detest and abhorre; and, "contrarye to the custome almost of all other natyons,

[1] *Bellum utpote rem plane beluinam.* A play covering an etymological derivation, which found favour with many mediæval opponents of war.

"they cownte nothinge so much against glorie, as glory "gotten in warre. And therefore, though they do daily "practice and exercise themselfes in the discypline of "warre, and that not only the men, but also the women, "upon certeyne appoynted dayes, leste they shoulde be "to seke in the feat of armes yf nead should requyre; yet "they never to goo to battayle, but other in the defence "of their owne cowntreye, or to dryve owte of theyr frendes "lande the enemyes that be comen in, or by their powre to "deliver from yocke and bondage of tyrannye some people "that be oppressed with tyranny. Whyche thynge they "doo of meere pytye and compassion....Truce taken with "theire enemies for a shorte time they do so fermelye and "faythfully keape, that they wyll not breake it; no not "though they be theire unto provoked. They do not "waste nor destroy their enemies lande with forraginges, "nor they burne not up theire corne. Yea, they save it "as muche as maye be from beinge overrune and troden "downe, other with men or horses; thynkynge that it "groweth for theire owne use and proffyt. They hurt no "man that is unarmed, onless he be an espiale. All cities "that be yelded unto them, they defende. And suche as "they wynne by force of assaute they nother dispoyle nor "sacke; but them that withstode and dyswaded the "yeldynge up of the same they put to death; the other "souldiours they punnyshe with bondage. All the weake "multitude they leave untouched. If they knowe that "anye cytezeins counselled to yelde and rendre up the "cities, to them they gyve parte of the condempned mens "goodes. The resydewe they distribute and gyve freely "amonge them, whose helpe they had in the same warre. "For none of themselfes taketh anye portion of the praye." Here we have the *Cyropaedia* of the early sixteenth century.

and recommends sundry mitigations in war practice, e.g. as to destruction,

non-combatants,

the storm of cities.

Utopia, Book ii. c. 8. Lupton's Edit. pp. 243, 263.

Foreign exiles are to be allowed to settle in vacant common lands.

Another of the Utopian doctrines was not without its influence upon Grotius himself. "They counte this the "moste just cause of warre, when any people holdeth a "piece of grounde voyde and vacaunt to no good nor "profitable use, kepyng other from the use and possession "of it, whiche notwithstandyng by the lawe of nature "ought thereof to be nowryshed and relieved."

Utopia, ii. c. 5. Lupton's Ed. p. 155.

Jean Bodin (c. 1530—96), elaborates the conception of the State.

§ 129. Whilst More found his inspiration in the *Republic* of Plato and the *Cyropaedia* of Xenophon, Jean Bodin fell back upon the *Politics* of Aristotle.

An Angevin lawyer, who had failed to obtain practice as an advocate at Paris, Bodin turned to literature, and obtained the patronage of Henry III., and subsequently of the Duke of Alençon. Settling at Laon he was chosen deputy to the States General for the Tiers État of Vermandois. In 1577 he published at Paris his most celebrated book, *De la République.* The book promptly ran through several editions[1], was translated into various languages, and was adopted as a text-book in political science alike in French and foreign Universities. Though by no means a work of supereminent genius, it is not undeserving of the attention accorded to it.

Les Six Livres de la République, 1577.

The first book is of special interest to the historian of International Law.

Definition of a Republic,

Liv. i. c. 1, *Quelle est la fin principale de la République bien ordonnée.*

In his opening chapter Bodin defines a Republic as being a legitimate government (*droit gouvernement*) of several Households (*mesnages*) and of that which is common to them, with sovereign power. Legitimate government is to be contradistinguished from such societies as those of brigands or pirates.

and of its constituent, the Household.

Liv. i. c. 2, *Du Mesnage et la différence entre la République et la famille.*

A Household is a legitimate government of several subjects under the obedience of the Head of a Family, and of that which is proper to them. Sovereignty is essential to the conception of a Republic, but over and above Sovereignty there must be something in common. *Ce n'est pas République s'il n'y a rien de public.*

Nature of Family Government.

Turning to family government Bodin treats of the nature and expediency of the power of husband, father,

[1] A Latin version was published by the author in 1586. Amongst other French editions was one printed at Lyons in 1593. This is the edition followed in the text.

Liv. i. c. 3, *De la puissance maritale.* c. 4, *De la puissance paternelle.* c. 5, *De la puissance seigneuriale.*

and lord, in dealing with which last he impugns the reasons commonly alleged in support of slavery, and in particular the favourite justification based on the preservation of the life of the captive.

The Head of the Family as the Citizen.

Liv. i. c. 6, *Du citoyen et la différence d'entre le subject, le citoyen, l'estranger, la ville, cité, et République.*

Classification of Citizens.

The union of Heads of Families constitutes the first natural body of citizens. Republics originate in a measure of subjection. The Citizen may in fact be defined as "the free subject, holding under the sovereignty of another." Citizens are natural born or naturalised. In the assignment of citizenship by birth, states follow different rules. A naturalised citizen is "one who has avowed the sovereignty of another and been by him received." Citizens natural born and naturalised, together with freedmen, when they are governed by the sovereign power of one or more common sovereign lords, constitute a Republic, even though they be diverse in respect of laws, language, customs, religion or nation; if all the citizens are governed by the same laws and customs, their union is not only a Republic but a City, distributed though they be through many towns, villages, and provinces. So we may distinguish between Subjects, Citizens, Townsmen, and Strangers; and between the Republic, the City, and the Town. The Republic and the City are legal, the Town is a local conception. Except on just occasion, the rights of the Burgess are not lost, nor yet the power of the Prince over his subjects, by change of place or country, any more than the vassal can exempt himself from faith to his lord or the lord relinquish the protection of the vassal without consent on both sides, the obligation being mutual and reciprocal. But if the one or the other has secured consent, express or tacit, and the subject, quitting his Prince, has been avowed by another by the sufferance of the first, he is no longer bound to the obedience which he formerly owed. Mere residence for the qualifying length of time does not work a change of rights without the obtaining of letters of naturalisation. If a stranger, who has obtained letters of naturalisation abroad, does not continue to reside there, he loses the right to which he

Definition of the City.

Change of Citizenship, how effected.

pretends, for a double fiction is not admitted in law. Not only are the rights of citizen and non-citizen distinguishable, but citizens differ amongst themselves in respect of privilege.

Rights which distinguish the Citizen from the Stranger:

The most notable privilege which the citizen possesses as contrasted with the stranger is that of making a testament and disposing of his property according to the customs, or of leaving his nearest relatives heirs; the stranger is devoid of right in either particular, and his property passes to the lord of the place where he dies.

droit d'aubaine;

The *droit d'aubaine* is no new creation of French law, but common to Naples, Sicily, and the Empire of the East. In England particular lords have the right within the limits of their lands.

limitation upon right of ownership;

The laws of various states differ in respect of the rights which they allow to strangers: some states refuse to strangers the right to hold a single foot of land. The kings of France have with extraordinary goodness remitted the *droit d'aubaine* in favour of merchants attending particular marts, and the Hanseatic merchants are exempt by privilege granted by Louis le Jeune and confirmed by Charles VIII.

security in litigation

Strangers resorting to law as plaintiffs are everywhere required to give special security for appearance and to abide judgment; defendants, whether subjects or strangers, give no security for abiding judgment at common law, but such security is now required of strangers by Arrêt of the Parliament of Paris of 1567.

droit de marque;

Reprisals cannot be exercised against subjects, but strangers are exposed to the effects of the *droit de marque*.

expulsion of strangers;

Strangers may be expelled from the country not only in time of war, when even Ambassadors are dismissed, but in time of peace.

detention of strangers;

In time of open war the stranger may be detained as an enemy *suivant la loy de guerre*; at other times he cannot be detained, unless he be bound by contract or by delict or have become the subject of another prince without the leave of his own, in which last case the lord possesses the right to arrest. The best defence which the Imperialists urged for the murder of Rinçon and Fregoze was that the one, a Spaniard and natural born subject of the Emperor, the other a Genoese under his protection, had entered into the service of his enemy, and report went that they were going to stir up a new war against him. A subject cannot exempt himself from the power of his natural lord even by becoming a Sovereign prince in a foreign land. The Queen of England recalled the Earl of Lennox and his son the King of Scotland, and, upon their disobedience, confiscated their property. The subject is bound by the personal regulations of his prince even in respect of proceedings abroad. In the enforcement of their rights in this particular princes are accustomed to employ among themselves rogatory commissions or *droit de marque*, to compel their subjects to obey them or to avoke action commenced against them otherwise than in cases permitted by law. As to differences in rights between subject and subject they are infinite.

impossibility of throwing off natural allegiance; personal obligation of the subject.

Differences between subject and subject in point of rights.

The bond of Protection between states constitutes a species of Confederation.

Liv. i. c. 7, De ceux qui sont en protection; et la différence entre les alliés, estrangers et subjects.

A clear definition of the meaning of Protection is essential to the right understanding of the facts as to Republics. The word Protection in general extends to all subjects who are within the obedience of one prince or lordship, but in treaties the word has a special application and imports no subjection on the part of him who is under protection or of command on the part of the protector. It imports on the side of the protected, honour and reverence only. The right of protection is the grandest, most honourable and most magnificent of rights. Protection is to be distinguished from patronage and vassalage. Protection is, in fact, as between sovereigns a species of confederation. An unequal alliance does not involve subjection, though it may imply superiority and honorary prerogative.

Alliances classified.

Referring by way of further explanation to the nature of alliances and treaties in general the author distinguishes treaties as made with friends, with enemies, or with neutrals. Treaties with enemies are for peace and friendship, or truces, or for some particular settlement. Treaties with friends are for equal or unequal alliance; they are defensive only, or offensive and defensive. Treaties of neutrality are made between subjects of hostile princes: they may be perpetual or for a limited time. Under the name of enemy must be understood one who has denounced, or upon whom has been denounced, war in open fashion by word or deed. In ancient days treaties of alliance had sometimes for an object the granting of mutual justice, but little by little the door of Justice has now been thrown open to strangers. Of confederations deserving of special examination may be put forward those of the Romans and Latins, of the Swiss Cantons, of the Amphictyonic cities, of the republics of ancient Gaul, of the Achaeans, of the Ionic towns, of the Ætolians and of the Grisons. The Empire is not a Monarchy, but a pure Aristocracy composed of Princes of the Empire, the Seven Electors, and the Imperial Cities.

Who is our enemy?

Examples of Confederations.

In these discussions the author makes frequent instructive reference to recent events, treaties, and enactments. A single example may be cited. "*Quand le subject d'un Prince se retire en la terre d'un autre, il est aussi en sa protection, de sorte que s'il est poursuyvi par l'ennemi, et pris prisonnier en la terre d'un autre Prince souverain, il n'est point prisonnier du poursuyvant, comme il fut jugé par la loy des armes, au pourpalé de paix, qui fut entre le Roy de France & l'Empereur Charles V., l'an M.D.LV. quand il fut question des prisonniers Imperiaux, que les François avoyent pris au Comté de Guynes, qui estoit lors en la subjection des Anglois: il fut soustenu par le Chancelier d'Angleterre, qu'ils ne pouuoyent estre tenus prisonnier estans en la terre et protection des Anglois: combien que le contraire se pouuoit dire: car jaçoit qu'il ne fust permis de quester, ny leuer la proye en la terre d'autruy, si est ce qu'il est permis l'ayant leuee en sa terre, la poursuyure sur le fond d'autruy: vray est qu'il y a une exception, si le seigneur ne l'empesche, comme de faict le Milor Grey Gouuerneur de Calais & de Guynes, estoit suruenu durant la poursuite, & print en sa garde ceux que les Francois avoyent pris.*"

Neutral territory affords protection to belligerents.

Bodin, *De la République*, i. c. 7, p. 104.

What is Sovereignty? *Liv. i. c. 8, De la souveraineté.*

Sovereignty, continues Bodin, is the principal foundation of every Republic. No mandatory for a limited period, however great his power, is sovereign. The Roman Dictator was not sovereign. Sovereignty has no limit either of power, change or time. Power conferred for life, though very great, if it be restricted in any fashion, is not sovereignty, but he is sovereign upon whom a people has conferred for life absolute and unlimited authority. A sovereign cannot be under the command of another, and must have power to give the law to subjects and to abolish laws which are not beneficial in order to make others. But the absolute power of the sovereign does not extend to the laws of God or of Nature. Is a prince subject to the laws which he has sworn to keep? He is not bound by his own laws nor by the laws of his predecessors, but he is bound by his conventions, they being just and reasonable, and in the observance of which the subjects in general or in particular have an interest. The sovereign prince is bound by the law to which he has sworn so long as it continues just. He cannot set aside any laws which concern the state of the kingdom or its establishment, in so far as they are annexed and united to the crown. If the so-called sovereign prince be subject to the estates of the realm, he is neither prince nor sovereign, and the Republic is neither kingdom nor monarchy but a pure aristocracy. But the sovereignty of the monarch is in no wise altered or diminished by the mere presence of estates, but is rather rendered the more illustrious. Being bound by the law of nature, the sovereign cannot take the goods of another without just and reasonable cause. If a sovereign prince have in the quality of sovereign contracted in respect of a matter which touches the state and for the profit of the state, his successors are bound; moreover if the treaty be made with the consent of estates, of the towns and principal communities, of Parliaments, or of the princes and great lords, even although the treaty be prejudicial to the public, the faith and obligation of the subjects are required. But if the prince have contracted

It is unlimited, *secus* the Laws of God and of Nature.

When does a sovereign prince bind by his contracts his successors in title?

without the consent of those before mentioned with a foreign state, or even with a subject, on a matter which touches the public and the contract is very prejudicial to that public, the successor in the state is in no way bound.

Classification of tributary and feudatory princes. *Liv.* i. c. 9, *Du Prince tributaire ou feudataire.*

In his ninth chapter, treating of tributary or feudatory princes, Bodin draws a distinction between princes who are merely under protection and princes who hold by faith and homage. He recognises amongst princes six grades short of absolute sovereignty: (1) the tributary prince who retains all the rights of sovereignty save the payment of tribute; (2) the protected prince; (3) the sovereign prince of one country who owes service to another as vassal in respect of some particular fief; (4) the vassal prince who, holding no other lordship, is not a subject of the lord of whom he holds; (5) the liege vassal who is not a natural subject of his sovereign lord; (6) the vassal who is a natural subject of his sovereign lord. These distinctions introduce an interesting detailed examination of feudal ties existing amongst contemporary states. Here, it may be noted, he makes short work of the claims of the Emperor as World Lord. "*Bartol a laissé par escrit que tous ceux-là sont heretiques, qui ne croyent pas que l'Empereur soit seigneur de tout le monde: ce qui ne merite point de responce: veu que les Empereurs de Romme ne furent jamais seigneurs de la trentiéme partie de la terre; et que l'Empire d'Allemagne n'est pas la dixiéme partie de l'Empire des Rommains.*" He is somewhat more lenient towards the pretensions of the Pope, in view of the frequent successes of Pontiffs in wresting acknowledgments of their title, but his French patriotism rises superior to his Roman Churchmanship. "*Mais quoy que le Pape pretende la souueraineté non seulement spirituelle ains aussi temporelle sur tous les Princes Chrestiens, & qu'il ait acquis ceste puissance sur les uns par tiltres & cessions, sur les autres par prescription et jouissance, si est-ce que le Royaume de France s'est toujours garenty, quoy qu'ils se soyent efforcés de l'assubjectir à eux, excommuniant noz Roys qui n'y vouloyent point entendre, à fin*

The World Lordship of Emperor

De la République. *Liv.* i. c. 9, p. 189.

and Pope challenged.

de faire revolter leurs subjects, commes ils faisoyent és autres pays."

De la République, i. c. 9. p. 201.

Precedence amongst Sovereign Equals.

The chapter closes with a brief account of the degrees of honour observed amongst princes who are sovereign equals. The first place amongst Christian princes after the Pope belongs to the Emperor, the second to France, who has lately vindicated her title against the novel assertions of Spain.

The notes of Sovereignty. *Liv.* i. c. 10, *Des vrayes marques de Souveraineté.*

In the final chapter of this first book Bodin seeks to ascertain the distinguishing notes of sovereignty. He finds that they are principally five: (1) the power of legislation for all in general and each in particular, without the consent of superior, equal or inferior; (2) the power of declaring war and making peace; (3) the power of instituting principal officials; (4) the power of final appeal; (5) the power of pardon. These powers should never without strong reason be delegated either by title of office or by commission. Other powers, such as that of coining money and that of taxation, naturally attend upon the power of legislation, but are not so essentially reserved for the hand of the sovereign. "*Mais les droits de la mer n'appartiennent qu'au Prince Souuerain, qui peut imposer charges jusques à XXX lieues loing de sa terre*[1], *s'il n'y a Prince Souuerain plus pres qui l'empesche: comme il a esté jugé pour le Duc de Sauoye: & n'est permis qu'au Prince Souuerain de bailler bref de conduire, que les Italiens appellent guidage, ny de prendre le droit de bris, ou de Vvarech, qui est l'un des articles porté par l'ordonnance de l'Empereur Frideric II. qui n'estoit point anciennement usité entre les Princes Souuerains: neantmoins est aujourd'huy commun a tous ayans port sur mer. Et me souuient auoir entendu que l'Ambassadeur de l'Empereur fit plaintes au privé conseil du Roy Henry II. l'an M.D.LVI. de deux galeres prises par Jourdan Ursin, qui avoyent souffert bris en Corsegue: le Connestable luy remonstra que*

The maritime rights of a Sovereign Prince: jurisdiction, dues, *guidage*, wreck,

[1] Bodin cites as his authority for this proposition Baldus in *Rub. de rer. divis. col.* 1, and in l. *cum proponas. de naut. fœnore*, C. Compare *ante*, p. 163, note.

le bris est confisqué au seigneur souuerain, & que c'est la coustume generale, non seulement és pays de l'obeïssance du Roy, mais aussi en toute la mer du Leuant & du Ponent. Aussi est-il certain que Antoine Doria ne fit jamais instance du bris de deux galeres confisquées par le Prieur de Caporia." *De la République, Liv.* i. c. 10, p. 246.

"*Quant au droit de marque, ou de represailles, que les Princes Souverains ont privativement à tous autres, il n'estoit pas anciennement propre au Prince Souverain, ains il estoit permis à chacun sans congé ny du Magistrat, ny du Prince user de represailles, que les Latins ce semble appelloyent* Clarigatio: *toutesfois les Princes peu à peu donnerent ceste puissance aux Gouverneurs et Magistrats: et en fin ils ont reservé ce droit à leur majesté pour la seurté de la paix et des trefves, qui souvent estoyent rompues par la temerité des particuliers, abusans du droit de marque.*" *De la République, Liv.* i. c. 10, p. 248.

Letters of marque.

The second and subsequent books of *De la République* are of less interest to the student of International Law than to his fellow of Political Philosophy[1]. The first book alone would, however, sufficiently establish the claim of the author to a high place amongst the contributors to the literature of the Law of Nations. Apart from his very considerable influence in the general spread of

Value of the work of Bodin for the historian of International Law.

[1] In his second book Bodin classifies Commonwealths as being Monarchies, Aristocracies or Democracies. Treating successively of the three forms of Monarchy, viz. Seigneurial, Royal and Tyrannical, he discusses the question whether it is lawful to assassinate a tyrant. Analysing the nature of Aristocracies and of Popular Governments, he refers to the one or to the other various constitutions of antiquity or of his own day. Book III. deals with the functions and authority of senates, of various offices and magistracies, and of the qualities necessary in their members or occupants. It touches also upon the nature of corporations. Book IV., which treats of the beginnings, rise, prosperity, decay and ruin of states, comprises a curious consideration of the influence of stars upon the fortunes of commonwealths. In Book V. Bodin considers the methods which must be followed to accommodate the form of the state to the diversity of men and the means by which the genius (*naturel*) of a people may be ascertained. Book VI. comprises discussions concerning the Censorship of the Press, finance and other matters, including Justice, which is classified as distributive, commutative, and harmonic.

clearer notions as to the nature of Sovereignty and of State-Being, his frequent references to recent events and repeated citations of documents examined by him in person or communicated by named responsible authorities are of the very greatest historical value as throwing the most welcome side-lights upon contemporary international practice.

(δ) The Forerunners.

§ 130. The way was now prepared for the appearance of systematic treatises upon the laws regulating the relations of State and State.

They are mainly men of action who treat of subjects falling within their spheres of active labour.

First came the early forerunners. These were, in general, distinguished men of action, diplomatists and judges, who published comprehensive treatises upon subjects suggested by the course of their active labours. Thus considered works upon *Jus Legationis* came to compete for popular attention with extended examinations of *Jus Belli*.

Conradus Brunus (*circ.* 1491—1563) treats in comprehensive fashion of *Jus Legationis*.

§ 131. Conrad Brunn or Braun, a native of Kirchen, in Würtemberg, after studying the Civil and Canon Law at Tübingen, passed seven years at the Episcopal Court at Würtzburg, whence he removed to the Bavarian service. He was employed in special consultation by Charles V. and Ferdinand I. and appeared with distinction at the Diets of Augsburg, Worms, Spires and Ratisbon. His collected works were reissued in 1561, two years before his death. His fame as a writer upon subjects of international legal interests rests upon a treatise published originally at Mayence in 1548, which deals with the rights and obligations of the legatine office[1].

Moreri, *Grand Dict. Historique.*

His *De Legationibus*, 1548,

Handling his subject well-nigh entirely in the light of Roman Law and of precedents drawn from ancient history, his tractate is mainly of historic interest as illustrating the passage from the mediæval to the modern. Leading the way into a field which was soon to be enriched by a particularly copious literature, it is noteworthy, over and above its recognition of the time-

a link between the mediæval and the modern.

Ompteda, *Litteratur*, pp. 419, 491, 502, 537, 547, 562, 564.

[1] *Conradi Bruni De Legationibus Libri* v. *Mogunt.* MDXLVIII.

honoured general inviolability of legates and their belongings, in its references to the regular credentials of ambassadors, i.e. letters of instruction, of credence and of commendation, and to their usual reception and forms of audience. Incidentally Brunn complains of the wars of his day as being unjust and without declaration, a declaration (*diffidatio*) being in his view essential to a just war. His conception of *Jus Gentium*, as an expansion of *Jus Naturæ* by virtue of usage and the common approval of peoples, has been already referred to.

De Legat. Lib. i. cc. 11, 12.

Lib. iii. c. 8.

Lib. ii. c. 9.

§ 132. Ferdinand Vasquez (1509—1566), an eminent Spanish official and jurist, published at Venice in 1564 a notable treatise, *Illustrium Controversiarum aliorumque usu frequentium Libri tres*[1].

F. Vasquez (1509—1566).

Illustrium Controversiarum Libri Tres, 1564.

Casting aside the notion of World Sovereignty, and repelling expressly the world claims of the Roman emperor[2], Vasquez in his first book asserts the sovereignty of the King of Spain within the limits of his own kingdom. He recognises a composite *Jus Gentium* (*jus gentium primævum, jus gentium secundarium*) or *Jus Naturale et Gentium* as governing the relations of princes and free peoples *inter se*. And he raises and briefly discusses various problems of international legal interest. The question *Bellum an utrinque justum esse possit* advanced likewise by Franciscus a Victoria was familiar to mediæval casuistry. The inquiry *Delictum extra fines regni commissum an puniatur*, descending from canonical glosses *de foro competenti*[3], touches more nearly modern ideas.

He rejects the notion of World Sovereignty.

Lib. i. cc. 20—22.

He recognises a composite *Jus Gentium*.

Lib. i. c. 10, ss. 17, 18; c. 41, s. 30; ii. c. 51, s. 30.

Can war be just on both sides?

Lib. i. c. 9.

May a crime be punished outside the kingdom within which it was committed?

Lib. i. c. 8.

[1] Subsequent editions appeared in 1572, at Antwerp (folio), and in 1595 at Leyden (4to), under the title *Illustrium Controversiarum Aliorumque usu frequentium Libri tres: Authore D. Fernando Vasquio Menchacensi Hispano Jureconsulto præstantissimo, et in summo dominicæ rei Philippi Hispaniarum regis catholici prætorio Senatore.*

I have not seen the Venice edition, but it is referred to in the preface of the subsequent issues.

[2] Vasquez unites with Victoria in the denial that infidels, although they do not recognise Pope or Emperor, may on that account be spoiled of their goods. *Illustr. Controv.* Lib. I. c. 23.

[3] Hostiensis in this connection recognises with peculiar clearness the

Vasquez leads the crusade for *Mare liberum*.

The first place in abiding importance must, however, be assigned to the challenge by Vasquez upon the ground of incompatibility with *Jus Gentium Primævum* of the claims advanced by the Venetians and Genoese to prohibit the navigation by foreigners of the Adriatic and Ligurian seas. *Quod sit contra illud jus, constat, quia non solum maria aut æquora eo jure communia erant, sed etiam reliquæ omnes res immobiles. Et licet ab eo jure postea recessum fuerit ex parte, puta quō ad dominium et proprietatem terrarum, quarum dominium jure naturæ commune, distinctum, et divisum, sicque ab illa communione segregatum fuit* (l. ex hoc jure, §§ de justit. & jur. § jus gentium & § jus autem gentium. Institu. de jure naturali), *tamen diversum fuit, et est in dominio maris, quod ab origine mundi ad hodiernum usque diem est, fuitque semper in communi nulla ex parte immutatum, ut est notum, et quamvis ex Lusitanis magnam turbam sæpe audiverim, in hac esse opinione, ut eorum rex ita præscripserit navigationem Indici occidentalis, ejusdemque vastissimi maris, ita ut reliquis gentibus æquora illa transfretare non liceat, et ex nostrismet Hispanis vulgus in eadem opinione fere esse videatur, ut per vastissimum immensumque pontum ad Indorum regiones, quas potentissimi reges nostri Hispaniarum subegerunt, reliquis mortalium navigare, præterquam Hispanis jus minime sit, quasi ab eis id jus præscriptum fuerit, tamen istorum omnium non minus insanæ sunt opiniones, quam eorum, qui quo ad Genuenses et Venetos in eodem fere somnio esse adsolent, quas sententias ineptiri vel ex eo dilucidius apparet, quod istarum nationum singulare contra se ipsas nequeunt præscribere, hoc est, non respublica Venetiarum contra semet ipsam, non respublica Genuensium contra semet ipsam, non regnum Hispanorum contra semet ipsum, non regnum Lusitanorum contra semet ipsum*[1].

Vasquius, *Illust. Controv., Lib.* ii. c. 89, s. 31.

territorial principle. *Forum censetur secundum fines territorii cujuslibet loci. Et ponitur territorium pro tota terra, in qua quis habet jurisdictionem. Summa Hostiensis*, Lib. II. Rub. 2.

[1] A Franciscan monk, Francis Alphonso de Castro, would appear to have shared with Vasquez the honour of this early challenge of the Genoese and Venetian maritime claims. See Nys, *Les Origines*, p. 382.

Balthazar Ayala (1548—84) treats of the Law of War.

§ 133. Balthazar Ayala (1548–84), Judge Advocate of the Spanish Army in the Netherlands, dedicated to Alexander of Parma from the camp before Tournay, in November 1581, a considerable treatise in three books, *De Jure et officiis bellicis et disciplina militari*, which was published with the significant censorial note, "*Tres hi libri utiles sunt ad conservandum hoc tempore calamitoso disciplinam militarem*[1]."

Lib. i. *De Jure et Officiis Bellicis. Cap.* i. *De Ratione Belli indicendi. Cap.* ii. *De Bello Justo et Justis Belli Causis.*

Prefacing his work with the declaration that there are rights of war as well as of peace, and with the justification of war by Old Testament citation, Ayala begins his first book[2], the only one of the three which is of much international legal interest, with a brief historical sketch of the Roman method of declaring war. Turning forthwith to the definition of *just war* and the *just causes of war*, he advances certain characteristic views. Wars are to be undertaken that men may live in peace. Even from just wars many evils arise. An honest war is nevertheless to be preferred to a shameful peace. *Justa bella sunt jure gentium indicta: et tum jure canonum, tum etiam jure divino permissa.* A Just War predicates the presence of (1) the authority and command of the sovereign prince, in whose hands is reposed the right to make war and peace, and (2) a just and necessary cause. The former may be dispensed with in view of the imminent needs of self-defence; just causes never. Of just causes many may be enumerated. Such are: (i) the defence of empire, person, friend, ally or property; (ii) the recovery of property unjustly and forcibly detained; (iii) the punishment of tort-feasors; (iv) the vindication of wrong, as, for example, the refusal of the right of innocent passage; (v) rebellion. In this last case war is not properly war. Rebels have no claim

What is a "just war"?

[1] *Balthazaris Ayalæ, J. C. et Exercitus regii apud Belgas Supremi Juridici, De Jure et officiis bellicis, et disciplina militari, Libri III.* The first edition seems to have been published at Douay in 1582: a later appeared at Antwerp in 1597.

[2] In his second and third books Ayala treats of the necessary qualities and practical duties of a commander, with strategy and military discipline.

to the rights of war, as, for example, to the advantages of *postliminium*. *In ipsos vero jure belli sævire, multoque magis quam in hostes licet: sunt enim odio digni majore.* Rebellion is worthy of the strongest condemnation: men are in duty bound to obey the prince, who holds from God alone. It is not just to declare war against infidels on the mere ground of their infidelity, even at the command of the Emperor or of the Pope[1], but (vi) war is justly made on heretics. Thus far just causes have been discussed rather with reference to equity and the duty of a good man than to the effect of law. The term "just" has, however, various significations. It does not always refer to equity and justice; it may refer to perfection of power: e.g. *justæ nuptiæ, justa ætas.* So that is called a just war which is waged publicly and lawfully by those who have the right to make war[2]. That the rights of war may have place it thus suffices that hostilities be waged by those who belong to the class of enemies and have the right of making war.

Lib. i. c. ii. 15.

When are Reprisals proper?

Having in his third chapter dealt shortly with the institution of Single Combat, Ayala engages in his fourth in a brief discussion of the subject of Reprisals (*de pignerationibus quas Represalias vocant*). The modern custom of making reprisals has, he notes, succeeded the ancient custom of pledge seizing, of which *Androlepsia* was an example. Reprisals directed against innocent *persons* can be no longer justified, but in respect of *property* the exercise of reprisals is just, provided such action be taken (1) under proper authority, to wit, the authority of a sovereign, and (2) for just cause.

Lib. i. c. 4.

The law of prize

His next chapter constitutes a comprehensive and authoritative code on the law affecting prize of war and

[1] Ayala, as becomes an orthodox Spaniard, approves the theory of "the two swords" of the Pope, in whom he recognises the Vicar of God on earth, whilst repudiating the World Lordship of the Emperor. *Imperator non est totius mundi dominus.* Lib. I. c. ii. 28, 29.

[2] *Justum bellum dicitur, quod publice legitime geritur ab iis qui belligerandi jus habent.* Lib. I. c. ii. 34.

recapture. He distinguishes in respect of the right of conquest between moveables and immoveables, assigns the distribution of booty to the determination of the commander, and deals at length with the condition of the prisoner of war. Christians no longer enslave their captives, *except in wars with infidels.* Women and children may be taken. A prisoner may not be put to death without public authority. He is bound by his promise of ransom. If his ransom exceeds the amount of 10,000 crowns, he is, by the ancient custom of Spain, France, and England, the prisoner of the sovereign. The prisoner who escapes to his own party recovers his former liberty, unless he has passed his word. Goods taken by pirates are not acquired, and therefore if recovered must be restored to their former owner. *Contra,* however, the constitutions of the kingdom of Spain.

and the treatment of prisoners of war.

Lib. i. c. 5.

In subsequent chapters Ayala discourses in careful and judicial fashion of the duty of keeping faith with an enemy, of treaties and truces, of the distinction of stratagem and fraud, and of *jus legatorum.* In this last connection he once again displays the lawyer's prejudice against insurgents. A rebel is not inviolable, even though he perform the functions of an envoy. Charles V. rightly imprisoned the envoys of the Duke of Milan. The doing to death of Rincon and Fregoze was justifiable, although the deed was in fact perpetrated without Imperial orders.

The duty of keeping faith.

Ayala's main sources of authority throughout are Roman military precedent and the decisions of Roman Law, supplemented here and there by a reference to Canon Law, to *Jus Naturæ, Jus Divinum* or *Jus Gentium,* or to Spanish municipal legislation.

§ 134. With Albericus Gentilis we reach a new stage in historic evolution.

A new stage is reached with Albericus Gentilis (1552—1608).

Albericus Gentilis was born in 1552 at Castello di San Genesio, a provincial town of the mark of Ancona. Educated at Perugia, where he graduated as Doctor in Civil Law in 1572, he practised for a time as an advocate in his native place. His father, Matthæus Gentilis, a physician of some note, having in consequence of heretical leanings found it advisable to retire from Italy, Albericus accompanied him into Austrian exile, and ultimately in 1580 found his way to Oxford. Under the patronage of Leicester, then Chancellor of the University, he was incorporated in January 1581, and at once began to deliver lectures. In 1584 his reputation was sufficiently great to secure his consultation by the royal Council as to the proper treatment of the peccant Spanish ambassador Mendoza. This incident led to the publication in the next year of a treatise, *De Legationibus*[1].

T. E. Holland, *Studies in International Law*, I.

He handles (i) *Jus Legationis*.

De Legationibus, 1585.

§ 135. This work, a slim quarto volume, dedicated in the prevalent fulsome fashion to Leicester's famous nephew, Sir Philip Sidney, is divided into three books. The third, which treats of the qualities and conduct of a model ambassador, is of comparatively small legal interest. To the other two a higher value attaches.

Definition of Legation.

In the first Gentilis deals with the definition and history of Legation. Opening with a brief account of various meanings attaching to the word *legatus*, he defines his legate as one *qui publico, aut sacratiori nomine ad rempublicam personamve aliam sacratiorem ob rem publicam, aut sacratiori missus sine imperio est rei dicendæ, agendæ caussa.* Dismissing lightly Divine missions, he passes to the classification of missions between men and men. Such missions may, he decides, be distributed by reference to the person of the sender or to that of the receiver. A mission may be (1) from a free republic or prince to an equal power, (2) from a republic or prince not in the enjoyment of freedom to a republic or prince in the like condition, or (3) of a mixed nature. Missions may be further distinguished *secundum mandata.* A mission may be titular, being created for some private

De Legationibus, Lib. I. c. 2.

Classification of missions.

[1] *Alberici Gentilis De Legationibus Libri Tres. Londini, Excudebat Thomas Vautrollerius,* MDLXXXV. The work was contemporaneously published by Wolfius, the printer of many others of the works of Gentilis: see T. E. Holland, *Studies*, p. 33.

reason. It is then *legatio libera. Legatio libera est ejus qui publico legati nomine commendatus, ornatusque, re ipsa ob privatam exiit occasionem.* Missions created for a public object are variously *negotii, officii* or *temporis.* Under missions "of matters" would appear to fall Extraordinary Embassies, whether for a peaceful or a warlike purpose; under "officious" missions are ranged embassies of compliment, condolence and the like; legates "of time" are those *quos Residentes vulgari sermone nominare solemus.* These general considerations introduce a short sketch, drawn from Livy, Tacitus, Xenophon and other classical historians, of the history of Embassage amongst the Romans, Greeks and other ancient peoples.

Lib. i. c. 8.

Lib. i. c. 5.

Jus Legationis amongst the ancients.

In his second book Gentilis deals directly with *Jus Legationis.* Here his work becomes of particular historical interest.

He decides that Legates are not inviolable except amongst the people to whom they are sent, but that nevertheless as men of peace they ought to be everywhere courteously treated. Legates sent for purposes of espionage and perfidy may be refused admission, or, if they have been admitted, may on the discovery of their characters be expelled; they are not, however, to be accorded harsher treatment. A sovereign may refuse to receive an embassy, but only for some good cause. He may, Gentilis thinks, refuse to receive titular, officious and time embassies (*liberæ legationes, officiosæ, et temporariæ*). So Henry VII. of England rightly refused to receive resident ministers. The sovereign who violates *jus legationis* in the persons of foreign ambassadors must look for retaliation upon his own ministers. Robbers and pirates can claim no legatine rights, nor may revolted subjects as against their ruler. Heretics, however, are not denuded of such rights, and offences committed by individuals before their assumption of the legatine office are not to be visited upon them when they have put on their public character. Not only the legate himself, but his company and goods are sacred, and to

The limits of legatine immunity.

Lib. ii. c. 4.

The right to refuse to receive a mission.

Lib. ii. c. 12.

Who have the right of legation?

The immunities of the suite.

the term company (*comites*) Gentilis would, contrary to the views of some, give a generous interpretation. In respect of the civil liabilities of the public agent Gentilis would admit but very restricted privileges. A contract made by an ambassador during the time of his embassy should, he is clear, be held enforceable; otherwise (1) the ambassador is endowed with power to defraud another of his goods, (2) no one will contract with an ambassador. But a public agent is absolutely exempt from the operation of the local criminal law of the land to which he is sent. Even if he conspires against the prince to whom he is accredited, his punishment at the hands of that prince is limited to dismissal. So the conduct of the English Government in respect of the Spanish ambassador who plotted against the life and throne of the Queen was most precisely correct.

Lib. ii. c. 15. Contracts and criminal offences of ambassadors. *Lib.* ii. c. 18.

(ii) The Law of War. *De Jure Belli*, 1588, marks an epoch.

§ 136. In 1587, after some service in Germany with Horatio Pallavicino, Elizabeth's envoy to Saxony, Gentilis was appointed to the chair of Regius Professor of Civil Law at Oxford. In 1588 appeared at London the first portion of his best known work, *De Jure Belli*, the second and third parts following in 1589[1].

Nature of *Jus Gentium*. *Lib.* i. c. 1. *De Jure Gentium Bellico.* Definition of "War." *Lib.* i. c. 2. *Belli definitio.* What is a "just war?" *Lib.* i. c. 3. *Principes bellum gerunt.* Answer, A war waged between sovereigns on just occasion.

After a brief reference to the nature of *Jus Gentium*, the sources of which he finds in Custom and Nature Gentilis advances his definition of War. *Bellum est publicorum armorum justa contentio.* War is a contest;—to deserve the name of war a contest must needs be (i) by force of arms, (ii) public, and (iii) just. What is to be understood by the term "just?" *Justum non solum quod a jure est, sed et quod est ex omni parte perfectum, significat.* The arms engaged must be public on both sides, and the contesting parties sovereigns (*principes*). A sovereign has no judge: he is not a sovereign over whom another exercises authority. Disputes between sovereigns

[1] The combined parts were issued at Leyden in 1589. The complete work passed through the press at Hanover in 1598. See Professor Holland's Preface to his edition of 1877.

can only be settled by discussion (*disceptationem*) or by force. Sovereigns do on occasions submit to arbitration, and such conduct is most proper, but in the last resort recourse may be justly had to war. The justification of war is thus grounded on necessity. *Si necessitas non subsit, bellum esse justum nec possit. Nam ex necessitate inductum dicitur. Voluntario compromisso antea est disceptandum, et ratione naturali, arbitra illa (ut inquit Seneca) bonorum, atque malorum; etiam et aliis rationibus, quae antea notatæ sunt.* Whether such rulers as the dukes of Mantua, Parma, and Ferrara, and various German princes have the right to make war, they having feudal superiors, is a question of fact to be decided by the terms of their investiture.

The justice of war is grounded on necessity.

Certain powers whose right to make war may be questioned,

The operations of pirates, robbers and deserters are not entitled to the name of war. They have no rights who violate all rights. *Ille hostis est, qui habet rempublicam, curiam, ærarium, consensum et concordiam civium, et rationem aliquam, si res ita tulerit, pacis et fœderis.* The Frenchmen who in the last Hispano-Portuguese war were made prisoners when fighting for the expelled claimant Antonio, were improperly treated as pirates by the Spaniards.

Lib. i. c. 4. *Latrones bellum non gerunt.*

or altogether denied.

A war may be just though vindicative or offensive. But can war be just on both sides? Yes, if there be reasonable doubt as to the right; so Victoria and others. The causes of war are manifold. A war waged by direct command of God is necessarily just. But may war be justly made on behalf of Religion? No, says Gentilis; religion is a matter between God and the individual; no man is wronged by the Faith of another. A sovereign may not justly employ force to compel the conformity of subjects who embrace another creed, unless the state suffers injury therein (*nisi quid detrimenti illinc respublica capiat*). Unity is desirable indeed, but not unity which is the product of coercion. Subjects, on their side, may not justly make war on their ruler on account of his desire to adopt a new, or to retain an old, religion. God

Wars may be just though vindicative or offensive.

Lib. i. c. 5. *Bella juste geruntur.*

Can a war be just on both sides?

Lib. i. c. 6. *Bellum juste geri utrinque.*

Causes of war considered.

Lib. i. c. 7. *De caussis bellorum.*

Divine Command

Lib. i. c. 8. *De caussis divinis belli faciendi.*

and religion as causes of war.

Lib. i. c. 9. *An bellum justum sit pro Religione.*

Lib. i. c. 10. *Si Princeps Religionem bello apud suos juste tuetur.*

Lib. i. c. 11. An subditi bellent contra principem ex caussa religionis.

can compel, Who is above all. One who is neither subject nor private individual may defend himself in the last resort in the possession of his religion as on other grounds.

War is not a natural condition.

Lib. i. c. 12. Utrum sint caussae naturales belli faciendi.

Is war the natural condition of men? Is there naturally, as Philip of Macedon said, and various great writers have alleged, war between Greeks and Barbarians? Were the Canaanites naturally enemies of the Jews, the Saracens of the Christians, the Romans of all external peoples? No: by nature men are all kin. There is no natural discord between man and man. The Spaniards had no natural cause of war with the Indians, nor was the warfare of Barbarians and Greeks natural. What of the Turk? Well, war of Christian upon Turk is not indeed natural, but it is very nearly so. The Turks deem us enemies, plot against us, threaten us, rob us by every perfidious device at all times, and so give us perpetually just cause of war. Faith pledged to them is not to be broken. War is not to be made on them when they are quiet, keep the peace and attempt no ill against us. But when do the Turks so act? *Silete theologi in munere alieno.*

Nature approves certain causes of war:

Lib. i. c. 13. De necessaria defensione.

(1) Self-defence.

Lib. i. c. 14. De utili defensione.

Albeit war is not the natural condition of men, Nature approves certain things as causes of war. Self-defence is a natural cause of war; so also the denial of anything which nature grants. War is just when it is necessary. It is not essential, however, to just defence that we await attack. That is a just defence which anticipates peril already designed, prepared, or even, although not designed, probable, possible. No one but a fool will wait to be knocked down. There must, however, be reasonable fear to justify anticipatory action; mere suspicion is not enough. The Turk and the Spaniard, who meditate universal dominion, may be justly resisted, and a common peril is to be met in common. Furthermore it is not alone in the defence of ourselves that war is just. Let it be remembered that all men are members of one body, that the world is a great republic. Men as individuals owe each other mutual service, and the rule holds for

(2) The defence of others.

Lib. i. c. 15. De honesta defensione.

princes. If one member of the body design the injury of another, it becomes all to assist the injured. "*Plena est justitia quæ defendit infirmos.*" And one may justly aid him who is threatened with harm.

Is it proper to defend subjects against their lord?

Lib. i. c. 16. *De subditis alienis contra dominum defendendis.*

May the subjects of a foreign sovereign be defended against their lord? The author desires no confusion of dominion nor any surveillance exercised by sovereign over sovereign. In questions between individual and individual it were improper to have recourse to other than the natural sovereign, and between subject and sovereign magistrates may in general decide; but, when the state itself is in debate, there is and can be no appropriate state judge. When so large a number of subjects have opposed themselves to their sovereign that there is actual war, the matter is public. In this event it may be proper for foreign sovereigns to intervene on behalf of justice. But what of subjects whose cause is unjust? May foreign aid be accorded to them? Kingdoms are not made for kings but kings for kingdoms. Aid may be given to subjects whose cause is unjust to moderate the cruelty of their sovereign or temper excessive punishment. The sovereign is to be protected against himself. Occasions for such interference will, however, be rare. Good reason existed for the interference of the English on behalf of the Netherlanders. There were close ties of mutual need between England and the Netherlands; there was old friendship with the Dukes of Burgundy; there were the ties of familiarity and ancient consanguinity between the peoples. If the Netherlanders were conquered their position would be entirely changed: an important consideration. No one is to be prohibited from favouring liberty, and a good neighbour is of great consequence. Lastly, it is not lawful to deal with subjects in such sort that harm or danger ensues for men who are not subjects.

Wars classified: (*a*) wars of necessity.

Lib. i. c. 17. *Qui bellum necessarie inferunt.*

War may be waged from motives of necessity, of profit, or of honour (*aut necessarie, aut utiliter, aut honeste*). War is waged of necessity, (1) if without war we cannot exist, e.g. by the Romans in their earliest days when refused *connubium* by their neighbours; (2) by exiles in search of new settlements after forcible ejection from their own seats. The occupation of vacant territory is deemed to be in accordance with the law of Nature. Uncultivated lands may well be allotted to immigrants, but subject to the jurisdiction of the original prince. Exiles are not always to be admitted. Their admission may be justly refused when their reception would (i) endanger the state, or (ii) entail war by giving occasion of quarrel with their conquerors.

(b) Wars advisable.

Lib. i. c. 18. *Qui utiliter bellum inferunt.*

War may be profitably waged to avenge injury received. It is profitable, because he who fails to avenge one injury provokes another. And to remedy loss is beneficial. Kings and kingdoms stand by name and reputation. Their good name must be protected.

They are justified by (1) The vindication of violated natural rights.

Lib. i. c. 19. *De naturalibus caussis belli inferendi.*

When, however, can we fairly say that our rights are violated? Our rights are violated in the first place when men deny what Nature grants. Examples are afforded by the denial of passage, of port shelter, of market, of trade, of intercourse.

Examples:

i. The right of passage.

(i) The subject of right of passage is full of difficulty; opinions are divided and precedents various. Gentilis holds with Augustine in admitting the existence of the right, if there be no reason to fear that injury will result from the grant. If no good reason exists for the denial of passage, denial is a just cause of war. But note in what passage consists. It is lawful to cross another's field; it is not lawful to hunt there in face of the owner's prohibition. So, whilst passage is lawful, the lord of the territory may forbid the exercise within his territory of acts of war. It will be said that the fact remains that sovereigns cannot pass through foreign territory with safety, and hence the custom of asking safe conducts. If sovereigns have established any such law amongst themselves, they cannot accuse one another of breach of *jus gentium*. But George Buchanan affirms that James, King of Scotland, who was taken by the English when driven upon the English shores, was captured *contra jus gentium*.

Buch. *Hist. Scot.* 10.

(ii) He who denies port, market, or intercourse offends against human society. The Spaniards had thus just cause for war against the inhabitants of the New World, who refused intercourse with them. The Spaniards fought, however, be it noted, not for commerce but for dominion. To constitute a just cause of war the prohibition must be general. It is in no way improper to prohibit the importation of particular goods which the inhabitants deem injurious. Foreigners have no right to change local manners and regulations. Intercourse cannot be said to be refused when a nation refuses to foreigners internal trade, whilst admitting them to their frontiers; so the Britons formerly acted, and so the Chinese act at the present day. The exportation of particular products, such as gold or silver, may likewise be forbidden: the Spaniards and the English have alike in time past issued such prohibitions.

ii. The rights of port, of market, and of intercourse.

(iii) The sea is, like the air, naturally open to the common use of all mankind. So too is the shore, the river bank, the flowing stream. The usage of the French, the English, and other peoples as to wrecks is *jus injurium.* Some contend that, whilst the use of these things is common to all, possession thereof may be acquired by particular men, and these may, as possessors, forbid the use of their possessions by others. In accordance with this view the Venetians may, not as *domini maris* but as *possessores*, close the Adriatic to foreign navigation. The contention is to be rejected: *lædit per inanes logos jus naturæ.* If the sea is naturally open to all, the attempt to close it is mere usurpation. The Venetians may exercise a right of jurisdiction or protection in the Adriatic and other peoples in other seas, but the use of those seas is common to all; proprietorship therein there is none. The prince who denies the use of the sea gives good cause of war.

iii. The right of navigation.

Our rights are further violated by the refusal of that which is granted by human law. The violation of positive legal rights constitutes just cause of war. War is not, however, to be begun on light occasion.

(2) The vindication of violated positive legal rights.

Lib. i. c. 20. *De humanis caussis belli inferendi.*

When is a state responsible in respect of the acts of the individual subject?

Lib. i. c. 21. *De malefactis privatorum.*

So far of the offences given by sovereigns to peoples; now of the offences of private persons. The injurious act of a private individual is not *per se* a cause of offence against his state, but a state itself offends, which, being at once bound and able to restrain the offences of its subjects, knowingly neglects so to do. A state is in default, not only when it expressly refuses to give satisfaction to the injured, but when it for a long time, although without common deliberation, allows injury to be done. A state is rightly held responsible in respect of the oft-repeated offences of its citizens. They were guilty of repeated offences who, to the great peril and loss of the kingdom of England and its allies, supplied the Spaniards with provisions, including articles of regular warlike use. They strove to continue their traffic when requested to discontinue it; they resisted the demand made upon them, on the ground that it was *contra jus gentium* and a violation of freedom of trade. An all-important question this. Equity was with the English; strict law was with the traders. The latter wished to avoid the loss of the profits of their commerce; the former objected to the doing of that which imperilled their safety. The rights of traders are to be respected, but still more is the safety of the state. *Est illud gentium jus: hoc naturæ est. Est illud privatorum: est hoc regnorum. Cedat igitur regno mercatura, homo naturæ, pecunia vitæ.* These considerations advanced on behalf of the English the author would likewise advance against the English and others, who at the time of writing supply munitions of war (*commoda bello*) to the Turk, who is belligerent against the Emperor. *Quod tibi fieri non vis, alteri ne feceris.*

When is an act public?

When is an act public, when private? That is public which is determined by a corporate body in legitimate assembly.

Prescriptive right amongst nations.

Lib. i. c. 22. *De vetustis caussis non excitandis.* *Lib.* i. c. 23. *De regnorum eversionibus.*

Old causes of war are not to be raked up. Prescription avails in public as in private affairs[1]. A war is

[1] Through the discussion of the foundation of prescriptive right Gentilis is led on to an interesting examination of the historical claims of the Holy Roman Empire. Lib. I. c. 23.

legitimate against the successors in title of those who have given offence: individuals die, but states partake of immortality.

A war is just against successors in title.

Lib. i. c. 24. *Si in posteros movetur bellum.*

It remains to discuss wars begun from motives of honour. A war is honourably (*honeste*) undertaken when it is waged not on our own private behalf but *communi ratione et pro aliis*. War is honourably undertaken against cannibals and against peoples who indulge in human sacrifices. War cannot be said to have been undertaken by the Spaniards against the Indians from motives of honour when based on the ground of their refusal to hear the preaching of the Gospel, nor does charity afford just cause for war against infidels. War is justly made on pirates; they are violators of the common Law of Nations.

(*c*) Wars dictated by motives of honour.

Lib. i. c. 25. *De honesta caussa belli inferendi.*

Subjects are excused if they carry on war without just cause: they are excused without distinction of offensive and defensive. Not so others.

Subjects are excused in their war-waging by the fact of obedience to orders.

War must not only be justly undertaken but justly waged. And justice demands in the first place that we make our determination known to him against whom we have determined upon war. A declaration of war should never be omitted, if it can be safely made; a demand for redress should, after the praiseworthy fashion of the ancient Romans, precede recourse to arms; and, following upon the demand, a reasonable delay for deliberation should be accorded. Declaration may, however, in certain cases be omitted. Declaration may be omitted in the case of war undertaken in necessary self-defence. It is unnecessary as against those who already conduct themselves in a hostile manner. It is unnecessary as against rebels. But he who omits to declare war, when a declaration is due, acts in a treacherous fashion, and his war is unjust, detestable and internecine. Stratagem and guile which would be improper in a listed duel are not illegitimate in war. Formerly the business of war was much simpler: the place and time of battle were often settled beforehand. We have departed from such practices, but not all guile is even now legitimate against

War should in general be preceded by declaration,

Lib. ii. c. 1. *De bello indicendo.*

but in certain cases such declaration may be omitted.

Lib. ii. c. 2. *Si quando bellum non indicitur.*

Stratagem is legitimate.

Lib. ii. c. 3. *De dolo et stratagematis.*

an enemy. It is hotly disputed whether faith should be kept with robbers and men of that order, but no one is hardy enough to contend that faith need not be kept with an enemy. *Dolus est fraus, fallacia ad circumveniendum.*

Verbal trickery in negotiating is to be eschewed. *Lib.* ii. c. 4. *De dolo verborum.*

And guile may be verbal or by deed. Let there in agreements with an enemy be no captious interpretation, no subtlety, but the utmost good faith. Verbal trickeries are for lawyers, not for honest soldiers. Many examples of disgraceful verbal trickery may be culled from the treaty making of antiquity. In the present age Charles V. and Louis XII. have had recourse to interpretations of words and treaties more befitting scriveners than princes. Stratagem is to be approved, but stratagem is one thing, perfidy another.

Apart from negotiation it may be just to lie to an enemy. *Lib.* ii. c. 5. *De mendaciis.*

There are many cases in which it may be justifiable to deceive an enemy by a lie. Themistocles furnished an illustrious example of such legitimate lying. When contracting, however, it is not lawful to lie to any enemy.

The use of poison in war is illegitimate: *Lib.* ii. c. 6. *De veneficiis.* so too of magical arts,

Of guile in act the use of poison is an example. It is a form of warfare which is altogether to be condemned. So too is the use of venomous beasts and of magical arts.

Lib. ii. c. 7. *De armis et mentitis armis.* and of assassins. *Lib.* ii. c. 8. *De Scævola, Juditha, similibus.*

Assassins and the hirers of assassins are equally blameable. An enemy may be slain indeed, but not at any time nor in any fashion, and not every enemy. The actions of a Scævola or a Judith are in no way to be approved.

The employment of spies is legitimate, but spies may be severely handled. *Lib.* ii. c. 9. *De Zopiro et aliis transfugis.*

To spy upon an enemy and to employ spies are alike legitimate: spies may nevertheless on account of the peril they represent be hardly handled by their captors. Simulated deserters and spies may be treated like subjects found in the territory of the enemy. It is lawful to employ the services of traitors against traitors.

What power to treat is vested in a military commander? *Lib.* ii. c. 10. *De pactis ducum.*

The commander-in-chief alone can treat with the enemy, and his powers of treating are by no means unlimited. It does not belong to a commander-in-chief to make a definitive peace. A commander may treat for a truce of limited extent only. In the absence of their superiors subordinate officers are deemed invested with similar power. The powers of the commander are in general limited to matters appertaining to his military command. A general may indeed be specially endowed with a fuller commission, but his conventions will in all cases be necessarily subject to ratification.

Captured soldiers may give their parole or enter into contracts of ransom. *Lib.* ii. c. 11. *De pactis militum.*

Captured soldiers are wont to be released on condition that they shall not serve again either at all or for a limited time against their captors. They are released too on contract of ransom. Many authorities contend that such undertakings are not binding, but accepted custom is to the contrary. The contract must nevertheless to be valid be made with a just enemy, not with a rebel or with robbers. If the undertaking be against the public or military law of the prisoner's state, the promise is not to be fulfilled, but the prisoner must return to his captivity.

Truces and their legal consequences. *Lib.* ii. c. 12. *De induciis.* *Lib.* ii. c. 13. *Quando contra inducias fiat.*

Truces are undertakings for the mutual cessation of hostilities for a short and present time. Truces in general bind from the moment of their establishment. The breach of truce by one party justifies hostile action on the part of the other. What is a breach of truce is to be ascertained primarily from the terms of the agreement. Truces are contracts *bonæ fidei.* The act of a private individual does not constitute a breach of truce, but the offender must be surrendered for punishment and reparation must be made. Forces are not to be advanced or retired in time of truce. During a truce soldiers are not to be introduced into a besieged town.

A safe-conduct is a species of truce. *Lib.* ii. c. 14. *De salvo conductu.*

A safe conduct is a species of truce. Safe conducts are, in general, grantable by a commander-in-chief alone. The interpretations of the terms of the privilege must be *ex bono, et ex æquo, et absque cavillationibus, et large.*

Exchanges and ransom, how to be effected. *Lib.* ii. c. 15. *De permutationibus et liberationibus.*

Exchanges are to be effected in good faith and in accordance with equity. Ransoms ought not to be excessive: it is difficult, however, to establish any hard and fast rate. If a released prisoner die before his ransom is paid, the ransom is due from his heir.

How should

A man is not deemed a prisoner of war until he is

the prisoner of war be treated? *Lib.* ii. c. 16. *De captivis et non necandis.*

brought *intra præsidia hostium*, but one who has surrendered is nevertheless not to be slain, even though he has not yet come *intra præsidia*, provided always that he abstain from force and do not attempt escape. To slaughter, except in such cases as just suggested, is altogether cruel and unjust. He is unjust who chooses to kill those whom he might make captive. Prisoners are not to be put to death. So says Law Natural and Law Divine, whatever may have been the practice of peoples. Granted that the slaughter of prisoners be lawful, "*Non omne, quod licet, honestum est.*" Henry II. of France, having taken a town by storm, hanged prisoners of war, who had resisted too obstinately. It is disgraceful and cruel thus to act towards those who execute the orders of their prince. The slaughter in Ireland of the Spanish prisoners was *contra jus belli.*

Enemies should be admitted in generous fashion to surrender, and to slaughter those so submitting is, in general, illegitimate. *Lib.* ii. c. 17. *De his qui se hosti dedunt.*

The belligerent who surrenders would seem to tacitly stipulate for the preservation of his life. Humanity and military law alike enjoin the sparing of the surrendering. Surrender is surrender, although it follow after hard fighting or be induced by fear. Cæsar announced to the Aduatici that their state would be preserved, provided they surrendered "before the ram touched the wall." So in these days the time for surrender is deemed to have passed when siege cannon are brought up against a weak place. But unless, as is possible, special reason exists for the rejection of surrender, surrender should in any case be admitted. A surrender made after common consultation by a majority or by those endowed with the necessary authority protects even those who opposed submission. The terms of capitulations afford subject-matter for endless disputes, and call for particular consideration. The author nevertheless contends that in any event such terms as *arbitrium, manus, voluntas, potestas, discretio, judicium, sapientia, gratia, misericordia, æquitas, conscientia, declaratio,* when employed in a capitulation, necessarily imply action within the limits of law and in accordance with the qualities of a good man.

In certain cases special severity towards prisoners taken or surrendering may be excused. Thus it may be justified, (1) towards those who employed abusive language towards the captor, (2) by way of reprisals, (3) towards foes guilty of perfidy, (4) towards violators of the laws of war, (5) towards deserters and other subjects of the captor, (6) towards released prisoners taken a second time. The supply of provisions to a besieged place is sometimes brought forward as affording occasion for sharp action, and Charles of Burgundy actually hanged persons captured when attempting thus to assist his enemy. But, except possibly in the case of foreigners led on by mere avarice, no sufficient reason for such severity appears. And some other common excuses are of equally questionable validity.

In certain cases, however, special severity towards prisoners is excusable.
Lib. ii. c. 18. *In deditos et captos saeviri.*

Hostages are not properly prisoners. According to ancient practice, upon breach of faith upon the part of the enemy, hostages were exposed to the penalty of death. It has seemed cruel to many of the greatest generals thus to punish the innocent for the guilty. A hostage, however, may well be sharply handled in respect of his own fault, such as an attempt at flight, and it is both just and expedient that the hostage should be held punishable in respect of the offences of his countrymen, since belligerent good faith, an object of the utmost importance, is thereby secured. Bodin seems to think that the disuse of the custom of putting to death hostages followed upon the appearance of habitual ill faith, the terrible slaughter which would be the consequence if all perfidy were not so punished deterring belligerents therefrom. But the truth rather is that good faith disappeared when perfidy was no longer punished.

Hostages may on occasion be put to death.
Lib. ii. c. 19. *De obsidibus.*

Philosophers, legislators, theologians, poets, and historians, Roman, Greek, and Barbarian, unite in approving the sparing of the suppliant. Common religion may protect fugitives to sacred places, they fleeing as it were to the bond which is not dissolved by war. Nature's communion pleads for suppliants everywhere. *Parcendum est supplicibus.* But be it remembered that belligerents

Suppliants should be spared.
Lib. ii. c. 20. *De supplicibus.*

may by their conduct exclude themselves from mercy.

So too women and children. *Lib.* ii. c. 21. *De pueris et fœminis.*

Young boys are to be spared, as are likewise women. An exception must be indeed made in the case of Amazons, of Zenobias or Artemisias, who assume masculine functions, and there are particular circumstances where severity would not be amiss, but in general women are not to be slain. A long line of famous commanders unite in the condemnation of attacks upon female honour.

What of peasants?

Some few belligerents have on occasion accorded immunity to peasants, and the respectable jurisconsult Arrian declares it to be improper to seize upon the cultivators of land, or to destroy their produce. To the same effect run provisions of the Canon Law. But if the peasants are not harmless (*insontes*) but armed, there exists no reason why they should be spared. *Non indulgetur versutis hodie rusticis.*

Foreigners found with the enemy are not necessarily enemies. *Lib.* ii. c. 22. *De agricolis, mercatoribus, peregrinis, aliis similibus.*

A foreigner may put on the character of an enemy by domicile upon belligerent soil,

Foreign merchants found amongst the enemy are not to be regarded as enemies. But residents who, with the intention of permanent stay, have fixed their domicile and seat with the greater part of their fortunes in any state, may be properly called citizens of that state, although they fall short of the exact definition of the citizen as a participator in the obligations and honours of the state. The rights of war may, that is to say, be exercised against inhabitants (*incolas*) of a hostile state. The foreigner, whether merchant or not, however long he remains with the enemy, is not an enemy; but he is an enemy who has become a citizen of the enemy's state, whether by habitation or by incorporation (*allectione*). Present practice harmonises with the law thus laid down.

but the mere sojourner with the enemy is not an enemy. Goods found on hostile soil are not necessarily hostile.

The goods of foreigners who are in Spain are not wont to be captured by the English: the goods of foreigners who are in England are not taken by the Spaniards. Such is the law, whether the goods be found on hostile soil or elsewhere. Goods taken on hostile soil, they not being hostile property, cannot reasonably be deemed *quasi hostium*, if sojourners with the enemy are not enemies. Locality does not affect the matter. It is the cause which makes the enemy. As far as the enemy himself is concerned, he may well be slain anywhere, and hostile goods may well be taken anywhere. Foreign territory gives rise to a different question. Foreign territory affords security, and therefore it is laid down that goods captured within foreign territory do not pass to the captor, but are to be restored upon the demand of the lord of the territory. Nor does it make any difference that the flight began where capture was legitimate: change of territory works change of power. So it was adjudged that Spaniards fleeing before French enemies to English territory should not fall under the hand of their pursuers, and the precedent was followed in the year 1588, when the Spaniards fled before the English fleet to the French coast, and were there protected.

The territory of a third power affords protection against the exercise of belligerent rights.

The goods of those who are not enemies (*non hostium*) cannot be anywhere legitimately captured: he who is not an enemy cannot be anywhere legitimately slain. It nevertheless behoves a foreigner to see to it that he wittingly does nothing to assist the enemy, lest he make himself an enemy, as does any other who brings aid to the enemy. They who supplied to Saracens goods apt for war against Christians or lent ships to Saracen invaders were excommunicated by decree of the Lateran Council, were despoiled of their property, and even made slaves of by their captors. He is to be deemed an enemy, who does that which pleases the enemy: so Agathias. He is a member of the enemy's army, who supplies to that army the necessaries of war: so queen Amalasuintha to Justinian. And queen Elizabeth, in reply to the Hanseatic States, who complained that their ships were despoiled by the English fleet contrary to treaty, which provided that the States might safely be friends of the enemies of England and trade with them, declared that injury to one and aid to the other were incompatible with friendship to both, *at imo hoc esse auxiliari hostibus, et cum hostibus adversum alios facere.* Only they, however, are made citizens of the enemy who become such *simpliciter et hoc volentes principaliter.*

The persons and goods of *non hostes* are free everywhere. It nevertheless behoves the *non hostis* to see to it that he does not become an enemy by active assistance of a belligerent.

The citizen of a belligerent state who is living abroad is an enemy, unless he has in some way apart from that residence laid aside his original character.

What now of the citizen of the enemy who is resident abroad? He is a Spaniard who lives elsewhere than in Spain, if he have not ceased in some independent fashion (*alias*) to be a Spaniard. *Non mutatur origo, nec deseritur patria facile. Incolatus, allectio, addit civitatem civitati, non tollit priorem. Potest quis allectione civis esse variorum locorum. Potest alibi civis esse allectione, et item alibi, atque alibi: et alibi item adoptione et in pluribus item locis per domicilium: et alibi nativitate, et alibi origine.* Subject character is assigned by reference, not to origin or to incorporation (*allectio*), but to domicile. A domicile is not acquired by a residence of a thousand years in default of the *animus habitandi perpetuo*, but in a doubtful case the intention to reside permanently may be presumed from a ten years' residence. Subject character acquired by residence or other like means is lost with much greater ease than subject character arising by origin or nativity: it is lost in fact by any desertion. Natural citizenship is never lost, except penally in the single case of desertion in the time of danger.

The international importance of domicile.

What is the legal position of property which is merely subject to belligerent control?

Property hired, pledged, or lent to, or deposited with the enemy may be captured, but *cum sua causa*, provided that it had not been handed to the enemy during or at the commencement of war. The former handing over to an enemy of some article of property is no offence against us, but present delivery to our enemy is an offence, if the article delivered be of warlike service.

The destruction of hostile property is legitimate by way of deterrent reprisals.

Lib. ii. c. 23. *De vastitate et incendiis.*

Turning particularly to the legal position of hostile property, Gentilis notes the declaration of Polybius, that, whereas it is permissible by the laws of war to destroy castles, gardens, towns, villages, ships and produce when the strength of the enemy is thereby lessened or our own strength increased, it is the act of a mere madman to destroy objects such as temples, porticos, statues, and the like, whose destruction neither profits the destroyer nor injures the enemy. With this opinion Gentilis is only in general accord. Temples are, he thinks, in general to be preserved, but they are not to be spared

(1) if the enemy has not spared them, (2) if the enemy has already profaned them, (3) if they are impediments to victory, or (4) if, in parallel cases, the enemy has acted contrary to the laws of war. Destruction is justifiable by way of deterrent reprisals. The ancient prohibition of the destruction of fruit-bearing trees was commendable, but such destruction may be in particular circumstances legitimate.

Humanity demands the burial of the dead.

Lib. ii. c. 24. *De caesis sepeliendis.*

Lastly, the author asks, are the bodies of the slain the property of the enemy? They, he answers, have ceased to be enemies who have ceased to be men. The universal sense of humanity voiced by poets, historians, doctors and fathers, brands as barbarous the refusal of sepulture to the fallen foe.

Peace is the end of war.

Lib. iii. c. 1. *De belli fine et pace.* Aristot. *Polit.* 14. 13. Cic. *De Officiis,* 1. 11.

Having in his first and second books dealt with the commencement and actual waging, Gentilis turns in his third to the termination of war.

Peace is the end to which all belligerent operations should be directed: so Aristotle, Cicero, Augustine, and the Canonists. It was a laudable custom which dictated that trophies should not be constructed of durable material, whereby the memory of battle might be perpetuated. Punishment is legitimate, but let the victor use his power with moderation. *Est pœnæ modus, sicut rerum reliquarum, et quædam mediocritas,* quoth Cicero. *Parcendum subjectis:* so Virgil. Let vengeance be stayed when the injurer repents him of his wrong-doing; the end of vindicatory action is the withholding of the offender from the repetition of his offence and the deterring of others from similar conduct. The due limits of vengeance are thus easily appreciated: compensation (*solatium*) for injury received, security from the offender and from others for the future, and the sinner's deprivation of gain. Let vengeance overtake the actual offender alone, and such monstrous punishments as the lopping of feet and hands, the tearing out of eyes, branding and mutilation, punishments exacted by cruel Athenian generals or a barbarous Basil, are altogether to be abhorred. What says Augustine? *No-*

The victor should use his power with moderation.

Lib. iii. c. 2. *De ultione victoris.*

cendi cupiditas, ulciscendi crudelitas, impacatus atque implacabilis animus, libido dominandi, culpantur hic: et contra sunt pœnarum regulas. These are the things which make the termination of war no termination.

He may exact a war indemnity, *Lib. iii. c. 3. De sumptibus et damnis belli.* take territory and impose tribute. *Lib. iii. c. 4. Tributis et agris multari victos.*

The victor may well exact an indemnity for expenses incurred and damage suffered. He may impose tribute and other monetary payments upon the conquered. He may, *pace* Alciati and certain theologians, or rather matæologians, take to himself lands and other property of the enemy. But let him remember that he exercises all these rights *pro arbitrio boni viri:* if security is to be consulted, he shall be satisfied when fear is at an end; if damages are to be repaired, he shall ask nothing over.

When a state is completely absorbed, it passes subject to existing obligations. *Lib. iii. c. 5. Victoris adquisitio universalis.*

In some cases the victor's title is universal, as was that of Alexander in the property of the Thebans on the destruction of the Theban state; in some it is particular, as is that of an invading army in occupied lands. When a state passes in its entirety from prince to prince, it passes *cum omnibus suis qualitatibus.*

The victor may take the ornaments of the conquered. *Lib. iii. c. 6. Victos ornamentis spoliare.*

The ornaments of the conquered may be taken as spoil, and that without distinction of things sacred and profane, but this in strict law. Modesty and honour may here well dictate abstention from the exercise of full legal right.

He may under certain circumstances level walls or even destroy towns. *Lib. iii. c. 7. Urbes diripi, dirui.*

History tells of the total destruction of many conquered cities. If towns captured cannot be held and may become again hostile and renew the war, they may be deprived of their walls or even levelled to their foundations. The future, that is to say, must be looked to. Revolt is a common cause of severity.

He is not, unless under very special circumstances, to put to death the enemy's commanders. *Lib. iii. c. 8. De ducibus hostium captis.*

The ancient Romans were wont to put to death captive hostile generals, whether with an eye to the prevention of renewed strife or to the propitiation of the *manes* of their own fallen warriors. In these days the commanders are preserved; it is the common soldiers who are slain! The general of a just foe ought not in any event to be put to death, unless special reasons dictate it. Nor ought he to be perpetually detained in custody, if the victor can otherwise secure his conquest.

Slavery is not recognised as a consequence of warfare between Christians, but it is not incompatible with *jus gentium*, and it is actually the lot of prisoners taken in wars between Christians and non-Christians. Even the Turk approves the kindly treatment of the slave.

Slavery is recognised by *Jus Gentium* but Christians do not enslave Christian captives.
Lib. iii. c. 9. *De servis.*

Policy may well induce a victor to leave to the conquered complete liberty, but he may deem it proper to so change the form of government of the conquered state as to bring it into closer harmony with his institutions. The pleas advanced in support of the compulsory change of the religion of the conquered are commonly but specious, but a conqueror may very properly prohibit that which is contrary to Nature. It is contrary to *jus naturæ* to destroy the harbours of a conquered state. The conquered may, however, be disarmed. In all cases of the exercise of the victor's rights equity is to be preferred to strict law, honour to bare utility.

The victor may change the form of government in a conquered state.
Lib. iii. c. 10. *De statu mutando.*
He ought not, in general, to interfere with the religion of the conquered.
Lib. iii. c. 11. *De religionis aliarumque rerum mutatione.*
Equity is to be preferred to strict law, honour to utility.
Lib. iii. c. 12. *Si utile cum honesto pugnet.*

In subsequent chapters Gentilis treats of the general principles which should guide the victor in dictating terms of peace. Peace should be settled on such conditions that it can be perpetual. Saving the Law of Nature, the victor may adopt any expedient which can make his victory stable and establish a just peace alike for himself and the vanquished.

Terms of peace should not be over-strict.
Lib. iii. c. 13. *De pace futura constituenda.*

Agreements should as far as possible cover all the ground of controversy. The agreements of princes are *bonæ fidei*. They are not vitiated by fear, provided that such fear be not improperly induced. The conventions made by captive princes are binding, provided their makers have been justly taken. Subjects are not, however, bound to obey the orders of their captive rulers. A treaty may be ratified by deed and silence. Fraud and error vitiate the contracts of sovereigns as of private individuals. New disputes excuse the execution of the terms of treaty. The treaties and conventions of princes are to be expounded, so far as possible, *a lege et ratione civili.*

Agreements of sovereigns are *bonæ fidei*.
Lib. iii. c. 14. *De jure conveniendi.*

Duelling is forbidden by the Canons and by the Civil

The powers of

sovereigns to make terms are not unlimited.

Lib. iii. c. 15. De quibus cavetur in foederibus: et de duello.

Law, but single combat is legitimate in war, and two pretenders to rule may well resolve to abide the issue of such a contest. Sometimes, however, it is to the interest of subjects not to change their lord, when their consent may be required to any alienation. Jacques Cujas most justly says that, although no special law prohibits the alienation of national property or of the kingdom itself, yet such alienation appears to be forbidden by a general law of all kingdoms, which comes into being with the kingdoms themselves and is *quasi jure gentium. Hallucinantur theologi, adulantur juris consulti, qui persuadent, omnia principibus licere, summamque eorum et liberam esse potestatem. Ridiculum est affirmare, pontificibus absolutam in subditos potestatem competere: quæ nec ipsi imperatori in Italos competit: a quo isti causam habent.* Let imperial power be as free as possible: it remains a power of administration, not of domination. And he who has unrestrained power of administration has not the power of donation. A king cannot alienate a people or give them another king; a people is free, though it be ruled by a king.

Certain common stipulations explained.

Lib. iii. c. 16. De legibus et libertate.

Many stipulations common in treaties require particular explanation. It is frequently stipulated that each contracting state shall enjoy its own laws. *Et quum est comprehensum, ut alter alterius majestatem comiter conservaret: tum nec quidquam de libertate, de æqualitate multum minuebatur, ut Brissonius, Sigonius, alii ista exposuerunt.*

Unless it be otherwise stipulated, ownership is regulated by the rule of *uti possidetis.*

Lib. iii. c. 17. De agris et postliminio.

Unless it be otherwise expressly stipulated in the treaty, lands, places and buildings remain in the power of him who held possession at the time when peace was made. So if no stipulation be made concerning captives and other property, all remain in the enemy's power. Thus ships, arms, garments do not return to their former ownership.

What is involved in a treaty of friendship?

Lib. iii. c. 18. De amicitia et societate.

Stipulations for friendship or fraternity impose serious obligations. On the analogy of private friendship, friends by treaty would seem to be bound to mutual assistance.

Princes are wont to expressly stipulate as to the amount of assistance due, and this is the wiser course. It should be noted that alliances are of two varieties, *συμμαχίαν* and *ἐπιμαχίαν*; according to the species so is the obligation to merely defensive or to defensive and offensive common action. If war breaks out between two states to both of whom a third power is bound by treaties of friendship, the third power might well be guided in the lending of aid by certain general rules. (1) Let aid be given to him who is not only friend but subject, although he be later in time; (2) let aid be given to one when the condition of the allies would be otherwise unequal; (3) let aid be given to the just cause; (4) in case of doubt, let order in time have a certain influence, the older ally having the preference; (5) when it is doubtful which of the applicants for aid acts most in accord with the treaty (*pro jure fœderis*), each citing it in support of his demand, let aid be given to none; (6) let one ally be defended against the other's offensive action; (7) by no means let aid be given to opposing belligerents; *secus* aid in provisions, money and such like, which both may and ought to be accorded; (8) if both sides cannot be satisfied, and no reason exists why one should be assisted rather than the other, aid neither.

What shall a third power do if war breaks out between two sovereigns to each of whom he owes aid?

May a league be rightly made with men of another religion? The question is partly theological, partly political (*civilis*). A general treaty of commerce with such men is legitimate, and even such a special treaty of intercourse as Isaac made with Gerar, David with the king of the Ammonites and with Tyre, and Solomon with Hiram. It is legitimate to hold those of another faith in the bonds of an unequal league, i.e. as tributaries and servants. *Et ex hoc dico, etiam posse non stipendarios habere qui nobis militent infideles: ut ita cum rege Neapolitano, etiam et Bononiæ Veneto stipendio turma fuit Turcarum non admodum pridem.* It is lawful to make a league of the order in question, when a believer is forcibly subjected to the Infidel. There are to-day

It is legitimate to make a treaty of commerce with the unbeliever,

Lib. iii. c. 19. *Si fœdus recta contrahitur cum diversae religionis hominibus.*

Christian princes and republics which pay tribute to the Turk. When the question is of an equal alliance and an alliance of arms, the issue is two-fold: the alliance may be that of a believer with an Infidel against another Infidel or against another believer. The Maccabees, the kings of Judah, and in these days the Portuguese have made leagues of the first kind. But such leagues denounced when made by kings of Judah are illegitimate. It is improper to aid Infidels or to seek aid from Infidels against Infidels; then how much the more against the Faithful? Be at peace with all men, even with the Infidel, but make no league with the Unbeliever. The league of the king of France with the Turks cannot be approved. No man can trust the Infidel.

but not a treaty of military alliance.

What is involved in a treaty clause affecting "arms," "a fleet,"

Lib. iii. c. 20. *De armis et classibus.*

A stipulation of a treaty touching "arms" is to be understood as referring to legitimate weapons of war. An "army" may be defined as *cœtus militaris uni duci subjectus*: it must be composed of some particular number of soldiers: it is wise to fix the number by special clause. Mere number of vessels does not constitute a "fleet": the character of the ships is more to the purpose. A stipulation that no "fortress" (*arx*) shall be made upon a frontier is not infringed by any construction which is not fortified against arms and warlike force. No one does a wrong who merely provides for his own security; but if places are built which are calculated to injure, they offend against the treaty. A stipulation concerning "defences" (*prœsidia*) is to be interpreted in the like fashion.

"fortresses," "defences"?

Lib. iii. c. 21. *De arcibus et prœsidiis.*

Whether a treaty binds the successors of the contractors is a question to be determined by particular considerations.

Lib. iii. c. 22. *Si successores fœderatorum tenentur.*

Is a treaty binding upon the successors of the contracting parties? The question is to be resolved by reference to the contractual powers of the framers and the name in which the treaty was made. Except in the case of an absolute despot the contractual powers of a prince are not unlimited, and a prince may treat as for himself or as for his state. In general a stipulation making peace is binding on successors, a stipulation for friendship and alliance calls for renewal if successors are to be bound. It is sometimes laid down that the contracts of peoples are perpetually binding, since peoples always remain the same, whilst the contracts of kings do not bind succeeding kings. Gentilis disapproves any such distinction. If kings are not bound by the contracts of their predecessors, neither are peoples bound by their treaties with deceased kings. The formal renewal with new sovereigns of treaties made with their predecessors is a very commendable custom.

Ratification is required when terms are made on behalf of absent principals.

Lib. iii. c. 23. *De ratihabitione privatis, piratis, exsulibus, adhærentibus.*

Care must be taken to restrain breaches of treaty by subjects.

Stipulations made by contractors on behalf of absent parties are not binding upon the absentees until ratified by them. But stipulations made by sovereigns are without ratification binding upon subjects from the moment of the making of peace. The acts of mere private individuals subsequent to the signature do not constitute a breach of a peace, but it behoves the states to exercise a preventive supervision over their subjects. Treaties are not violated by the slaughter of pirates: so the English on one occasion justly replied to Scottish complaints. Whether the reception of banished exiles or of fugitives constitutes a breach of treaty were best expressly determined by the terms of the treaty.

What circumstances justify departure from or renunciation of a treaty?

Lib. iii. c. 24. *Quando fœdus violatur.*

A treaty is not violated if it be departed from for just reason. If some condition of the alliance be unfulfilled, or if it be impossible to enjoy that for which the alliance was contracted, the union may be renounced. If a part of the convention be not observed, the whole may be disregarded. Necessity and *vis major* excuse breach of treaty on the part of an ally.

What is the penalty of breach of faith?

What is the penalty of breach of faith? There are penalties pointed out by law, and penalties may be fixed by convention. It is scarcely necessary to add that the offender is no more to be trusted. Faith may justly be broken with him in the same and connected negotiations. But let not faith be broken with him in a distinct affair; heap not perfidy on perfidy. *Deus optimus maximus faciat principes imponere bellis omnem finem et jura pacis ac fœderum colere sancte.* '*Pax plenum virtutis opus, pax* '*summa laborum, pax belli exacti pretium est, pretiumque*

God grant peace and good faith!

'*pericli: sidera pace vigent, consistunt terrea pace: nil* '*placitum sine pace Deo.*' *Etiam Deus, etiam impone tu bellis finem: tu nobis pacem effice: placatus iniquitatibus nostris: propitius nobis in Filio tuo, servatore nostro, Jesu Christo.*

(iii) The Law of Neutrality.

Hispanicae Advocationis Libri II. 1613.

§ 137. In 1605 Gentilis was appointed to represent as advocate before the English Court of Admiralty the interests of Philip III. and his subjects. The treatise *Hispanicae Advocationis Libri Duo*[1], in which Gentilis collected and examined a number of questions coming before him in the exercise of the duties of his office, reveals a very considerable advance towards the definition of the mutual rights and duties of belligerent and neutral. "*Postliminium an sit apud amicum communem?*" "*An* "*hostem liceat capere in territorio alieno?*" "*An hostem* "*captum liceat ducere per territorium alienum?*" "*Utrum* "*caedamus juste eos, qui proficiscuntur ad militiam nostro-* "*rum hostium?*" "*An Rex jure velit, Hispanos tuto in* "*Belgium navigare, qui male habiti ab Hollandis ad* "*portum Regis fuerunt?*" Not only does Gentilis deal at length with these and other kindred legal problems, but his resolutions are well-nigh always, if not in every case, identical with the decisions of modern international law.

Gentilis apprehends in clear fashion the territorial rights of the neutral.

Founding his arguments in the main upon citations from the Roman civilians and their mediæval commentators, he bases his system upon a clear apprehension of the conception of Territorial Sovereignty. A reference to one only of his decisions, that with regard to the belligerent right of capture within foreign territory, will suffice to demonstrate at once the soundness of his method and the independence of his judgment. *Licitum videtur*, he writes,

[1] *Alberici Gentilis Juriscons. Hispanicæ Advocationis Libri Duo. Hanoviæ, Apud haeredes Guilielmi Antonii*, MDCXIII. The work was also published at Frankfort in the same year. T. E. Holland, *Studies*, p. 35. Albericus Gentilis had died in 1608. The work was published by his brother Scipio, and by him dedicated to the Spanish ambassador Zuniga.

capere hostem in territorio alieno. Scilicet liceat ingredi alienum agrum, venandi feras caussa, itaque liceat quoque alienum ingredi territorium, venandi hostes causa (*Bar. Ang. Castr.* l. 16, *de ser. rus. prae.*). *Nam bellum venatio est* (Xen. 2, *Cyrop.*; Arist. 1, *Polit.*). *Et territorium nihil est aliud quam dominium* (*Bar.* l. 48, *de ser.*; *Bal.* l. 10 *C. eod.*). *Etiam invito domino ingressus agrum facit praedam suam. Quid si persecutio capiendi fuerit cœpta in territorio permisso, hostis vero continuata fuga in alieno est captus. In delinquente, qui ita fugerit, et ita captus sit, adfirmatur licitum per Mynsingerum in observationibus Cameræ Imperialis ex Angelo, aliisque* (*Myns.* 2 *Obs.* 28). *Et adfirmatio potest generalis esse ex illa regula, quod attendendum sit ad principium licitum, non ad finem illicitum* (*l. quod ait. ubi Bar. de adult.*). *Cœterum hœc conclusio falsa est in hoste. Et sic docui in libris meis bellicis* (*Alb.* 2, *de Ju. Bell.* 22). *Alienum territorium securitatem præstat. Et mutato territorio mutatur potestas.*

Albericus Gentilis, *Hispan. Advocat.* i. c. 5. Cf. *De Jure Belli*, ii. c. 22.

Estimate of the work of Gentilis.

§ 138. The foregoing *résumé* of the three most interesting of the works of Gentilis will, incomplete although it inevitably is, perhaps suffice to make clear how great is the advance made by him upon the efforts of his predecessors. Gentilis raises numerous problems which had exercised earlier pens; he refers to the same ancient authorities, ranges for precedents the history of Greece and Rome, and cites in the like copious fashion the opinions of poets and philosophers, moral and political, of fathers, schoolmen and civilians; he is as familiar with the pages of Thomas More and Bodin as with those of Augustine and Aquinas, Bartolus, Baldus, and Alciati. But with Gentilis discussion has become no longer mainly a mere display of dry academic learning or of logical acumen; it is ever thoroughly practical. He turns at every step to pressing international questions of the day, and brings to their consideration a sound judgment and a remarkable independence of thought, which, coupled with a vigorous style, directness of attack, and a vein of shrewd humour, lend to his pages at once a singularly grateful vivacity and a high permanent value.

His three above-cited works represent excursions into the three great divisions into which the field of International Law may be divided, and in each he makes his mark. In *De Legationibus* he shakes well-nigh entirely off the purely municipal entanglements with which the use of the Latin tongue had hitherto involved the rights and duties of ambassadors, entanglements to which Brunus fell an easy victim. In *De Jure Belli* in like fashion he frees his subject from that connection with military discipline, tactics and other heterogeneous matters which had clung to it from the day of Isidore to that of Ayala. In his partial treatment of the Law of Neutrality he displays the clearest grasp of that territorial principle which lies at the root of all sound conceptions of neutral right and duty. It did not fall to Gentilis to weld all into a single complete system, but the constituent factors of such a system were under his hand, and it is but small justice that we accord him, when we recognise in him the first of a long line of international jurists properly so called. How great were the obligations to him of Grotius a comparison of *De Jure Belli ac Pacis* with *De Jure Belli* will render abundantly apparent. Withal Gentilis was possessed of a lightness of touch, coupled with a firm grip of his subject-matter, which is hardly compensated for by the often overloaded scholarship of Grotius; and in the close relevancy at once of argument and illustration, and in the avoidance of side issues, he set an example which not only his more celebrated successor, but more than one of the successors of that successor would have done well to imitate.

Holland, *Studies*, Essay II.

John de Carthagena.

§ 139. But another writer need be referred to before we treat of Grotius.

His *Propugnaculum Catholicum De Jure Belli*,

In 1609 Father John de Carthagena published at Rome a treatise in four books under the title *Propugnaculum Catholicum De Jure Belli Romani Pontificis adversus Ecclesiæ Jura violantes.* Issued from the Papal Press with the strong approval of the Curia and dedicated to Paul V, this short work is in its main positions a striking example of the worst products of casuistry. The author, a Spanish Franciscan[1], declares the injustice of any war against the Pope on the part of *violatores Sacræ Libertatis. Privilegium amittit, qui eo abutitur; igitur cum Princeps vel Respublica volens gerere bellum contra Romanum Pontificem supremum caput Ecclesiæ, eo quod jura ecclesiastica libertatis illæsa servare contendit, crimen læsæ majestatis Pontificiæ incurrat: procul dubio amittit privilegium potestatis, quo gaudet ad bellum authoritative indicendum, et sic etiam hac ratione redditur bellum ex parte ejus omnino injustum propter defectum prædictæ potestatis et authoritatis, quæ est prima omnium conditionum requisitarum ad justitiam belli.* No person may without mortal sin assist in such a war, even though probable reasons be offered to him in proof of its justice.

1609, illustrates a particular portion of the field of thought of the age which brought forth Grotius.

It is unjust to make war upon the Pope,

Propugnaculum Cathol. Lib. ii. c. 1.

On the other hand, the Pope possesses as fully as the greatest Christian lay monarch the power to declare war, and there are numerous causes sufficient to render just his waging of war against violators of the liberties of the Church. The prince or republican magistrate who impedes the Roman Pontiff in the punishment of violators of the Canons or of persons holding wrongly concerning the Catholic Faith gives adequate cause of war; and so, too, the princely or republican ruler who has broken faith and treaty with the Church that nothing shall be done in prejudice of ecclesiastical immunities and liberty.

but the Pope may make war.

Lib. i. cc. 3, 4.

The rejection of the Papal temporal jurisdiction *in ordine ad finem supernaturalem* is sufficient cause of war. The Pope may with secure conscience call infidel soldiers to his aid, and may enforce against his enemies the full rights accorded by the laws of war to lay belligerents. Nay, he may even reduce his prisoners to the condition of slaves, and a captive so reduced to servitude would in

The rejection of the Papal temporal jurisdiction *in ordine ad finem supernaturalem* is good cause of war.

Lib. iii. c. 6.

The Pope may enslave captives.

[1] *Ordinis Minorum de Observantia, Sacræ Theologiæ Lector generalis de mandato Sanctissimo, in Regali Conventu S. Petri Montis Aurei.*

escaping from the hand of his master be guilty of mortal sin! Clerics are forbidden to bear arms by Human Law indeed, but by no rule of Law Natural or Divine. Waging war lawfully they may without sin slay, maim, and share in plunder. And how good and glorious a thing it is to be a soldier in a war against the violators of the Church's rights[1]. Interesting in the fiery light which it throws upon the mental condition of Roman churchmen[2] in the days of the formation of the fateful rivals, the Protestant Union (1608) and the Catholic League (1609), Carthagena's treatise with its constant and often arbitrary citation of Scriptural precedent and ancient authority, is incidentally valuable in the general sanction which it gives to standards of belligerent right set up by Victoria and other sixteenth century writers on the Laws of War, in particular in respect of the treatment of non-combatants.

Lib. iii. c. 8. Clerics are not forbidden by Divine Law to bear arms. *Lib.* iv. *Lib.* iii. cc. 4, 5.

Hugo Grotius (1583—1645). *Mare Liberum*, 1609, challenges the Portuguese monopoly of Eastern trade and navigation. Nations have a general right to trade and navigate. c. i. *Jure gentium quibusvis ad quosvis liberam esse navigationem.*

§ 140. In the same year which saw the issue of Carthagena's treatise there appeared at Leyden an anonymous brochure entitled *Mare Liberum*.

Aiming, as his title indicates[3], to demonstrate the right of the Dutch to navigate and trade with the East Indies, the author commences by laying it down as a certain rule of *Jus Gentium Primarium* that it is lawful for any one people to visit and trade with any other. This principle agrees, he declares, with the purpose of God which is revealed by the different natural endowments and consequent mutual needs of various peoples. The winds

[1] *Quam utile et gloriosum sit militare in bello adversus jura Ecclesiæ violantes.* Lib. IV. *cap. ult.*

[2] The attestation of the Papal Censor is not without a curious interest: *Nihil in eis a Catholica fide et Ecclestica* (sic) *doctrina alienum, vel bonis moribus contrarium reperi, sed insignem doctrinam, pietatemque singularem observavi eosque dignissimos existimo.*

[3] *Mare Liberum, seu de jure quod Batavis competit ad Indicana commercia Dissertatio, Lugd. Bat. ex offic. Ludovici Elzevirii*, 1609. Other editions appeared at Leyden in 1618, 1632, and 1633, and at Amsterdam in 1633.

blowing in changing directions teach the same lesson. The principle is recognised by jurists, who deny the possession by princes of the power to forbid all foreign intercourse with their subjects, and by poets who denounce inhospitality. Wars have been begun by peoples on account of the denial of intercourse, the rights of the Spaniards themselves in America having been actually supported by the fact of such denial by the Indians. The denial of the right of passage was made a cause of war by the Israelites against the Amorites, by the Greeks under Agamemnon against the king of the Mysians, by Christendom against the Saracen. Even, therefore, were the Portuguese lords of the regions with which the Dutch seek intercourse, they would act wrongly in forbidding approach and commerce to the Dutchmen. How much more iniquitous is it to prohibit commerce with peoples anxious to trade, when neither the people nor the channel of access is subject to dominion!

Mere discovery constitutes no valid legal title.

c. ii. *Lusitanos nullum habere jus dominii in eos Indos ad quos Batavi navigant titulo inventionis.*

The Portuguese cannot be the owners of lands of which they are not in possession and to which they have no title. And Java and the greater part of the Moluccas they never directly or by agents possessed. Those islands have their own kings, polity, laws and rights. The Portuguese hold their right to commerce there equally with other peoples under concession of the local princes. And the Portuguese have in those parts not so much as a bare titular claim, which is not overthrown by the decision of doctors even amongst the Spaniards. If they set up title by discovery, they fail alike in law and in fact. *Invenire enim non illud est oculis usurpare sed apprehendere.* For valid title by discovery there must be actual occupation. And in point of fact the Portuguese did not discover the Indies, which had been known to mankind for centuries before they appeared there. Furthermore title by discovery can be claimed only in *res nullius*; the Indians, when the Portuguese appeared, were indeed some idolaters, some Mahometans, but they were nevertheless capable of public and private ownership. Victoria contended upon behalf of the Indians of the West that they were not to be robbed of their lands by Christians, except as a consequence of some actual wrong committed, and the Indians of the East are civilised.

Papal grant constitutes no valid title.

c. iii. *Lusitanos in Indos non habere jus dominii titulo donationis Pontificiæ.*

The Portuguese have no right in the Indies by virtue of Papal donation. The Pope might give a judgment between two nations as elected arbiter, when that judgment in no way affected the rights of third parties; but, even should the Pope have made a donation to the Portuguese, that donation were of no avail without *traditio*, and for *traditio* there must be *possessio*. The authorities who attribute the highest power to the Pope ascribe it *in ordine ad spiritualia.* No title to lay dominion can be based upon Papal spiritual pretensions.

The Portuguese have no title in the Indies by right of war.

c. iv. *Lusitanos in Indos non habere jus dominii titulo belli.*

The Portuguese have no right of ownership in the Indies by title of conquest. They were not so much as at war with many of the peoples with whom the Dutch entered into intercourse. War against Barbarians is commonly justified either in respect of the denial of commerce or of the rejection of the true Faith. In the first particular the Portuguese have no occasion of complaint, and for proof that the rejection of the true Faith is no just cause of war see the burning words of Cajetanus, but one amongst many authorities. In point of fact the Portuguese have been far from teaching the true Faith either by preaching or example. From the foregoing considerations we may finally conclude that the Indian peoples are free and *sui juris.*

Having proceeded thus far with an argument which recalls at every stage the positions of Victoria, the author next adopts and amplifies the contentions of

Occupation may constitute a valid title to lands,

c. v. *Mare ad Indos aut jus eo navigandi non esse proprium Lusitanorum titulo occupationis.*

F. Vasquius with regard to dominion in the sea. The sea-way to the Indies or the right of navigating it is not, he declares, appropriated to the Portuguese by title of occupation. *Jure Primo Gentium* no property is appropriated, but all things are common: so the poets as to the Golden Age. Private property arises by occupation, and *Occupatio in mobilibus est apprehensio, in immobilibus instructio aut limitatio.* When politics come into being a further division arises; property is (1) public, *i.e.* appropriated to a people, or (2) private. *Occupatio autem publica eodem modo fit, quo privata.* But (i) things which cannot be *occupied* cannot be the subjects of proprietorship. (ii) Those things which by Nature are so ordered that when used by one they equally suffice for the use of all others are, and ought to be, in that legal state in which they were when first naturally created. To this order belong: (1) Air, which cannot be occupied, and ought to be held of promiscuous use; (2) the Ocean, which is so boundless as to be incapable of possession, and to be fitted for the use of all, whether in respect of navigation or fishing. So Cicero, Virgil, Plautus, *in var. loc.* An individual may indeed occupy a portion of the sea, so long as his occupation does not injure the common right of user; so too a people may occupy. But no part of the sea can be held *in territorio* of any people. *Territoria sunt ex occupationibus populorum, ut privata dominia ex occupationibus singulorum.* Authorities who state that the sea belonged to the Roman Empire are to be understood to mean that it so belonged in respect of *protection and jurisdiction.* States can by convention appropriate portions of the sea to particular jurisdictions, but these conventions do not bind third parties[1]. The claim of the Portuguese is to an immense ocean expanse, and one who should refuse to another a light from his light would sin against human society. Further, if the Portuguese sailor who first navigated the eastern seas could claim a right by occupation, every sea were occupied, since some first sailor there must needs be in every case; and circumnavigators might claim the world. A ship leaves on the sea no more *law* than *track.* Much of the sea in question was navigated by others before the Portuguese; for example, by Alexander and the Phœnicians. They who claim the Indian seas by discovery merely lie; and for a

but the sea cannot be occupied.

[1] A curious anticipation of the modern "sphere of influence" treaty.

rediscovery the Portuguese have reaped a sufficient reward alike in wealth and renown. Lastly, in other seas claims were set up by possessors of shores: the Portuguese have but petty territorial possessions in the East.

Papal grant cannot confer that which is incapable of ownership.

c. vi. *Mare aut jus navigandi proprium non esse Lusitanorum titulo donationis Pontificiæ.*

The seaway to the Indies or the right of navigating it is not appropriated to the Portuguese by title of Papal donation. A gift is without effect if it respects *res extra commercium.* The Pope is not lord of the world in things temporal, and has no authority to do that which conflicts with the Law of Nature.

Prescription confers no title as between princes,

c. vii. *Mare aut jus navigandi proprium non esse Lusitanorum titulo præscriptionis aut consuetudinis.*

and the Portuguese have in fact no prescriptive rights in the Indies.

The seaway to the Indies or the right of navigating it, is not appropriated to the Portuguese by title of prescription or custom. Prescription belongs to *Jus Civile,* and has therefore no place between kings or free peoples; and one may not acquire by prescription a thing which is incapable of legal possession. In this last case a claim rested on immemorial prescription is of no avail. Custom is a species of positive law which cannot abrogate a perpetual law; and such a perpetual law there is requiring the common use of the sea. The opinion of Vasquius, *decus illud Hispaniæ,* was sound, and the claim of the Portuguese is weaker than those of the Genoese and Venetians which Vasquius repelled. The Portuguese cannot set up a claim of immemorial possession. Their first discoveries began in 1477; twenty years later their navigators rounded the Cape; subsequently they reached the Moluccas, to which the Dutch began to sail in 1595. The Spaniards allege a misty Portuguese possession of the seas about the Moluccas from the year 1519. The French and English, however, publicly opened a way into those seas, and the inhabitants of the African and Asiatic shores regularly fished and navigated their waters without Portuguese prohibition.

Free trade is natural.

c. viii. *Jus Gentium inter quosvis liberam esse mercaturam.*

So far of land and maritime dominion: lastly of commerce. *Jus gentium primarium* commands free trade.

Exclusive trading rights

The trade to the Indies is not appropriated to the Portuguese by title of occupation. Commerce is not a corporeal thing; and if the Portuguese have any exclusive right of trade it must be by express or tacit convention.

cannot be acquired by occupation,

The trade to the Indies is not appropriated to the Portuguese by title of Papal grant. The Pope cannot give what is not his. If he wished to create a Portuguese monopoly he would wrong the Indians, who are not his subjects, and all men Christian and non-Christian.

c. ix. *Mercaturam cum Indis propriam non esse Lusitanorum titulo occupationis.*

Papal grant,

c. x. *Mercaturam cum Indis propriam non esse Lusitanorum titulo donationis Pontificiæ.*

The trade to the Indies is not appropriated to the Portuguese by right of prescription or custom. So Vasquius very rightly. The attempt of the Portuguese to monopolise the Indian trade is a display of grasping greed, and it behoves the Dutch to vindicate their trading rights and the Law of Nations in peace, in truce, and in war.

or prescription.

c. xi. *Mercaturam cum Indis non esse Lusitanorum propriam jure præscriptionis aut consuetudinis.*

The Portuguese monopoly is altogether inequitable.

c. xii. *Nulla æquitate niti Lusitanos in prohibendo commercio.*

c. xiii. *Batavis jus commercii Indicani qua pace, qua induciis, qua bello retinendum.*

§ 141. The veil of anonymity was speedily rent aside and the author of "*Mare Liberum*" was known to be Hugo Grotius.

Born in 1583 at Delft, educated at Leyden and Orleans, and when yet a boy introduced at Paris to diplomatic life under the auspices of Oldenbarnevelt, Grotius had already in 1603 established a reputation which secured for him unsought the post of historiographer of the United Provinces, an appointment which he justified by the preparation of his *Annales et historiæ de Rebus Belgicis*[1]. The treatise *Mare Liberum* would appear to have been a chapter published with or without the author's permission of a dissertation *De Jure Prædæ*[2] which had been composed in 1604.

The career of Grotius before the appearance of *De Jure Belli ac Pacis.*

Encyclop. Britannica, Article "Grotius." Nys, *Les Origines*, p. 383.

Appointed in 1607 Advocate-General to the Fisc of Holland and Zealand, Grotius settled in 1613 at Rotterdam with the dignity of Pensionary. After taking a leading

[1] Published at Amsterdam in 1657, in folio, and in 1658 in duodecimo. An English translation, entitled "*De Rebus Belgicis, or the Annals and History of the Low Country Warrs, faithfully rendered into English by T. M., of the Middle Temple,*" was published at London in 1665. The translator was T. Manley. Casaubon saw the original work in some form as early as 1613.

[2] Published in 1868.

part in maritime discussion with England he was in 1618–9 involved in the fall of Oldenbarnevelt, and, whilst his early patron suffered upon the scaffold, he himself underwent sentence of forfeiture and perpetual imprisonment. Escaping in 1621 through the devotion of his wife from the castle of Loevesteins, he fled to France, where he was granted a pension by Lous XIII. At Paris he resumed the work begun in 1604, and in 1625 appeared in that city with a dedication to Louis the Just the epoch-making *De Jure Belli ac Pacis*[1].

The occasioning cause of the preparation of the work.

§ 142. Grotius in his Preface sets out the occasioning cause of his labours. He was excited, he states, to the preparation of his work by the uninformed and unhappy state of the public opinion current in his time on the subject of the Law of Nations, and by the wild lawlessness and barbarity in war practice which was the natural outcome of the popular darkness. There were not wanting those in his and preceding ages for whom the law which regulates the relation between various peoples or between the rulers of peoples (*jus illud quod inter populos plures aut populorum rectores intercedit*) was an empty name. The evil-sounding diction of Euthydemus was in every mouth, "For a king or a sovereign city nothing profitable is unjust"; everywhere the opposition of law and arms was held necessarily irreconcilable, and the worse than barbarous practice of professedly Christian combatants cried shame on the Christian world in the face of Heaven. *Videbam per Christianum orbem vel barbaris gentibus pudendam bellandi licentiam; levibus aut nullis de caussis ad arma procurri, quibus semel sumtis nullam jam divini, nullam humani juris reverentiam, plane quasi uno edicto ad omnia scelera emisso furore*[2].

De Jure Belli ac Pacis, Proleg. 3, and 29.

Proleg. 28.

[1] *Hugonis Grotii De Jure Belli ac Pacis Libri Tres. In quibus Jus Naturale et Gentium: item juris publici præcipua explicantur. Parisiis, Apud Nicolaum Buon, in via Jacobæa, sub signis S. Claudii, et Hominis Silvestris.* MDCXXV. *Cum Privilegio Regis.*

[2] It is probable that in these words, although they have an exact application to the general war practice of the day, we hear a particular

So terrible was the prevailing licence that Erasmus and other good men had been led to doubt whether war was in any case permissible to a Christian man.

It was the task of Grotius to show that there was a law at once of peace and of war, that men were not, as members of different states, released from all control in their mutual dealings, that Justice was not silent amidst the clash of arms; to prove, in brief, the existence of a definitely ascertainable and active Law of Nations. In *De Jure Belli ac Pacis* he stands forth as the Prophet of Justice to an age of lawlessness.

Grotius the Prophet of International Justice.

§ 143. Treating first of "the Right of War," Grotius commences with the definition of his understanding of the terms *War* and *Right*.

Analysis of *De Jure Belli ac Pacis*, 1625.

War, its definition.

War, described by Cicero as "a contest by force," is, says Grotius, rather "the condition of those contending by force."

Jus, its meanings:—

Lib. i. c. 1. *Quid Bellum, quid Jus.*

1. "That which is just."

The term *Right* (*jus*) primarily and in the phrase "the Right of War" (*jus belli*) signifies "that which is just," or rather, "that which is not unjust," that is to say, that which is not repugnant to the nature of a rational society. *Right* has, however, two other meanings. As applied to a person it signifies a moral quality enabling to just having or doing. If the moral quality be perfect, it is properly a faculty (*a right*); if it be imperfect it is an aptitude (*a capacity for right*). Rights strictly so called, i.e. faculties, include the rights severally described by the terms *potestas*, *dominium*, and *creditum*, and may be classified as (1) common or private, and (2) eminent or public. Aptitude represents the Aristotelian *worth* or *fitness*. Rights strictly so-called belong to Expletive, aptitudes to Attributive Justice.

2. A right or a capacity for right.

In its third signification the term *Right* is equivalent

3. A rule of moral action (*lex*).

echo of those Low Country wars with which the historiographer's studies had made the writer specially familiar, wars which for relentless savagery and unbridled brutality vied with the worst experiences of ancient or mediæval barbarity.

to *lex* in the largest sense of that word. It then signifies "a rule of moral action obliging to that which is right.' *Jus* in this sense does not belong to the sphere of Justice alone, but to that of other virtues. So understood it is best divided, with Aristotle, into *jus naturale* and *jus voluntarium*.

In the last sense we have

(1) *Jus Naturale.*

The distinction drawn by Ulpian between *jus naturale*, as common to man and beast, and *jus gentium* as respecting men only, is quite worthless. *Jus naturale est dictatum rectæ rationis indicans actui alicui, ex ejus convenientia aut disconvenientia cum ipsa natura rationali, inesse moralem turpitudinem aut necessitatem moralem, ac consequenter ab auctore naturæ Deo talem actum aut vetari aut præcipi. Actus de quibus tale exstat dictatum, debiti sunt aut illiciti per se, atque ideo a Deo necessario præcepti aut vetiti intelliguntur: qua nota distat hoc jus non ab humano tantum jure, sed et a divino voluntario, quod non ea præcipit aut vetat quæ per se ac suapte natura aut debita sunt aut illicita, sed vetando illicita, præcipiendo debita facit.…Est autem jus naturale adeo immutabile ut ne a Deo quidem mutari queat.*

Lib. i. c. i. s. 10.

It follows from this definition that we may prove *a priori* that anything is or is not in accordance with the Law of Nature, by showing the necessary agreement or disagreement of the thing with a Nature which is reasonable and designed for society. We may, however, proceed in another fashion: we may with very great probability, although not with perfect certainty, conclude that to be an effect of the Law of Nature which is generally believed to be so by all, or at least by all the more civilised (*omnes moratiores*) nations. For an universal effect requires an universal cause, and there cannot well be any other general cause for this general opinion than a certain general sense which is common to all mankind.

(2) *Jus Voluntarium.*

Jus Voluntarium, being the expression of some Will, is either human or Divine.

i. *Jus Voluntarium humanum* includes:—

Jus Voluntarium humanum is of three species. There is (α) *Jus Civile.* This is the law of a particular state proceeding from the governing authority, the Civil Power, of that state. A state is definable as *cœtus perfectus liberorum hominum, juris fruendi et communis utilitatis causa sociatus.* (α) *Jus Civile;*

(β) Law narrower than *Jus Civile*, subject to, although not derived from, *Jus Civile*, e.g. the power of a father over his child. (β) Law of a particular condition.

(γ) Law wider than *Jus Civile*, viz. *Jus Gentium. Jus Gentium, id est quod gentium omnium aut multarum voluntate vim obligandi accepit. Multarum addidi quia vix ullum jus reperitur extra jus naturale, quod ipsum quoque gentium dici solet, omnibus gentibus commune. Imo sæpe in una parte orbis terrarum est jus gentium quod alibi non est, ut de captivitate ac postliminio suo loco dicemus. Probatur autem hoc jus gentium pari modo quo jus non scriptum civile, usu continuo et testimonio peritorum.* (γ) *Jus Gentium.* *Lib.* i. c. 1, s. 14.

Jus Voluntarium Divinum is derived from the express Will of God made known by Revelation to all mankind, or to a particular people. God has made known His Will to men by direct legislation on three occasions: immediately after the Creation, upon the reinstatement of Mankind after the Flood, and in the more perfect re-establishment by Christ. The laws given on these three occasions are of universal obligation. A Divine Law was specially given through Moses, but by that law the Israelites alone were bound. Still (i) the Jewish Law, being Divine, cannot be in conflict with the Law of Nature; (ii) Christian princes may now, in general, legislate to the same effect as the Mosaic Code; and (iii) whatsoever is enjoined by the Mosaic Law with respect to the virtues required by Christ in His disciples is incumbent as much, if not more, upon Christians. ii. *Jus Voluntarium Divinum.*

Having laid down these general premises, Grotius turns to the discussion of the time-honoured question, whether war-waging may ever be just. Referring the question successively to the Law of Nature, to *Jus Gentium Voluntarium*, and to the Law of God, he concludes that war, There may be a just war. *Lib.* i. c. 2. *An bellum unquam justum sit.*

not incompatible with the Law of Nature, and recognised by the usage of civilised nations, is not altogether forbidden by the Law of Christ.

Classification of Wars.
Lib. i. c. 3. *Belli partitio in publicum et privatum. Summi imperii explicatio.*

Grotius then proceeds to classify wars as private, public and mixed. Private war is not prohibited by the Law of Nature, which admits the right of self-defence. Even after the establishment of courts of justice, recourse in certain cases may be had to private force. That private war may be lawful may be further seen by reference to (1) the Mosaic law concerning the nocturnal thief, which seems to represent the Law of Nature, (2) the consent of all known people, which allows a person assailed to defend himself against the aggressor, and (3) Divine Voluntary Law.

Public Wars are solemn or less solemn.
Lib. i. c. 3, s. 4.

Public wars are either solemn or less solemn. To be entitled to the term solemn a war must (1) be made on both sides by the authority of the sovereign power of the state, and (2) be carried on in accordance with certain particular formalities. A less solemn war is one made without these formalities, against private men, or by an inferior magistrate. The municipal laws of most states forbid the making of war except by the authority of the sovereign, and it may be questioned whether war begun by any other than the holder of supreme power can be fitly styled public. That power is supreme whose acts are not so subject to another's right that they may be made void by the operation of any other human will. The opinion that the supreme power resides everywhere and without exception in the people is to be rejected. A people may choose what form of government it deems best, and in the exercise of this right it may resign all right of self-government. History, both sacred and profane, clearly testifies that there may be kings who are not subject to the will of the people, even collectively taken. It is not true that all government exists for the sake of the governed. Nor is it correct to say that people and kings are mutually subject; subjection being conditioned upon good rule. For one who would determine to whom in any

A Public War must be begun by the Supreme Power.
What is the Supreme Power?
Lib. i. c. 3, s. 7.

nation the sovereign power belongs certain cautions are necessary. (1) Mere names or external appearances constitute no certain test. The military chiefs of the Spartans after they were subjected to the ephors were still styled kings. The Roman emperors after they had openly assumed regal power were still styled but princes. The fact that succession is hereditary or elective is no sufficient means of discrimination between sovereign and less than sovereign authority. (2) Sovereignty and the manner of holding sovereignty are different things. A Roman dictator possessed supreme power although his tenure was but temporary. Some supreme governments are held in patrimonial right, with full power of alienation; other supreme governments are inalienable; many governments which are not supreme are held by fullest freely alienable title. (3) Sovereignty does not cease to be because he who holds it promises something to his subjects or to God, even though that something belong to the very root of his government. The Persian king was adored as the image of God, yet could not change laws passed in a particular form. (4) Sovereignty, although one and *per se* undivided, may be divided, whether by parts potential or parts subjective. The Roman Empire was one, although a Western and an Eastern emperor ruled. A people when choosing a king may reserve to itself the exercise of certain acts. It does not follow, however, that because some kings will not allow their acts to be valid until ratified by the Senate or some other body that there has been a partition of power. Whatever acts are in this way repealed must be judged to be repealed by the royal authority. These principles being premised, certain questions may be considered.

Lib. i. c. 3, s. 16.

Is the bond of an unequal alliance incompatible with sovereignty?

Lib. i. c. 3, s. 21.

(*a*) Can one bound by an unequal alliance be possessed of sovereignty? By an unequal alliance is to be understood not the union of confederates of unequal strength, nor a league which implies some transient act, but a confederation in which one party gives to another some permanent preference (*prælationem*). Such is the case when one state receives the patronage, protection or defence of another. If a people bound by such an alliance remains free and is not subjected to the power of its ally, it follows that it retains its sovereignty. Protection is not necessarily dominion. The payment of tribute, although as an acknowledgment of weakness it reduces dignity, is not incompatible with sovereignty.

Is feudal tenure incompatible with sovereignty? *Lib.* i. c. 3, s. 23.

(*b*) Can a prince who holds in fee possess sovereignty? The ties of mere personal obligation in no way reduce the power of the prince over his own subjects. Though a government may be lost by the happening of a particular event, it may none the less be sovereign; for, as aforesaid, the *res* is one thing, the manner of holding another.

War against superiors is in general illegitimate, *Lib.* i. c. 4. *De bello subditorum in superiores.*

War may be made by private men upon private men, by sovereigns upon sovereigns, by private men upon sovereigns other than their own, and by sovereigns upon private men, whether their subjects or strangers. But may war be lawfully made by subjects, whether private or public persons, against those set over them? War may be made against superiors by commission from a higher authority, and, when the sovereign commands that which is contrary to Nature or to the Law of God, a subject may be under a moral objection to disobey; but war against superiors as such is contrary alike to the Law of Nature, to the Mosaic Law, to the Law of the Gospel and to the practice of primitive Christians with regard to the worst of the Roman emperors. Some writers of the age think that inferior magistrates may in certain cases authorise, and are bound to authorise, resistance, but wrongly. Extreme necessity may furnish excuse, but we must spare the king's person and refrain from speaking ill of him. Be it noted, however, that (1) a free people may make war upon their ill-doing ruler, (2) subjects may war against a king who (i) has abdicated or deserted his throne, (ii) would alienate his inalienable kingdom, (iii) designs the utter destruction of his people, or (iv) violates the condition of his tenure. It is lawful for subjects to resist a king who, having constitutionally

but may be lawful in certain special cases.

but one part of the sovereign power, invades another, or who upon his accession granted license to his subjects to resist upon the happening of particular events.

The right of resistance to an usurper; its extent.

An usurper of sovereign powers may be killed (1) in the course of war waged in resistance to his claims upon their first assertion, (2) by antecedent law, and (3) by commission from the rightful sovereign. But in a case of controverted right no private person ought to determine; he should obey the *de facto* possessor.

Classification of the parties to a War.

Lib. i. c. 5. *Qui bellum licite gerunt.*

The parties to a war may be principals, assistants or agents. Kinship, neighbourhood and citizenship oblige men to mutual assistance: the call of common humanity is enough to justify the lending of aid to the distressed. As agents in war-waging all subjects may be naturally employed: by particular law some are nevertheless excused.

The causes of War may be assimilated to the grounds of private actions at law.

Lib. ii. c. 1. *De belli causis, et primum de defensione sui et rerum.*

The violation of right (*injuria*) constitutes the only just cause of war. The grounds of war are identical in number with the grounds of actions at law. Violation of right threatened justifies a preventive action; and violation of right complete may be ground for reparation or ground of punishment.

(I) *Causes of war grounded in preventive action.*

First, of threatened violation of right as a cause of war. A violation of right may affect body or property.

Preventive action is justifiable in (*a*) Defence of Person,

(*a*) It is lawful for a private person to kill another in defence of life, member, or chastity imperilled by an immediate and otherwise unavoidable danger. The right of self-defence may nevertheless on occasion be properly resigned; to kill an aggressor whose life is of great public benefit were sinful, and it does not become a Christian to kill a man on account of a box on the ear or to avoid the ignominy of running away.

(*b*) Defence of Property.

(*b*) In defence of property it may be lawful to kill: so the Law of Nature and the Mosaic Law concerning the nocturnal thief.

The above principles apply particularly to Private War: they are likewise applicable to Public War. Public authorities, however, have not only the right to defend, but the right to avenge, and they may justify action upon dangers merely threatened. It is the opinion of some (e.g. Albericus Gentilis, *De Jure Belli*, I. c. 14) that war may be rightly undertaken to diminish a growing power which threatens future danger. The question here is not of the just but of the expedient. Equity assuredly abhors the notion that we may forthwith employ force because force may perchance be employed against us in the future. Nor can we adopt that other contention of Gentilis, that it may be just to defend those who carry on an unjust war (Alb. Gentilis, *De Jure Belli*, I. c. 13).

(II) *Causes of War grounded in reparative action.* Action for reparation is justifiable in respect of (a) *Property Rights.* I. Common Property. *Lib. ii. c. 2. De his quæ hominibus communiter competunt.*

Secondly, of overt violation of right as a cause of war. In the first place, such violation may affect *property.* Property may be either common or private. Taking first common property, we may distinguish between the right over a corporeal thing (*jus in rem corporalem*) and the right to certain acts (*jus ad actus aliquos*). Corporeal things may be devoid of owners or already appropriated. And things which are devoid of owners may be incapable of ownership or capable of ownership.

We may begin by determining what is the nature of that right of ownership which jurisconsults term *Dominium.*

i. Common rights over corporeal things. What is Dominion?

In the early days of mankind all things were common: subsequently first moveables, then immoveables were recognised as appropriated either expressly, by division, or tacitly, by occupation. The sea is naturally incapable of ownership, whether as a whole or in respect to its principal branches. Of this its inexhaustibility and boundlessness afford moral proof. Among things which may be but are not yet appropriated may be enumerated many uncultivated places, islands, wild animals, and so forth.

Be it noted that occupation is of two kinds, *per universitatem* and *per fundos.* Land may be occupied *per universitatem* although not assigned to an individual proprietor.

Dominion is subject to:— 1. The right of necessary use,

The introduction of property did not put an end to:—

1. *The right of necessary use.* Necessity justifies men

in using as things common the property of others; but the necessity alleged must be unavoidable, it must yield to the equal need of the first possessor, and its claims are subject to the obligation where possible of restitution. He that is engaged in a just war may possess himself of a fort in a neutral country provided that there is an evident danger of its falling into his enemy's hands and that irreparable harm would ensue therefrom. Such a seizure must be subject to the conditions that (1) only that be taken which is necessary for security, and (2) restoration be made as soon as the danger is over.

2. *The right of innocent use.* Men have a right to use the property of others, if thereby no detriment results to the proprietor. Running streams within the bounds of one people may on this principle be utilised by foreign navigators. So too land and any portion of the sea which has become the property of a single people ought to be deemed to be open to the free passage of those who have just occasion therefor. The right of passage may be denied to one who wages an unjust war, or to one who would bring with him the enemies of the territorial ruler, but the right in general exists not only for persons but for merchandise. Duties can only be fairly levied on passing goods by way of compensation for actual services rendered, e.g. protection. Amongst other examples of innocent use may be mentioned the temporary sojourn of the passing stranger, such as that involved in recourse to a port for shelter from sudden storm. The right of permanent settlement is not to be refused to exiles driven from their own seats, provided that they will subject themselves to the existing local government.

2. The right of innocent use.

Lib. ii. c. 2, s. 10.

The second order of common rights, viz. common rights to actions, includes (1) the right to all acts whereby are procurable things without which we cannot conveniently subsist. There is a common right to purchase such things at a reasonable price, although there is no like right on the part of a possessor to insist on the purchase of his goods. And there is a similar common

ii. Common rights to actions.

right of intermarriage. (2) The right to all actions which a nation permits to foreigners at large.

II. Private Property. How are rights acquired? Acquisition is original or derivative.

Acquisition is original or derivative.

Things are now originally acquired by *Occupation* only.

Original acquisition might in the early days of the human race ensue upon division, now it arises by occupation alone.

Occupation of empire and occupation of property distinguished.

There may be occupation of empire, whose subjects are (1) persons, (2) territory, or occupation of property. Empire and property are often acquired by the same act, but the two are distinct.

Lib. ii. c. 3. *De acquisitione originaria rerum, ubi de mari et fluminibus.*

It is naturally possible to occupy rivers s. 7. and portions of the sea, but *jus gentium* may limit the right.

Rivers may be occupied, even although their upper and lower courses lie beyond our bounds. It is sufficient that the water is shut up between our banks and that by comparison with our lands the stream is small. In like fashion it would appear that sea is capable of occupation by the possessor of land on either hand, including the cases of gulfs and straits, provided that the sea expanse is not so great that compared with the land it cannot be deemed a portion of it. But many things which are naturally permissible, may be prohibited by *jus gentium* by a certain common consent. Accordingly, wherever such *jus gentium* is in force and has not been repealed by common consent, no portion of the sea, however inconsiderable it may be in extent, and howsoever nearly shut in by shores, can ever become the property of a particular people. Even where such *jus gentium* is not received or has been repealed, it does not necessarily follow that a sea is occupied by a people because they have occupied the neighbouring land: the intention to occupy must be set out in overt act, or, in default, the sea will revert to its ancient condition of common use. It is certain that, even when a sea has been occupied, it is open to harmless and innocent navigation, since the like passage cannot be refused in the case of land, in which case the necessity is commonly less and the consequences are more dangerous.

To establish a claim in the sea an overt act of occupation is essential.

The right of the occupier does not override the right of innocent use.

s. 12. Sea dominion does not necessarily imply proprietorship.

It may very easily happen that there is empire over a part of the sea without any other proprietorship. Sea empire is acquired in the same fashion as land empire, to wit, through persons or through territory: it may be acquired by a fleet riding thereon, or by the command from the land of those making use of the water. It is not contrary either to *jus naturæ* or to *jus gentium* that those who have assumed the burden of protecting navigation should impose a reasonable tax upon navigators. Treaties have been made between particular peoples imposing restrictions upon their use of particular seas, but such arrangements prove nothing concerning the occupation of the sea or the general right of navigation. The difficulties which frequently arise between neighbouring states in consequence of a change in the course of a stream must be settled by reference to the nature and manner of acquisition. The ownership of lands divided and marked out by artificial boundaries, or comprised within recognised measures, such as hundreds or acres, is unaffected by the change of a river course. The ownership of lands defined by natural boundaries is altered by a change of course of the bounding river: whatever the river adds to particular land is annexed to the empire of the ruler of that land. The case is entirely altered if the river entirely forsake its former channel and force a new one. If a dividing river be entirely dried up, the boundary is to be determined by the middle of the bed. In doubtful cases lands which reach to a river are to be considered as naturally bounded by the river: it may happen, however, that the entire stream belongs to the owner of a single bank. It remains to observe that things which are derelict by abandonment, or which are vacant by the extinction of their owners, are proper subjects for original acquisition. Furthermore original acquisition is sometimes so made by a people or prince that, not only the *dominium eminens* hitherto spoken of, but the actual ownership remains in the people or prince, the possession being subsequently assigned to individuals by one or other of various dependent titles.

How sea is occupied. *Lib.* ii. c. 3, s. 13.

The fair limits of taxation upon navigation.

How changes in the course of a stream affect territorial rights. *Lib.* ii. c. 3, s. 16.

Derelict property may commonly be acquired by occupation.

Usucapion and prescription properly so called there

Long continued possession furnishes a good international title.

Lib. ii. c. 4. De derelictione præsumta et eam secuta occupatione et quid ab usucapione et præscriptione differat.

cannot be between free peoples or their governors, since they are institutions of municipal law. Long-continued possession is nevertheless wont to be alleged as a title between states.

Legal effects, which depend upon the human mind, cannot be determined by the mental act alone: reference must be made to words and to facts. That is taken as derelict which is abandoned, unless it appears from the circumstances that the relinquishment was intended to be temporary. Forbearance may take rank as a fact: silence may give consent. That dereliction may be presumed from silence, however, it is necessary that the silence be witting and that of the possessor of free will. In this connection lapse of time is of the highest importance. Lapse of time exceeding the memory of man is commonly deemed sufficient to raise a presumption of abandonment of claim, and it may probably be laid down, not only as a matter of presumption but as an institution of *jus gentium voluntarium*, that possession for time out of mind, uninterrupted and unchallenged, conveys absolute ownership. A right may thus be transferred from king to king or from people to people by dereliction followed by assumption of possession, as well as by express consent. Even the rights of sovereignty may be so acquired.

(β) Rights over Persons.

Lib. ii. c. 5. De acquisitione originaria juris in personas.

Rights over persons are originally acquired by (1) generation, (2) consent,

Rights may be acquired over persons as well as over things.

There are three methods of original acquisition of rights over persons:

(1) *By generation*, whence arises the right of parents over children.

(2) *By consent*, whence the right of husbands over wives and rights over particular societies of which a State is the most perfect example. The power of the State over its members is most complete. In default of prohibition an individual subject may quit the State, but for reasons connected with the interests of the State the withdrawal of subjects may be forbidden. A State has no power over exiles.

Voluntary subjection is private or public. Of private

voluntary subjection examples are afforded by *arrogatio* or *adoptio*, and by voluntary self-surrender to slavery. By public subjection a people yields itself up to some person, to some body of persons, or to another people.

(3) delict.

Involuntary subjection, whether of an individual or of a people, arises by forfeiture upon some misdemeanour. So we have the third form of original acquisition: (3) *By misdemeanour* (*ex delicto*).

Derivative Acquisition arises:—

Derivative acquisition arises by act of man or by act of law.

(1) By act of man.

Lib. ii. c. 6. *De acquisitione derivativa facto hominis, ubi de alienatione imperii, et rerum imperii.*

(1) Derivative acquisition by act of man arises by conveyance. For a valid conveyance there is required on the part alike of the transferror and transferree an act of will and an actual setting forth of that will.

Essentials of a valid conveyance.

Sovereignty like anything else may be conveyed: it may be conveyed by the king if the State be patrimonial, otherwise by the people with the assent of the king. In the alienation of a part of a State there is required the consent of the part which it is proposed to alienate. On the other hand a part cannot separate from the body, unless it plainly cannot otherwise preserve itself from destruction.

The empire over any particular place, that is any piece of territory, which lies uninhabited and waste may be alienated at will by a free people or by a king with the sanction of the people. But, if a free people may not convey the empire over a part of the people without the assent of that part, much less may a king.

Infeoffment is a species of, to wit a conditional, conveyance, so also is a testament.

(2) By act of law:

Lib. ii. c. 7. *De acquisitione derivativa quæ fit per legem, ubi de successionibus ab intestato.*

(2) Derivative acquisition by act of law arises under the Law of Nature, the Voluntary Law of Nations or Civil Law. The last may be neglected as leading us too far afield.

(i) Under the Law of Nature,

Under the Law of Nature alienation is effected in two ways; (1) by the satisfaction of a claim of right, and (2) by succession. In the former case some other thing of equal value is accepted in lieu of a thing due. In the latter, he to whom it may be reasonably inferred that the late owner would have desired it to pass succeeds to property.

Children naturally succeed to parents. Kingdoms in respect of succession are distinguishable according as they are patrimonial or held by popular consent. In each case, in default of express regulation, succession proceeds by certain well-recognised inferential rules.

(ii) Under the Voluntary Law of Nations, *Lib. ii. c. 8. De acquisitionibus quæ vulgo dicuntur juris gentium.*

Through the Voluntary Law of Nations arises the acquisition which comes by right of war. The Roman lawyers improperly enumerated as belonging to *jus gentium* several modes of acquisition, which are in fact the creation of the Law of Nature or of Municipal Law. They classified for example as *juris gentium,* (i) acquisition by occupation of things without owner (*res nullius*), a purely natural title; (ii) acquisition by alluvial accretion, which is recognised by the particular laws of some nations; (iii) acquisition by the rule *partus ventrem sequitur*, a maxim of municipal origin; (iv) acquisition by virtue of the combination of materials belonging to different owners (*confusio, specificatio*); and (v) acquisition by delivery, both which last belong to Civil Law.

(iii) Under Municipal Law.

Empire and property alike cease

Empire and property, acquired in one or other of the foregoing fashions, cease in the following ways:—

(1) by abandonment,

(1) By abandonment (*derelictio*).

(2) by extinction of the subject-matter. *Lib. ii. c. 9. Quando imperia vel dominia desinant.*

(2) By the extinction of the subject-matter. A people may become extinct either by the annihilation of its corporate body or by the annihilation of its corporate species or spirit. The first occurs upon the destruction of the essential parts of the people, or upon the voluntary or compulsory dispersion of its constituents; the second upon the loss of corporate legal community. A people does not cease to be by mere migration, if the corporate form be retained, much less by the destruction of its walls. Nor does it signify whether its government be that of Monarch, of Aristocracy, or of Demos. A debt contracted by a free people remains a debt still due when the people has passed under the rule of a king. If two nations are united their several rights are not lost but combined, and that whether they be really united, or merely joined by an alliance, or by the rule of a common king.

If, on the other hand, a state be divided, whether by mutual consent or by force of war, the divided parts must be deemed so many sovereignties, each with its particular authority; if anything were held by them in common, it must now be administered in common or divided *pro rata*. In this connection may be discussed the famous question as to the present vesting of the rights of the Roman Empire. In the author's opinion, the rights of the Roman Empire are still ultimately vested in the Roman people. *Lib.* ii. c. 9, s. 11.

General duties which arise upon the establishment of rights.

Lib. ii. c. 10. *De obligatione quæ ex dominio oritur.*

Obligations arise (*a*) Under the Law of Nature:— (1) By pact.

Lib. ii. c. 11. *De promissis.*

Lib. ii. c. 12. *De contractibus.*

Lib. ii. c. 13. *De jure jurando.*

Turning now to the duties attendant upon established rights over things, we may note, in general, that (1) he who has in his hands an object belonging to another, by whatever means the holder may have obtained possession, is bound to do his utmost to secure its passing into the owner's power; (2) he who has been enriched by the consumption of another's property lies under an obligation to recoup that other for his loss. Obligations may be created by contract, by misfeasance, or by law. The fulfilment of promises is a duty rooted in the nature of immutable Justice. Thus we introduce the detailed consideration of the essentials and consequences of promises, of contracts and of oaths.

The promises, contracts and oaths of kings are binding in cases in which private men might claim *restitutio in integrum*.

Lib. ii. c. 14. *De eorum qui summum imperium habent promissis et contractibus et juramentis.*

There are those who argue that the same reasons, e.g. fraud, mistake, or fear, which excuse a private individual from the performance of his promise, contract, or oath, do in like fashion excuse a king. This is true indeed of the private acts of a king, and, where a king is not possessed of absolute power, his acts may be avoided entirely or in part as being contrary to constitutional law; but, in general, the act of the king must be deemed the act of the whole people, and in the case of contracts made by the king *restitutio in integrum*, which is a creation of Municipal Law, has no application.

Promises which are full, absolute and accepted, convey rights in the mouths of kings, as in the mouths of private men. Kings are bound by their promises, though made without consideration (*causa*).

Classification of Public Conventions:— *Lib.* ii. c. 15. *De fœderibus ac sponsionibus.*

Public Conventions include leagues, public engagements (*sponsiones*) and other pacts. Leagues are made by direct command of the Sovereign Power. A public engagement is an undertaking made concerning some public matter by one who is without a commission in that regard.

1. Leagues. Their varieties.

Leagues either stipulate for that which is in accordance with the Law of Nature or add somewhat to that law. Amongst leagues of the first order may be mentioned treaties stipulating for hospitality and freedom of commerce. Conventions of the latter order are either equal or unequal. There may be an equal or an unequal treaty of peace, and an equal or unequal treaty of alliance. An unequal treaty of alliance may or may not diminish sovereign rights.

With whom they may be made.

The making of a treaty with an enemy of the true religion is permissible by the Law of Nature, and is not wholly forbidden either by the Mosaic Law or by the Law of Christ. On the other hand, all Christians ought undoubtedly to make common cause against the advance of enemies of the Faith.

Obligations arising therefrom.

If war breaks out between two of our allies we must assist him who wages the juster war. If the cause of both be unjust we must abstain from taking any part.
s. 13. If both have just cause, we must as far as possible aid both.

A league entered into for a limited time is not to be presumed as tacitly renewed, except in the presence of acts which can bear no other interpretation. If one party violates a league, the other may withdraw from it.

2. Public engagement (*sponsiones*).

Public engagements (*sponsiones*) are, in respect of subject-matter, as various in kind as leagues. If a public engagement be disapproved, the state is not obliged either to make it good or to restore matters to their original condition; but the promiser is bound to satisfaction in person and in goods. If a public engagement be made subject to the condition of ratification, it is in the absence of ratification of no force. And even in the case of an engagement unconditionally made, silence on the part of the sovereign power cannot *per se* be held to be consent.

In the interpretation of promises certain definite rules are to be followed.
Lib. ii. c. 16. *De interpretatione.*

The terms of promises are to be interpreted by certain definite rules. Thus:—

(1) In default of special evidence to the contrary, words are to be understood in their common popular sense.

(2) Terms of art are to be understood in accordance with the understanding of experts in the art.

(3) Words or sentences which are equivocal or ambiguous must be interpreted by presumptions based upon (i) their subject-matter, (ii) their effect, (iii) their original occasion and place of employment.

(4) Words are to be variously interpreted according as they are odious, favourable, or mixed in operation.

(5) Where the design is clear, its fulfilment may justify departure from the letter of the promise. A restrictive is in this regard more readily admissible than an extensive interpretation.

(6) An extrinsic restrictive interpretation may be based upon presumed original defect of the will of the promiser, or upon the happening of an event inconsistent with that will. Original defect of will may be presumed from an absurd result, from the failure of motive, or from defect in the matter. Inconsistency with design may be assumed: (i) in pursuance of natural reason, when literal interpretation leads to an illegal or intolerable result; (ii) from other signs of the will of the promiser, as when the words to be interpreted are inconsistent with other words of the promiser. In this last connection: (1) a mere permission must yield to a command; (2) that which is to be done at a time certain is to be preferred to that which may be done at any time; (3) a prohibition outweighs a command; (4) a particular takes precedence of a general pact; (5) the more outweighs the less honourable; (6) in the last resort, the later is to be preferred. A pact on oath it may be added is to be interpreted in accordance with the common meaning of words, and with the exclusion of all tacit or unnecessary restrictions; and

a pact so fortified is to be preferred to one entered into in any less formal fashion.

The Roman Law is not, except on strong evidence of its applicability, to be taken as particularly valuable in interpreting the language of princes.

(2) By wrong-doing. *Lib.* ii. c. 17. *De damno per injuriam dato, et obligatione quæ inde oritur.* If, by reason of any act or omission conflicting with the duty incumbent upon men in common or upon the man in particular, damage ensues, there arises a natural obligation of reparation. The obligation extends not only to principals but to accessories, and not only to the simple fact but to consequential injury. Kings and magistrates, to whom it belongs to restrain robberies and piracy, are bound to reparation, should they neglect to employ in this regard all the means in their power.

(*b*) Under the Law of Nations:— So far of duties arising by the Law of Nature. But duties are likewise imposed by the Voluntary Law of Nations.

(1) *Jus Legationum.* *Lib.* ii. c. 18. *De legationum jure.* Here the first place belongs to the law with respect to the rights and duties of Embassage. These rights and duties, in so far as they are matter of *jus gentium*, affect those ambassadors only who are employed by Sovereign Powers *inter se.* In Civil Wars, more particularly where the opposing parties are so equally divided as to make it difficult to determine with whom rests the sovereignty, necessity may compel departure from this principle, but that irregularly.

Ambassadors are endowed with The Law of Nations accords to ambassadors, (1) a right of admission, (2) immunity from violence.

1. A right of reception. Ambassadors may be refused admission, but not without particular cause. Good cause may be found in (1) the person of the sender, (2) the person of the envoy, or (3) the subject of the mission. *Optimo jure rejici possunt quæ nunc in usu sunt legationes assiduæ, quibus quam non sit*
s. 3. *opus docet mox antiquus cui illæ ignoratæ.*

2. A right of immunity. What is the extent of legatine immunity? The subject of the extent of legatine immunities is very variously handled by contemporary authorities of eminence. Some hold that under the Law of Nations the person of an ambassador is protected against unjust

force only. Others contend that force may only be applied to an ambassador when he has personally violated the Law of Nations; a contention which is sufficiently sweeping, since, the Law of Nature being included in the Law of Nations, an ambassador would thus be punishable in respect of all offences except those created by mere municipal law. Others again restrict the field of legitimate force to offences aimed at the state-being of the republic, or at the dignity of the prince to whom the ambassador is sent. There are those who think that even this position is perilous, and would have complaint made to the accrediting sovereign, and the ambassador remitted to that sovereign for punishment. There are yet others who would have appeal made to disinterested kings or peoples; a suggestion which may be well enough from the point of view of prudence, but hardly touches the question of law.

The answer must be derived from the practice of nations.

The question raised is to be resolved by reference not to the firm ground of Natural Law, but to the free will of nations. Nations might have granted to ambassadors immunity, either absolute or subject to limitations. What nations have in fact resolved on cannot be determined from precedents alone, these being by no means consistent. Recourse must be had to the judgment of wise men and to considerations of probability. Led by these, the author is of opinion that nations have been pleased that the common custom, whereby every person being within foreign territory is subjected to the territorial law, shall suffer exception in the case of ambassadors, insomuch that, just as these are by a certain fiction held representative of the persons of their accreditors, so also, by a like fiction, they are made as it were extra-territorial. Accordingly, if an ambassador commit some unimportant offence, it may be winked at; or the ambassador may be ordered to quit the country. If the crime be heinous, and such as injuriously affects the public weal, the ambassador must be sent to him who accredited him, with a request that he shall either punish him or surrender him for punishment. In case of extreme necessity, nevertheless, not by way of punishment but by way of preventing some grave, especially a public, evil, an ambassador may be apprehended and examined; and, if he be guilty of armed assault, he may be slain in self-defence by the person assailed. It is only at the hands of the sovereign to whom he is accredited, and by whom he has been granted admission, that the ambassador is thus sacred. His character in no way ties the hands of other sovereigns through whose territories he passes without permission (*non accepta venia*).

The immunity is confined to the territory of the receiver.

Lib. ii. c. 18, s. 5.

An ambassador is not to be subjected to retaliation.

An ambassador may not be put to death by way of retaliation for similar treatment of an ambassador by his principal. The Law of Nations looks not only to the dignity of the accreditor, but to the security of the envoy.

The immunity of the ambassador's suite and personal effects.

Within the immunity of the ambassador are comprehended his suite and personal effects (*vasa*), but these are privileged only as being accessory, and consequently so long as the ambassador deems proper. Accordingly, if members of his suite commit a heinous offence, the ambassador may be asked to hand them over to justice.

An ambassador is not endowed *jure gentium* with any jurisdiction *in familiam*, nor his house with any *jus asyli*.

Whether the ambassador has jurisdiction over his household, or whether there exists any *jus asyli* in his house for those fleeing thither, must depend upon the concession of the sovereign with whom he is resident. The Law of Nations confers no such rights. It is the better opinion that the moveables of an ambassador and other articles annexed to his person are exempt from all seizure by way of pledge, or for the satisfaction of a debt, whether by process of court or by the royal hand. Nor is there ground for the fear expressed by some that, if such be the law, none will be found willing to contract with an ambassador. Kings, whom none can force to payment, never want for creditors.

Lib. ii. c. 18, s. 8. The civil immunity of the ambassador's goods.

s. 9.

s. 10.

Profane and sacred history alike tell of numerous wars begun on account of the ill-handling of ambassadors. And Cicero deems that there can be no more just cause.

(2) The right of burial.

A second duty arising by the Voluntary Law of

Nations is that of burying the dead. It is due to open enemies. Ancient authorities agree with one consent that its refusal constitutes a just cause of war.

So far, dealing with the causes of war, we have considered violations of right as furnishing ground for reparative action. A violation of right may have, however, another aspect, viz. the punitive. So war may be justifiable by way of punishment. Punishment is *malum passionis quod infligitur ob malum actionis.* It properly belongs to the sphere of expletive justice. Nature fails to determine the person to whom the right to punish belongs, but a man certainly ought not to be punished by one who is equally guilty. The end of human punishment is threefold: (1) the good of the offender, (2) the good of the sufferer, (3) the good of men at large. The good of the offender is secured by his amendment, the good of the sufferer by the prevention of the like offences against him in future, (3) the good of men at large by the protection afforded by the fear of punishment. Punishment should be proportioned to the offence. In this regard consideration must be had to the impelling and the restraining motive, and to the openness of the person to the influence of each.

(II) *Causes of War grounded in punitive action.* Violations of Right furnish ground not only for reparative but for punitive action.

Lib. ii. c. 20. *De poenis.*

War may be justly waged by way of punishment;

There are certain considerations affecting the waging of war by way of punishment which ought not to be overlooked.

subject to certain limitations.

War is not to be waged for an offence merely inchoate, unless the matter affected be of great concern, and some injurious consequences or some great peril have already ensued.

Kings and those who are equal in power to kings may exact punishment, not only for injuries done to themselves or to their subjects, but in respect of acts which constitute in respect of any person whatever a grievous violation of the Law of Nature or of the Law of Nations (*quae jus naturae aut gentium immaniter violant*). The right to consult by punishment the good of human society in general, a right belonging in the beginning of

Sovereigns may exact punishment on behalf of any injured person from any grievous violator of the Law of Nature or the Law of Nations.

things to individuals, has, since the institution of states and magistrates, come to be reposed in the holders of sovereign power. It is in very truth more honourable to avenge the injuries of others. Wars may thus be justly begun against those who are impious to parents, who slay the passing stranger, who practise cannibalism or piracy. So the author contends against Victoria, Vasquez, Molina and others, who seem to hold it essential to the justice of a war that he who undertakes it shall either be injured in his own person or in his state, or shall have jurisdiction over the wrong-doer. The right of punishment arises not, as these think, from municipal jurisdiction, but from the Law of Nature.

The Law of Nature must, however, be distinguished from municipal customs generally received, and from Voluntary Divine Law not known to all mankind, and the obvious must be distinguished from the less obvious principles of Natural Law.

Certain cautionary remarks are here necessary. The first is, that municipal customs, though they be received with good reason among (*inter*) many peoples, must not be mistaken for Natural Law. The second is, that amongst things forbidden by Nature must not be rashly enumerated some, the evidence concerning which is insufficient to do more than show that they conflict with the Voluntary Law of God. The third is, that a distinction is to be carefully maintained between general principles and inferences therefrom, obvious although some of these last be.

May wars be made in respect of offences against God? Violators of the simplest religious notions are rightly punished,

May wars be made in respect of offences against God? Some authorities decide in the negative, on the ground that the right of punishment predicates jurisdiction, or on the stronger ground that God is sufficient for the punishment of offences committed against Him. But religion is the cement of human society. Its utility is even greater in the larger society of mankind in general than in the limited society of any particular state, where its place is partly supplied by laws. The two notions that God is, and that He cares for the affairs of men, are universally received, and are essential to any religion, whether true or false. They who first attempt to overthrow these notions may well be restrained in the name of human society. Other simple notions of the true religion, e.g. that there is but one God, that God is invisible, that God created the world, are not equally patent, and the knowledge of them has become obliterated amongst some peoples. They accordingly are not proper subjects for human punishment who worship the stars of heaven or other natural objects. It follows that war may not justly be begun upon peoples because they refuse to accept the truths of Christianity. They who persecute the teachers or professors of Christianity sin against reason, and are properly punishable by war. Heretics are not to be so forcibly coerced. A more just punishment were that of those who are irreverent and irreligious towards the God Whom they accept.

but not so those who refuse to embrace Christianity. War may be made on persecutors of Christians but not on heretics.

They who are accomplices in an offence are properly punishable as for positive wrong-doing. A state, like any other corporation, is only accountable in respect of the conduct of its members by reason of its own act or omission. A ruler becomes responsible in respect of a crime by tolerance (*patientia*) or the grant of protection (*receptus*). He is responsible by tolerance, if, being at once cognisant of the offence and able to prohibit, he fails to prohibit. He is responsible by the grant of protection when he harbours a fugitive criminal, and fails either to punish him or deliver him up on demand to the state which seeks his punishment. The right of asylum exists for the undeservedly distressed (*qui immerito odio laborant*), not for offenders against human society or against the rights of their fellows.

Guilt may be communicated between sovereign and subjects.
Lib. ii. c. 21. *De poenarum communicatione.*

Subjects in like fashion make themselves responsible for the crime of their sovereign, if they consent thereto, or act illegally under his persuasion or command. There may be communication of guilt between individual members and a whole community. The offences of a community are not to be visited upon succeeding generations.

A distinction may be drawn between *causae justificae* and *causae suasoriae*, i.e. between the justifying occasions and the impelling motives of war. They who begin war without either, from the mere love of the thing, are no better than brute beasts. The majority of belligerents

Certain pretexts not uncommonly put forward furnish no just cause of war, e.g.:—
Lib. ii. c. 22. *De causis injustis.*

are at least actuated by *causae suasoriae*, but since some from time to time allege as *causae justificae* matters which on examination prove to furnish no just occasion of war, enumeration may be made of a few *causae injustae*.

1. Fear of the growing strength of a neighbour,

(1) The dread of a neighbour's increasing strength affords no legitimate cause for war. Nothing short of moral certainty that he has not only the power but the intention to injure will justify recourse to arms.

2. Refusal of matrimonial alliance, 3. Desire after change of seat, 4. Discovery in the case of lands already inhabited,

(2) The refusal of matrimonial alliance furnishes a no better occasion, nor does (3) the desire after a change of national seat bring us to firmer ground. It is equally unjust to embark upon war in virtue of (4) alleged title by discovery, when the territory in question is already inhabited, even though it be by worthless, impious or degraded peoples. *Inventio est eorum quae nullius sunt. Neque ad dominium requiritur, aut virtus moralis, aut religiosa, aut intellectus perfectio: nisi quod hoc videtur posse defendi si qui sint populi omnino destituti a rationis usu, eos dominium non habere, sed ex caritate tantum iis deberi quae ad vitam sunt necessaria: nam quae alibi diximus de sustentatione dominii, quam pro infantibus et amentibus facit jus gentium, ad eos populos pertinet, cum quibus est pactorum commercium: tales autem non sunt populi si qui reperiuntur toti amentes, de quo merito dubito.*

Lib. ii. c. 22, s. 10.

5. Natural Liberty,

(5) Liberty, whether of individuals or that freedom of states which is called *αὐτονομία*, cannot be legitimately alleged, in the light of a natural and always claimable condition, as good ground for war. When individuals or peoples are said to be naturally free, the reference is to that state of Nature which preceded all human action.

6. The subjugation of natural slaves,

(6) It is unjust to subject by force of arms, as being only fit for servitude, those whom the philosophers sometimes styled "slaves by Nature."

7. The Universal Dominion of the Roman Emperor,

(7) The title to Universal Dominion, ascribed by some to the Roman Emperor, were too vain for notice if Bartolus, long held the prince of jurisconsults, had not gone so far as to declare its denial heresy. The Roman

Emperor has now a legal right not even to all those territories which once belonged to the Roman people. Some have been lost by war, some alienated by treaty, others have passed by dereliction to various kings and peoples. Some states, which were formerly fully subject, have since become but partially so, or have assumed the position of confederates in an unequal alliance.

8. The Universal Dominion of the Pope.

(8) The claim to legal rights over the peoples of the undiscovered parts of the earth, asserted on behalf of the Church, is equally futile. Christ's Kingdom was not of this world, and, were He now to claim legions, they were of angels, not of men. And a Bishop should be no striker.

Be it in conclusion noted, that a war, for which just cause exists, does not cease to be just because the belligerent is really actuated by an evil motive.

War should be if possible avoided. *Lib.* ii. c. 23. *De causis dubiis.*

When there is doubt as to the justice of competing courses in a matter of importance, and one alternative must be taken, he acts justly who selects the safer. War is a matter of the highest import; by it the innocent suffer many afflictions. It follows that war should where possible be by all means avoided.

Misunderstandings between sovereigns may be cleared up by (1) conference, (2) arbitration, or (3) lot.

There are certain methods short of war by which misunderstandings between princes may be cleared up. They are (1) conference, (2) arbitration, and (3) the casting of lots. Akin to this last is single combat, which may well be accepted as a method of decision when two princes, whose controversy would otherwise involve whole peoples, are ready to commit their dispute to the fortune of the lists.

Possession gives superior claims.

Although both parties in a case of doubt are bound to seek out the conditions for averting war, the possessor has the stronger claim. When neither claimant is in possession, or when both are equally so, he who refuses to divide the subject in dispute must be reputed unjust.

Let Christian and prudent men hesitate to make war. *Lib.* ii. c. 24. *Monita de non temere etiam ex justis causis suscipiendo bello.*

Very many considerations, based on Christian Charity or on prudence, dictate moderation in asserting by war even the soundest claims. War is only in fact to be undertaken when the conditions upon which peace is obtainable are worse than war itself.

War may be justly made, not only on behalf of our own violated rights, but on behalf of

Lib. ii. c. 25. *De causis belli pro aliis suscipiendi.*

Subject to the foregoing principles, war may be justly undertaken not only on behalf of self but of others.

1. Subjects,

1. War may be made on behalf of subjects. A sovereign is not, however, obliged to take up arms in respect of the just claims of any one of his subjects, except when many or all his subjects would otherwise suffer inconvenience. One innocent subject may actually be surrendered to preserve the rest.

2. Allies,

2. Allies may be defended next to, or equally with, subjects, when the terms of the alliance so require. But the obligation ceases when their war is unjust, or if there be absolutely no hope of a successful issue.

3. Friends,

3. War may be waged for the protection of friends apart from any express promise.

4. Fellow men.

4. Common humanity may call to war. If the wrong be patent, it may even be legitimate to assist subjects of a foreign state against the oppressive action of their prince.

But no alliance for war is just apart from the justice of the cause of war.

Military alliances which are entered into for mutual assistance, without reference to the causes of war, are altogether illegitimate, and no course of life is more reprehensible than that of mercenaries, who wage war without regard to cause purely for pay.

Superior orders will not justify war-waging if the war be unjust.

Lib. ii. c. 26. *De causis justis ut bellum geratur ab his qui sub alieno imperio sunt.*

War may be well waged by subjects under the orders of their sovereign, but, if the war be obviously unjust, it is the moral duty of the subject to disobey. Moreover, if a man be persuaded that a certain course is unjust, it is unjust for him. In cases of doubt it may be argued that the subject will do right in obeying orders, but it were the safer course to refrain from war. Declarations of war were formerly wont to be made public, in order that all mankind might judge of the justice of the proceeding. It were an act of grace on the part of a prince to dispense with the personal service of scrupulous subjects, substituting, should he think proper, an extraordinary tax. Even in an unjust war, subjects assailed may take up arms in their own defence.

But men may in all cases defend themselves when assailed.

What force is allowable in war?
Lib. iii. c. 1. *Quantum in bello liceat, regulae generales ex jure naturae: ubi et de dolis et mendacio.*

We are now in a position to consider what is allowable in war, the extent of permissible force, and the methods by which it may be applied.

The problems thus indicated may be dealt with as entirely unaffected, or as affected, by antecedent promise. Considered under the former condition, we must examine, first, the requirements of the Law of Nature.

[I.] Apart from special undertaking.

(a) Under the Law of Nature it is legitimate to have recourse against an enemy to 1. All means necessary to the just end, 2. Or to the prosecution of supervening rights, and 3. All means incidental to the prosecution of just rights.

Here we may lay down certain clear general principles.

1. Those means are just which are morally necessary to the attainment of a just end.

2. The belligerent's right in war-waging is not defined by the beginning of the war alone: it may be affected by events subsequently transpiring.

3. Proceedings, which were illegitimate if the outcome of direct design, may be proper when they arise as incidental consequences of the prosecution of legal right.

By the application of these general rules it is possible to ascertain the measure of force which it is naturally legitimate to exercise against an enemy.

Lib. iii. c. 1. s. 5.
What of a third party who supplies an enemy?
Distinction of the articles supplied,

But there are those who are not enemies, or who at any rate wish not to be so styled, who cater for the enemy's needs. What force may be legitimately exercised against them? Here we must distinguish amongst the articles which may be supplied. Some things, such as arms, are useful in war only; some, such as articles of luxurious living, have no warlike use; some, such as money, provisions, ships and ships' furniture, are useful alike in war and in time of peace. He who furnishes to an enemy articles of the first order is a direct partaker in that enemy's war. The supply of articles of the second order is obviously innocent. In the case of the supply of articles of the third order, i.e. articles of ambiguous use (*ancipitis usus*), regard must be had to the state of the war. If I cannot protect myself without intercepting the articles sent, necessity gives me the right to seize them, but subject to the obligation of restitution unless reason to the contrary supervene. If the supply sent hinder the execution of my lawful designs, and the supplier might and the position of belligerent affairs.

have known as much; for example, if I hold a town under siege, approach is cut off and surrender or peace is looked for, the supplier is as much bound to give me satisfaction as he who releases my debtor from prison, or aids him in his escape. Accordingly I may seize his property, and hold it in satisfaction to the extent of my loss. If he actually occasioned me no loss, but designed so to do, justice will bear me out in compelling him, by the detention of his goods, to give security for the future, by pledge, hostages or the like. Furthermore, if the injustice of my enemy in my regard is obvious, and a third party encourages him in an iniquitous war, that third party is not only civilly obliged to satisfaction for damage but criminally punishable, being in the condition of one who rescues from the hands of justice a notorious malefactor. In this event, he may be dealt with agreeably to his offence; so he may be pillaged by way of penalty. Belligerents have been wont, in view of these facts, to issue public intimations (*significationes*) to other peoples setting out, not only the justice of their cause, but their reasonable hopes of successful prosecution of their right.

Force and terror are the specially appropriate agents in waging war. Fraud is justified within certain limits. It is illegitimate to compel or solicit illegal action.

Force and terror are the specially appropriate agents in the waging of war. Fraud is likewise legitimate, but within certain limits. Stratagem is often to be commended. The impropriety of a lie is founded in repugnancy with another's right. It is, thus, lawful to lie to an enemy, but not in words promissory, nor in words fortified by an oath. It is illegitimate in the prosecution of war to compel or solicit another to do that which is illegitimate for him: it is illegitimate, for example, to force or persuade a subject to kill his prince. But it is not illegitimate to employ for the doing of an act, which is legitimate for the employer, the freely offered services of an agent for whom the doing is illegitimate.

(β) *Under the Law of Nations.*

Lib. iii. c. 2. *Quo modo jure gentium bona subditorum pro debito*

The Law of Nations introduces certain further regulations as to the carrying on of war, some of these being general, others affecting particular species of war.

Contrary to the principle of Natural Law, which requires

that no man, except the heir in respect of one deceased, shall be held bound in respect of the debt of another, the Voluntary Law of Nations imposes liability in respect of the obligations of any civil society, or of its head, upon all the property, corporeal and incorporeal, of the subjects of that society or head. Of legal execution in virtue of this principle the Athenian *Androlepsia* furnished an ancient example. Another is supplied by that international pledge-taking which modern lawyers refer to under the name of *jus repressaliarum*, and the French, with whom authorisation was wont to be sought from the king, as *literae Marcae*. This mode of proceeding is proper when right is denied, either by unreasonable delay or by a judicial sentence clearly unjust. The right does not, however, reach to the lives of innocent subjects, except in so far as these are incidentally killed whilst resisting its exercise. By the Law of Nations all subjects of a wrong-doer, whether they be natives or incomers, are exposed to the exercise of this right, provided that they be permanently subjects, and not mere passing travellers or temporary sojourners. By Municipal Law particular classes of persons are exempt. By the Municipal Law of some states authority to seize must be obtained from the sovereign; elsewhere it may be obtained from a judge. By the Law of Nations the property in the goods taken immediately accrues to the captor to the extent of the debt due and of expenses, and any balance ought to be restored. Under Municipal Law all interested persons are wont to be cited and the goods sold and adjudged under authority of the State.

imperantium obligentur: ubi de repressaliis.

The property and persons of subjects are held responsible in respect of the obligations of their government.

Examples are furnished by 1. Androlepsia, 2. Reprisals.

A war to be just must be a contest of sovereign states; and not only so, it should furthermore be publicly declared, and that in such sort that the one party makes known his intention to the other. A clear distinction must here be drawn between the requirements of the Law of Nature, of Honour, of the Law of Nations and of the institutions of particular peoples. By the Law of Nature no declaration is required, when war is begun by way of repelling hostile force or of exacting punishment. When, however, one

A Declaration of War, not required by the Law of Nature, is called for by the Law of Nations

Lib. iii. c. 3. *De bello justo sive solenni jure Gentium, ubi de indictione.*

object is seized in lieu of another, or the property of a debtor is taken in respect of a debt, a prior demand is necessary; much more then is notice requisite before the property of subjects is attacked in respect of the debts of the prince, or *vice versa.* Motives of honour may induce the giving of notice, where by the Law of Nature notice is not strictly necessary. Notice may be required under the Municipal Law of a particular state, as was the case amongst the Israelites. The Law of Nations is satisfied if notice be given on the part of one of the belligerents.

at least on one side.

Forms and effect of declaration.

A declaration of war may be conditional or absolute. The Municipal Law of some states lays down a particular ceremonial for the declaration of war. War duly declared upon a sovereign is deemed to be declared upon his subjects and allies. The necessity for a declaration of war is grounded not in the prevention of secret or crafty dealing, but in the need that it be certainly known that the contest is begun, not by private daring, but by the express will of both peoples or of their rulers. Hostile operations may be begun immediately after the declaration of war.

The extent of the right of a belligerent in respect of (1) *the person.*

Lib. iii. c. 4. *De jure interficiendi hostes in bello solenni, et alia vi in corpus.*

A proceeding may be lawful in two senses: (1) as being altogether right and worthy, although another course might be more laudable; (2) as being adopted with legal impunity, albeit not without some moral taint. In this latter sense, a sense in which the lawful and the proper may be opposed, the right of the belligerent to injure his enemy alike in person and property is practically unlimited.

It reaches to (i) all bearing hostile arms, (ii) all subjects of the enemy, (iii) all those remaining within hostile borders after notice of war.

This right extends, in the first place, to the person. It extends, not only to those who bear arms or who are the subjects of a belligerent power, but to all those who are within the hostile borders. Foreigners who came within the belligerent borders before the outbreak of war appear by the Law of Nations to be entitled to a reasonable time within which to withdraw, but foreigners who come into belligerent territory after war is proclaimed, and with full knowledge of it, may indubitably be treated as subjects of the territory. Those who are permanently subjects of the enemy may, as far as their own persons are concerned, be under the Law of Nations assaulted anywhere. They may be killed with impunity on their own soil, on hostile soil, on soil which is *res nullius* and on the sea. The rule which forbids their slaughter or injury on neutral soil (*in territorio pacato*) is grounded, not in respect for their own personality, but in regard for the rights of the local sovereign. The extent of the strict belligerent right may be gauged from the fact that women and young children may in virtue of that right be slaughtered with impunity. Women and children were in fact not infrequently slaughtered in the wars of Antiquity. Prisoners, alike male and female, were not exempt from this licence; nor by the Law of Nations is the power to put these to death taken away, albeit by the Municipal Laws of states it be more or less restrained. Suppliants and enemies who have surrendered at discretion have been treated in times past with equal harshness. Historians have on occasion excused such severity, as being the outcome of retaliation or of an over-obstinate defence. Such considerations concern the actuating motive, not the justification. Retaliation would properly reach the offenders only, whereas belligerent reprisals have a wider operation. An obstinate defence is so far from criminal, that its opposite was by the Romans deemed a capital crime.

It reaches the enemy anywhere, saving respect for the sovereignty of third powers.

It extends to the slaughter of

i. Women and Children,

ii. Prisoners,

iii. Suppliants and foes surrendering at discretion,

The right of the belligerent in respect of the person has been extended to hostages, as well those who have been handed over by others as those who have bound themselves voluntarily.

iv. Hostages.

Thus the Law of Nations tolerates many things which are expressly forbidden by the Law of Nature. On the other hand, it prohibits some proceedings which the Law of Nature allows. So the Law of Nations, at least as practised by the more civilised peoples, prohibits the slaying of an enemy by poison, a proceeding which would appear in no way opposed to the Law of Nature. The use of poisoned arms *contra jus est gentium non universale sed gentium Europaearum et si quae ad Europae melioris*

The Law of Nations prohibits certain belligerent proceedings which the Law of Nature allows, e.g. :—

i. The use of poison,

s. 16. *cultum accedunt.* Florus declares the poisoning of springs to be contrary not only to *mos majorum* but to *fas Deorum.* The mere contamination of waters so as to render them undrinkable is on another footing, as Solon and the Amphiktions declared.

ii. Assassination, being the *treacherous* slaughter of a foe,

It is questioned whether an enemy may be under the Law of Nations slain by a private emissary. The problem is to be resolved by considering whether the act of the emissary involves or does not involve a breach of pledged faith. The act of a Scaevola and an Eleazar is in no way illegitimate. The punishment meted out to individuals detected in such attempts proves nothing to the contrary. Spies in like fashion may be lawfully employed under the Law of Nations: they may equally under that law be severely handled, if captured. The treacherous assassination of a foe in a solemn war is, alike in the assassin and in his employer, an offence against the Law of Nations.

iii. The dishonour of women.

Some authorities hold the dishonouring of women to be in war allowable, but others assert the contrary, and with these last is the Law of Nations, not indeed of all, but of the more civilised peoples. The Law of Nations, permitting the slaughter of an enemy, naturally allows also the destruction and pillage of his property. The Law of Nations *per se* makes no exception in favour of things sacred or religious. The property so exposed to attack may be taken, not only by open force, but by guile, provided always the guile do not involve treachery.

The extent of belligerent rights in respect of (2) *property.*

Lib. iii. c. 5. *De rebus vastandis eripiendisque.*

The Law of Nations permits:—

(i) The destruction and pillage of the property of the enemy.

By the Law of Nature such property may be acquired in a just war as represents a fair equivalent for a debt due to us, payment of which we cannot obtain, or a fair punishment of an offender. By the Law of Nations, not only he who wages war for a just cause, but every combatant in a solemn war is lord of that of which he makes prize. Moreover it is agreed that a thing must be deemed taken, when it is so detained that the owner has lost all probable hope of recovering it, the thing having escaped pursuit. Moveables are held taken when they are brought *intra fines id est praesidia hostium.* Property taken at sea is deemed

When does property in prize vest?

The case of moveables and immoveables distinguished.

to be taken when brought within the enemies' port, or to the station occupied by their fleet: by later European practice such property is deemed captured when it has remained for 24 hours in the power of the captor. For the conquest of land firm possession is deemed essential. That land will be held taken which is so enclosed by permanent fortifications that approach thereto is cut off until these be forced.

The property of third parties is not good prize.

Property to pass by conquest must belong to the enemy. Property of which the owners are not subjects of our enemy, even although it be found within the enemies' towns or garrisons, is not good prize. The common saying, that goods found in hostile ships must be deemed hostile, must not be taken as a hard and fast rule of the Law of Nations, but as setting out a presumption, which can be overruled by sound proof to the contrary. And so it was adjudged in Holland in full Senate in the year 1338, war being then waged with the Hanse Towns.

The case of neutral property found on the enemy's ship. *Lib.* iii. c. 6. s. 6.

Property taken from our enemy passes to us, albeit that property have previously been taken by the enemy from a third party. Real property is commonly taken by public act alone, and, accordingly, it does not fall under the denomination of booty. Moveables, if taken otherwise than in public service, become the property of the captor, unless the municipal law of the captor's state otherwise ordain. But goods taken by the soldiers in the course of public service accrue, unless the municipal law of the state otherwise provides, to the State, which may distribute it at will.

In whom is the property in prize?

Property taken in territory not belonging to either belligerent may indeed pass to the captor, but the local sovereign may prohibit any such prize-taking, and demand satisfaction should his prohibition be disregarded.

The neutral sovereign may demand restitution of property taken within his bounds.

In pursuance of a practice deemed by the Romans universal all persons taken in war were, as soon as they were brought within the captor's lines, reputed slaves; the right of the lord extended to the subsequent issue of the captive to all generations, and his power over his slave

(ii) The ransom of prisoners. Prisoners of war are not now enslaved, *Lib.* iii. c. 7. *De jure in captivos.*

was unlimited. All property taken with the prisoner passed to the captor. The captor was endowed with these extensive rights by way of inducement to abstain from the exercise of the extreme right of slaughter. The practice so set out has not been at all times or amongst all peoples accepted. Amongst Christians it is universally agreed that war confers no right to enslave prisoners; for them Christian charity should furnish inducements to restraint sufficiently powerful without the support of another motive. But even amongst Christians the custom remains of retaining the prisoner in custody until the payment of a ransom fixed, unless it be otherwise agreed upon, at the will of the captor. This last right is commonly granted to individual captors, except in the case of prisoners of high rank, whose ransom is, by the custom of many peoples, deemed to belong to the State.

but ransoms are still exacted.

(iii) The acquisition of sovereignty by conquest. *Lib.* iii. c. 8. *De imperio in victos.*

By conquest sovereignty itself may be acquired, and the victor may not only succeed to the full rights of the conquered, but assert a more despotic power. Just as the property of individuals passes by the right of war to those who overthrow them, so the property of the State, whether corporeal or incorporeal, passes, if he so please, to the conqueror.

Belligerent rights cease by *postliminium.* *Lib.* iii. c. 9. *De postliminio.*

The right as attached to persons

Postliminium is a right which arises out of return within the *limen*, that is, within the public bounds. The bounds in question may be those of the original state or of a state allied in the war. Return to neutral territory will not avail except in pursuance of special compact. The right is annexed alike to persons and to property. Subjects of third parties surprised upon belligerent territory and retained during the war become immediately free upon the return of peace. Slaves and other property taken during the war are upon the return of peace restored to their original owners only if it be so expressly stipulated. During the time of war a free man is invested with the right of *postliminium* by return with a view thereto in whatever fashion. He thereby returns not only to freedom, but to the possession of all property, corporeal or incorporeal, which he holds in any country which is at peace. The right of *postliminium* is not, however, enjoyed by those who have surrendered at discretion or in time of truce. The right may attach to a people as well as to an individual. It may be limited by the municipal law of the captive's state. Slaves are recovered by right of *postliminium* when they return within the actual or potential power of their owner. Lands are recovered by the same right when the enemy is beaten out of their occupation. Moveables in general are not recoverable by right of *postliminium*. Exception was wont to be made by many ancient nations in favour of particular objects, e.g. ships of war and ships of burden, pack-saddle mules and other objects of warlike use, but this distinction would appear to be now disused.

and as attached to property.

Moveables in general are not recoverable by *postliminium*.

In the case of property which was never carried *intra praesidia hostium* there is no need for recourse to the right of *postliminium*. In like fashion, property recovered from pirates can be claimed at any time by the former owner, unless Municipal Law otherwise ordain.

In certain cases of return or recovery the right is not called into exercise.

The Romans recognised the right of *postliminium* as arising not only in time of open war, but as between the Roman and foreign peoples. The possibility of captivity outside the condition of belligerency has ceased to be recognised amongst Christians, and even amongst Mahometans, but the right might still be called into exercise should we have to do with a people so barbarous as to assert a legal right to treat in a hostile fashion without declaration or any cause given all foreign persons and property. And, even as the author writes, it is adjudged by the highest Court of Paris, that the goods of French subjects taken by Algerines are lost to their owners, and become the property of their recaptors.

So far of belligerent rights under the Law of Nations. But Honour and Moral Justice may forbid what Law permits.

(γ) *Under the Codes of Honour and Moral Justice (justitia interna).*

In the first place, let the war be undertaken in solemn fashion; if its cause be unjust all acts done therein are

Honour and Moral

Justice may forbid what Law permits.

morally unjust, and the doers of the acts and the authors of the war are alike bound to restitution.

1. They forbid all proceedings in a war devoid of just cause.

Lib. iii. c. 10. *Monita de his quae fiunt in bello injusto.*

2. They command moderation in a just war.

Lib. iii. c. 11. *Temperamentum circa jus interficiendi in bello justo.*

Moderation is to be shown: in the employment of certain measures, towards women and children; towards priests and students; towards husbandmen and merchants; towards prisoners; towards yielding foes;

Secondly, even in the exercise of belligerent rights in a just war, moderation should be shown. A distinction may well be made between the authors of the war and those drawn into it. A distinction may even be made amongst authors of war by reference to their actuating motives. Where Justice fails to require it, it often becomes a good, a modest, an exalted soul to forgive. Pity will dictate the refraining from lawful measures which may occasion the death of innocents. *Puerum aetas excuset, feminam sexus:* so Seneca. And all males, whose mode of life is foreign to arms, should be equally spared. Amongst these should be included priests and those who apply themselves to literary pursuits or other studies beneficial to the human race. To these the Canons of the Church would add husbandmen and merchants. Mercy should likewise be shown to the captive. Quarter should be granted alike in the besieged town and upon the open field. The Romans granted quarter to besieged towns surrendering before the battering ram touched the wall. Contemporary custom dictates the like, in the case of weak places if they surrender before the batteries open fire; in the case of fortified places if they yield before the advance of storming parties. Natural equity would approve a yet further relaxation of strict belligerent rights. Equity would equally demand that suppliants and those who surrender unconditionally should be spared. Against these demands of equity exceptions are wont to be urged which are but little just, exceptions grounded, for example, in retaliation, in the necessity to strike terror, in the pertinacity of the resistance offered. A yet weaker excuse for the shedding of blood is grief for loss sustained in the war.

in the presence of death on a large scale; towards hostages; in recourse to combat.

When there is the best reason for severity, the greatness of the number of the offenders may well furnish cause for leniency. Hostages should be spared, unless personally guilty of some crime. And all needless combats should be avoided.

Devastation is endurable if it be such as to lead the enemy quickly to sue for peace. It ceases to be justifiable: (1) in the case of fruit-bearing property of which we are in possession in such sort that the enemy cannot profit by it; (2) in the presence of great hope of a speedy decision of the contest which will assign the property to the victor; (3) if the enemy can secure sustenance elsewhere; (4) if the property is of a species which is of no utility for warlike purposes, *e.g.* public ornaments, to which may be assimilated places of worship and the sepulchres of the dead. Considerations of personal profit would reinforce the call of virtue to moderation in this particular; it is foolish to drive an enemy to despair, whilst clemency wins over opponents.

Moderation is to be shown in the devastation of hostile property, *Lib.* iii. c. 12. *Temperamentum circa vastationem et similia.*

The goods of the subjects of an enemy taken in war should only be retained by way of payment for debt due, including the necessary expenses of the war, and not by way of punishment for the offence of their ruler. And humanity would bid us not squeeze the poor debtor to the utmost.

in respect of prize captures, *Lib.* iii. c. 13. *Temperamentum circa res captas.*

In like fashion, he who wages a just war has in equity a right over his prisoners only to the extent of satisfaction for original debt and consequent charges, except in the case of individuals personally guilty of some crime. Very many considerations, moral, religious, social and practical, dictate the fair treatment even of the slave. Amongst nations which do not permit the enslaving of prisoners of war exchange constitutes the best expedient; after which follows ransom, the ransom being fixed at a reasonable rate. The ransom of a common soldier in the author's day is a month's pay.

and in respect of the ransom of prisoners. *Lib.* iii. c. 14. *Temperamentum circa captos.*

The moderation displayed towards individuals is becoming in a yet higher degree towards peoples. Sovereignty may be acquired by conquest, but it is laudable to use the right with moderation. The end of war is peace. The conquered may be combined with the conquerors, as was the policy of the ancient Romans. The conquered may be left in possession of their own form of

Moderation is to be shown in the acquisition of sovereignty by conquest. *Lib.* iii. c. 15. *Temperamentum circa acquisitionem imperii.*

government. It will sometimes suffice to place garrisons in the conquered territory, or to impose a tribute by way of security. Such moderation is not only humane but politic, a fact which is proveable by numerous examples. If it be not judged safe to leave the conquered in possession of their sovereign rights, a part thereof may well be left to them; they may be indulged with some remains of their old constitution, with their old laws, with the exercise of their religion. Finally, if the last relic of sovereignty be taken away, let the conquered be treated with such clemency that the profit of the conqueror be one with that of his new subjects.

Moderation should be shown towards peoples oppressed by the enemy. *Lib.* iii. c. 16. *Temperamentum circa ea quae jure gentium postliminio carent.*

Equity requires that goods taken from the enemy be restored to their original proprietors, should they have been taken by the enemy in an unjust war, and in practice this has been often done. The cost of recovery may, however, be charged to the owner. Under like circumstances, peoples and parts of peoples should be restored to the rule of their former sovereigns. The length of time which works the extinction of this right must between citizens of the same sovereignty be referred to their municipal law, between strangers to presumption of dereliction.

The mutual rights and obligations of belligerents and neutrals. *Lib.* iii. c. 17. *De his qui in bello medii sunt.*

Under plea of necessity burdens are sometimes imposed in time of war upon those who take no part in the contest, particularly upon near neighbours. But it must be remembered that, to confer a right over another's property, (1) the necessity must be extreme; (2) it must not be opposed by an equal necessity on the part of the owner; and (3) the supply taken must not exceed the measure of the exigency.

On the other hand, it is incumbent upon those who abstain from war to do nothing whereby he who prosecutes an ill cause may be strengthened, or the movements of him who wages a just war may be impeded. In a dubious cause they should treat both combatants alike, in the matter of allowing passage, of the supply of provisions to troops, and of refraining from aiding the besieged.

We may now ask what share in belligerent operations may be taken by a private person? As far as the laws of Nature and Equity are concerned, it would appear open to any person to do in a just war, within the limits of just war-waging, such things as would be beneficial to the innocent party. Sometimes private individual subjects are endowed with special power to slay, over and above the general right of self-defence. Not only may they be specially authorised who receive pay, but others also who fight at their own charges, or who do what is more, to wit, bear a share in the expense of the war. Amongst these last must be classed individuals who equip and maintain ships at their private cost, who are wont to be reimbursed by grant of the property of which they make prize. How far this proceeding is in accordance with abstract justice (*justitia interna*) and charity may well admit of question.

How far may private individuals take part in war? *Lib.* iii. c. 18. *De his quae in bello publico privatim fiunt.*

Thus far we have considered the just modes and measure of belligerent force apart from special undertaking. It remains that we consider the extent of belligerent right as affected by antecedent promise. Faith is always to be kept with enemies; the obligation of good faith is grounded on the very nature of human society; they who are enemies are yet men and capable of rights. It constitutes no excuse for breach of faith pledged in a solemn war that the promise was occasioned by fear, provided that the fear was such as the Law of Nations allows of. In two cases alone is the non-performance of a promise compatible with good faith, namely, when the condition of the promise fails, and when compensation is given.

[II.] In view of particular promise.

Faith is to be kept with enemies, *Lib.* iii. c. 19. *De fide inter hostes.*

except when the condition of the promise fails or compensation is accorded.

All agreements between enemies depend upon faith either expressed or implied. Faith expressed is either public or private. Public faith is pledged either by supreme or subordinate powers. The pledged faith of supreme powers either terminates war or binds during its continuance. Amongst things which terminate war some are principal, some accessory. Such things are principal as directly finish the contest, either by their own

(a) *Faith expressed:* **1. Public.**

Lib. iii. c. 20. *De fide publica qua bellum finitur.*

(1) Pledged by Sovereigns.

A war may be terminated

i. By direct agreement, *i.e.* Treaty of Peace.

Who has the power to make peace?

To what does the power extend?

operation, *e.g.* actual agreement, or by consent referring to some other decisive test, such as lot, the fate of a battle, or the judgment of an arbitrator. They have the power to end by agreement who have the power to begin a war. The power to end war belongs accordingly to the exerciser of supreme power (*summum imperium*). The power of most kings is now limited, and the power of alienation in particular may be restrained. Under these circumstances the consent of the whole people is required for the alienation of entire sovereignty, the consent both of the whole people and of the particular part for the alienation of the sovereignty over the part. The ruler of a patrimonial kingdom may in general freely alienate the kingdom. The property of individual subjects may for the good of the State be under the terms of a peace disposed of by the sovereign in virtue of his eminent domain, subject to the obligation attaching to the sovereign to make good the loss to the subject. The contention of Vasquius, that the State is not bound to repair losses incurred by subjects during war, is not to be generally admitted, although municipal laws may so ordain.

How are the terms of a treaty of peace to be interpreted?

The principle of *uti possidetis*,

and the principle of *in statu quo*.

Effect of return to the peace-footing.

In the interpretation of the terms of a peace that meaning is to be assigned which regulates the condition of the parties most nearly in accordance with the justice of the war. The effect, in general, is to regulate possession, either in accordance with ancient right or by reference to the facts of actual tenure. In a doubtful case the presumption is in favour of the latter arrangement. When the restoration of possession disturbed by the war is agreed upon, the condition last preceding the war is to be taken as meant. In default of express stipulation to the contrary, no action will lie after peace for damage suffered in the course of war. Private debts incurred before the war revive upon the signature of peace. Punishment due in respect of acts preceding the war is, as between state and state, held to be remitted upon the return of peace. Punishment due at the demand of a private prosecutor is not in the same case, but a very slight presumption based upon the terms of the peace will be admitted in favour of oblivion.

Property captured after the signature of peace must undoubtedly be restored. In dealing with stipulations concerning the restoration of property captured stipulations which are mutual are to be more widely interpreted than stipulations which confer rights on one party only; stipulations concerning men are to be more favourably received than stipulations concerning property; amongst these last, stipulations concerning lands are to be more favourably received than stipulations concerning moveables, stipulations concerning property in the possession of the State than stipulations concerning property in the hands of private individuals, and amongst stipulations concerning property in private hands those which restore property held by lucrative title than those affecting property held by onerous title.

He who takes a thing under a treaty takes with it the fruits of the thing from the time of the grant.

Some further rules of interpretation.

Geographical names are to be received in the acceptation current amongst experts.

Unforeseen necessity alone justifies delay in the fulfilment of articles.

Where the sense is ambiguous the interpretation should be against him who imposes conditions, since it was within his power to speak more plainly.

What constitutes a breach of a treaty of peace?

Constant disputes arise as to the circumstances which may be held to constitute a breach of treaty of peace. Such breach may come about in three ways:—(1) By the doing of that which is incompatible with any peace. Renewed hostile assault by the foe upon ourselves or upon such of our allies as were comprehended in the terms of peace thus constitutes a breach of treaty. The acts of individual subjects are not, however, in all cases chargeable to State account. (2) By the doing of that which violates the express terms of settlement. Some particular punishment may well be annexed to offences of less moment by way of saving the peace, but in strictness no distinction in importance can be admitted amongst terms. An absolute necessity, such as the destruction of the subject-matter of an article, must nevertheless be admitted as a valid saving condition. (3) By the doing of that which is incompatible with the nature of the particular peace. An unfriendly act is incompatible with an article stipulating for friendship.

ii. By reference to the chance of lot.

A war may well be ended by lot if a sovereign unjustly assaulted, judging himself upon due examination to have no hope of resistance, elect to escape a certain by an uncertain danger. The decision of a war by single combat can only be justified if it be highly probable that the wager of an unjust cause would come off the victor, and his victory be accompanied by a great slaughter of the guiltless.

iii. By single combat.

iv. By reference to arbitration.

Proculus tells us that there are two species of arbitration, the one where the decision is final whether right or wrong; the other when reference is made to the judgement of a good man and true. It must be determined in each case whether the arbitrator occupies the post of a judge or of a moderator. In general, it may be laid down that, in doubtful cases arbitrators must follow the ordinary principles of law. By surrender at discretion a form of arbitration is constituted. A hostage given to secure the release of another is released by the death of his principal. Whether a hostage given to secure a covenant be released by the death of the covenanting ruler must be dependent upon the character of the treaty as being personal or real. Contracts concerning pledges are not so strictly taken as the like undertakings concerning hostages. No lapse of time will operate to take away the right of redemption of the pledge, provided the condition in respect of which the deposit was made be performed.

Accessory sureties of agreement: hostages,

and pledges.

Faith may be pledged during time of actual war.

Lib. iii. c. 21. *De fide manente bello, ubi de induciis, commeatu, captivorum redemptione.*

Sovereigns are wont to mutually grant what Virgil and Tacitus term *belli commercia*, such as Truces, Safe-conducts, Ransom of Prisoners.

i. Truces.

A truce is a rest, not a peace. Accordingly upon the expiration of a truce no new declaration of war is needed. Truces are wont to be made, either by the mention of a continuous length of time or by the determination of a final time. In the former case the reckoning must be made by moments of time: in the latter the question may be raised whether the fixed day, month or year be included or excluded. In this last connection it is more natural to consider the determining time as part of the period. Their species.

Truces begin to bind the contracting parties from the time the contract is concluded; the subjects on either side, when the truce puts on the form of law by publication. If publication be made in one place only, a reasonable time must be allowed for notice to reach other localities. For an infraction in the meantime of the terms of the truce the subject is not liable, though the contracting party ought none the less to repair the injury. When they bind.

During the time of truce all warlike acts are illegitimate, whether against persons or against property. To retreat, to repair a wall, or to enlist soldiers is not incompatible with truce, unless it be expressly stipulated. It is illegitimate, however, to secure a town during time of truce by the corruption of its garrison, or to occupy an unguarded post. Particular conduct may, moreover, be forbidden by express agreement or by the special nature of the truce. What is permissible during a truce?

If a truce be broken by one party, the opponents may resume hostile operations without any notice, unless breaches of the truce be guarded against by penalties agreed upon, and those penalties be exacted. The acts of private individuals constitute no infraction of truce, unless they be in some way publicly approved. Effect of breach of a truce.

The right of passing and repassing (*jus commeandi*) otherwise than in time of truce is a special privilege, and so to be defined by rules of interpretation applicable to privileges. But, not being a privilege injurious to a third person or very grievous to the grantor, it calls for benevolent interpretation. A licence during pleasure is valid until notice is given of changed counsels. A passport avails not only within the territory of the grantor, but generally against the rights of war. ii. Passports and Safe-conducts.

iii. Ransom contracts.

The ransoming of captives is a proceeding which is regarded by Christians with particular favour.

(2) Pledged by Subordinates. The proceedings of subordinates are binding

Lib. iii. c. 22. De fide minorum potestatum in bello.

i. within the ordinary limits of the duties of their offices,

ii. within the limits of their special commissions.

Men are bound by the acts of those whom they delegate to be ministers of their will, whether that will be specially expressed or to be gathered from the nature of the commission. Subordinates accordingly bind their sovereigns by the doing of that which may be reasonably deemed to be within the sphere of their office, or of that for which they have a special commission, either public or known to those with whom they treat.

Sovereigns furthermore may be bound by a subsequent ratification of the proceedings of their officers, or by the acceptance of benefits accruing from their agreements. Sovereigns are bound by the proceedings of their agents in the exercise of their public functions, even though those proceedings contravene secret instructions given to the delegate. If an agent exceed the limits of his commission, he himself is bound to full restitution, unless some well-known law prevent it. In any case the other contracting party is obliged by the terms of his contract.

The general contractual powers of commanding officers.

It does not, in general, belong to a commanding officer to make a final peace: a commander may, however, make a truce, and thereby oblige the forces under his orders. It does not belong to a commanding officer to dispose of conquests, whether of men, of governments, or of lands, but he may stipulate concerning objects still unconquered. The contracts of such officers are in all cases to be strictly interpreted.

2. Private. In certain cases private persons have the power to contract on matters of public interest.

Lib. iii. c. 23. De fide privata in bello.

Faith pledged to an enemy by private individuals is to be kept equally with public faith. It is somewhat difficult to decide how far the contractual power of a private individual extends. The promise of a prisoner to return to his captivity is certainly binding, and prisoners are now frequently released on condition that they shall not again bear arms against the releaser. A promise not to attempt escape binds a prisoner. The fraudulent interpretation of the terms of such promises is rightly scouted.

Faith, public or private, may be tacitly pledged. He who demands or admits a parley tacitly promises that the parleying agents shall be secure. Certain dumb signs are by custom significant. So the hoisting of the white flag is now a tacit demand for parley, and binds as exactly as do spoken words. The *sponsio* of a commanding officer may be tacitly confirmed. Mere silence is insufficient to establish the remission of a penalty.

(β) *Tacit faith.* Signs may be as significant as spoken words, and import the like consequences. *Lib.* iii. c. 24. *De fide tacita.*

In conclusion, as men were before admonished to avoid war by all means possible, so now may they be adjured, by arguments valid alike during and after war, to the keeping of faith and the preservation of peace: to the keeping of faith especially, because without faith hope of peace there is none. For by faith not only stands, as Cicero says, every State, but the great society of nations. Take away faith, and men are reduced to the level of the brutes, whose rage is dreaded of all. More particularly does it concern monarchs to religiously keep their faith, first for conscience' sake, then for the sake of that repute whereon is founded the authority of a kingdom. It is by the continual looking forward to peace alone that the soul can during the course of war repose secure and confident in its God. A safe peace is not too dearly bought, if it be purchased at the price of the forgiveness of offenders and the overlooking of loss and expense, especially amongst Christians, to whom the Lord bequeathed His Peace. And Paul bade us, as much as in us lies, to live peaceably with all men. Peace is good for the weaker, who must carry on war at his peril; it is good for the stronger, since in peace he will enjoy his own in plenty and prosperity; and, if parties are equally balanced, then is the fittest time of all for the making of peace. Finally, if peace be made, let the conditions be observed with every circumstance of good faith. Away not only with perfidy, but with whatsoever may exasperate! God grant that these precepts be written on the hearts of the rulers of Christendom!

Conclusion: keep faith, *Lib.* iii. c. 25. *Conclusio cum monitis ad fidem et pacem.*

and seek peace.

Estimate of the work of Grotius.

§ 144. We are now in a position to attempt an estimate of the indebtedness of the world to Grotius.

1. There is little new in his general treatment of his subject. His system is that of Suarez.

Grotius, like Suarez, conceives of a society of nations, of a law amongst the society, *Proleg.* 23.

In the first place, we may remark, that there is little or nothing new in his general treatment of his subject. His system is fundamentally identical with the ideas outlined by Suarez. Grotius like Suarez conceived of a society of nations. Like Suarez too he advanced a stage further in alleging the necessity of law to such a society: "If there is "no community which can be preserved without Law, as "Aristotle proved by that remarkable instance of robbers, "certainly that likewise which joins Mankind in general, "or several Nations, together in one society must stand "in need of Law." It is in the certain assurance that such a law (*aliquod inter populos jus commune*) there *must be*, that Grotius sets out upon his quest after its actual dictates.

Proleg. 28.

As to the motive for its observance, he is equally clear. "As that citizen is no fool who obeys the law of his city, "though out of reverence to that law he must and ought "to pass by some things that might be advantageous to "himself: so neither is that people nor nation foolish who, "for the sake of their own particular advantage, will not "break in upon the laws common to all nations (*com-"munia populorum jura*); for the same reason holds good "in both. For as he, that violates the laws of his country "for the sake of some present advantage to himself, "destroys that which is made for the perpetual security "of what himself or his posterity shall be able to acquire; "so that people which violates the Laws of Nature and "Nations breaks down the bulwarks of their future happi-"ness and tranquillity."

Proleg. 18.

Justice is approved of, injustice condemned by all good men, and, over and above the strength resulting from a good conscience, there is no city so strong or well-provided but it may need foreign aid in peace or in war.

and of that law as *jus inter gentes*.

On occasion Grotius employs language which recalls the ancient conception of *Jus Gentium* as Law Universal rather than that of law international, but elsewhere in passage after passage he proves his firm apprehension of another notion. His Law of Nations is "the law which is between nations," *jus quod inter populos plures intercedit, jus inter civitates aut omnes aut plerasque.* *Proleg.* 1 and 17.

Grotius recognises the historic facts that (1) states are independent,

It could not escape Grotius, son that he was of revolted Holland, that the states of the Europe of his day were *de facto* independent communities. He proves his recognition of the actual interpolitical situation by his delimitation of the conception of sovereignty. Sovereignty, the essential attribute of State-being, combines two notions, positive and negative: the positive notion of Government and the negative notion of Independence. The positive right of ruling Grotius analyses under the name of the Civil Power: the negative right of independence he denotes as the characteristic feature of Supremacy. His Sovereign is the one governor, or body of governors, exercising the civil power personally or by delegates[1]. He casts to the winds the conception of World Empire and World Church, of a *dominus totius mundi.* The figures in his international field are independent sovereigns. So he, uniting with the distinguished company of challengers of Imperial or Papal claims, anticipates the Peace of Westphalia. *De Jure Belli ac Pacis. Lib.* ii. c. 22 s. 13.

and (2) all states do not observe a single *corpus* of international rules.

It could as little escape Grotius that Independence alone must constitute an unsatisfactory outer pale for the field of his science, that not all States in practice observed a common international law. He drew his boundary, where alone it could be drawn, by reference to civilisation. *Jus Gentium* arises by virtue of the practice, not of all peoples, but of *omnes moratiores.*

He conceives of a society of *civilised* states.

The field was then clear: a society—an International Circle—of States independent and civilised. But the moment Grotius approached the laying down for that society of positive rules of law he encountered a serious difficulty. His primary objects were confessedly those of

[1] *Summa autem illa dicitur, cujus actus alterius juri non subsunt, ita ut alterius voluntatis humanæ arbitrio irriti possint reddi. Alterius cum dico, ipsum excludo qui summa potestate utitur; cui voluntatem mutare licet, ut et successorem, qui eodem jure utitur, ac proinde eandem habet potestatem, non aliam. De Jure Belli ac Pacis,* Lib. I. cc. 6, 7.

Seeking for a definite and high moral standard, he seizes upon the conception of the *Law of Nature*,

a Reformer. To have accentuated at the outset the territorial independence of States would have been to imperil the foundations of the legal system which he proposed to construct. To have referred for the evidence of his International Law to actual practice alone would have been to defeat his aim as a preacher of better things. The lauding of simple usage to Mansfeld and Christian of Brunswick had been merely futile. Grotius would lay his foundation upon ground at once sure and capable of sustaining the platform of the advocate of moral progress. He fell back accordingly upon the Law of Nature and Natural Justice, and his first care was "to refer the "proofs of those things that belong to the Law of Nature "to some such certain notions as none can deny without "doing violence to his judgment."

Proleg. 39.

and retains it in reserve as an ultimate test, when referring to usage as the source of *Jus Gentium*.

The *Jus Gentium* of Grotius was built and necessarily built upon usage. Its rules were rules of conduct actually observed and to be observed in their mutual dealings by all, or by the greater number of, civilised peoples possessing national independence; rules of conduct operating, therefore, within the field of that independence, within the sphere, that is, of Territorial Jurisdiction. Grotius taking the stern figures of Practice and National Independence draped them in the coverings of Conscience and Good Opinion. Behind his Law of Nations he never lost sight of the Law of Nature with the approving and attesting witness, the Rational Just Man. Conradus Brunus had conceived of *Jus Gentium* as the streamlet of *Jus Naturæ* swollen by the tributaries, Usage and Common Consent. *Ex hoc jure (jure naturæ) jus gentium derivatur: Quod fit cum quod leniter a natura tractum est, majus facit usus et velut communis gentium approbatio.* Grotius recognised in one at least of the tributaries a possible source of contamination. Referring for the evidence of his *Jus Gentium* to continued Usage, he traced the course of the suspected current through the gathering pool of Consent to the mountain spring of the Moral Sense of Rational Humanity, and filled his pitcher

C. Brunus, *De Legationibus*, Lib. ii. c. 9.

once and again with the pure Law of Nature. Crowding his pages with references to poets, philosophers and orators, as proofs of the existence of a common opinion, which could only arise either from the dictates of Nature or from Consent, he added the confirmation of Holy Writ, of Canons of Councils, of the interpretations of Fathers, and of the dicta of Schoolmen. History supplied him at once with examples and with decisions. And, in the last resort, he preached the blessings of *temperamenta* whilst he acknowledged a stricter *right*.

De Jure Belli ac Pacis. Proleg. 40 and 46.

§ 145. If there was little novel in the legal system of Grotius, there was equally but little original in either the arrangement or the matter of his work. The arrangement of Books I. and II. of *De Jure Belli ac Pacis* closely follows that of the *De Jure Belli* of Gentilis. The matter of Grotius is largely borrowed from the writings of various predecessors.

2. There was but little original in either his arrangement or his matter.

In respect of arrangement he is largely indebted to Gentilis.

In respect of matter his work is a Digest.

It is the main task of *De Jure Belli ac Pacis* to identify the Law which can claim the allegiance of struggling independent nations: the author would show that *Jus inter gentes* is by showing *what* it is. Accordingly he ransacks all history for precedents and dicta, and very noteworthy will one find it, who shall search afresh the records of antiquity, that every precedent of value which he shall encounter has already been drawn within the net of Grotius. Grotius helped himself freely wherever information was to be obtained. Victoria, Covarruvias, Vasquius, Ayala, Gentilis, Bodin and others amongst his immediate forerunners are laid under contribution equally with classical authors, mediæval Fathers, Schoolmen, Canonists and Civilians. Again and again the reader of the pages of Grotius, who shall have made the acquaintance of the lights of moral and legal learning of the sixteenth century, will catch the echo of their opinions and their very phrases. And, as he advances, he will gradually understand that the work of Grotius is in fact a species of digest, and he may even be at times tempted to think of the famous Dutchman, as Dumont thought of Mirabeau,

Dumont, *Recollections of Mirabeau*, p. 15.

But the work of Grotius is not a mere compilation.

that if each who had contributed to *De Jure ac Pacis* were to claim his own but little would remain as the author's share. It were unjust, however, to regard the work of Grotius as that of a mere compiler; it is that of one who brings together the varied products of several lines of independent thought and weaves them into a harmonious whole. Even as in the valley full of bones, very many and very dry, Ezekiel saw the bones come together, bone to his bone, sinews and flesh come upon them and the skin cover them, and at the word of prophecy they lived and stood upon their feet, an exceeding great army, so we may see in the pages of *De Jure Belli ac Pacis* the labours of jurists and theologians, moralists and political philosophers, poets and historians of every generation and race come together in one consistent entity, and in the voice of Grotius recognise the life-summoning call.

Ezek. xxxvii.

Grotius goes beyond all his predecessors in the detailed elaboration of principles.

His use of old material was a main cause of his success, *e.g.* his use of Roman Law.

§ 146. In the detailed elaboration of his principles Grotius advances far beyond all his predecessors. He traces out in exhaustive fashion the broad generalisation at which Suarez stayed. The very fact that he employed old material was a primary condition of his success. His use of Roman Law furnishes a salient example. The Roman Law, like the Roman Faith, had resisted the shocks of the Middle Ages by the strength of an innate moral power. It had trickled through Barbarian Codes, and come in full stream through the Basilika and the Western commentators from the founts of Justinian. It had had its Professors in every great mediæval University, and the common lawyer, who repudiated its sway, had borrowed on occasion largely of its dictates. What meaning was attached by Grotius to *Jus Gentium* in the mouths of Roman jurists it is of little more than curious interest to decide. Grotius, whilst he drew on all antiquity for precedents and proofs, had in the Roman Law an unfailing supply of principles; and he used it unsparingly. He did so with success because, made known by generations of mediæval legal thinkers, the principles of pure Roman

Ante, p. 150.

Maine, *International Law*, pp. 16, 97.

Civil Law yet spoke in the day of Grotius with the authority of *lex scripta*. The obligatory force which men acknowledged in these principles as rules of a municipal legal system was accorded them when they were enunciated as laws of international conduct. The system of Grotius lived because it was grafted on a living tree.

Some criticisms upon the work of Grotius.

His use of the *Law of Nature*.

His numerous citations.

His excursions into side issues.

His use of the term *Jus Gentium*.

§ 147. It is easy to multiply criticisms of every kind upon the method of Grotius. The Law of Nature, as the foundation of a scientific system, would seem to be a veritable quicksand. The materials borrowed by Grotius from the stores of poetry and general literature appear to the modern eye to lend to his work no strength and little grace. His argument is often overweighted, his illustrations seem superfluous. He indulges in long and apparently irrelevant excursions into side issues. His very employment of the term *Jus Gentium* is not beyond the reach of reproach. In the mouths of Roman writers that term was not, we have seen, without a certain ambiguity, and the theologians and civilians of the Middle Ages, defining by different methods the relation of *Jus Gentium* and the Law of Nature, had imported into its usage further possibilities of confusion. Grotius himself distinguishes aptly enough between the Law of Nature, whose evidence is the Moral Sense of Rational Mankind, and the Law of Nations, which is of human ordinance and evidenced by practice. But the method of Grotius rendered it eminently likely that his *Jus inter gentes* would, through the Law of Nature, become entangled with matters belonging to other fields of study. Grotius, in fact, is personally not guiltless of the confusion, and International Law was with Puffendorf lost in *Jus Naturae et Gentium*. The best justification of any method of teaching is, however, its success. The prompt and universal applause which hailed the appearance of *De Jure Belli ac Pacis*, coupled with its obvious permanent influence in the field of practice, constitutes the fullest and highest proof of the correctness of its author's diagnosis

The success of Grotius the best justification of his method.

at once of the needs of his day, and of the moral qualities of men. Modern International Law may date its beginnings as a distinct branch of scientific study from the labours of Hugo Grotius.

Grotius and the Science of International Law.

§ 148. The Prophet had appeared. In some quarters a disposition was shown to question, at least in certain particulars, the inspiration of his message. Already in 1617 Angelus Mattheaceus had advanced to defend the claims of the Venetians in the Adriatic against the assaults of Vasquius and the author of *Mare Liberum*. After the appearance of *De Jure Belli ac Pacis*, Selden, Burgus, Pontanus and others, with whose works it will fall to us to deal in a later chapter, came forward to challenge other impugned maritime jurisdictions. Discussion still proceeded on the old lines in other directions by the publication of special tracts. And much indeed remained to be done, not only in the further elucidation of numberless points of detail, but in the settlement of sundry notorious contested causes, and in the laying down of important general principles. The Law of Neutrality, handled by Johann Wilhelm Neumayr von Ramsla[1] in a treatise published at Frankfort in 1620, was barely touched upon by Grotius, an omission not without its significance. But the message was delivered[2], and found growing accept-

[1] Joh. Wilh. Neumayr von Ramsla, *Von der Neutralitet und Assistenz oder Unpartheilichkeit und Partheilichkeit in Kriegszeiten.* Frankf. 1620. For an account of this book see Nys, *Les Origines.*

[2] The later career of Grotius was not without its pathos. Tiring of the splendid poverty in which he found himself at Paris, in consequence of the precarious nature of the royal doles, he in 1634, after a brief visit to his native Holland and a temporary sojourn in Hamburg, accepted the offer of employment made on behalf of Christina of Sweden, the famous daughter and successor of his admirer, Gustavus Adolphus. Subsequently resident for eight years as Swedish ambassador at Paris, he in 1645 retired from the service of the Northern Court to die at Rostock, after suffering shipwreck on the Pomeranian coast. His remains were deposited in his native Delft. Over and above his legal and historical work, he was a prolific writer on theological subjects, a much admired Latin poet, and no mean dramatist.

ance. Of *De Jure Belli ac Pacis* edition followed edition[1]. And more important than the flattering reception of scholars was that accorded by practical statesmen. It is a matter of well-known anecdote, how the Hero-King of Sweden carried the book with him as his constant camp companion, and Charles Lewis, the Elector Palatine, returning to his war-worn capital, called in 1661 to a newly-founded chair of Natural Law in the University of Heidelberg Samuel Puffendorf, who had won his favour by his published studies of the work of Grotius. The great Dutchman had not lived in vain, when within sixteen years of his death *Jus Naturæ et Gentium* had won a place as a subject of systematic University study side by side with the texts of Justinian.

Puffendorf, Professor of *Jus Naturæ et Gentium*, 1661. Rose, *Biog. Dict.* Art. "Puffendorf."

[1] Amongst early editions of *De Jure Belli ac Pacis* may be enumerated those of Frankfurt, 1626 and 1691; Amsterdam, 1632, 1646, 1647, 1702, 1704; the Hague, 1680.

INDEX.

Cambridge:
PRINTED BY J. AND C. F. CLAY,
AT THE UNIVERSITY PRESS.

35349355R00223

Made in the USA
Lexington, KY
07 September 2014